HOT SPOTS

HOT SPOTS

AMERICAN FOREIGN POLICY
IN A POST-HUMAN-RIGHTS WORLD

AMITAI ETZIONI

Transaction Publishers
New Brunswick (U.S.A.) and London (U.K.)

Library of Congress Catalog Number: 2012009455
ISBN: 978-1-4128-4963-0
Printed in the United States of America

Library of Congress Cataloging-in-Publication Data

Etzioni, Amitai.
  Hot spots : American foreign policy in a post human rights world / Amitai Etzioni.
    p. cm.
  Includes bibliographical references and index.
  1. United States—Foreign relations—21st century. I. Title.
JZ1480.E92 2012
327.73—dc23
                                                        2012009455

Contents

Preface

This book seeks to identify the most important challenges faced by American, and more generally Western, foreign policy. In each case, it holds that there are strong reasons for major change in the treatment of these hot spots. Moreover, it holds that there is no one treatment that fits all. Each treatment requires a distinct yet significant course adjustment.

The book starts with a discussion of the role of China in the changing global order. In early 2012, the United States "pivoted" to make the Far East its military and strategic first priority and downgraded the Middle East. This change in priorities is particularly important as it was accompanied by a curtailed military budget and the end of the two-war doctrine. Hence if the United States is making the Far East (actually China) its first priority, it must downgrade the Middle East. Indeed the change was symbolized by the fact that as the United States completed the withdrawal of its troops from Iraq and began the drawdown of its forces in Afghanistan, it opened a new military base in Australia and shipped Marines there.

The book argues that such pivoting toward the Far East is premature. China can and should be treated for the near future as a potential partner in a changing global order rather than contained and made into an enemy which whom a military clash is expected. At the same time, the truly hot spots continue to be in the Middle East, albeit not in Iraq or Afghanistan, but in Iran and Pakistan. The book suggests a rather different way to deal with both.

Less urgent but of great importance are the ways the West deals with the complex and varied Muslim world, with political Islamic parties and social movements, and with the Arab Awakening. Here the distinction between security and nation building becomes of great relevance for both normative and prudential reasons, as we shall see.

The threat of nuclear weapons has long been recognized as posing the gravest danger to our security, especially if terrorists are able to acquire them. However, the approach of seeking zero nuclear arms and focusing on the strategic weapons of the United States and Russia is completely misfocused. More innovative is the suggestion to create a transnational fuel bank. However, both ideas are light-years away from the urgency of the hot threats of nuclear weapons not well protected in Pakistan and Russia (especially tactical ones) and the threats posed by North Korea and soon Iran.

Less "hot" but still more likely to overheat than the Far East in the near future is the EU, which suffers from a major design flaw that is unlikely to be corrected. One must expect the EU to be troubled over the next years, troubles that will spill over to other nations' economies.

One must expect that there will be few armed humanitarian interventions of the kind we saw in 2011 in Libya and did not see in Syria. The main reason is the tendency of the United States and the rest of the West to scale back its commitments overseas. There is nevertheless room for explaining when such interventions are justified.

The book closes with an examination of the policies that threaten and favor the promotion of human rights. Determining which rights should take precedence and examining their relationship to security raises many important questions that go well beyond the elementary notions that human rights ought to be promoted because their virtue is self evident.

Acknowledgments

This manuscript was compiled by Courtney Kennedy. Several essays have been updated and modified for this publication. The author gratefully acknowledges the following publishers and publications for permission to use previously published material:

"Life, the Most Basic Right," previously published in *Human Rights Journal* 9, no. 1 (January 2010): 100–110. Reprinted by permission of Taylor & Francis, www.tandfonline.com.

"China: Making an Adversary," previously published in *International Politics* 48, no. 6 (November 2011, Macmillan Publishers Ltd.): 647–66. Reproduced with permission of Palgrave Macmillan.

"Is China a Responsible Stakeholder," previously published in *International Affairs* 87, no. 3 (May 2011): 539–53.

"Who Is Violating the International Rules?" previously published in a shortened version as "Is China More Westphalian than the West: Changing the Rules," as part of an exchange with G. John Ikenberry. Reprinted by permission of *Foreign Affairs*, 90, no. 6 (November/December 2011): 172–76. Copyright 2011 by the Council on Foreign Relations, Inc. www.foreignaffairs.com.

"Are Iran's Leaders Rational Actors?" previously published as "Can A Nuclear-Armed Iran Be Deterred?" in *Military Review* (May/June 2010): 117–25.

"Can the U.S. Prevent Iran from Lording Over the Middle East?" previously published as "Shifting Sands," in *Journal of International Security Affairs* 20 (Spring/Summer 2011): 87–97.

"Pakistan: A New, Geopolitical Approach," previously published as "Rethinking the Pakistan Plan" in *National Interest* 117 (January/February 2012): 55–65.

"Tunisia: The First Arab Islamocracy," previously published in *National Interest* online (October 26, 2011).

"Illiberal Moderate Muslims Are the Global Swing Vote," previously published as "The Global Importance of Illiberal Moderates" in *Cambridge Review of International Affairs* 19, no. 3 (September 2006): 369–85. Reprinted by permission of Taylor & Francis Ltd, www.tandfonline.com.

"Should We Support Illiberal Religious Democracies?" previously published in *Political Quarterly* 82, no. 4 (October–December 2011): 567–73.

"The Salafi Question," previously published online as "The Salafi Question: Egypt's Constitutional Moment" in *Boston Review* (June 11, 2012).

"Why There Cannot Be a Marshall Plan for the Middle East," previously published as "No Marshall Plan for the Middle East" in *Prism* 3, no. 1 (December 2011): 75–86.

"Nationalism: The Communitarian Block," previously published in *Brown Journal of World Affairs* 18, no. 1 (Fall/Winter 2011): 229–47.

"Zero Is the Wrong Number," previously published in *World Policy Journal* 26, no. 3 (Fall 2009): 5–13.

"A Deeply Flawed Fuel Bank," previously published in *World Policy Journal* (Winter 2010/2011): 103–10.

"The Lessons of Libya," previously published in *Military Review* 92, no. 1 (January/February 2012): 45–54.

"The Case for Decoupled Armed Interventions," previously published in *Global Policy* 3, no. 1 (February 2012): 85–93.

"Terrorists: Neither Soldiers nor Criminals," previously published in *Military Review* (July–August 2009): 108–18.

"Drones: Moral and Legal?" previously published as "Unmanned Aircraft Systems: The Moral and Legal Case" in *Joint Force Quarterly* 57 (2nd Quarter 2010): 66–71.

"Is the Normativity of Human Rights Self-Evident?" previously published as "The Normativity of Human Rights is Self Evident" in *Human Rights Quarterly* 32 (2010): 187–97.

"Pirates: Too Many Rights?" previously published as "Somali Pirates: An Expansive Interpretation of Human Rights" in *Texas Review of Law & Politics* 15, no. 1 (Fall 2010): 39–58.

Part I

The China Hedge: First—A Partner?

1

China: Making an Adversary[*]

At the end of the first decade of the twenty-first century, *The Economist* issued a report that asked: "China—friend or foe?" However, the cover of the same issue, referring to the same report, stated, "The danger of a rising China."[1] Many others in the Western media, the US Congress, and academia increasingly contend that the verdict on China is out: that it is on its way to becoming a threatening global force, an adversary, and potentially an enemy. This chapter examines who is most justified—those who view China as an adversary or those who are much less alarmed—and explores alternative American responses to China's rising power.

Adversarial Predispositions

There are strong a priori reasons to critically examine all claims that a nation is turning into an adversary, because there are considerable political, sociological, and psychological forces that push nations to find adversaries and make enemies where there either are none or when the evidence is ambiguous. These are widely known, having found their way into popular literature and movies, such as *Wag the Dog*, and are hence merely briefly listed. Those who frame a nation as an opposing force achieve several "secondary gains," i.e., benefits one derives from what is otherwise a loss. A nation whose people (at least the majority of them, the elite, and the mainstream media) have come to regard other nations as a threat is likely to be more able to suppress differences and achieve national unity, and its populace more likely to be willing to fight and make sacrifices for the common good than a nation without an adversary. Thus, a typical headline reads, "Poland, lacking external enemies, is turning on itself."[2] Moreover, finding an adversary rewards special interests, such as the defense community, arms manufacturers, and those who oppose free trade. And politicians who champion the view that another nation is an adversary often do better than those who seek to refute it, at least in the United States.

One had also take into account the limited capacity of futurists and other scholars to foretell the course of a nation. Several highly influential predictions about the rise and fall of global powers turned out to be far off the mark. These include the well-known forecasts by Paul Kennedy and Ezra Vogel that Japan would rise to global preponderance.[3] For decades, American estimates of the military power and political stability of the Soviet Union were vastly inflated. And the misjudgments concerning Saddam's weapons of mass destruction are well documented. Ergo, one ought to take predictions that we have entered a "Chinese century"[4] and the China is poised to "rule the world"[5] with considerable caution.

Not less important is the fact that characterizing China as an adversary is one factor that can make it into one. While it is somewhat of an overreach to argue, "Treat China like an enemy and that's what it will be,"[6] social scientists have shown that nations do respond to being defined and treated as an adversary with moves that confirm the initial claims of the adversary-makers, leading to a vicious cycle.[7] Already, military, economic, and political moves by the United States and China reveal some early aspects of this phenomenon. For example, China responded to the US-India nuclear deal by implementing a deal to supply Pakistan with two nuclear reactors.[8] And China responded to close surveillance by harassing American surveillance ships and warplanes, leading to incidences that made the United States see China as belligerent.[9] In other situations, moves by China led to American responses. Thus, Chinese missile tests over the Taiwan Strait in the mid-1990s caused the United States to respond by deploying aircraft carriers to the region.

The Debate by Sector

The significance of subjecting adversarial predispositions to critical analysis has thus been established, but there remains the question of whether, in the case of China, there is a real emerging adversary. The examination proceeds by summarizing the arguments of those who consider China an adversary in the making, if not an enemy, and the responses of those who hold China is leaning toward a peaceful development and should be engaged by the United States. Lacking better terms, I refer to the former as "adversarians" and to the latter as "engagers." The first group tends to consider the rise of China as threatening to US interests and to the world order, although they do not rule out the possibility of "socializing" China into the prevailing international institutional framework. The second group tends to consider China as a nation that seeks to focus on its own development and can be engaged to work with the United States and other nations to advance shared interests and the common good, although they do not rule out that China may turn into a formidable adversary. As the following analysis indicates, one can as a rule discern whether the basic outlook of the various scholars, think tanks, and public leaders who comment on China's rise fall into the adversarian or engager camp.

The following discussion is organized into three segments, each analyzing the debate with regards to the different sectors of power: military/geopolitical, economic, and ideational. This categorization is based on a study of power, initially undertaken with reference to domestic politics,[10] and applied to China in a seminal essay,[11] and later as the basis of a major book on China.[12] Though all forms of power have been invoked in the popular debate over whether or not China is becoming an adversary, military power is widely regarded as the most threatening and influential in deliberations over China's rise, and is thus accorded the most detailed analysis.

Military/Geopolitical Assessments

Assessments of whether China is becoming a military threat consider both its capabilities and intentions. Adversarians usually stress capabilities given the ambiguity in determining China's current and future intentions, while engagers often emphasize that China has benign intentions.

First, regarding capabilities, adversarians contend that peace will be best maintained if the United States sustains a strategic military advantage over China at all levels of potential conflict escalation in order to deter it from any aggressive action. They contend that the military balance has been shifting in China's favor in recent years and that without urgent US military investment aimed at countering China, conflict will become more likely.[13] In support of this thesis, the following evidence is cited:

- China has increased its military investment. Its defense budget grew by an average of 12.9 percent per year between 1996 and 2008, while its GDP only grew at a rate of 9.6 percent.[14] It is "proceeding at a rate . . . to be of concern even with the most benign interpretation of China's motivation," a State Department task force concluded in 2008.[15] These funds are being used for extensive military modernization which raises the question: who is China's target, considering China faces no

5

direct threats nor does it undertake global responsibilities? Moreover, China's nontransparent military build-up has centered on war-fighting capacities, many designed specifically to counter US forces.[16]

- At the same time, the US military has been in decline and is facing a budgetary squeeze. US defense spending as a percentage of GDP is at an almost all-time low in American history, despite ongoing military operations in Iraq and Afghanistan.[17] The size of the American military has declined by a third over the past two decades,[18] and its platforms, including ships and aircraft, are antiquated and in decay.[19] With 280-some ships, the navy has been reduced by more than 500 ships since 1989 and is smaller than at any time since 1916.[20] The US military is said to be headed for a "train wreck."[21]

- Although US defense spending far exceeds that of China (the US defense budget is almost as large as that of all other nations combined, China included), the United States has substantially more global commitments and responsibilities, as opposed to China's current narrow interest in its neighboring lands and seas.

- China's military is gaining a strategic advantage by focusing on lower-cost "asymmetric" capabilities,[22] meaning that it could effectively counter the United States even if its defense spending does not quite catch up to America's. In this regard, of particular concern is that China has already made advances in anti-access/area denial (A2/AD) systems, notably including anticipated anti-ship ballistic missiles (ASBMs). China could employ such missiles to demolish the much more expensive US aircraft carriers, compelling US forces to retreat from Chinese coasts[23] and leaving American officials with few options other than to surrender or dramatically escalate the conflict, for example, by bombing China's mainland.[24] And it successfully tested an anti-satellite missile in 2007, proving it might be able to take out US space-based reconnaissance and missile defense systems.

- Other troublesome developments of China's military include that it has developed advanced cyberwarfare and cyber espionage capabilities, which could be used to sabotage infrastructure run on information systems, including power grids, and steal sensitive military information.[25] China has increased its submarine fleet at a rate of about five per year.[26] And China has modernized its nuclear arsenal—moving from a purely land-based force to include also sea and air-based ones, while strengthening its survivable second strike capabilities.[27] In addition, China is set to deploy its first aircraft carrier and has already conducted a test flight of its first stealth fighter jet.

By contrast, engagers, pointing to the same data, come to much less alarmed conclusions and make the following observations:

- Adversarians tend to exaggerate China's defense spending, for example, by citing only the highest estimates, like the DOD figure of

$150 billion in 2009, rather than the figure of $100 billion the same year as suggested by the highly regarded Military Expenditure Database of the Stockholm Peace Research Institute (SIPRI).[28] China's defense spending as a proportion of overall government spending has remained at roughly 8 percent through the 1990s and into the first decade of the new millennium.[29] As China's economic growth slows and the cost of its social problems (widening income inequality, environmental degradation, health care inadequacies, ethnic tensions, etc.) rises, it is likely to curb its defense spending.

- Adversaries also exaggerate China's capabilities, ignoring that China's military modernization began at a low baseline.[30] China's highly bureaucratic and inefficient military-industrial complex lags behind even its own nonmilitary and nonstate-owned counterparts.[31] Thus when Russia refused to sell China nuclear submarines, China attempted to build its own ones that turned out to be rather noisy,[32] like "sitting ducks," according to one analyst.[33]

- China's military faces many logistical shortcomings and problems in its command and control systems.[34] It also faces daunting challenges in making fully operationally capable its anti-ship missiles, for which it has yet to conduct a successful public test over water against a maneuvering target.[35] Moreover, the US Director of Naval Intelligence, David Dorsett has stated that China's stealth fighter will not be fully operationally capable for years.[36] And China still does not have its nuclear submarines on regular patrols,[37] and its nuclear-armed bomber fleet is woefully obsolete.[38]

- The US defense budget has increased by 68 percent since 2001, excluding the cost of the Afghanistan and Iraq wars. And it is spends six times as much as China on defense.[39] While China is developing its first aircraft carrier, the United States already has eleven.[40] While the Chinese are seeking to build up their nuclear stockpile, the United States will have 1,550 deployed nuclear warheads (as per the new START limitations), whereas China possessed 186 in 2009.[41]

- US power is augmented further when one considers the combined power of its various regional allies and strategic partners (including Japan, Singapore, Malaysia, Indonesia, the Philippines, South Korea, Thailand, Australia, and Taiwan) who could join the United States in a fight and/or provide it with air, naval, and port facilities. In contrast, China has very few allies that can augment its military might.[42] It could be noted further that China's increased assertiveness has not significantly increased its leverage over the region, but often to the contrary—it has pushed several of these countries closer to the United States.[43]

- US naval intelligence holds that China's weapons are being designed to "defend its coasts, not to contest the United States in the air or on 'the blue water.'"[44] Indeed, "China's navy rarely leaves its home waters; when it does patrol farther afield, it still does not cross the Pacific."[45] And

China certainly does not have the ability to strike the US mainland, except with a small percentage of its nuclear forces.[46]

- Some of the expansion of China's military is dedicated to tasks such as "counterterrorism operations, participation in UN Peacekeeping operations, noncombatant evacuation operations, emergency disaster relief operations, international humanitarian assistance, and counterpiracy patrols."[47]

When it comes to assessments of intent, some adversaries see China's character as innately expansionist. Thus Edward Timberlake and William Triplett write in their book *Red Dragon Rising*, "If the Communist Chinese can gun down thousands of innocent civilians [in Tiananmen Square] in order to ensure the regime's survival, it is only a matter of time before they turn their guns on the rest of the world to satisfy their territorial ambitions."[48] Retired Navy Admiral James Lyons believes that "China intends to challenge the United States for global military supremacy. In short, China's goal is to make the world 'safe' for the continued survival of the Chinese communist dictatorship."[49]

Other adversaries highlight China's attempts to dominate its region as its way to become a global power. Robert Kaplan writes that "Once it becomes clear, a few years or a decade hence, that the United States cannot credibly defend Taiwan, China will be able to redirect its naval energies beyond the first island chain in the Pacific (from Japan south to Australia) to the second island chain (Guam and the Northern Mariana Islands) and in the opposite direction, to the Indian Ocean."[50] Others point to China's 2010 declaration that much of the South China Sea is its Exclusive Economic Zone (EEZ) as a major sign of growing Chinese aggressiveness. China has increased naval patrols in the area, pressured foreign energy companies to halt operations in contested waters, and imposed fishing bans on parts of the sea,[51] in some cases seizing fishing boats and arresting sailors from other countries.[52] In addition, China has sought to restrict passage of peacetime military vessels in international waters outside the limits of its territorial waters, harassed Japanese and American military vessels in its neighboring seas, likewise outside of its territorial zone,[53] and warned foreign militaries not to conduct naval exercises in its EEZ.[54]

Adversaries also point out that China has used force in a number of its border disputes, rather than seeking resolution through mediation, arbitration, or some other peaceful internationally legitimate process. The Chinese attacked India in 1962 over a border dispute, a war that resulted in thousands of casualties. China captured the

Paracel Islands from Vietnam in 1974, and in 1988, China's military sunk several Vietnamese ships, killing seventy sailors, while defending its claim to the Johnson Reef in the disputed Spratly Islands. And in the mid-1990s, China ignored protest by ASEAN when it occupied Mischief Reef, within the Philippines' EEZ, and built military-like structures there. In September 2010, a Chinese fishing trawler rammed a Japanese ship patrolling the disputed Senkaku (Diaoyu) Islands in the East China Sea.

By contrast, engagers point out that China has greatly improved its relationship with neighboring countries as compared to earlier eras and is seeking to allay their concerns by settling differences peacefully and joining regional organizations and forums, such as the ASEAN Regional Forum (ARF), ASEAN + 3, and the East Asia Summit Group (ASEAN + 6). In addition, China has initiated a Free Trade Area with ASEAN states and improved its ties with neighboring Russia, South Korea, and Mongolia.[55]

Engagers add that China settled seventeen of its twenty-three territorial disputes with other governments, usually gaining control over less than half of the contested land, and offering "substantial compromises in most of these settlements."[56] Moreover, in 2003 China signed the Treaty of Amity and Cooperation with the ASEAN countries, whose main tenet is to "settle such disputes among themselves through friendly negotiations," and not through "the threat or use of force."[57] That year, it also signed the Declaration of Conduct of Parties in the South China Sea, which resolved that future conflicts between the parties to the declaration would be worked out through dialogue and cooperation.

With regards to whether China has global ambitions, engagers argue that evidence does not support the claim. China is reported to have concluded from the experience of the USSR and its own history that military build-up is not the preferred route to follow, but that economic development is. David Lampton points out that China took to heart what happened when the USSR engaged in an arms race with the United States, which it was unable to maintain due to its comparatively smaller and weaker economy.[58] Moreover, Chinese authorities hold that unless they attend to the economic needs of their people as well as maintain the government's legitimacy, they will face internal pressures that will lead to their undoing. Doug Bandow of the Cato Institute holds that "If Beijing poses a threat, it is to U.S. domination of East Asia, not the country itself." And Kenneth Lieberthal writes that

"Both leaderships [of the U.S. and China] want the bilateral relationship to go smoothly. Neither is seeking to cause a major problem for the other as a key objective of national policy."[59]

Economic Assessments

Adversarians level five major charges against China with regard to the ways its economic policy affects the global economy. (a) China is charged with manipulating its currency, which prevents it from appreciating, thus making it difficult for other nations to enter China's markets. (b) China's trade barriers include unfavorable regulations, import restrictions, unjustifiable customs requirements, and especially buy-Chinese-only directives by the government. (c) China is not acting to "rebalance" the world economy by encouraging its people to consume more (and save less) thus increasing imports and making its economy less export-oriented. (d) Chinese companies acquire the latest Western technologies by various means, many of which are illegal (such as reverse engineering Western productions, industrial espionage, and piracy). (e) China benefits from cheap labor because it pays its workers little and grants them few benefits, while allowing corporations to abuse the environment.

Engagers do not deny the basic facts concerning these charges; however, they point to a trend of improvement on all of these fronts. China has allowed its currency to appreciate, its domestic consumption is rising, workers are better paid, piracy of Western products is curbed, and it is moving to protect the environment.[60]

Engagers also point out that China continues to act as a major source of savings for the United States, by financing a good part of the American debt and that it has not abused the power it has over the United States as a result. Indeed, "a simple announcement that China was cutting back its dollar holdings could put huge pressure on the U.S. dollar and/or interest rates."[61] However, China refrained from doing so even when the United States was most vulnerable in 2008 and 2009. (Some argue that if China would have acted otherwise, it would have damaged its own interests. However, the damage to the United States would have been much greater.)

Ideational Assessments

Adversarians warn that China's model of authoritarian capitalism has a growing appeal to nations who previously saw democratic capitalism as the model to follow. China's rapid economic growth and increasing wealth, almost twice that of the largest democracy, India, and much higher than that of any Western nation or Japan, is reported to win the respect of other nations and invite imitation. Similarly, while the politics of the United States and several other democracies seem to be gridlocked, China is viewed as being able to make strategic decisions expeditiously. Finally, China fared well when in 2008, the United States caused a Great Recession that unsettled many other parts of the world. In short, observers argue that what used to be a growing Washington Consensus that the world is marching to form regimes similar to those of the United States—a consensus that was particularly strong after the collapse of the USSR in 1990—is increasingly being replaced by a Beijing Consensus that sees China as the model to emulate.[62]

Engagers point out that authoritarian regimes often invite their own destruction; that one should be weary of linear projections especially concerning future economic growth of China[63] that China is facing increased tensions among the very large poorer rural parts and the affluent ones,[64] among various ethnic groups, and a young generation that is tech-savvy and may undermine the authoritarian regime. The Cato Institute's Leon Hadar put it well in an article entitled: "Don't Fear China." He writes: ". . . very much like the Japanese, German, French, Scandinavian, Indian, or, for that matter, the Anglo-Saxon or American 'models' the Chinese 'model' cannot be 'exported' to, say, Somalia, Brazil, or Iran (which are developing their own 'models') or even to its neighbors in East Asia."[65]

Responses

Given the compelling cases of both the adversaries and the engagers with regards to the different sectors of power, the following section discusses the appropriate responses to China's rise in each of these sectors that the West ought to consider.

Military/Geopolitical Responses

The analysis of China's military threat has shown that a case can be made both that China is embarking on a course that would make it at least a powerful regional military force, and potentially a global one, and that China is not seeking to challenge the United States, is focused on domestic economic development, and is merely seeking to play a growing regional role but not to dominate its region. Complicating matters, whatever course China is set on now can change. Under most circumstances as ambiguous as this one, it would be best to prepare for the worst given the serious consequences of a misjudgment on the scale of Pearl Harbor or Britain's poor preparedness at the eve of World War II.

But, it is also worthy of consideration that there are in fact grave costs to such a hedging strategy.[66] It could deteriorate US-China relations and lead to an arms-race,[67] which would amount to a bottomless pit of increased economic burdens and not necessarily increased security, especially troublesome in a tight-budget era. Moreover, if the United States seeks to counter all potential threats worldwide through military superiority, it will become overstretched—as some argue it already is. In addition, cooperation with China is important for the achievement of other US national security priorities, such as dealing with the Iranian and North Korean nuclear stand-offs, countering terrorism and piracy, and providing humanitarian assistance. In fact, by reducing tensions and laying the groundwork for military cooperation in some of these areas, the United States and China could reach a greater level of mutual trust, further decreasing the likelihood of conflict.[68]

More importantly, all but the most ardent adversarians do not see a significant Chinese military threat to core US interests in the near or even intermediary future. Even Robert Kaplan in his alarmed 2005 essay, "How We Would Fight China," concludes, "China has committed itself to significant military spending, but its navy and air force will not be able to match ours for some decades."[69] Robert Ross finds, "The transformation of the PLA into a region-wide strategic power will require many decades . . . The transformation of the PLA into a global strategic power is an even more distant prospect."[70] And Lieberthal contends, "There is no serious military man in China or in the United States who thinks that China has any prayer of dominating the U.S. militarily in the coming three or four decades."[71] Hence, the United States can safely continue to seek to turn China into a partner before concluding that a course of confrontation is unavoidable. The importance of the long lead time in the case of China stands out when one compares its rise to that of Iran. Here many agree that if one seeks to prevent Iran from acquiring nuclear arms, which would be a "game changer" for the region and beyond, the United States and its allies must act in the very near future.

At the same time, there are changes in the US military that have a long lead time and that recommend themselves anyhow, regardless of which course China follows. One may refer to them as a "generic hedge" in distinction from a "China hedge," which holds that the United States should develop capabilities specifically geared to a potential war with that country. The main change central to what is referred to here as a generic hedge is to move away from "big platforms" (aircraft carriers, bomber wings, and armored divisions) that are costly and vulnerable to new technologies, and towards investing in high-tech, low-cost weapons (such as drones and the tools of cyberwarfare), building of highly mobile rapid deployment forces and tactics, and increasing the relative role of Special Forces.[72]

Major factors that hinder these changes are not located in China, but with traditionalists in the US military. They tend to see glory in flying jet and are contemptuous of "drone pilots"; their advancement is based on commanding aircraft carriers and not Littoral combat ships or fleets of speed boats; and they exhibit a strong preference for "classical warfare," relying on conventional forces and ways of making war, to the new "asymmetrical" and irregular modes of warfare.[73] These traditionalists are strongly supported by industries that garner much greater profits from producing big platforms, but have little to gain from the new means of warfare. And from politicians who can insert line items for building the big tickets that building big platforms involve (and ensure that the funds are spent in their states), but have little to show if the funds go to expanding say, the Special Forces or to mass production of small items (such as Kevlar vests) in which competitive bidding is possible and earmarking much more difficult.

At this point, the military posture issue must be reviewed within the much more encompassing geopolitical strategy that is applied to China. Engagers tend to favor treating China as a full fledged partner; adversarians hold that it must be contained and balanced. Current US policy rhetorically favors a partnership approach to China; however, its actions often bespeak of a containment approach. Zbigniew Brzezinski has advocated the development of a G-2, comprising China and the United States, which "could address the international financial crisis, tackle climate change, limit the proliferation of weapons of mass destruction and maybe even help resolve the Israeli-Palestinian conflict."[74] Similarly, James Blaker argues that "U.S. policy should be bolder in pushing the relationship toward greater collaboration."[75] Some even refer to the coming age as one of Chimerica[76] or a condominium.[77]

President Obama stated that the "United States welcomes China's efforts in playing a greater role on the world stage"[78] and Secretary of State Hillary Clinton said, "We believe the United States and China benefit from, and contribute to each other's successes."[79] And they have toned down public criticisms of China's human rights violations. President Hu was celebrated in January 2011 during a visit to the White House.

At the same time, US actions are focused on "balancing" China and containing it. American sources discuss quite openly that the United States should seek to balance China, especially by courting India. As for containment, the United States often seems to act not merely to prevent China from becoming a global superpower or a regional hegemon, but even from becoming a major regional player. Thus, when China sought to settle its differences regarding the South China Sea with neighboring countries in a bilateral way, the United States encouraged these nations to insist on multilateral negotiations, forming what some have called an "anti-China alliance," and arming neighboring nations that have border disputes with China in this area, such as the Philippines.[80]

Forward positioning of US military forces very close to China, including moving aircraft carriers into nearby waters and military exercises in the same parts as well as close daily surveillance, are a particularly pronounced expression of the containment approach.

Economic Responses

China's economic rise is considerable and has many consequences that require distinct responses, none of which require adversarial approaches and which may well be undermined by these. Many analysts agree that the best response is for the West, particularly the United States, to put its own house in order. This requires reducing its deficits and debt, saving more and consuming less, and reducing its dependency on imported oil.[81] These responses would gradually decrease the leverage China has over the United States as a major financier of its debt.

While it is true that China's ravenous demand for resources is likely to put pressure on the world's commodities, this is also the case with the income growth of populations in other large nations, such as India and Indonesia. However, historically such increased demand for commodities has led to increased extraction, more economical use of resources, and technological innovation, rather than to lasting shortages.

Urging China to help "rebalance" the global economy by saving less and consuming more makes little sense to a sociologist. The Chinese are likely to learn to do so quickly, by their own volition, while the US public will be much slower to accept the changes in behavior required for it to consume less and save more.

The issue of China's alleged manipulation of its currency is part of a more encompassing matter. As previously discussed, there is ample evidence that China is acting as an unfair competitor. A simple response would be for the West to demand that either China allow other nations to compete within its markets on a near-equal basis ("near," taking into consideration that all nations favor their home industries to some extent) or face similar countermeasures by nations that import its products. However, for various reasons, both Western corporations and governments often choose to allow China to continue with its discriminatory politics. The reasons included US dependence on Chinese financing; that American and other non-Chinese corporations are willing to let China appropriate their trade secrets, violate their patents, require that they hire local laborers, and siphon off much of their profits in order to not be excluded from the Chinese market, which the corporations see as likely to contribute greatly to their growth[82]; that so far there has been relatively little that Western industrial espionage can gain from spying on Chinese corporations compared to what the Chinese and their government do to the United States; lack of hard evidence that can be presented to the WTO[83]; and economic theories that if a nation like China is intervening in the market, it will suffer and free market economies will benefit. In other words, the West is acting as a major enabler of China's multi-faceted discriminatory economic policies. But this finding hardly makes China into an enemy.

Ideational Responses

That some nations might find the Chinese model of authoritarian capitalism more compelling than democratic capitalism, does point to a competition of ideas, but one which the West has little reason to fear losing in the longer run. Nations that resisted democracy and human rights find themselves under constant pressure to engage in regime change. The idea that the world is marching toward an American kind of regime, as argued by Francis Fukuyama, is too simplistic; however, despite considerable retrogression in Russia and several countries in Latin America and Africa, there has been an overall trend toward democratization globally.[84] Indeed, China is moving, however gradually, and with occasional retrogression, in this direction.[85] This movement was captured by President Hu's response when asked about China's human rights record during his January visit to Washington: "China recognizes and also respects the universality of human rights. And at the same time, we do believe that we also need to take into account the different and national circumstances when it comes to the universal value of human rights."[86] Although his conception of human rights may be different from that of the West, he nevertheless paid homage to these rights, rather than attack them as bourgeois ideas as his predecessor did.

Moreover, there are compelling theories that suggest China will be unable to sustain its authoritarian model due to technological developments, especially the Internet and tensions among various ethnic groups and between the poor countryside and the richer urban centers, all of which call for increased toleration for political expression and inclusion if violence is to be limited.

In Conclusion

Several scholars view the US-China relationship through the lens of power transition theory.[87] They see China as a rising power and the United States as a declining one, and see confrontation as likely because empirically, declining powers rarely cede their position in the power hierarchy in a peaceful manner. In contrast, others expect China's rise to falter and hold that the decline of the United States is overstated and that the United States is poised to rebuild itself. Still others hold that if the West acts strategically, it can facilitate the "socialization" of China into the existing world order or one that will be modified to take the views and interests of both countries into account. All of these perspectives treat China as a unitary actor. But the different sectors of China's power each merit there own analysis to assess whether China is to be an adversary, and call for alternative ways the West can respond to it as a rising power.

China's growing military power can be interpreted as both threatening to US regional or even global interests and as mainly defensive and compatible, with its focus on domestic economic development and peaceful rise. There is much less difference of opinion about the fact that whatever are China's current intentions and capabilities, it will take decades before it could catch up to the West. This lead time provides a window for focusing on true engagement (as distinct from rhetorical engagement), holding back on containment, and above all, moving away from forward positioning of US forces and other acts that China considers to be provocative. At the same time, the United States can engage in a "generic hedge" that will bring its forces into the twenty-first century without specifically grooming them to fight China.

China's economic policies call for a combination of different responses. The United States is called upon to put its own economic house in order and may have little reason to fear that China's increased need for commodities and energy will post lasting difficulties for other nations. At the same time, the United States and the rest of the West have strong reasons to challenge China to greatly curtail its numerous unfair economic practices or face appropriate reactions. However, this is not to suggest that China is acting like an enemy in the economic sector, one in which such terms are rarely employed and rarely apply. It is acting as a discriminatory competitor, and pressuring it to become a fair competitor through economic means is one way to even the economic relationship rather than treating it as an enemy in the making.

Last, the West can do much to improve its promotion of human rights and democracy by nonlethal means throughout the world. However, it has no reason to fear that over the longer run it will lose the ideational competition. Indeed, there are signs—despite some setbacks—that China itself will gradually move toward a less authoritarian regime.

Most important, the lessons of the sectoral analysis reinforce the view that one must guard against the many forces that push a nation to seek an adversary and declare one when it is far from clear that there is a true enemy, and one can safely proceed by working towards a cooperative relationship and focusing on self-improvement, while making only limited and necessary hedging preparations.

Notes

* I am indebted to Marissa Cramer for extensive research assistance and editorial comments and to Avery Goldstein, Jonathan Holslag, and Brantly Womack for comments on a previous draft.

1. *Economist* 397, no. 8711 (December 4, 2010).

2. Michael Slackman, "Poland, Lacking External Enemies, Turns on Itself," *New York Times* (November 27, 2010).

3. Paul Kennedy, *The Rise and Fall of the Great Powers: Economic Change and Military Conflict from 1500 to 2000* (Random House, New York, 1987); Ezra F. Vogel, "Pax Nipponica?" *Foreign Affairs* 64, no. 4 (Spring 1986): 752–67.

4. Ted Fishman, "The Chinese Century," *New York Times Magazine* (July 4, 2004); Michael Elliott, "The Chinese Century" *Time* (January 11, 2007); Patrick Buchanan, "The Chinese Century," *American Conservative* (April 22, 2010).

5. Martin Jacques, *When China Rules the World: The End of the Western World and the Birth of a New Global Order* (New York: Penguin Press, 2009); "The Fourth Modernization," *Economist* 397, no. 8711 (December 4, 2010): 7.

6. Joseph Nye, "The Case against Containment: Treat China Like an Enemy and That's What It Will Be," *Global Beat* (June 22, 1998).

7. Charles E. Osgood, "Reciprocal Initiative," *Liberal Papers* (New York: Doubleday & Company, 1962).

8. Geoff Dyer and Farhan Bokhari, "China-Pakistan Reactor Deal to Open Fresh US Rift," *Financial Times* (September 23, 2010).

9. Seymour M. Hersh, "The Online Threat," *The New Yorker* (November 1, 2010).

10. Amitai Etzioni, *A Comparative Analysis of Complex Organizations* (New York: The Free Press, 1961 and revised edition 1975).

11. G. William Skinner and Edwin A. Winckler, "Compliance Succession in Rural Communist China: A Cyclical Theory," in *A Sociological Reader on Complex Organizations*, 2nd ed., ed Amitai Etzioni (New York: Holt, Rinehart, and Winston, 1969), 410–38.

12. David Lampton, *The Three Faces of Chinese Power: Might, Money, and Minds* (Berkeley, CA: University of California Press, 2008).

13. Aaron Friedberg, "Here Be Dragons," *National Interest* no. 103 (September/October 2009): 19–34; Dan Blumenthal, "Detecting Subtle Shifts in the Balance of Power," *American Enterprise Institute* (September 3, 2010).

14. Friedberg, Here Be Dragons.

15. "China's Strategic Modernization," Report of the International Security Advisory Board (ISAB) task force, United States Department of State (October 2008), 1.

16. For instance, Blumenthal ("Detecting Subtle Shifts") contends, "Beijing has been focused like a laser beam on how to coerce and intimidate Taiwan while deterring U.S. and Japanese intervention."

17. Matthew Foulger, "No to Further Cuts in the Defense Budget," *The Foundry*, The Heritage Foundation (November 22, 2010), http://blog.heritage.org/?p=47081 (accessed June 18, 2012).

18. Jim Talent and Mackenzie Eaglen, "Shaping the Future: The Urgent Need to Match Military Modernization to National Commitments," The Heritage Foundation (November 4, 2010), http://www.heritage.org/Research/Reports/2010/11/Shaping-the-Future-The-Urgent-Need-to-Match-Military-Modernization-to-National-Commitments (accessed June 18, 2012).

19. Jim Talent, "Don't Cut Military Spending," *National Review* (November 4, 2010), http://www.nationalreview.com/articles/252458/don-t-cut-military-spending-jim-talent (accessed June 18, 2012).

20. See note 18.

21. William Perry and Stephen Hadley, statement before the House Armed Services Committee, Hearing on Quadrennial Defense Review Independent Panel, United States Congress (August 3, 2010), 4.

22. Eric Sayers, "Military Dissuasion: A Framework for Influencing PLA Procurement Trends," *Joint Force Quarterly* 58 (July 2010): 89–93.

23. This hypothetical scenario is discussed in James Kraska, "How the United States Lost the Naval War of 2015," *Orbis* 54, no. 1 (2010): 35–45.

24. See for example, Jan van Tol with Mark Gunzinger, Andrew Krepinevich, and Jim Thomas, "Air Sea Battle: A Point-of-Departure Operational Concept," Center for Strategic and Budgetary Assessment (May 18, 2010); David A. Shlapak, David T. Orletsky, Toy I. Reid, Murray Scot Tanner, Barry Wilson, "A Question of Balance: Political Context and Military Aspects of the China-Taiwan Dispute," *Rand Corporation* (2009).

25. United States-China Economic and Security Review Commission (USCC), 2010 Report to Congress (November 2010), http://www.uscc.gov/annual_report/2010/annual_report_full_10.pdf (accessed November 17, 2010); Siobhan Gorman, "Electricity Grid in U.S. Penetrated By Spies," *The Wall Street Journal* (April 8, 2009).

26. Adm. James A. Lyons, "China's One World?" *Washington Times* (August 24, 2008).

27. Peter Brookes, "National Review: Beijing's Build-up and New START," *National Public Radio* (December 9, 2010), http://www.npr.org/2010/12/09/131928912/national-review-beijing-s-build-up-and-new-start (accessed June 18, 2012).

28. Michael Chase, "The Dragon's Dilemma: A Closer Look at China's Defense Budget and Priorities," Policy Memo, The Progressive Policy Institute (March 4, 2010), 3.

29. M. Taylor Fravel, "China's Search for Military Power," *Washington Quarterly* 31, no. 3 (Summer 2008): 137; See also "China's Military Power," Council on Foreign Relations, Independent Task Force on Chinese Military Power (May 2003), 7: "China's armed forces must compete for resources and attention with social security, education, public health, science and technology, and large-scale public works projects."

30. Ivan Eland, "Is Chinese Military Modernization a Threat to the United States?" *Policy Analysis* no. 465 (January 23, 2003), The Cato Institute.

31. "China's Military Power," Council on Foreign Relations, Independent Task Force on Chinese Military Power (May 2003), 6.

32. John Pomfret, "Military Strength Eludes China, which Looks Overseas for Arms," *Washington Post* (December 25, 2010).

33. Hans M. Kristensen, director of the Nuclear Information Project at the Federation of American Scientists, cited in Ibid.

34. Michael Chase, "Not in Our Backyard: China's Emerging Anti-Access Strategy," Policy Memo, The Progressive Policy Institute (October 2010), 5.

35. Ben Ianotta, "Navy Intel Chief: Chinese Missile Is Effective," *C4ISR Journal* (January 5, 2011).

36. Karen Parrish, "Navy Intel Chief Discusses China's Military Advances," *American Forces Press Service* (January 6, 2011).

37. "Annual Report to Congress: Military and Security Developments Involving the People's Republic of China, 2010," Office of the Secretary of Defense, 34, http://www.defense.gov/pubs/pdfs/2010_CMPR_Final.pdf (accessed June 18, 2012); Hans M. Kristensen, "China's Noisy Nuclear Submarines," Strategic Security blog, Federation of American Scientists (November 21, 2009). http://www.fas.org/blog/ssp/2009/11/subnoise.php (accessed June 18, 2012).

38. Keir A. Lieber and Daryl G. Press, "The Rise of U.S. Nuclear Primacy," *Foreign Affairs* (March/April 2006): 48–49.

39. Gregg Easterbrook, "The Pentagon and Wasteful Defense Spending," *New Republic* (November 10, 2010); Nicholas Kristof, "The Big Military Taboo," *New York Times* (December 26, 2010).

40. Fareed Zakaria, "A Military for the Real World," *Newsweek* (July 26, 2009). http://onfaith.washingtonpost.com/postglobal/fareed_zakaria/2009/04/a_military_for_the_real_world.html (accessed June 18, 2012).

41. Chris Buckley, "China Military Paper Spells Out Nuclear Arms Stance," *Reuters* (April 22, 2010).

42. Robert Ross, "The Rise of Chinese Power and the Implications for the Regional Security Order," *Orbis* 54, no. 4 (2010): 541; Ross, "Myth," *National Interest* no. 103 (September/October 2009).

43. Edward Wong, "China's Disputes in Asia Buttress Influence of U.S.," *The New York Times* (September 22, 2010); Jeremy Page, Patrick Barta, and Jay Solomon, "U.S., Asean to Push Back against China," *Wall Street Journal* (September 22, 2010).

44. Adm. Gary Roughead, Chief of Naval Operations, cited in Easterbrook, "Waste Land," 20.

45. Drew Thompson, "Think Again: China's Military," *Foreign Policy*, no. 178 (March/April 2010): 86–90.

46. Michael Richardson, "China Tips the Nuclear Balance," *NZ Herald* (February 3, 2011). http://www.nzherald.co.nz/world/news/article.cfm?c_id=2&objectid=10385486 (accessed June 18, 2012).

47. Michael Chase, The Dragon's Dilemma.

48. Edward Timberlake and William C. Triplett, *Red Dragon Rising: Communist China's Military Threat to America* (Washington, DC: Regnery Pub, 1999), 42.

49. Adm. James A. Lyons, "Countering China's Aggression: Communist Dictatorship Presents Trouble in Asia and Abroad," *Washington Times* (October 18, 2010).

50. Robert D. Kaplan, "While U.S. Is Distracted, China Develops Sea Power," *Washington Post* (September 26, 2010); See also John Mearsheimer, "The Rise of China Will Not Be Peaceful at All," *Australian* (November 18, 2005).

51. Bronson Percival, "Threat or Partner: Southeast Asian Perceptions of China," Testimony before the U.S.-China Economic & Security Review Commission, United States Congress (February 4, 2010).

52. John Pomfret, "Beijing Claims 'Indisputable Sovereignty' over South China Sea," *The Washington Post* (July 31, 2010).

53. The most noted such incident for the United States occurred in March 2009 and involved the US surveillance ship, the *Impeccable*. Other examples include the 2006 incident when a Chinese submarine stalked the *USS Kitty Hawk* and surfaced within a torpedo's firing range and two incidences in 2009 involving the *USS John S. McCain* and *The Victorious*. Regarding Japan, in April 2010, a Chinese helicopter buzzed (flew dangerously close to) a Japanese destroyer near Japan's coast.

54. Ian Johnson and Martin Fackler, "China Addresses Rising Korean Tensions," *New York Times* (November 26, 2010).

55. Michael Yahuda, "The Evolving Asian Order" in *Power Shift: China and Asia's New Dynamics*, ed. David Shambaugh (Berkeley, CA: University of California Press, 2005), 347.

56. M. Taylor Fravel, "Regime Insecurity and International Cooperation: Explaining China's Compromises in Territorial Disputes," *International Security* 30, no. 2 (2005): 46.

57. Bates Gill, "China's Evolving Regional Security Strategy," in *Power Shift*, ed. Shambaugh (Berkeley, CA: University of California Press, 2005), 257.

58. Lampton, *The Three Faces of Chinese*, 253; See also Zheng Bijian, "China's 'Peaceful Rise' to Great-Power Status," *Foreign Affairs* 84, no. 5 (2005): 18–24. "U.S.-China Relations: An Affirmative Agenda, a Responsible Course," Task Force Report, Council on Foreign Relations, April 2007: "The Task Force finds that China's foreign policy is focused for the near to midterm on securing the inputs for and maintaining a peaceful environment in which to achieve domestic economic and social development. China wants to avoid conflict."

59. Kenneth Lieberthal, "Is China Catching Up with the US?" *ETHOS* no. 8 (August 2010): 8.

60. For example, changes in China's conduct are already reflected in its rise in the annual rankings of countries in terms of their level of intellectual property rights protection. China moved from 53rd to 27th place of 139 countries between 2008 and 2011: *The Global Competitiveness Report 2010–2011* (Geneva: The World Economic Forum, 2011); *The Global Competitiveness Report 2008–2009* (Geneva: The World Economic Forum, 2009).

61. Roger Altman and Richard Haass, "American Profligacy and American Power," *Foreign Affairs* 89, no. 6 (November/December 2010): 30.

62. Stefan Halper, *The Beijing Consensus: how China's Authoritarian Model Will Dominate the Twenty-First Century* (New York: Basic Books, 2010); see also Jacques, *When China Rules the World*.

63. Josef Joffe, "The Default Power: The False Prophecy of America's Decline," *Foreign Affairs* (September/October 2009); Lieberthal, Is China Catching Up with the US?

64. Yang Yao, "The End of the Beijing Consensus: Can China's Model of Authoritarian Growth Survive?" *Foreign Affairs* (February 2, 2010). http://www.foreignaffairs.com/articles/65947/the-end-of-the-beijing-consensus (accessed June 18, 2012).

65. Leon Hadar, "Don't Fear China," *American Conservative* (December 17, 2010). http://www.amconmag.com/blog/dont-fear-china/ (accessed June 18, 2012).

66. Evan S. Medeiros, "Strategic Hedging and the Future of Asia-Pacific Stability, *Washington Quarterly* 29, no. 1 (Winter 2005/2006): 145–67.

67. Paul Godwin, "Perspective: Asia's Dangerous Security Dilemma," *Current History* no. 728 (September 2010): 264; See also "China's Military Power," Council on Foreign Relations, Independent Task Force on Chinese Military Power (May 2003) 1.

68. Jonathan Holslag, "Embracing Chinese Global Security Ambitions," *Washington Quarterly* 32, no. 3 (July 2009): 105–18.

69. Robert Kaplan, "How We Would Fight China," *Atlantic* 295, no. 5 (June 2005): 49–64.

70. Ross, The Rise of Chinese Power, 545.

71. "Connect the World," CNN International (January 20, 2011). http://archives. cnn.com/TRANSCRIPTS/1101/20/ctw.01.html; see also Avery Goldstein, Testimony before the U.S. Economic and Security Review Commission, July 21, 2005: "A rush to judgment about the nature of the China we are likely to face several decades from now is not only unwise, it is also unnecessary."

72. This paradigm was advanced by the RAND Corporation and especially Andy Marshall: See Zalmay Khalilzad, John White, and Andy W. Marshall, eds. *Strategic Appraisal: The Changing Role of Information in Warfare*, RAND Corporation 1999; See also, John Nagl, "Let's Win the Wars We're In," *Joint Force Quarterly* 52 (First Quarter 2009): 20–26.

73. James R. Blaker and Steven J. Nider, "Why It's Time to Revolutionize the Military," *Blueprint Magazine* (February 7, 2001).

74. Elizabeth C. Economy and Adam Segal, "The G-2 Mirage," *Foreign Affairs* 88, no. 3 (May/June 2009): 14–23.

75. James R. Blaker, "Avoiding Another Cold War: The Case for Collaboration with China," *Perspectives*, American Security Project (November 2008).

76. Niall Ferguson, "What 'Chimerica' Hath Wrought," *American Interest* 4, no. 3 (January/February 2009), http://www.the-american-interest.com/article. cfm?piece=533.

77. David Shambuagh, "Introduction" in *Power Shift*, 15; C. Fred Bergsten, 'Two's Company," *Foreign Affairs* 88, no. 5 (September/October 2009): 169–70.

78. "President Obama Delivers Joint Press Statement with President Hu Jintao of China," *Washington Post* (November 17, 2009).

79. Mark Landler "Clinton Seeks Shift on China," *New York Times* (February 13, 2009).

80. Ross, The Rise of Chinese Power.

81. Michael Mandelbaum, *The Frugal Superpower: America's Global Leadership in a Cash-Strapped Age* (New York: Public Affairs, 2010).

82. Keith Bradsher, "Sitting Out the China Trade Battles," *New York Times* (December 23, 2010).

83. According to an article in *Bloomberg Business Week* ("The Runaway Trade Giant," April 24, 2006, http://www.businessweek.com/magazine/content/06_17/b3981039.htm [accessed November 15, 2010]), a reason why the United States has not been more persistent in using the WTO to halt Chinese piracy is that "the WTO lacks clear standards on adequate progress towards enforcement" of intellectual property rights. To prove China's inadequate enforcement of anti-piracy laws, the United States would need hard data from companies that do business in China. But the problem is that even if these companies are being harmed by intellectual property rights violations, they also do not want to be seen as cooperating with the US government. "Besides risking retaliation against their mainland operations,

executives aren't sure a successful WTO ruling will solve anything, given China's weak rule of law." Moreover, if the suit were to fail—a not unlikely prospect—an even worse scenario could arise: China would probably be emboldened to become even laxer about enforcing its intellectual property rights laws. See also Bradsher, "Sitting Out the China Trade Battles."

84. Daniel Deudney and G. John Ikenberry, "The Myth of the Autocratic Revival: Why Liberal Democracy Will Prevail," *Foreign Affairs* 88, no. 1 (January/February 2009).

85. Bijian, "China's 'Peaceful Rise;'" See also Randal Peerenboom, *China Modernizes: Threat to the West or Model for the Rest?* (New York: Oxford University Press, 2008) for an argument that China is not doing so badly in law/governance for its level of development, and Yu Keping, *Democracy is a Good Thing* (Washington, DC: Brookings Institution Press, 2008) as an example of a moderate democratizing position within China. Cf. James Mann, *The China Fantasy: How Our Leaders Explain Away Chinese Repression* (New York: Viking Adult, 2007); Andrew J. Nathan, "Authoritarian Resilience," *Journal of Democracy* 14, no. 1 (2003): 6–17.

86. "Press Conference with President Obama and President Hu of the People's Republic of China," Office of the Press Secretary, the White House (January 19, 2011). http://www.whitehouse.gov/the-press-office/2011/01/19/press-conference-president-obama-and-president-hu-peoples-republic-china

87. Robert Ross and Zhu Feng, eds., *China's Ascent: Power, Security, and the Future of International Politics* (Ithaca, NY: Cornell University Press, 2008).

2

Is China a Responsible Stakeholder?*

China recently has been criticized as not being a "responsible stakeholder," as not being a good citizen of the international community, and as not contributing to global public goods. China "is refusing to be a responsible stakeholder in the international political system, cultivating, as it has been, good relations with some of the world's most odious regimes," according to Robert Kaplan, writing in *The Atlantic*.[1] An editorial in the *Wall Street Journal* asserts "China won't be a responsible stakeholder" and acts as a "free rider."[2] Observing China's growing assertiveness in foreign policy and purported attempts to undermine the current liberal world order, Elizabeth Economy writes in *Foreign Affairs*, "China is transforming the world as it transforms itself. Never mind notions of a responsible stakeholder; China has become a revolutionary power."[3]

This article explores the application of the concept of stakeholding and all it entails to China's international conduct. It proceeds by applying sets of criteria to evaluate whether China is acting as a "responsible stakeholder" in the international system. In the process, the article raises questions about frequently employed criteria on the subject. The article first utilizes a communitarian set of standards of international responsibility that distinguishes between the status of a member of a community and that of a citizen of a state. The article then briefly studies China's conduct from a less demanding standard, one that considers whether China has fulfilled its duties as a partner in projects in which it has shared or complementary interests with other nations. The article's last section examines China's conduct from a third set of criteria that involves conceptions of power, rather than value or interest-based considerations.

Within History

The first major break in the American view that China is part of the Soviet-run global communist threat, came with the well-known "opening to China" during the Nixon Administration. In a 1967 essay in *Foreign Affairs*, Richard Nixon wrote that China should be drawn into the community of nations, because a globally engaged China would act in a more "civilized" and less dogmatic manner.[4] However, many Americans and others in the West continued to see China as an aggressive, expansionist, communist nation until the end of the Cold War. During the Clinton administration, Secretary of Defense, William Perry argued that engagement was a strategy for getting China to act like a "responsible world power," and Secretary of State Madeleine Albright called on China to become a "constructive participant in the international arena." The W. Bush administration's view of China was less optimistic; Secretary of State Condoleezza Rice declared that China was not a status quo power.[5] However, it was during this administration, in 2005, that Deputy Secretary of State Robert Zoellick called on China to become a "responsible stakeholder" of the international community—a phrase that echoed widely.

The concept "stakeholder" is a highly communitarian one as it holds that while the members of a given community are entitled to various rights, these go hand in hand with assuming responsibilities for the common good. The term "stakeholder" was used in recent decades mainly in reference to corporatism and societies. Communitarian economists argued that the corporation should be viewed not as belonging to the shareholders, but to all those who have a stake in it and are "invested" in it, including the workers, creditors, and the community in which the plants are located. Tony Blair championed a stakeholder society in the year leading up to his election to British government and during his first years of service, an economy "run for the many, not for the few . . . in which opportunity is available to all, advancement is through merit, and from which no group or class is set apart or excluded."[6]

In Zoellick's speech urging China to become a "responsible stakeholder" of the international system, he listed a very extensive number of changes that China would have to undertake in its domestic policies, indeed regime, and in its foreign policy in major areas—from North Korea and Iran to trade—in order to qualify. A critic may argue that basically he asked China to become like the United States and to do its bidding, all in the name of service to the common good of the world. (A similar idea is often expressed in the argument that after World War II, the United States erected a set of "liberal" global rules and institutions that, while tying its own hands to some extent, helped promote world peace, order, human rights, and democracy, and that China should now buy into these arrangements.) Several other authors have employed the term, seeking to determine whether or not China is becoming a responsible stakeholder based on more universally applicable criteria. The article joins this examination from the viewpoint of a global community.

In the same years during which American policymakers urged China to become a more "responsible" or more "status quo" international power, academics set out to analyze its conduct in similar terms. Robert Ross argued in a 1997 essay in *Foreign Affairs* that China is acting as a "conservative power" even though it may also be considered "revisionist" in the sense that it is dissatisfied with aspects of the status quo in Asia, especially with regards to Taiwan and Japan.[7] Alastair Johnston in a 2003 article in *International Security* concluded that China is a status quo power and criticized the notion that it is a revisionist power, one currently outside the international community that must be brought in. He held that there is not a well defined global community with well defined norms. Nonetheless Johnston defined criteria of what would make a status quo power, and that despite some problem areas, China meets them. For example, China's participation in international institutions and organizations increased dramatically in the post-Mao era. He criticized those who describe grandiose Chinese goals of regional hegemony. For example, while some of China's actions with regards to the Spratly Islands raised red flags, "China is like the Spratlys' other claimants. Indeed none of the claimants has sound legal basis."[8] And when it comes to potential for conflict with the United States, Johnston argued that China seeks to constrain US behavior, not violently push against US power.[9]

Chinese policymakers themselves have sought over the past couple of decades to show that China intends to act responsibly. President Jiang Zemin stated, "China needs a long-lasting peaceful international environment for its development." And in 1997, he initiated China's "New Security Concept," which stresses "mutual respect" and "peaceful coexistence." Since then, Chinese leaders, such as Hu Jintao and Wen Jiabao, have declared that they are seeking a "peaceful rise" and that they seek to focus on domestic development, not international expansion. The concept was furthered by Chinese scholar Zheng Bijian in a *Foreign Affairs* article entitled, "China's Peaceful Rise to Great Power Status," in which he wrote,

> Beijing remains committed to a 'peaceful rise': bringing its people out of poverty by embracing economic globalization and improving relations with the rest of the world. As it emerges as a great power, China knows that its continued development depends on world peace—a peace that its development will in turn reinforce.

Also, the concept of a China as a "responsible great power" has been widely discussed by Chinese intellectuals.

Critics argue that China is merely trying to "pull the wool over Western eyes," that is, to generate the impression that it has peaceful inclinations, while it is preparing to come out as an aggressor once it gains the capabilities to carry out its true intentions.[10]

In the current context one cannot avoid asking, by what criteria is one to judge the extent to which a nation is acting responsibly? The article turns next to grapple with this key question from the viewpoint of key values, interests, and power relations.

Stakeholder Unpacked and Evaluated

Membership and Citizenship

From a communitarian viewpoint the term "stakeholder" is best unpacked, because the assessments that employ it often conflate two distinct precepts by blurring the differences between being a member in good standing of a community and an upstanding citizen of a state. The expectations from members are significantly higher than those from citizens. Moreover, contributions to the common good are voluntary and undergirded by informal norms and informal social controls (such as appreciation for those who contribute and criticism of those who fail to do so) while citizens' duties are set by law and serious violations are punished by financial penalties (or sanctions) and coercive means (e.g., armed interventions). By conflating membership with citizenship, critics tend to be unduly condemning and may rush to call for penalties and coercive measures—when only stronger moral appeals are justified.

To highlight the distinction between these concepts, it is fruitful to first examine how they apply to individuals. An upstanding citizen pays the taxes due, serves as juror when called to, and abides by the laws of the land. (I deliberately avoid the term "good citizen," because good implies a moral standing, which is appropriate for community membership, but not for a pure citizen role.) Such citizens may also keep up with public affairs and vote regularly; however, these requirements already move the analysis from a pure citizen notion toward a membership status. A good member—aside from being an upstanding citizen—also contributes to the common good of the community by volunteering, making donations, heeding the informal norms of the community, and helping to enforce them by exerting informal social controls over those who do not. One reason citizenship and membership is often conflated is in part due to the fact that a given societal entity can be both a state and a community. Indeed this is a widely used definition of a nation.

When these concepts are applied to international affairs, one must take into account that the international community is a very nascent one. At the same time, although there is no global state of which one can be a loyal citizen, there is a non-trivial and growing body of established international law and institutions, which nations are expected to heed. Hence, in the international realm too, it is important to distinguish between being a "bad" member (e.g., a nation that makes few or no donations to countries devastated by earthquakes or does not contribute troops to peacekeeping operations) and a nation that acts like a poor citizen, one that violates widely held international laws or disregards the rulings of international institutions such as the World Trade Organization (WTO) and the United Nations (UN). Such acts of poor citizenship include engaging in hostile activities, such as supporting terrorism or invading other countries without due cause and the authorization of world institutions, and failing to live up to agreed treaties.

The discussion next turns to examine several areas of China's conduct with this dual perspective in mind. The analysis is deliberately limited in two major ways. Firstly, it does not seek to encompass all or even most areas of international conduct, but merely to examine a sufficient number to highlight the difference between membership and citizenship, and to gain a preliminary assessment of China's conduct in both capacities. Secondly, the discussion focuses almost exclusively on conduct and not declarations and statements. One can readily find belligerent statements by both Chinese and American military officials, statesmen, and observers. Behaviors speak more clearly, although they too are open to different interpretations.

China Is neither a Good Member nor a Good Citizen

China is reported to have contributed very little to whatever is considered the common good (or "public goods") of the global community. It was roundly criticized for providing very little help when nations donated relief aid to those struck by the 2010 earthquake in Haiti and the 2004 Indian Ocean tsunami. For example, according to *Foreign Policy*, the low levels of China's pledged relief aid at the UN donors' conference following the earthquake in Haiti were pitiful. "More than 50 countries kicked in $5.3 billion in all, at least a billion dollars over their initial goals. But the world's fastest-growing economy ponied up a miserly $1.5 million, comparable to the donations made by Gambia and Monaco—hardly top-three economies—and less than the cost of a house in some of the tonier suburbs of Shanghai."[11]

After the tsunami struck, China's initial emergency aid amounted to less than $3 million. It was raised to about $60 million in the following week, arguably so as not to be outdone by Taiwan who pledged $50 million.[12] This sum plus its decision to dispatch medical teams marked China's largest relief operation.[13] In comparison, Australia granted the equivalent of US $810 million in grants and loans to the tsunami affected countries; Germany, about $700 million; Japan, $500 million; and the United States, $350 million.[14]

One should note though that such donations are expected from good members, but not making them—unlike avoiding paying taxes—does not make a nation into a bad global citizen. The same holds for China's failure to support interventions to stop genocides. China opposed humanitarian intervention in Kosovo, continued to sell arms to Sudan while it was committing genocide, and made a concerted effort to block UN Security Council authorization to send peacekeeping troops to Darfur.[15] In short, China is indeed a rather deleterious member.

Turning to examine China as a citizen, one ought to consider that, although international law is subject to different and changing interpretations, there is a body of law that is widely recognized and that China itself does not contest, but often violates.

China has used force in a number of its border disputes, rather than seeking resolution through mediation, arbitration, or some other peaceful internationally legitimate process. The Chinese attacked India in 1962 over a border dispute, a war that resulted in thousands of casualties. China captured the Paracel Islands from Vietnam in 1974, and in 1988, China's military sunk several Vietnamese ships killing seventy sailors, while defending its claim to the Johnson Reef in the disputed Spratly Islands.[16]

In addition, China used force, albeit of much lower scale, to reinforce its claims to rights over large parts of the South China Sea and territories in other of its surrounding waterways. It seized fishing boats and arrested sailors from other countries in these areas.[17] In the mid-1990s, China ignored protest by ASEAN when it occupied Mischief Reef, within the Philippines' EEZ, and built military-like structures there. And in September 2010, a Chinese fishing trawler rammed a Japanese ship patrolling the disputed Senkaku (Diaoyu) Islands.[18]

Moreover, on some occasions, China attempted through harassment to deny passage to US surveillance ships and aircraft in waters and airspace outside the country's territorial limits—in violation of international conventions. In April 2001, a Chinese plane collided with an American one, bringing it down.[19] Similarly, Chinese ships maneuvered dangerously close to American ones. The most noted such incident occurred in March 2009 and involved the US surveillance ship, the *Impeccable*. According to defense analysts, there have been numerous other such incidences in the high seas outside of China's territorial waters.[20] The Japanese military has reported similar confrontations with China at sea.[21]

Beyond these occasional uses of force, which were spread over decades and limited in scale, serious demonstrations of China's poor global citizenship are revealed by its industrial espionage, violations of intellectual property rights, and hostile acts in cyberspace.

The Chinese government "has been a major beneficiary of technology acquired through industrial espionage," concluded the U.S.-China Economic and Security Review Commission (USCC).[22] For example, Google reported one such intrusion in December 2009.[23] Later it was revealed by investigators that this was part of a "larger computer network exploitation campaign . . . with perhaps 33 or more other victim companies,"[24] among them Yahoo and Adobe.[25] According to the Commission's 2010 report, China is placing requirements on firms operating in China that are designed to force them to expose "their security measures or even their intellectual property to Chinese competitors" as the price of doing business in China.[26]

Moreover, China's inadequate enforcement of intellectual property rights laws has led to rampant piracy and counterfeiting. Chinese trade in illegal copies of software, films, records, books, pharmaceuticals, and a variety of other goods—ranging from luxury items to shampoo—is reported to cost US companies[27] billions of dollars a year.[28] The Motion Picture Association of America estimates that the industry was cheated out of $2.7 billion in one year alone.[29]

Hostile acts by China in cyberspace are reported to pose a serious threat to US security. According to the report of the House of Representatives Select Committee on U.S. National Security and Military/Commercial Concerns with the People's Republic of China (the Cox Commission report), China "has stolen classified information on all of the United States' most advanced thermonuclear warheads, and several of the associated reentry vehicles."[30] In April, 2010 a state-owned Chinese telecom firm "re-routed traffic sent to about 15% of the Internet's destinations, including branches of the U.S. armed services."[31] In 2007, hackers, believed to potentially be Chinese agents,[32] stole several terabytes of information—nearly equal to the amount of information in the Library of Congress—from, among others, the Departments of State and Defense.[33]

China has targeted other countries besides the United States as well. Thus according to the 2010 report of the USCC, "A China-based computer espionage network targeted primarily Indian diplomatic missions and government entities; Indian national security and defense groups; Indian academics and journalists focused on China; and other political institutions in India, as well as the Office of His Holiness, the Dalai Lama."[34] A German intelligence officer stated in 2009 that Chinese spying operations are costing the German economy billions of Euros a year and warned that China was capable of "sabotaging" German infrastructure, including its power grids.[35]

Much has been made of China's 2010 claim to "indisputable sovereignty" over the South China Sea, seeking to treat the body of water as if all of it was part of its Exclusive Economic Zone from which it can extract oil and mineral resources also claimed by its neighbors. This position has been treated with considerable alarm as a sign of rising Chinese assertiveness, if not aggression,[36] despite the fact that many other nations have made what some consider extraordinary territorial claims about seas or lands, including recently about the Arctic.

Statements aside, the main test of Chinese citizenship in this area is how these disputes will next be resolved. To the extent that China is making these extravagant claims merely as opening moves in a legal dispute, a far from unprecedented move among lawyers. The key question is if China will turn next to negotiations with the countries involved, such as Vietnam, Malaysia, and the Philippines, to international mediation or courts to come to an agreed solution, or—if it will employ force to make these claim stick. (Favoring bilateral over multilateral negotiations is acceptable if the other nation agrees.) If China follows the first course, it is quite in line with an upstanding citizen role. If not, it surely will be a major piece of evidence that China is far from ready to become a citizen in good standing.

In short, both those who rate China as a rather poor member of the global community, and those who see it is as far from an upstanding citizen, have considerable bases for their judgments—at least as long as one accepts the precept that nations ought be good members of the international community and good global citizens.

Aspirational Standards

So far the evaluations of China were based on the concept of a stakeholder and the normative assumptions packed into it. However, in evaluating China's conduct, one should take into account that the standards involved are aspirational standards, especially regarding community membership but also regarding citizenship. Aspirational standards means expressions of norms and even laws employed by those who argue that nations ought to abide by them and that the world would be a better place if they were more widely honored. These aspirational standards are far from mere lip service. The global community, despite being very weak, does recognize and reward those who live by them and chastise and sometimes punish those who do not. It uses approbations and censures, which have an effect. Nations do care whether their acts and regimes are considered legitimate and respected by others, and the ways a government is viewed by the world affects domestic politics. Thus, the ways many nations reacted to the 2003 US invasion of Iraq, had considerable adverse "real" consequences. They are an element of what is considered soft or persuasive power. However, one must assume that often various actors will not fully heed the norms, try to circumvent them, or change them.

At the same time one best take into account that even in the most closely knit communities, in families and villages, members vary in the extent to which they heed the norms and contribute to the common good. The same holds for members of a national community. All this holds, only many times over, when one deals with the international community, which is in a very preliminary state, its norms still young and being formed. In short, it is productive to have such norms and to promote them; however, before one condemns—let alone seeks to punish—those who do not live up to them, one best take into account their aspirational nature. For example, China is properly criticized for doing little to stop genocides. However, while the United States and its allies are credited for stopping the ethnic cleansing in Kosovo, they failed to do so in Cambodia, Rwanda, the Congo, and Sudan.[37] In a class in which many get a C or a lower grade, including the class leaders, those with a D should not be treated as if they were outliers in a class full of A students—but all should be expected to improve their standing.

Some of the same points apply to global governance. There obviously is no global state and hence the concept of a citizen barely applies. At the same time, although the expectations and demands of nations as citizens are much more circumscribed than those of membership, they are relatively more codified and the mechanisms for enforcements are clearer. Considering this context, China's various violations of established international laws might have been encouraged because they have not encountered a strong response. Most times, the nations attacked sought peaceful resolutions or simply yielded. Those whose economies were robbed, responded with rather mild complaints and did not reciprocate nor retaliate.[38] These weak responses further dilute the already weak concept of citizenship—and lessen the reasons to criticize China for not being a better global citizen.

Contextual Factors

So far the article assumes that all nations can be expected to abide by the same standards as far as their international roles are concerned. However, it is common to take into account differences in capabilities such as stages of development and magnitude of assets in making such judgments. How do these particularistic adjustments affect the applications of universal normative standards in evaluation of China given its recent, current, and expected capabilities?

Relative affluence: Even in well formed communities, contributions expected from community members are scaled according to their affluence and thus ability. Among the nations that did make substantial contributions to the tsunami and Haiti relief are the more affluent countries, such as the United States, Germany, and Japan. Although China is the world's second largest economy, it does not see itself—and by many measures is not—an affluent nation. It points to its income per capita as well below that of the main donor nations, a point that is confirmed by the most recent (2009) data from the CIA World Factbook, which shows that the average per capita GDP in the OECD countries is above $35,000, compared to about $6,700 in China.[39] At the same time, given China's rapid economic growth, one would expect it to become more giving in the future.

China improving: Bates Gill, Director of the Stockholm International Peace Research Institute, carefully reviewed in detail China's conduct in many areas, including regional and international security, energy security, economic development and assistance, peacekeeping, trade and economic affairs, and human rights. He concluded in a 2007 memo that "Looking back over the past 15 years and looking ahead to the next 10 or 15, the trend is clear that China is becoming a more responsible stakeholder."[40]

Turning first to membership, China has decided to increase the number of troops it sends to peacekeeping operations.[41] China has also increasingly participated in counter-piracy operations in Somalia, sending its naval fleets to help in the endeavor[42] and committing to share intelligence and conduct humanitarian rescue operations in coordination with other countries involved in anti-piracy efforts.[43]

In terms of becoming a better global citizen, China is improving with regards to its protection of intellectual property rights. Although piracy and counterfeiting remain widespread in China, the government has taken increased steps to put a halt to the practice since it joined the WTO in 2001.[44] Moreover, senior level Chinese officials vowed in December 2010 to more effectively tackle the issue, through new stricter laws on Internet piracy and cracking down on landlords who rent space to counterfeiters.[45] Changes in China's conduct are already reflected in its rise in the annual rankings of countries in terms of their level of intellectual property rights protection. For example, China moved from 53rd to 27th place of 139 countries between 2008 and 2011.[46]

Moreover, China is exhibiting a more positive attitude toward international organizations and laws. A review of such transformations by two leading scholars concluded that China accepts international law, actively participates in the UN, and represents itself ably in a variety of multilateral institutions—a drastic improvement from past decades when it "rejected what it called the 'bourgeois' rules and institutions that dominated the world community" and silenced its international law experts. Moreover, they demonstrate that China is playing "a responsible role" in multilateral organizations that deal with maritime issues, where China has many disputes with its neighbors, but tries to restrict its actions to "at least its own understanding of international law." They point out that China participated in the drafting of the UN Convention of the Law of the Sea (UNCLOS) and ratified it in 1996 (in contrast to the United States, which has yet to do so) and joined regional organizations protecting maritime environments in East Asia.[47]

Moreover, while China is often portrayed as expansionist and aggressive, unwilling to settle its disputes through peaceful means, these scholars point out that China reached a successful agreement with Japan for a joint hydrocarbon project in waterways disputed between the countries, and another one with Vietnam over the maritime boundary in the Gulf of Tonkin, whereby the body of water was divided about equally between them.[48] As already indicated, this trend will be next tested in the ways China resolves the disputes over its claims to the South China Sea.

Additionally, China is the first country to buy newly issued bonds from the International Monetary Fund to help countries worldwide weather the global financial crisis, spending $50 billion, as its voting rights in the IMF have been increased.[49]

Different interpretation of norms and duties: China by and large ceased to claim that human rights are bourgeois, Western ideas, and now tends to argue that it is observing them, or that it advances first socioeconomic rights with the legal and political rights to follow, once development is more advanced. Nor can one ignore that many other nations violate human rights at the same or even greater scale than China and that Western nations—quick to chastise China for violations of human rights—are most times turning a blind eye to such violations by other nations, for instance, Saudi Arabia.[50]

Finally, one ought to take into account the way nations perceive themselves, albeit as a mitigating factor and not as one that absolves them from the responsibilities of good members and the duties of upstanding citizens. China views itself as a nation that has been humiliated, exploited, and occupied for generations by Western powers and Japan,[51] a view that has much history to draw on. It views many of the demands now laid on it as an attempt to keep it in a weakened status. Gradually, as China's economic status is improving, and it is gaining in respect, China is moving to liberate itself from these sensibilities. However, they continue to affect its international conduct.

China, in some occasions, identifies itself with the South and sees itself as part of the global struggle to move toward a less tilted distribution of resources and assets that favors the North. Thus for instance, its $50 billion bond purchase from the IMF was dedicated to a program that focuses on the developing and emerging market countries of the South.[52]

China as a Partner

Strong communities are based on a core of shared values and a web of bonds of affinity among their members.[53] However, a measure of community can also be based on shared or mutual complementary interests. China is often accused of not even living up to this lower, less aspirational, more interest-driven standard. For instance, Minxin Pei writes that "China enjoys the practical benefits of the current world order but refuses to share its costs."[54] Others argue that China will benefit from peace and stability in Afghanistan, purchasing its minerals, while it refuses to contribute to the pacification of that country.[55] However, a closer examination shows that often what the critics see as shared interests, are not shared or at least are not so perceived from China's viewpoint.

From China's viewpoint, for example, for the US military to be mired in a war in Afghanistan (and before that in Iraq) and being further occupied with a proliferating Iran, is in line with in its interests, especially given statements by American military officials that define China's military as a major threat to the United States,[56] implying that China is an adversary.

A similar problem arises with regard to Iran's proliferation. China has no reason to fear that it or its allies (of which there are not many) will be targeted by Iran's nuclear arms. The notion that if Iran will acquire nuclear arms, this will lead other nations in the Middle East to acquire nuclear arms and will destabilize the region, is again not a course that troubles China nearly as much as the United States. At the same time, China is very concerned about energy sources, and Iran is a significant such source. Nevertheless, China has voted—albeit reluctantly and only after pressure was expended—to support several rounds of sanctions imposed on Iran.

Many view free trade as a clear case of a shared interest: all nations that open their markets are said to benefit. China is often chided for damaging others and itself by limiting access to its markets and by controlling its currency. However, even free trade theory is more complicated than it often is made out to be. The benefits to one and all are easy to demonstrate when full-blown free trade is achieved, however, not when nations merely move from more to less managed trade. And the benefits gained by free trade are not the same to all participants and there are considerable transition costs.[57]

Second, no nation is engaging in free trade, although they differ greatly in the extent and the ways they affect their trade. Finally, China has been moving in the desired direction, allowing the value of its currency to slowly rise and opening up its markets gradually, albeit surely not nearly at the pace the US favors. Thus, even in this area China may earn a C+, moving up from a C−, while quite a few nations have lower standing and the others hardly deserve a B.

Climate change is another topic for which China is criticized as not pulling its weight in service of a shared interest. China was blamed by various observers for sabotaging the 2009 UN Climate Change Summit in Copenhagen.[58] At the same time, China set a national target for 15 percent of its energy needs to come from renewable power sources by 2020.[59] And it is investing hundreds of billions of dollars in the clean-energy sector and is providing subsidies to domestic manufacturers of clean-energy products.[60]

In short, it is a bit simplistic to measure China by an idealized image of a community in which shared interests are clearly established and each member does its share. A better assessment recognizes that at least in some key areas there are different interests—or only a rather limited overlap therein—and that China is moving to pay more mind to such interests.

China as a Power: Challenge or Transformative?

So far China's international conduct was examined from relatively high aspirational standards, asking whether it does live up to that which is expected from a good member of the global community and an upstanding citizen of global governance, or at least a partner who realizes the value of serving shared or mutually complementary interests. China's conduct (and that of other nations) is however also assessed by much more real politics standards that concern the actual and changing power relations among the nations of the world.

Some who apply such standards see the United States as the de facto world government, as Michael Mandelbaum explicitly does.[61] Rising new powers and their assertive demands are seen from this viewpoint as upsetting the global order and hence are to be kept in line. In contrast, to the extent that one views the global architecture as moving from a unipolar to multipolar one, in which various powers become the focus of one region or another (e.g., France, Germany, and the United Kingdom as the main drivers of the EU) or—as several powers centers that share among them remaking a new world order (e.g., the G-20 or some other such number), the same policies by new powers seem much more acceptable, indeed transformative. Others, for good reason, prefer to point to "depolarization." One would reach still different assessments if one would use as one's frame for assessment the G-2 concept that some referred to as a condominium[62] and others as Chimerica.[63]

Two rather circumscribed situations illustrate the importance of this difference in the criteria employed in assessing China. When conflicts arise between China's claims to the South China Sea and its islands and counter claims by other countries in the region, including Vietnam, Malaysia, and the Philippines, China preferred to work out these differences with one nation at a time, while the United States threw its weight to support the position of the nations involved, to deal with China collectively. If one sees the United States as a hegemon, this move makes sense as it reflects the precept that the United States needs to contain and "balance" China, as a new upstart, assertive if not aggressive power, to maintain global order as headed by the United States.

In contrast, if one views the world as increasingly multipolar, especially along regional lines, and does not view this change as threatening, one sees no obvious reason that the United States should be involved at all, in what might be considered East Asian issues, other than delight in the commitment of all involved to resolves matters peacefully.

Similarly, if one views the United States as the hegemon that needs to contain and balance china, it makes sense that the United States would seek to push its armed forces to the border of China if the North Korean regime collapses and the two Koreas are unified. In contrast, if one views the world as moving toward a multipolar one, and sees China as a legitimate regional power (albeit not as a regional hegemon), one would favor the United States committing itself to keep its troops at the demilitarized zone or even removing them from Korea altogether over time.

In Conclusion

China is surely not a responsible stakeholder, but then few nations are. Urging China to become a better member of the global community and a better global citizen is quite legitimate, as long as one recognizes the aspirational nature of these expectations. And one ought to take into account China's history, low income per capita, and improving conduct. Moreover, the judgment that China does not even carry its share when shared interests are involved, often do not take into account that these interests are often not as shared as they may seem at first blush. Finally, if one views the United States as a hegemon, there are good reasons to seek to contain China. These reasons are much less evident if one accepts that the world is becoming more multipolar, and China is a legitimate regional power.

Notes

*   I am indebted to Marissa Cramer for extensive research assistance and editorial comments, and to Joshua Kurlantzick for comments on an earlier draft.

1.   Robert Kaplan, "Don't Panic About China," *The Atlantic* (January 28, 2010), http://www.theatlantic.com/magazine/archive/2010/01/don-apos-t-panic-about-china/7926/ (accessed June 18, 2012).

2.   John Lee, "China Won't Be a Responsible Stakeholder," *The Wall Street Journal* (February 1, 2010), http://online.wsj.com/article/SB100014 24052748704722304575037931817880328.html (accessed June 18, 2012).

3.   Elizabeth C. Economy, "The Game Changer: Coping with China's Foreign Policy Revolution," *Foreign Affairs* (November/December 2010): 142.

4.   Richard Nixon, "Asia after Viet Nam," *Foreign Affairs* (October 1967): 111–25.

5.   Alastair Iain Johnston, "Is China a Status Quo Power?" *International Security* 27, no. 4 (Spring 2003): 6–7.

6.   Tony Blair's 1996 speech in Singapore cited in Michael Hopkins, *The Planetary Bargain: Corporate Social Responsibility Matters* (London: Earthscan Publications, 2003), 18.

7.   Robert Ross, "Beijing as a Conservative Power," *Foreign Affairs* (March/April 1997): 33–44.

8.   Johnston, "Is China a Status Quo Power?" 28.

9.   Ibid.

10.   Erich Follath, "The Dragon's Embrace: China's Soft Power Is a Threat to the West," *Der Spiegel* (July 28, 2010), http://www.spiegel.de/international/world/0,1518,708645,00.html (accessed June 18, 2012).

11.   Evan A. Feigenbaum, "Beijing's Billions," *Foreign Policy* (May 20, 2010), http://www.foreignpolicy.com/articles/2010/05/19/beijings_billions (accessed October 18, 2010).

12. Srikanth Kondapalli, "Tsunami and China: Relief with Chinese Characteristics," *Asian Affairs* (January 17, 2005), http://rudar.ruc.dk/bitstream/1800/1446/4/Dokument.pdf (accessed June 18, 2012).

13. Drew Thompson, "Tsunami Relief Reflects China's Regional Aspirations," *China Brief*, Jamestown Foundation (January 17, 2005), http://www.jamestown.org/single/?no_cache=1&tx_ttnews[tt_news]=27394 (accessed October 21, 2010).

14. Kondapalli, Tsunami and China.

15. "China Must End UN 'Interference'," *Save Darfur* http://www.savedarfur.org/pages/press/china_must_end_un_interference/ (accessed November 17, 2010).

16. "South China Sea/Spratly Islands," GlobalSecurity.org, http://www.globalsecurity.org/military/world/war/spratly.htm (accessed November 17, 2010).

17. John Pomfret, "Beijing Claims 'Indisputable Sovereignty' over South China Sea," *The Washington Post* (July 31, 2010).

18. China is also said to have become more assertive in its claims over the South China Sea, labeling sovereignty over the sea a "core national interest." However, such claims are not discussed here in so far as they are only statements and not behaviors.

19. See on this "EP-3 incident" Seymour Hersh, "The Online Threat," *The New Yorker* (November 1, 2010).

20. Examples include the 2006 incident when a Chinese submarine stalked the *USS Kitty Hawk* and surfaced within a torpedo's firing range and two incidences in 2009 involving the *USS John S. McCain* and *The Victorious.*

21. The Chinese argue that in its interpretation of international law, surveillance and certain other military vessels are considered to be engaged in hostile activities and thus should not be afforded the same rights to free passage as peacetime vessels: See legal brief by Ji Guoxing, "The Legality of the 'Impeccable Incident'," http://www.chinasecurity.us/pdfs/jiguoxing.pdf (accessed October 5, 2010). However, China's viewpoint is not a widely accepted interpretation of the UN Convention on the Law of the Sea or other international agreements: See Glenn Tiffert, "By Provocatively Engaging the US Navy, Beijing May Be Trying to Change the International Rules," *Yale Global* (March 27, 2009), http://yaleglobal.yale.edu/content/china-rises-again-%E2%80%93-part-ii (accessed June 18, 2012).

22. Christopher Drew, "New Targets for Spies: Employers' Trade Secrets," *International Herald Tribune* (October 19, 2010).

23. David Drummond, "A New Approach to China," *Googleblog* (January 12, 2010), http://googleblog.blogspot.com/2010/01/new-approach-to-china.html (accessed November 17, 2010).

24. U.S.-China Economic and Security Review Commission (USCC), 2010 Report to Congress (November 2010), http://www.uscc.gov/annual_report/2010/annual_report_full_10.pdf (accessed November 17, 2010).

25. Robert McMillan, "Google Attack Part of Widespread Spying Effort," *Computerworld* (January 13, 2010), http://www.computerworld.com/s/article/9144221/Google_attack_part_of_widespread_spying_effort (accessed November 15, 2010).

26. USCC, 2010 Report to Congress.

27. US Assistant Secretary of Commerce put the estimate at nearly $24 billion a year in a 2004 statement: "US lashes out at Chinese Piracy," *Asia Times* (January 15, 2005), http://www.atimes.com/atimes/China/GA15Ad03.html (accessed November 15, 2010).

28. Henry Blodget, "How to Solve China's Piracy Problem," *Slate* (April 12, 2005), http://www.slate.com/id/2116629/ (accessed November 17, 2010).

29. Frederik Balfour, "U.S. Takes Piracy Pushback to WTO," *Bloomberg Business Week* (April 10, 2007), http://www.businessweek.com/globalbiz/content/ apr2007/gb20070410_466097.htm (accessed November 15, 2010).

30. US House of Representatives, Select Committee on U.S. National Security and Military/Commercial Concerns with the People's Republic of China, *U.S. National Security and Military/Commercial Concerns With the People's Republic of China*, 106 Cong., 1 sess., 1999, 60.

31. Michael R. Crittenden and Shayndi Rice, "Chinese Firm 'Hijacked' Data," *The New York Times* (November 18, 2010): A8.

32. James Lewis, "To Protect the U.S. Against Cyberwar, Best Defense Is a Good Offense," *U.S. News and World Report* (March 29, 2010).

33. "Cyber War: Sabotaging the System," *60 Minutes* (November 8, 2009).

34. USCC, 2010 Report to Congress.

35. Kate Connolly, "Germany Accuses China of Industrial Espionage," *The Guardian* (July 22, 2009).

36. Joshua Kurlantzick, "A Beijing Backlash: China Is Starting to Face Consequences for Its Newly Aggressive Stance," *Newsweek* (October 4, 2010).

37. Samantha Power, *A Problem from Hell* (New York: Basic Books, 2002).

38. According to an article in *Bloomberg Business Week* ("The Runaway Trade Giant" [April 24, 2006], http://www.businessweek.com/magazine/content/06_17/b3981039.htm [accessed November 15, 2010]), a reason why the United States has not been more persistent in using the WTO to halt Chinese piracy is that "the WTO lacks clear standards on adequate progress towards enforcement" of intellectual property rights. To prove China's inadequate enforcement of anti-piracy laws, the United States would need hard data from companies that do business in China. But the problem is that even if these companies are being harmed by intellectual property rights violations, they also do not want to be seen as cooperating with the US government. "Besides risking retaliation against their mainland operations, executives aren't sure a successful WTO ruling will solve anything, given China's weak rule of law." Moreover, if the suit were to fail—a not unlikely prospect—an even worse scenario could arise: China would probably be emboldened to become even laxer about enforcing its intellectual property rights laws. See also Keith Bradsher, "Sitting Out the China Trade Battles," *The New York Times* (December 23, 2010).

39. The CIA World Factbook, https://www.cia.gov/library/publications/the-world-factbook/rankorder/2004rank.html (accessed November 17, 2010).

40. Bates Gill, "China Becoming a Responsible Stakeholder," event resource, The Carnegie Endowment for International Peace (June 11, 2007), http://carnegieendowment.org/files/Bates_paper.pdf (accessed October 20, 2010). See

also Bates Gill, *Rising Star: China's New Security Diplomacy* (Washington, DC: Brookings Institution Press, 2007).

41. Andrew Higgins, "China Showcasing Its Softer Side," *The Washington Post* (December 2, 2009).

42. Maureen Fan, "China to Aid in Fighting Somali Pirates," *The Washington Post* (December 18, 2008).

43. Anne Barrowclough, "China Sends Navy to Fight Somali Pirates," *The Times* (December 26, 2008).

44. Balfour, U.S. Takes Piracy Pushback to WTO.

45. Sewell Chan, "China Agrees to Intellectual Property Protections," *The New York Times* (December 15, 2010).

46. *The Global Competitiveness Report 2010–2011* (Geneva: The World Economic Forum, 2011); *The Global Competitiveness Report 2008–2009* (Geneva: The World Economic Forum, 2009).

47. Jerome A. Cohen and Jon M. Van Dyke, "Finding Its Sea Legs," *The South China Morning Post* (October 26, 2010).

48. Ibid. See also David Shambaugh, "Return to the Middle Kingdom? China and Asia in the Early Twenty-First Century," in *Power Shift*, ed. Shambaugh (Berkeley, CA: University of California Press, 2005), 24.

49. "China to Buy $50 Billion of First I.M.F. Bonds," *The New York Times* (September 3, 2009). On China's economic leadership, see also David M. Lampton, *The Three Faces of Chinese Power* (Berkeley, CA: University of California Press, 2008), 111.

50. Jackson Diehl, "Obama's National Security Strategy Is Light on Human Rights," *The Washington Post* (May 31, 2010).

51. Shaun Narine, "State, Sovereignty, Political Legitimacy and Regional Institutionalism in the Asia-Pacific," *The Pacific Review* 17, no. 3 (2004): 14; Lau Guan Kim, "A Lie Repeated Often Becomes Truth," *China Daily* (April 14, 2004), http://www.chinadaily.com.cn/english/doc/2004-04/14/content_323217.htm (accessed December 3, 2010).

52. "China to Buy $50 Billion of First I.M.F. Bonds."

53. Amitai Etzioni, *The New Golden Rule: Community and Morality in a Democratic Society* (New York: Basic Books, 1996).

54. Minxin Pei, "China: The Big Free Rider," *Newsweek* (January 22, 2010); see also Stephanie T. Kleine-Ahlbrandt, "Beijing, Global Free Rider," *Foreign Policy* (November 12, 2009), http://www.foreignpolicy.com/articles/2009/11/12/beijing_global_free_rider (accessed October 18, 2010).

55. Robert D. Kaplan, "Beijing's Afghan Gamble," *The New York Times* (October 6, 2009); Anne Applebaum, "Making the World Safe for China," *Slate* (September 27, 2010), http://www.slate.com/id/2268833/ (accessed October 18, 2010).

56. For instance, Admiral Robert Willard of the US Pacific Command testified that China's military build-up is "aggressive" at the House Armed Services Committee in January 2010: Bill Gertz, "Harsh Words from Chinese Military Raise Threat Concerns," *The Washington Times* (March 5, 2010). Similarly, Joint Chiefs of Staff Chairman Admiral Mike Mullen said in June, 2010 that he was "genuinely concerned" about China's military modernization: Huma

Yusuf, "US Concerned about China's Military Investments," *The Christian Science Monitor* (June 10, 2010). And the Department of Defense's 2010 Quadrennial Defense Review said that the lack of transparency in China's military modernization programs raises "legitimate questions regarding its long-term intentions": Department of Defense, *Quadrennial Defense Review Report* (February 2010), 31.

57. R. G. Lipsey and Kelvin Lancaster, "The General Theory of Second Best," *Review of Economic Studies* 24, no. 1 (1956): 11–32.

58. "China's Thing About Numbers: How an Emerging Superpower Dragged Its Feet, Then Dictated Terms, at a Draining Diplomatic Marathon," *The Economist* (December 30, 2009); Sam Coates, "China to Blame for Failure of Copenhagen Climate Deal, Says Ed Miliband," *The Times* (December 21, 2009); Tobias Rapp, Christian Schwägerl, and Gerald Traufetter, "How China and India Sabotaged the UN Climate Summit," *Der Spiegel* (May 5, 2010).

59. Jonathan Adams, "China's Climate Change Talks: What's Changed since Copenhagen," *The Christian Science Monitor* (October 5, 2010).

60. Economy, The Game Changer, 144.

61. Michael Mandelbaum, *The Frugal Superpower: America's Global Leadership in a Cash-Strapped Era* (New York: Public Affairs, 2010), 4–5.

62. David Shambuagh, Introduction to *Power Shift*, 15; C. Fred Bergsten, "Two's Company," *Foreign Affairs* (September/October 2009): 169–70.

63. Niall Ferguson, "What 'Chimerica' Hath Wrought," *The American Interest* (January/February 2009), http://www.the-american-interest.com/article.cfm?piece=533 (accessed October 15, 2010).

3

Who Is Violating the International Rules?

The question of whether China will buy into the prevailing liberal, rule-based international order—one promoted and underwritten by the United States—ought to be reversed with regard to one key element of this order: the Westphalian norm. Here the West is seeking major modifications that weaken the norm, while China is the champion of the established rule and the international order based on it. Several leading Western progressive leaders and public intellectuals have championed the legitimation of another major category of intervention: armed humanitarian intervention, referred to as the "responsibility to protect." And some in the West favor legitimizing interference in the internal affairs of other nations if they develop nuclear arms, referred to as the "responsibility to prevent." Both explicitly call on making sovereignty conditional on nation-states conducting themselves in line with new norms that directly conflict with the Westphalian one. Both entail not merely making exceptions on a case-by-case basis to the sovereignty norm as this or that crisis is faced (say as Qaddafi forces are about the overrun Benghazi and threaten to slaughter civilians there), but for categorical legitimation of interventions if they meet a priori criteria.

One should note from the onset that the support for both normative changes even in the West is far from universal, as reflected in reactions to the 2003 invasion of Iraq and opposition to military action against Iran even if it becomes even clearer that it is developing nuclear arms and maintaining its threat to "wipe off the map" another nation. The 2011 intervention in Libya also raised many questions, including in the United States.

The issue hence is not whether China will buy into the rule-based order, but whether it can be convinced or motivated to support major changes in the rules, which the West—and not China—are seeking.

45

Once I lay the groundwork on which the answer to this question may be built, I suggest that it depends to a significant extent on how high the bar interventions would need to clear is set in order to be considered legitimate and on the forum that will decide whether or not a given nation has lived up to its new responsibilities.

Throughout the discussion, it is important to keep in mind that both suggested normative changes seek to justify armed interventions; transnational nonlethal acts such as promoting human rights and democracy through mass media (e.g., Voice of America's China service) and cultural ones (e.g., student exchanges) are not at issue, or least should not be, because they do not violate the Westphalian norm. I keep referring to the Westphalian norm rather than the treaty because at issue is the contemporary understating of the principle that one nation ought not to use force to interfere in the internal affairs of another nation, and not the text of a document signed some 300 years ago.

China Viewed as the Challenger

A question often raised in American foreign policy discourse is whether China, as a rising power, will buy into the prevailing "liberal world order." The preeminent scholar on the subject, G. John Ikenberry, posed this question in a 2008 essay in *Foreign Affairs*, when he asked, "Will China overthrow the existing order or become part of it?"[1] Stewart Patrick, writing in *Foreign Affairs* in 2010, suggests that the answer to the question is that emerging powers, China included, "often oppose the political and economic ground rules of the post–World War II liberal order."[2] Elizabeth C. Economy goes a step further, arguing that Beijing is becoming a "revolutionary power" that is seeking "to remake global norms and institutions."[3] Stefan Halper contends in *The Beijing Consensus* that China is delivering a "mortal blow" to the assumption that the West holds "the power to shape the future of the international system to guide it gradually toward the norms and values that we imbue with a sense of universal destiny."[4] Others speak of China as if it were a feral child that needs to be "socialized" into the world order, echoing Richard Nixon, who wrote in *Foreign Affairs* in the late 1960s that China should be engaged into global institutions to encourage it to act with more "civility."[5]

Many of these authors do not refer specifically to the Westphalian norm nor do they necessarily spell out the key elements of the liberal, rule-based order that China ought to embrace. There are, however, several core values that appear in writings on the subject. Some scholars refer, in this context, to the ideas of the 1997 Manifesto of the Liberal International: "We believe that civil society and constitutional democracy provide the most just and stable basis for political order . . . We believe that an economy based on free market rules leads to the most efficient distribution of wealth and resources, encourages innovation, and promotes flexibility . . . We believe that close cooperation among democratic societies through global and regional organizations, within the framework of international law, of respect for human rights, the rights of ethnic and national minorities, and of a shared commitment to economic development worldwide, is the necessary foundation for world peace and for economic and environmental sustainability."[6]

What is the place of the Westphalian norm in the liberal order? Ikenberry correctly points out that the Westphalian norm deserves much credit because it serves as a "foundation" upon which the liberal world order has been forged through creating a "stable system of states."[7] Liberalism builds on this norm as it seeks peaceful conflict resolutions and multilateral cooperation amongst states. Similarly, English School theorists, such as Hedley Bull, posit that international society took shape around the Westphalian principle, which continues to guide international institutions.[8]

Who Is Seeking Change?

The 1990s and early 2000s saw numerous humanitarian crises around the world. The international community intervened with the use of force in some of these, such as Kosovo, but did not in others. Many liberals and supporters of human rights were particularly troubled by the fact that the international community did not act to stop the genocide in Rwanda, Sudan, Somalia, and the Democratic Republic of the Congo. In an influential book entitled *A Problem from Hell*, Samantha Power pointed to still other, earlier genocides that were ignored, especially the Armenian genocide and those in Cambodia, Bosnia, and Iraq.[9]

These humanitarian crises brought new attention to the issue of sovereignty. Among those who looked at the issue anew were Francis Deng and his associates, who published a 1996 book entitled, *Sovereignty as Responsibility*, which argues that when nations do not conduct their internal affairs in ways that meet internationally recognized standards, other nations not only have the right, but the duty to intervene.[10] In effect, such governments forfeit their sovereignty, making it conditional on good conduct. This idea has since been referred to in a sort of shorthand as "the responsibility to protect."

This major modification of the Westphalian norm was further advanced by a report of the International Commission on Intervention and State Sovereignty (the Evans-Sahnoun Commission), "The Responsibility to Protect," issued in 2001.[11] In 2004, the UN Secretary General's High-Level Panel on Threats, Challenges, and Change (the "High-Level Panel") issued its report, "A More Secure World—Our Shared Responsibility," which lends further support to this reformulation of sovereignty.[12]

The Commission's report puts sovereignty as responsibility at the center of its proposals. It argued, "The Charter of the UN is itself an example of an international obligation voluntarily accepted by member states. On the one hand, in granting membership of the UN, the international community welcomes the signatory state as a responsible member of the community of nations. On the other hand, the state itself, in signing the Charter, accepts the responsibilities of membership flowing from that signature. There is no transfer or dilution of state sovereignty. But there is a necessary recharacterization involved: from sovereignty as control to sovereignty as responsibility in both internal functions and external duties."[13]

While the UN Security Council had previously authorized interventions in states such as Somalia and Haiti, such authorizations have been rare and were made on an ad hoc basis; it had not developed a general case for degrading national sovereignty. Proponents of the new concept of sovereignty as responsibility sought to legitimate a fundamental shift in the international community's role in the internal affairs of states by establishing an a priori category of conditions under which interventions would be justified. To the extent that this change of the Westphalian norm was accepted, nations that called for armed humanitarian intervention no longer needed to justify them in principle but merely to show that a given nation had not lived up to its responsibilities, for instance, by allowing a genocide to take place.

In 2004, two leading American foreign policy mavens, Lee Feinstein and Anne-Marie Slaughter, sought to further scale back sovereignty by adding a second responsibility that sovereign nations had to discharge, referred to as the responsibility to prevent.[14] This responsibility entailed a nation's obligation to refrain from acquiring or developing weapons of mass destruction (WMDs). Moreover, the international community was put on notice that it was its role to ensure that nations acting irresponsibly in this regard lost the privileges of sovereignty and became subject to intervention.

In a sense, this new responsibility reflects the spirit of the nonproliferation treaty (NPT), according to which its 188 signatory nations agreed that nations that did not have nuclear arms committed themselves not to acquire them and those that had them committed themselves to give them up. However, the NPT per se has no enforcement mechanism. It leaves it to the International Atomic Energy Agency (IAEA) to report to the United Nations when nations deviate from the treaty and for the UN to decide what action, if any, to take. Nor does the NPT explicitly deal with nations that refused to sign it (such as India, Pakistan, and Israel) or that quit (such as North Korea). Thus, by defining a universal responsibility to prevent the acquisition of nuclear arms and call on the nations of the world to enforce it, Feinstein and Slaughter dramatically advanced the NPT precept.

In short, the agents of change, who are advocating a major break in one of the key elements of the normative international order, are either progressive voices in the West and UN officials or Western scholars, public intellectuals, and officials.

China: Supporting the Established Order

China, far from seeking to challenge or transform the global order in this regard, consistently opposed changes to the Westphalian norm either in the name of the responsibility to protect or to prevent. Ever since it abandoned its Mao-era policy of supporting communist and anti-imperialist insurgencies in other nations, China has argued repeatedly and strenuously that national governments should be the sole, legitimate users of force within their borders, which it holds, is the "universally recognized norm of international law."[15] Thus, Chinese President Jiang Zemin stated in a speech at the United Nations Millennium Summit on September 6, 2000, "Respect for each other's independence and sovereignty is vital to the maintenance of world peace. Countries would not be able to live in amity unless they follow the five principles of mutual respect for sovereignty and territorial integrity, mutual non-aggression, non-interference in each other's internal affairs, equality and mutual benefit, and peaceful coexistence."[16]

China's position on cases of armed humanitarian intervention, in line with the responsibility to protect, is based on the invocation of the Westphalian norm. China abstained from and was the only country not to vote in favor of resolutions 781 and 816 authorizing the establishment and enforcement of a no-fly zone over Bosnia and Herzegovina in 1992–1993 to prevent attacks by Serbian warplanes, arguing that "consent of all relevant parties" was lacking.[17] When considerations were underway for the international community to try to stop the genocide in Rwanda, China argued that any international intervention would require consent of the Rwandan government. When Western powers held that action was called for to stop ethnic cleansing in Kosovo, it worked via NATO and not the UN, because it anticipated that China, along with Russia, would have vetoed authorization for such a mission. In response, China's UN delegate Ambassador Shen Guofang stated that NATO created "an extremely dangerous precedent in the history of international relations . . . In essence, the 'human rights over sovereignty' theory serves to infringe upon the sovereignty of other States and to promote hegemonism under the purposes and principles of the United Nations Charter. The international community should maintain vigilance against it."[18]

On Darfur, China insisted that no UN peacekeepers be sent without the consent of the government of Sudan. This position enabled Sudan to reject a 2006 UN deployment of peacekeepers in that country. (While some argue that China played a constructive role by "persuading" the Sudanese government to eventually assent to a UN role in Darfur, such persuasion confirms rather than modifies the Westphalian norm. Once a nation agrees to allow peacekeeping forces or IAEA inspectors into its country, these acts do not constitute a violation of its sovereignty, and in this sense are not "interventions," antagonistic uses of force.)

Although China joined the heads of 150 governments at the 2005 UN World Summit who endorsed the "the responsibility to protect" doctrine, its interpretation of the concept is similar to its stance on Darfur: it sees it as a responsibility for the international community to provide mediation of conflicts that cause grave humanitarian tolls, but not through the use of force without consent of the concerned government. Still, the flexibility China showed on Darfur and the responsibility to protect doctrine—even if limited—suggests that there is some room for a normative dialogue with China on whether certain categories of armed humanitarian interventions could be viewed as legitimate.

China also showed flexibility on Somalia, Haiti, and East Timor, but these were all for very particular reasons, in which it was questionable if there was any breach of sovereignty. China argued that Somalia was a unique situation because the level of anarchy resulted in there was no functioning national government to give approval for a UN intervention. Haiti was a case in which the ousted (via coup) UN-recognized government was asking for international intervention even as the new military government opposed it. And Indonesia eventually gave its consent to intervention in East Timor (though this was "induced" consent under pressure, like in the Darfur case).

Regarding the responsibility to prevent, China joined France and Germany in criticizing President Bush's decision to wage war on Iraq. China's state-run newspaper, the *People's Daily*, reported that President Jiang Zemin considered it China's "responsibility to take various measures to avoid war" and push for a "political solution of the Iraq issue in the framework of the United Nations."[19] China took this stance even after supporting the 2002 Security Council Resolution 1441, which granted Iraq a last chance to disarm or face "serious consequences."[20]

China clearly favors political over military solutions to the nuclear weapons proliferation of Iran and North Korea. Various observers contend that when it has been willing to take measures against these countries, they were limited, e.g., watered-down sanctions, and China's support came only as a result of immense pressure from the West.

In short, there seems to be no indication that China is accepting the responsibility to prevent anymore than it is embracing the responsibility to protect. It is supporting the long-established, widely embraced, traditional Westphalian norm. It is clearly the conservative force in this matter. (I keep adding in this matter, because the same may not be true about other elements of the liberal rule-based order, not under discussion here.)

Next

If one accepts, even merely for the sake of argument, that the West is seeking major modifications to the Westphalian norm and China is seeking to uphold the traditional order, the question follows: what might be the next steps that could lead to an agreed change in the rule-based order?

First, it might serve if the West itself could achieve a higher level of shared understanding about the favored normative changes. The progressive interventionist voices have weakened since the 2003 invasion of Iraq, because they feared that demoting the sovereignty principle from its former preeminence could be used in future forced regime changes. As noted in *The Economist*, "The Bush year have also damaged the intellectual case for intervention."[21] And *Orbis* editor James Kurth wrote that "Among the casualties of the Iraq War has been the U.S. political will to undertake any new humanitarian interventions."[22]

When the United States championed and led an armed intervention in Libya in 2011, the Obama administration did not base its position on the responsibility to protect, arguing that Libya was a prime example of a case in which such action was justified, and it refrained from using such a categorical legitimation of the intervention. Instead, it stressed that the intervention in Libya was an exceptional case, and another intervention under similar circumstances was off the table. As the President put it, "It is true that America cannot use our military wherever repression occurs. And given the costs and risks of intervention, we must always measure our interests against the need for action. But that cannot be an argument for never acting on behalf of what's right. In this particular country—Libya—at this particular moment, we were faced with the prospect of violence on a horrific scale."[23] As Thom Shanker and Helene Cooper noted in *The New York Times* regarding Obama's justification for intervening, "these conditions seemed tailor made for Libya."[24]

Hillary Clinton promised during her presidential campaign to "operationalize"[25] the responsibility to protect doctrine and "adopt a policy that recognizes the prevention of mass atrocities as an important national security interest of the United States, not just a humanitarian goal"[26] and "develop a government-wide strategy to support this policy, including a strategy for working with other leading democracies, the United Nations, and regional organizations."[27] By contrast, when Obama was asked at a press conference about his thoughts on the responsibility to protect, he avoided embracing the new norm and stated instead, "There are going to be exceptional circumstances in which I think the need for international intervention becomes a moral imperative, the most obvious example being a situation like Rwanda where genocide has occurred."[28]

The Obama administration position on the responsibility to prevent is reflected in its position on Iran. It repeatedly announced that it was "unacceptable"[29] for Iran to acquire nuclear arms, and mobilized the international community to impose sanctions on Iran. Obama promised during his campaign, "I will take no options off the table in dealing with this potential Iranian threat."[30] However, so far the administration has not chosen to interfere by use of arms—and if it did, it would find very little support among its allies, not to mention in the third world, China, Russia, or world public opinion.

According to a 2011 report by the German Marshall Fund of the United States and Italy's Compagnia di San Paolo foundation, most US and European policymakers would prefer a nuclear-armed Iran to taking military action if the diplomatic track fails.[31] Only 42 percent of policymakers in the United States and 32 percent in Brussels support military action.[32] Consider that even former French President Nicolas Sarkozy, who pressed strenuously for tougher sanctions on Iran, has not endorsed a military option and urged Israel not to attack Iran in July 2009. Thus, before one can discuss what the United States can or should expect the role of China to be—not with regard to sanctions or humanitarian aid, but with regard to armed interventions to stop genocides and to prevent the proliferation of nuclear arms—the United States needs to sort out its current position and find out whether its allies and others will support its position to the extent that it continues to favor a scaled-back sovereignty. It then would be ready to see whether it can move China from its position as a strong supporter of the traditional liberal rule to a scaled back one if the United States still favors such a change.

The Forum and the Criteria

In the transnational give-and-take about changes to the Westphalian norm with China, and in effect with governments, publics, and institutions worldwide, two key issues arise: which authority will rule when the violations of national responsibilities reach the level that justifies an armed intervention and which a priori criteria ought they to employ? (I keep stressing a priori criteria, because ad hoc justifications make for weak legitimation.)

The UN Security Council is often cited as the appropriate forum for such ruling. Thus, when NATO intervened in Kosovo without UN authorization this action was referred to as legitimate by some, but also as illegal. The 2003 invasion of Iraq faced much condemnation in many parts of the world, because it was not fully authorized by the UN. In contrast, interventions in East Timor and the Congo were considered not only legitimate, but also legal, as was the 1991 rollback of Saddam from Kuwait.

Reliance on the UN raises many familiar issues, including that the Security Council veto power is held by five nations that were part of the alliance that won World War II two generations ago, but do not reflect the major nations today; that many of the UN members are themselves tyrannies and gross violators of human rights; and that the Security Council was deadlocked and unable to act when atrocities took place in Cambodia, the Kurdish parts of Iraq, and elsewhere. There were many other reasons for inaction, but the UN structure was one of them. Numerous suggestions have been made to make the Security Council more representative and thus enhance the legitimacy of its rulings. However, for various familiar reasons that need not to be revisited here, these reforms are not forthcoming.

One may hence fall back on applying to the UN what Winston Churchill said about democracy—a very flawed system and the best there is. There is no other international body, nor is one seriously suggested that could replace the UN Security Council, and hence all future discussions are very likely to be centered around the UN. China is both much more likely to support this body than, say, the Council of Democracies or NATO or any other body that comes to mind. And it is very unlikely to agree to dilute its veto power by adding other nations that will be granted such power. Indeed, Chinese President Jiang Zemin stated China's continued support for the central role of the UN Security Council in handling international disputes: "We should come together to safeguard the authority of the Security Council rather than to impair it . . . it is against the will of many member states for any country to bypass the Security Council and do what it wishes on major issues concerning world peace and security."[33]

In short, although the West may seek to change the forum, for instance, the United States stated that it favors the membership of India in the Security Council, realistically one must assume that for the foreseeable future, the UN Security Council will be the international body that will rule whether the responsibility to protect or to prevent has been violated and what armed responses are called for.

If the question of which forum is in effect is settled, one had best turn one's attention to the second question: what qualifies as a violation worthy of breaching sovereignty? If the West is seeking common ground with China and the international community, the key issues hence are what specific conditions justify action and how high to set the bar.

The major contributors to the sovereignty-as-responsibility conception vary in how they address this problem. Deng et al. go about defining nations in which outside powers could intervene by defining the opposite: nations in which intervention would be impermissible. These exempt nations are those with governments that "under normal circumstances, strive to ensure for their people an effective governance that guarantees a just system of law and order, democratic freedoms, respect for fundamental rights, and general welfare."[34] With the bar set so low and vague, there are few nations that would not be vulnerable to intervention.

Substantially more limiting criteria, which hold more promise of acceptance by China, were proposed by The Evans-Sahnoun Commission. It proposed that intervention require: " (a) large-scale loss of life, actual or apprehended, with genocidal intent or not, which is the product either of deliberate state action, or state neglect or inability to act, or a failed state situation; or (b) large-scale 'ethnic cleansing,' actual or apprehended, whether carried out by killing, forced expulsion, acts of terror or rape."[35] Moreover, both the Commission and the High-Level Panel assert that any intervention must be based on exclusively humanitarian intentions, be taken as a last resort, use only the minimum force necessary to complete the mission, and have reasonable prospects of success.

The importance of such a high bar to China is reflected in a 2006 statement by its UN ambassador, which supported the responsibility to protect doctrine as it pertains to "genocide, war crimes, ethnic cleansing, and crimes against humanity,"[36] but insisted that "it is not appropriate to expand, willfully to interpret or even abuse this concept."[37]

Whether the killing in Libya prior to the UN resolution authorizing a no-fly zone met the limiting criteria for the use of force is not self-evident. In any case, China abstained, which has usually been its way of opposing such armed interventions. It hence follows that if one is seeking common ground with China in the quest to modify the Westphalian norm, one had best consider stricter adherence to the high standards spelled out in the recommendations of the Evans–Sahnoun Commission and applying definitions of genocide and war crimes recognized in international law.

With regard to the duty to prevent, the problem is whether development or possession of any type of WMD by states "without internal checks" legitimates intervention, or whether only specific kinds of WMD qualify. Biological and chemical weapons are much more difficult to detect and control than nuclear ones. Hence an international regime dedicated to preventing all WMD would have to

55

be much more interventionist than one dedicated at least initially to preventing only the proliferation of nuclear arms. Given that chemical and most biological agents are reported to be less dangerous than nuclear ones, a strong case can be made that the threshold for intervention should, at least for now, be set at the nuclear prevention level.

It is worthy of note that China has not explicitly condemned the responsibility to prevent. When Former Vice-Premier and Foreign Minister Qian Qichen argued against the preventive war doctrine in an editorial in a state-run newspaper, the Foreign Ministry distanced itself from those remarks, stating that they were not commissioned. Moreover, China has spoken out against nuclear proliferation, though urged that solutions come only through the UN.

A normative give-and-take with China is much more likely to bear fruit the more one stresses that neither new responsibility justifies forced regime change and neither calls for bringing about democracy and enforcing human rights by the use of armed interventions. These kinds of regime changes are most abhorrent to China for obvious reasons, but they are not encompassed in either the responsibility to protect nor to prevent.

Indeed, there is a very rarely discussed deep normative principle that underlies and connects the two new responsibilities: both focus on saving lives and no more. They thus provide a much higher bar for interventions than those sought by neo-conservatives and others who favor promoting the "freedom agenda" by use of lethal means. This issue came up recently when the invasion of Libya was considered. There was much more support—in the Arab League, Europe, and even in the United States—for preventing a massacre of thousands of civilians in Benghazi than for using military force to push Qaddafi out, opening the door to a new regime. Indeed, when President Obama laid out the rationale for the intervention during his speech at the National Defense University on March 28, 2011, he stressed the saving-lives goal and added that the ousting of Qaddafi will be sought only with "nonmilitary means."[38]

However, as so often happens, once the shooting started, it escalated well beyond the original goal, demonstrating the danger of the slippery slope. That once one seeks to modify the Westphalian norm, one must set clear and strong markers to notch the slope. One can justify going to war to save lives (if all other means of stopping the massacres and the spread of nuclear arms have been exhausted), but it is much more taxing to make a normative case for advancing other rights by the use of force, such as to free speech, religious practices, and assembly.

The right to life has a special standing. Most obviously because all other rights are conditioned on it, but it is not conditioned on these other rights being observed. (Dead people lose all the other rights, while those who live may fight for and see the day their other rights will be realized.) The particularly high normative standing of the right to life is further revealed insofar as the criminal codes of numerous nations place a higher penalty on taking a life than on violating other rights. Finally, forced regime changes often do not lead to the hoped-for results and tend to cause great losses of life and numerous casualties, as we witnessed in Iraq and Afghanistan.

At the same time, the West has a strong case to reject China's claim that nonlethal transnational acts, by means of communication or educational and cultural exchanges, amount to intervention in a nation's internal affairs. China was clearly out of line when it argued in 2011 that a UN human rights agency violated its sovereignty by condemning the torture and arbitrary detention of Chinese human rights lawyer Gao Zhisheng.[39] Similarly, China misused the sovereignty argument when it vetoed a 2007 UN Security Council resolution, calling for the Myanmar regime in Burma to allow unimpeded access to humanitarian workers and the release of political prisoners, including Nobel laureate Aung Sun Su Kyi.[40] These do not amount to interventions that violate traditional conceptions of Westphalian sovereignty, nor do they violate any international laws or shared understandings. On the contrary, they are sound means to gradually build an international community, in which shared norms develop out of nations and people expressing their appreciation and censure across state lines, just as China often does.

Notes

1. G. John Ikenberry, "The Rise of China and the Future of the West: Can the Liberal System Survive?" *Foreign Affairs* (January/February 2008), http://www.foreignaffairs.com/articles/63042/g-john-ikenberry/the-rise-of-china-and-the-future-of-the-west (accessed January 19, 2012).

2. Stewart Patrick, "Irresponsible Stakeholders? The Difficulty of Integrating Rising Powers," *Foreign Affairs* (November/December 2010), http://www.foreignaffairs.com/articles/66793/stewart-patrick/irresponsible-stakeholders (accessed January 19, 2012).

3. Elizabeth C. Economy, "The Game Changer: Coping with China's Foreign Policy Revolution," *Foreign Affairs* (November/December 2010),

http://www.foreignaffairs.com/articles/66865/elizabeth-c-economy/
the-game-changer (accessed January 19, 2012).

4. Stefan Halper, *The Beijing Consensus: How China's Authoritarian Model Will Dominate the Twenty-First Century* (New York: Basic Books, 2010), 210.

5. Richard Nixon, "Asia after Viet Nam," *Foreign Affairs* (October 1967), http://www.foreignaffairs.com/articles/23927/richard-m-nixon/asia-after-viet-nam (accessed January 19, 2012).

6. "Oxford Manifesto 1997," Liberal International, adopted November 1997. http://www.liberal-international.org/editorial.asp?ia_id=537 (accessed January 19, 2012).

7. G. John Ikenberry, "Is a "One World" Order Possible? The Rise of China, the West, and the Future of Liberal Internationalism," Centre on Asia and Globalisation working paper 030 (June 2011), 13. http://www.caglkyschool.com/pdf/working%20papers/2011/CAG_WorkingPaper_30.pdf (accessed January 19, 2012).

8. Hedley Bull, ed. *Kai Alderson and Andrew Hurrell, Hedley Bull on International Society* (Basingstoke: Palgrave Macmillan, 2000).

9. Samantha Power, *A Problem from Hell: America and the Age of Genocide* (New York: Harper Perennial, 2003).

10. Francis M. Deng, Sadikiel Kimaro, Terrence Lyons, Donald Rothchild, and I. William Zartman, *Sovereignty as Responsibility: Conflict management in Africa* (Washington, DC: Brookings Institution Press, 1996).

11. Gareth Evans, Mohamed Sahnoun, et al., "The Responsibility to Protect," Report of the International Commission on Intervention and State Sovereignty (December 2001) http://responsibilitytoprotect.org/ICISS%20Report.pdf (accessed January 19, 2012).

12. United Nations, "A More Secure World: Our Shared Responsibility," Report of the High-level Panel on Threats, Challenges and Change (2004), http://www.un.org/secureworld/ (accessed January 19, 2012).

13. Gareth Evans, Mohamed Sahnoun, et al., "The Responsibility to Protect," Report of the International Commission on Intervention and State Sovereignty (December 2001), 13. http://responsibilitytoprotect.org/ICISS%20Report.pdf (accessed January 19, 2012).

14. Lee Feinstein and Anne-Marie Slaughter, "A Duty to Prevent," *Foreign Affairs* (January/February 2004). http://www.foreignaffairs.com/articles/59540/lee-feinstein-and-anne-marie-slaughter/a-duty-to-prevent (accessed January 19, 2012).

15. Wang Guangya, "Statement by H.E. Vice Foreign Minister Wang Guangya at the 58th Session of the United Nations Commission on Human Rights" (April 2, 2002). http://www.china-un.org/eng/zghlhg/jjhshsw/rqwt/t29329.htm (accessed January 19, 2012).

16. Jiang Zemin, "Statement by President Jiang Zemin of the People's Republic of China at the Millennium Summit of the United Nations" (September 6, 2000). http://www.un.org/millennium/webcast/statements/china.htm (accessed January 19, 2012).

17. Jonathan E. Davis, "From Ideology to Pragmatism: China's Position on Humanitarian Intervention in the Post-Cold War Era," *Vanderbilt Journal of Transnational Law* 44, no. 2 (March 2011): 243.

18. Ibid., 251.

19. "China Supports Joint Declaration by France, Germany, Russia on Iraq," *People Daily English* (February 12, 2003). http://english.peopledaily.com. cn/200302/12/eng20030212_111535.shtml (accessed January 20, 2012).

20. "Effect of a Recent United Nations Security Council Resolution on the Authority of the President Under International Law to Use Military Force Against Iraq," *Opinions of the Office of Legal Counsel in Volume 26* (November 8, 2002). http://www.justice.gov/olc/2002/iraq-unscr-final.pdf (accessed January 20, 2012).

21. "Protecting the vulnerable: What Congo Means for Obama," *Economist* (November 18, 2008). http://www.economist.com/node/12601948 (accessed January 20, 2012).

22. James Kurth, "Humanitarian Intervention After Iraq: Legal Ideals vs. Military Realities," *Orbis* 50, no. 1 (Winter 2006): 87–101.

23. "Transcript: President Obama's Address to the Nation on Military Action in Libya," *ABC.com* (March 28, 2011). http://abcnews.go.com/Politics/ transcript-president-obamas-address-nation-military-action-libya/story ?id=13242776&page=4#.Txl_mIHpbTo (accessed January 20, 2012).

24. Thom Shanker and Helene Cooper, "Doctrine for Libya: Not Carved in Stone," *New York Times* (March 29, 2011). http://www.nytimes. com/2011/03/30/world/africa/30doctrine.html (accessed January 20, 2012).

25. Hillary Clinton, Response to Citizens for Global Solutions 2008 Presidential Candidate Questionnaire, Citizens for Global Solutions. http://globalsolutions.org/08orbust/pcq/clinton (accessed January 20, 2012).

26. Ibid.

27. Ibid.

28. Jeffrey Gettleman, "Obama in Africa: Welcome Back, Son. Now Don't Forget Us," *New York Times* (July 11, 2009).

29. Michael Makovsky and Blaise Misztal, "Obama's Iran Policy Shifts to Containment," *Washington Post* (December 9, 2011). http://www. washingtonpost.com/opinions/obamas-iran-policy-shifts-to-containment/2011/12/09/gIQAUD8DjO_story.html (accessed January 20, 2012).

30. Barack Obama, "Transcript of Obama's Speech in Sderot, Israel," *New York Times* (July 23, 2008). http://www.nytimes.com/2008/07/23/us/politics/ 23text-obama.html?pagewanted=print (accessed January 20, 2012).

31. "Transatlantic Trends 2011," German Marshall Fund of the United States and Compagnia di San Paolo (2011). http://trends.gmfus.org.php5-23.dfw1-2.websitetestlink.com/?page_id=3189 (accessed January 20, 2012).

32. Ibid.

33. "UN Needs to Help All Nations Develop," *China.org* (September 7, 2000). http://www.china.org.cn/english/2000/Sep/1605.htm (accessed January 20, 2012).

34. Francis M. Deng, Sadikiel Kimaro, Terrence Lyons, Donald Rothchild, and I. William Zartman, *Sovereignty as Responsibility: Conflict Management in Africa* (Washington, DC: Brookings Institution Press, 1996), 223.

35. Gareth Evans, Mohamed Sahnoun, et al., "The Responsibility to Protect," Report of the International Commission on Intervention and State Sovereignty

(December 2001). http://responsibilitytoprotect.org/ICISS%20Report.pdf (accessed January 19, 2012).

36. Ramesh Thakur, "Law, Legitimacy and United Nations," *Melbourne Journal of International Law* 1 (2010), http://www.austlii.edu.au/au/journals/MelbJIL/2010/1.html#fn59 (accessed January 20, 2012).

37. Ibid.

38. "Remarks by the President in Address to the Nation on Libya," Transcript from the Office of the Press Secretary (March 28, 2011). http://www.whitehouse.gov/the-press-office/2011/03/28/remarks-president-address-nation-libya (accessed January 20, 2012).

39. Edward Wong, "China: Government Tells U.N. Agency Not to Interfere," *New York Times* (March 29, 2011). http://www.nytimes.com/2011/03/30/world/asia/30briefs-ART-zhisheng.html (accessed January 20, 2012).

40. "Double veto for Burma resolution," *BBC* (January 12, 2007). http://news.bbc.co.uk/2/hi/6257921.stm (accessed January 20, 2012).

Part II

Can a Nuclear Iran Be Deterred and Contained?

4

Are Iran's Leaders
Rational Actors?

Increasing evidence that Iran has embarked on a course that will lead it to develop nuclear arms in the near future has re-intensified the debate about the ways the world should react to such a danger. Questions concerning ways to deal with the proliferation of nuclear arms are of course not limited to Iran, but also include other nations or groups that might employ nuclear arms, especially North Korea and terrorists.

Four possible responses are commonly discussed in dealing with Iran: engagement, sanctions, military strikes, and deterrence. *Engagement* has been tried, especially since the onset of the Obama administration (and previously by European governments), but so far has not yielded the desired results. *Sanctions* are deemed an unreliable tool, as some nations, especially China, have so far refused to authorize them. Also sanctions, in the past, have often been readily circumvented and have not had the sought-after effect, even when imposed on nations that are more vulnerable than Iran, such as Cuba and Syria. And sanctions may help solidify the regime in place and subdue democratic opposition. *Military strikes* are said to be the measure most likely to fail. As Defense Secretary Robert Gates stated on April 13, 2009, "Militarily, in my view, it [a bombing of Iran's nuclear facilities] would delay the Iranian program for some period of time, but only delay it, probably only one to three years."[1] Hence the growing interest in *deterrence*; that is, in tolerating a nuclear-armed Iran but keeping it at bay by threatening retaliation in kind should they use their nuclear weapons. Although the Obama administration has not formally embraced this position, several observers believe that this is the direction it is headed. Indeed, a statement by Secretary of State Hillary Clinton in Thailand on July 22, 2009, was understood as implying such an approach. She stated, "If the U.S. extends a defense umbrella over the region . . . it's unlikely that Iran will be any stronger or safer, because they won't be able to intimidate and dominate, as they apparently believe they can, once they have a nuclear weapon."[2] In an interview with the *Wall Street Journal* on March 5, 2010, Zbigniew Brzezinski, the former National Security Advisor, also called for such an umbrella as the way to deal with Iran.[3]

Retired Gen. John Abizaid, former head of US Central Command, put it as follows: "We need to make it very clear to the Iranians, the same way we made it clear to the Soviet Union and China, that their first use of nuclear weapons would result in the devastation of their nation. I don't believe Iran is a suicide state. Deterrence will work with Iran."[4]

Fareed Zakaria, the editor of *Newsweek International*, a *Washington Post* columnist, and a frequent TV commentator, is a leading advocate of deterrence. In his article "Don't Scramble the Jets," he argues that Iran's religious leaders comprise a "canny (and ruthlessly pragmatic) clerical elite," and that military dictatorships like the one that is now forming in Iran "are calculating. They act in ways that keep themselves alive and in power. That instinct for self-preservation is what will make a containment strategy work."[5] Among academics, Columbia University professor Kenneth Waltz has written that, "It would be strange if Iran did not strive to get nuclear weapons, and I don't think we have to worry if they do. Because deterrence has worked 100 percent of the time. After all, we have deterred big nuclear powers like the Soviet Union and China. So sleep well."[6]

In the following paragraphs, I focus on the question of whether deterrence might work and, if not, what kind of military strike—if any—could have the required effect.

Rational Actors?

One of the few points on which there is wide agreement is that for deterrence to work, the leaders of the nations that command nuclear arms must be rational. The same holds for terrorists who may acquire nuclear arms one way or another. In effect, a small cottage industry has developed of popular authors and researchers who argue that both heads of states and terrorists do act rationally, and thus—fearing retaliation from other nuclear powers—they will not employ their nukes. (To those who may ask, if nations such as Iran do not intend to use their nuclear arms, why would they go through the cost and risk of acquiring them—these rationalist mavens respond by explaining that the nuclear weapons serve these nations by fending off attacks against them.)

The rationalist champions of deterrence often draw on the same assumption as does economics: that people are purely rational. One way economists protect this assumption from obvious criticism is by using one data point to assess both the intentions and the actions of the person involved. Thus, economists have argued that if a person who never drank wine—and had no intention of drinking wine—suddenly purchased a bottle of wine, this must have been a rational choice—because otherwise why would he have bought it? And they state that when a person chooses to become a criminal, he "must have" weighed the pros and cons and made a rational decision that being a criminal was the optimal choice. As Nobel Laureate George Stigler pointed out, "A reason can always be found for whatever we observe man to do," which "turns utility into a tautology."[7]

This approach violates a basic tenet of science—that propositions are to be formulated in ways that can be falsified. Using the same academic sleight of hand, the champions of deterrence maintain that whatever the leaders of a nation do is rational because one can find some reason according to which their actions make sense. However, this line of reasoning would also make dropping nuclear bombs and ignoring the effects of retaliation "rational"—say, because, like Herman Kahn, the leaders believe that their nation will fare better in such a war than their enemy would, or because such bombing would bring about a rapture that provides a shortcut to heaven.

The champions of deterrence further defend their position by suggesting that the only alternative to being rational is to be irrational, which is treated as tantamount to crazy. They then argue that Iran's leaders, terrorists, and even Kim Il-sung and his son Kim Jong-il are not insane people. They demonstrate this by showing that these leaders react, in a sensible way, to changes in the world around them. For instance, by far the most conciliatory offer made by Iran regarding its nuclear program was made in May 2003, after the US military wiped out Saddam's army within a few weeks with few casualties, something Iran had been unable to do even after an eight-year-long war. It is also when Iran was told in no uncertain terms by the President of the United States that it was on the same short list of members of the "Axis of Evil." In short, Iran had reason to expect to be attacked. Because by these proponents of deterrence, actors can act only either purely rationally or purely irrationally, showing that the leaders of Iran and other rogue states are not insane, seems to prove their assertion that they are rational.

Other scholars who have studied terrorism further uphold this line of thinking by explaining that terrorists act strategically and not irrationally. In an article entitled "Deterring Terrorism: It Can Be Done," UCLA professor Robert F. Trager and Columbia doctoral candidate Dessislava P. Zagorcheva observe that, "The assertion that terrorists are highly irrational is contradicted by a growing body of literature that shows that terrorist groups . . . choose strategies that best advance them. The resort to terror tactics is itself a strategic choice of weaker actors with no other means of furthering their cause."[8] Further, in "Explaining Suicide Terrorism: A Review History," Stanford professor Martha Crenshaw reports, "There is an emerging consensus that suicide attacks are instrumental in or strategic from the perspective of a sponsoring organization . . . They serve the political interests of identifiable actors, most of whom are non-states opposing well-armed states. This method is mechanically simple and tactically efficient . . ."[9]

The trouble with this line of reasoning is that it makes a jump from showing that the rulers of countries such as Iran and North Korea, as well as terrorists, are not irrational—they have clear goals, find means suitable to their goals, and respond to facts and logic—to assuming that they hence act rationally, and reach the same conclusions as the observers do. However, leading sociologists, notably Talcott Parsons, have long pointed out that there is a third category of decision-making and behavior, which they called "nonrational."[10] This may at first seem like typical academic hair-splitting, a weakness that is rather prevalent among social scientists. However, in this case it points to a major category of human behavior, where people act in response to deeply held beliefs that cannot be proven or disproven; for instance, their sense that God commanded them to act in a particular manner. People have long shown that they are willing to kill for their beliefs, even if they will die as a result. True, they respond to facts and pressures, but only as long as those factors affect the ways they implement their beliefs—not the beliefs themselves. Thus, a religious fanatic Iranian leader may well believe that God commands him to wipe out Tel Aviv, may calculate whether to use missiles or bombers, and what season to attack, but not whether or not to heed God's command to kill the infidels.

In "Can Iran Be Deterred? A Question We Cannot Afford to Get Wrong," *National Review* Deputy Managing Editor Jason Lee

Steorts writes, "[Iran's] religious zealotry causes it to exaggerate the significance of issues that are, objectively speaking, only tangentially related to its interests. The Israeli-Palestinian conflict, for instance, has no direct bearing on Iran's security, but much of the regime sees it as fundamental to Iranian interests and even to Iran's identity as a Muslim nation."[11] This is an example of nonrational, not irrational, thinking.

Nonrational behavior is not limited to one faith. The Israelis, for instance, who have been criticized roundly on many accounts, are usually not considered irrational. But they have a strong Masada complex, which led their forefathers to kill each other and commit suicide, rather than surrender. This is more than an idle piece of history. Many Israelis still hold to this fatalistic belief, further reinforced by the narrative about Samson, who pulled a building down on himself in order to kill his enemies, and by the strong commitment to "never again" go "like lambs to the slaughter" as Jews did (in the Israeli view) during the Nazi regime. Israelis model themselves after those few Jews in the Warsaw Ghetto who fought the Nazis—despite the fact that they had no chance of winning—until the bitter end. Such beliefs might lead Israel to attack Iran even when rational considerations indicate that such an attack would be extremely detrimental. Such an attack would serve their beliefs and is rational in this technical sense—but the beliefs themselves are based on nonrational commitments that one cannot argue with on the basis of facts and logic, and thus cannot be reliably deterred.

Does the Past Predict the Future?

Related to the rationality thesis is an argument based on the historical record. Waltz writes, "It is now fashionable for political scientists to test hypotheses. Well, I have one: If a country has nuclear weapons, it will not be attacked militarily in ways that threaten its manifestly vital interests. That is 100 percent true, without exception, over a period of more than fifty years. Pretty impressive."[12] In "Containing a Nuclear Iran," Zakaria writes, "Deterrence worked with madmen like Mao, and with thugs like Stalin, and it will work with the calculating autocrats of Tehran."[13]

Such arguments fail on several grounds. First, as we learn in Logic 101, the fact that all the swans you see are white does not prove that there are no black ones. The fact that so far no nukes have been employed (since 1945, when the deterrence system was instituted) does not prove that no such incident will occur in the future. This is especially true as the number of actors increases to include a considerable number of fanatics.

Moreover, the historical record reveals several occasions in which nations governed by leaders who are considered far from irrational came dangerously close to nuclear blows. India and Pakistan earned this dubious title several times. John F. Kennedy almost hit the "launch" button during the Cuban Missile Crisis in 1962. Moshe Dayan nearly did as well, readying the Israelis' nuclear arsenal for use in the Yom Kippur War. Mao planned to drop a nuclear bomb on the USSR during a 1969 border dispute.

The pro-deterrence champions point to the same incidents as demonstrating that deterrence did work; after all, the various nations pulled back from the brink, albeit some at the very last minute. However, as I see it, heads of states have shown themselves in the past to be very capable of making gross miscalculations that cost them their lives, their regimes, and all they were fighting for—take Hitler, for instance. Similarly, the Japanese, when they attacked Pearl Harbor, believed that they would be able at least to drive the United States out of their part of the world. And both the Germans and the French completely misjudged the course of World War I. History is further littered with numerous, less grand miscalculations, from Bernard Montgomery's "a bridge too far," to Lord Cardigan's Charge of the Light Brigade in the Crimean War, to Pickett's Charge in the American Civil War.

The leaders of nations may be more cautions when it comes to dropping nuclear bombs. But they may not. It is hence rational to apply here the rule that if the potential disutility is very large, avoiding it must govern the decision, even if the probability of suffering that disutility is very low. A simplistic way to highlight this point is to note that rational people will happily accept a bet for $1 if the probability of winning is 99 out of 100. They will do the same for $10, and even $100—but not for $1,000,000. The reason is that although the probability of losing remains the same and is very small, the cost of losing is so high (assuming those who bet will have to pledge their future income as collateral) that the disutility is so great that it makes sense to refuse such a bet. Only a reckless gambler would accept such a wager. Obviously the disutility of being attacked with nuclear arms is so high that even if the probability that deterrence will fail is very low, it makes sense to go a long way to avoid it. In plain words, we had better be safe than sorry.

I should add that the matter of probabilities is essential here. Many of the champions of deterrence use hedged wording to explain that the risk of attack is very low. In "Terrorism: The Relevance of the Rational Choice Model," George Mason economist Brian Caplan writes, "While millions believe that they earn vast rewards in the afterlife if they engage in terrorism or—better yet—suicidal terrorism, only a handful put their lives on the line."[14] Thus, when Waltz writes, "I don't notice that many religiously oriented people act in ways that will result in the massacre of thousands of people. I think people are people. I don't think heavenly rewards motivate very many people,"[15] one cannot but note that many hundreds of thousands of people have been slaughtered because of one faith or ideology or another; many thousands of Armenians by Turks, Jews by Hitler, Russians by Stalin, and many more. And even if not "many" people are motivated by heavenly rewards, it did not take many terrorists to bring down the Twin Towers, nor will it take many to place and activate a nuclear device under one of our cities.

Nor can one ignore the low probability that terrorists will get their hands on nukes and find ways to deploy them. One or more small nukes can be placed in one of the 6,000,000 containers that make their way to the United States each year and are only minimally screened, or they can be delivered by one of the more than 2,000,000 recreational boats and small private planes that enter the United States each year with next to no oversight (in the case of the boats), and rather attenuated screening (in the case of the small planes). As one Coast Guard commander told me, "The best way to bring a nuke into the U.S. is to put it into a ton of cocaine." In short, given that nobody is really denying that there is small probability of a very great disutility, we had better seek to prevent the proliferation of nukes than grow to learn to live with them.

Side Effects: Undermining the Norm

Clearly the more nations that command nuclear arms, even if one disregards the differences in the mentalities and predispositions of those who now seek nukes compared to older members of the club, the greater the danger that some nation will employ these catastrophic weapons. The champions of deterrence scoff at this danger and stress that rather few nations have acquired nukes over the last decades, in contrast to the fear voiced early in the nuclear age. Thus, President Kennedy observed that there might be "10, 15, 20" countries with a

69

nuclear capacity. And C. P. Snow wrote at the time that, unless there was a nuclear disarmament, a nuclear war would be "not a probably but a certainty." However, over the decades that followed, a considerable number of countries capable of developing nuclear weapons have refrained from progressing down this road, including Canada, Sweden, Italy, Brazil, Argentina, South Africa, South Korea, and Taiwan.

However, although it is true that proliferation has been slower than some initially feared, those who claim we have nothing to worry about disregard the fact that we are at a tipping point, at which the old restraining regime may give way to a nuclear free-for-all. For decades, we were able to promote a taboo on nuclear weapons, well depicted in *The Nuclear Taboo* by Brown University professor Nina Tannenwald.[16] Major segments of the population of the world and their leaders embraced the precept that nations should refrain from acquiring nukes, and that giving them up was the desired policy. When President Obama called for a world free of nuclear weapons and promised that the United States, working with Russia, would move toward zero nukes, he was widely cheered. The taboo is at the foundation of a treaty signed by 189 nations, the Nuclear Non-Proliferation Treaty (NPT). Both the taboo and the treaty were undergirded by various diplomatic and economic measures, as well as some arm-twisting.

In recent years, though, as North Korea thumbed its nose at the NPT and Iran seemed increasingly to move toward developing nuclear weapons, the taboo has weakened and respect for the NPT has waned. Moreover, the champions of deterrence in effect argue that the taboo and treaty are so yesterday, that more and more countries will obtain nukes, and that we ought to get over it, adjust to the world as it is now, and move on. Thus, Texas A&M University professor Michael Desch writes that, "If [during the Cold War] we could live with those rogue nuclear states [the Soviet Union and China], which were willing to sacrifice millions of their own people to advance an eschatological ideology, there is scant reason to think Iran poses a more serious threat. . . . To paraphrase the subtitle of Stanley Kubrick's great nuclear satire *Dr. Strangelove*, it might just be time to stop worrying and learn, if not to love, at least to tolerate the Iranian bomb."[17]

As I see it, the taboo and treaty are indeed being tested, but it is too early to write them off. If Iran can be stopped, which in turn would increase the chances that we could pressure North Korea to reconsider its course, we may be able to save the nuclear abstinence regime. In contrast, there is little doubt that if we allow Iran to develop nukes, other nations will seek them, including Saudi Arabia, Egypt and, some believe, even Jordan. Also, as a countermeasure against North Korea, Japan and South Korea would not be far behind if the taboo is broken so flagrantly in the Middle East. Brazil and Argentina may well also follow suit as more and more "important" nations acquire nukes. In short, applying deterrence to Iran rather than trying to dissuade it from developing nukes in effect entails opening the world to truly large-scale proliferation that would significantly increase the probability of nations coming to nuclear blows and terrorists finding places to get their hands on nukes.

Side Effects: Shield and Blackmail

Even if Iran never drops its nukes on anybody, once it demonstrates that it has acquired them—say, by testing them—these weapons would have considerable consequences for our security and that of our allies. Desch correctly reports, "The concern is that once Iran develops a nuclear capability, it would become even more aggressive in support-ing terrorist groups like Hezbollah in Lebanon or Hamas in Gaza. . . . Finally, many Americans fear that once Iran fields a nuclear weapon, it will become ever more meddlesome in Iraq."[18] The side effects of allow-ing Iran to obtain nukes are well spelled out by Emanuele Ottolenghi, the executive director of the Transatlantic Institute in Brussels. I hence quote him at some length. He writes, "The fact is that an Iranian bomb would enable Tehran to fulfill the goals of the revolution *without using it*. A nuclear bomb is a force multiplier that, as U.S. President Barack Obama aptly said, constitutes a 'game changer'. Iran's success will change the Middle East forever—and for the worse. Under an Iranian nuclear umbrella, terrorists will be able to act with impunity, and its neighbors will enter into a dangerous arms race. Less understood are the dynamics that will emerge if Iran chooses not to use the bomb against its enemies. It matters little that Tehran may act rationally. If Iran goes nuclear, the Western world will have to negotiate a Middle East Yalta with Tehran—one that may entail a U.S. withdrawal, an unpleasant bargain for the smaller principalities of the Gulf's shores and an unacceptable one for Israel and Lebanon's Christians."[19]

Last but not least is the risk that Iran, or some other rogue nation, will slip a nuke or two to terrorists, or they will obtain one without consent of the leaders with the help of one group or another, such as the Revolutionary Guard. The champions of deterrence argue that it suffices to deter such nations from sharing nukes with terrorists for us to declare that if terrorists use such weapons, we will hold responsible the nation that provided them. However, this argument assumes a much more reliable level of nuclear forensics than we command so far. We may well be unable to determine the source of a bomb, or it will take months, after which striking a nation with nuclear bombs in cold blood may well not seem a very credible counter-threat.

One hardly needs to elaborate any further that even if Iran can be deterred from employing its nukes directly, there are strong reasons to favor an Iran without WMDs.

Costs of Prevention

So far, the discussion has focused on the question of whether an Iran equipped with nuclear arms poses a serious security threat that cannot be reliably deterred by the threat of a second strike. However, even if one agrees that Iran does pose a significant threat, one still must ponder the costs of the only viable alternative to deterrence—a military strike. (We already suggested that engagement and sanctions are unlikely to have the required effect.)

Opponents of a military strike argue that (a) the location of some key sites may well not be known; (b) several sites are well protected; (c) some of the sites are in highly populated areas, and bombing them may cause a great number of civilian casualties; (d) in the past, bombing such sites was not very effective, and the bombing might delay the development of nuclear programs only slightly or even lead Iran to accelerate its program in reaction, as well as to refuse all future inspections by the IAEA; and (e) some even warn that bombing fully fueled nuclear plants could release radioactive materials into the atmosphere, resulting in disastrous levels of illness, deformity, and death among the population, both immediately and in years to come.

The fact that all these objections deal with bombing nuclear sites points to a different military option. It is one that has not been discussed in public so far and at first blush may seem very controversial. Note should be hence taken that it has been previously employed, indeed on several occasions. The basic approach seeks not to degrade Iran's nuclear capacities (the aim of bombing) but to compel the regime to change its behavior, by causing ever higher levels of "pain." It starts with demanding that Iran live up to its international obligations and open its nuclear sites up by a given date, to demonstrate that they are not serving a military program. If this demand is not heeded, the next step would entail bombing of Iran's non-nuclear military assets (such as the headquarters and encampments of the Revolutionary Guard, air defense installations and radar sites, missile sites, and naval vessels that might be used against oil shipments). If such bombing does not elicit the required response, the bombing of select dual-use assets will be undertaken, including key elements of the infrastructure, like bridges, railroad stations, and other such assets, just the way the United States did in Germany and Japan in World War II. If still more tightening of the screws is needed, Iran could be declared a no-fly zone, the way parts of Iraq were even before Operation Iraqi Freedom in 2003. This kind of military action is akin to sanctions—causing "pain" in order to change behavior, albeit by much more powerful means.

Critics are likely to argue that military action will help those in power in Iran to suppress the opposition, or make the opposition support the regime. However, the regime is going all out to repress the opposition anyway, and a weakening of the regime, following the military strikes, may provide an opening for the opposition. Moreover, experience in Cuba, the Dominican Republic, the USSR, and Burma, among other countries, shows that we tend to exaggerate the likelihood that the opposition will win against brutal domestic regimes. Also, as the head of the reformers made clear to me when I was his guest in Iran in 2002, the reformers do not plan to fold the nuclear program. All this suggests that trying to figure out the vagrancies of domestic policies should not be allowed to determine our foreign policy when vital national interests are at stake.

Above all, we cannot delay action much longer if we are to prevent Iran from crossing a threshold after which a military option will become much more dangerous to implement—for us and for them.

Legitimacy?

In considering the way other nations and international institutions, especially the UN, would react to such a policy, one must distinguish between the act of deciding to exercise a military option and the decision of which specific kind of military action is to be undertaken. This discussion assumes that military action of *some kind* has been deemed necessary and ordered by the president, has been authorized by the US Senate after due consultation with our military authorities, that allies have been consulted, and that the US government decided that it must act even if no UN approval can be obtained. Hence, the only question is if capacity-degrading military action is more likely to gain UN approval and international support than a behavior-changing strike.

Critics may argue that the behavior-changing approach amounts to "total" war, while striking the nuclear sites entails only "limited" war. However, this distinction has been largely erased in recent years, and it is particularly inappropriate in this case, given that an attack on nuclear sites may cause considerably more collateral damage than the suggested option.

Coping with Side Effects

Critics of a military strike fear that Iran will retaliate by unleashing Hezbollah and Hamas, making our lives more difficult in Iraq and Afghanistan, and disrupting the supply of oil to us and to our allies. These concerns do not apply to the decision of *which* military mode is the proper one, but to the question of whether a military option should be considered in the first place. In response, I suggest that a nation that holds that it cannot cope with such countermeasures should not only forego its claim to the status of a superpower, but also cease to see itself as much of an international player.

In Conclusion

Engagements and sanctions are very unlikely to suffice to stop Iran from becoming a nuclear power. Hence, increasing attention is devoted to containment. It may well work, but given the high disutility of a nuclear strike by Iran—even a relatively small probability is unacceptable. The argument that the rulers of Iran are not irrational disregards that quite a few national leaders "bet" their lives and regimes and lost. Hence, a military option should not be off of the table. However, bombing the nuclear sites might not be the most effective choice.

Notes

1.   William H. McMichael, "Gates: Strike on Iran Would Create Backlash," *Army Times* (April 14, 2009). http://www.armytimes.com/news/2009/04/military_iran_gates_041309/ (accessed January 20, 2012).

2.   Mark Landler and David E. Sanger, "Clinton Speaks of Shielding Mideast From Iran," *New York Times* (July 22, 2009). http://www.nytimes.com/2009/07/23/world/asia/23diplo.html (accessed January 20, 2012).

3.   Gerald F. Seib, "An Expert's Long View on Iran," *Wall Street Journal* (March 5, 2010). http://online.wsj.com/article/SB2000142405274870418720457510156080175615.html (accessed January 20, 2012).

4.   Interview with General John Abizaid, "Iran Is Not a Suicide State," *New Perspectives Quarterly* 25, no. 4 (Fall 2008), http://www.digitalnpq.org/archive/2008_fall/14_abizaid.html (accessed January 20, 2012).

5.   Fareed Zakaria, "Don't Scramble the Jets: Why Iran's Dictators Can Be Deterred," *Daily Beast* (February 18, 2010). http://www.thedailybeast.com/

newsweek/2010/02/18/don-t-scramble-the-jets.html (accessed January 20, 2012).

6.   Scott Sagan, Kenneth Waltz, and Richard K. Betts, "A Nuclear Iran: Promoting Stability or Courting Disaster?" *Journal of International Affairs* 60, no. 2 (Spring/Summer 2007): 138.

7.   George J. Stigler, *The Theory of Price*, 3rd edn. (New York: MacMillan, 1966), 57.

8.   Robert F. Trager and Dessislava P. Zagorcheva, "Deterring Terrorism: It Can Be Done," *International Security* 30, no. 3 (Winter 2005/2006): 93–94.

9.   Martha Crenshaw, "Explaining Suicide Terrorism: A Review Essay," *Security Studies* 16, no. 1 (January–March 2007): 141.

10. See Talcott Parsons, ed. Bryan S. Turner, *The Talcott Parsons Reader* (Hoboken: Wiley-Blackwell, 1999).

11. Jason Lee Steorts, "Can Iran Be Deterred? A Question We Cannot Afford to Get Wrong," *National Review* 58, no. 19 (October 23, 2006): 35.

12. Sagan, Waltz, and Betts, A Nuclear Iran, 137.

13. Fareed Zakaria, "Containing a Nuclear Iran," *Daily Beast* (October 2, 2009). http://www.thedailybeast.com/newsweek/2009/10/03/containing-a-nuclear-iran.html (accessed January 20, 2012).

14. Brian Caplan, "Terrorism: The Relevance of the Rational Choice Model," *Public Choice* 128 (2006): 92.

15. Sagan, Waltz, and Betts, A Nuclear Iran, 143.

16. Nina Tannenwald, *The Nuclear Taboo: The United States and the Non-Use of Nuclear Weapons since 1945* (Cambridge: Cambridge University Press, 2007).

17. Michael Desch, "Apocalypse Not," *The American Conservative* (May 19, 2009). http://www.theamericanconservative.com/article/2009/may/18/00006/ (accessed January 20, 2012).

18. Ibid.

19. Emanuele Ottolenghi, "Life after the 'Game-Changer,'" *Standpoint* (April 2009). http://standpointmag.co.uk/node/1063/full (accessed January 20, 2012).

5

Can the US Prevent Iran from Lording over the Middle East?

Years will have passed before we know the kinds of regimes that emerged from the uprisings that swept through the Middle East at the beginning of 2011. Observers are quick to project on them their fondest dreams (the rise of the elusive Arab democracy) or their worst fears (a region ripe for *jihadist* takeover).

One can, however, make four predictions with a considerable level of confidence. First, America's influence and leverage in large parts of the Middle East will be lower than they were before the uprising tidal wave (extending a trend, as we shall see, that started before 2011). Second, the influence and leverage of Iran over large parts of the Middle East will rise (similarly expanding a trend that began before 2011). In some cases, this influence has been concrete, such as the six-fold increase in Iranian trade with Turkey that took place between 2002 and 2007.[1] In others, such gains are less "real" but still significant, such as Iran's appeal among Shi'a in the Middle East.

Third, regional elites and the broader public believe that the United States is abandoning the region—and them—and are reacting to this perception in surprisingly different ways. Finally, it follows that America's future role in the Middle East will be determined to a large extent by the way it deals with Iran. If Iran's hegemonic and militaristic ambitions can be thwarted, the US allies and friends will be reassured significantly, and Washington will need to worry much less about the particular political direction taken by various regional regimes. On the other hand, if Iran is not defanged, it seems set on a course that will increasingly pull—or force—nations in its direction. Coping with Iran therefore is a critical test of American credibility and resolve in this increasingly volatile region.

Allies at Risk

It is already clear that the greatest effect of the convulsions that spread through the Middle East, beginning with the removal of the Tunisian autocrat Ben Ali early in 2011, has been a reduction in America's leverage—and a concomitant increase in Iran's potential influence there. To point to both developments is not to argue that the United States should oppose the transformation of these regimes (or that it could stop it, if it so desired), but to point out the consequences for the balance of power in the region and to the challenges they pose to US and its remaining allies.

The decline of US leverage is obvious. Regimes that were solid US allies, most notably Egypt, but also Jordan, Bahrain, and Yemen, either have been toppled or are being severely challenged. Ultimately, they may turn into stable democracies that find their way to becoming part of the free world. However, one cannot help but note that so far no Arab country has made such a transition. And while such transformations invariably take time—it took years or longer before the military regimes of South Korea, Turkey, Indonesia, and Chile turned into stable democracies—a range of unfavorable conditions, from high levels of unemployment to low levels of education and often weak civic bodies, make the prospect for substantive change in the Middle East daunting.

Indeed, a review of recent regional changes hammers home the point that American strategic interests are suffering significant setbacks, while those of Iran are (or could be) advanced in unprecedented fashion.

Egypt

Though some in the United States view the convulsions in Egypt as a step toward a Western-style democracy, Iran casts the unrest as an uprising inspired by its own 1979 Islamist revolution. Iran's Supreme Leader, the Ayatollah Ali Khamenei, has said that the "awakening of the Islamic Egyptian people is an Islamic liberation movement." The Egyptian political force that has the greatest pro-Iranian potential is the Muslim Brotherhood. Much has been made of the fact that the Brotherhood has greatly moderated its positions over the last decades and is now interested in political participation. Perhaps it has. But, in the same way the Brotherhood changed its stripes before, it can certainly do so again, especially once it no longer needs to fear brutal oppression by the Egyptian regime. Moreover, more attention should be granted to the fact that the Muslim Brotherhood is internally divided over how extreme its brand of political Islam ought to be. For example, during the 2011 uprising, Mohamed Badi, the Brotherhood's Supreme Guide, "pledged the Brotherhood would 'continue to raise the banner of jihad' against the Jews, which he called the group's 'first and foremost enemies.'"[2] Other Brotherhood figures have made similar points. Ragib Hilal Hamida, an Egyptian MP and Muslim Brotherhood member, has stated, "Terrorism is not a curse when given its true meaning. [When interpreted accurately] it means opposing occupation as it exists in Palestine, Afghanistan and Iraq. From my point of view, bin Laden, al-Zawahiri and al-Zarqawi are not terrorists in the sense accepted by some. I support all their activities since they are a thorn in the side of the Americans and the Zionists."[3]

These statements drive home a vital point: While many have pointed out that the current revolutions taking place in the Middle East are being led by secular, pro-democratic, youth groups, one should note that often, after revolutions, more extreme groups overrun the moderate ones, and extremists become even more radical. Examples of this trend include the Bolsheviks and Mensheviks of revolutionary Russia; the Nazis and Social Democrats of Weimar Republic in Germany; and the Revolutionary Guard of Iran, who led the 1979 revolution from the onset but later overwhelmed the reformers and became even more strident. True, such an outcome is not predetermined. Yet no one should ignore the potential for greater radicalism as a result of Mideast upheavals.

Iran, meanwhile, is busy exploiting Egypt's turmoil. In the wake of the Mubarak regime's collapse, it sent two warships through the Suez Canal—the first time it had done so since the 1979 revolution.[4] The Egyptian government acquiesced to this passage. The exchange was not lost on regional observers. "Egypt is signaling that it is no longer committed to its strategic alliance with Israel against Iran, and that Cairo is now willing to do business with Tehran," one analyst noted in London's *Telegraph* newspaper.[5] Cairo's unfolding dalliance with—or, at a minimum, its greater tolerance of—the Islamic Republic suggests that the current transformations open doors for Iran, even among traditional allies of the United States.

Bahrain and Saudi Arabia

The unrest now taking place in Bahrain has shaken the leaders of Saudi Arabia to their core, and for good reason. Bahrain is a majority

Shi'ite country ruled by a Sunni minority—one which is close to the Saudi leadership. If Bahrain's government were to fall, and a Shi'ite government rise to power instead, it would be—in the eyes of the Saudis—a major victory for their regional nemesis, Shi'ite Iran.[6] (The Saudi rulers also fear an uprising from their own Shi'ite population, which, although a minority within the country, is located mostly on the border with Bahrain.[7]) A political sea change in Bahrain also could pose a major challenge to America's strategic interests there, particularly as it seeks to keep an eye on the expanding naval power of Iran. The headquarters of the US Navy's Fifth Fleet are based in Bahrain, just across the Persian Gulf from Iran—one factor which has made Bahrain, in the words of a former US Navy Rear Admiral, "the enduring logistical support for the United States Navy operating in the Persian Gulf for 50 years."[8] Moreover, the Fifth Fleet protects the supply of oil which moves through the Persian Gulf and the Strait of Hormuz, which totals 33 percent of all seaborne traded oil and 17 percent of oil traded worldwide.[9] The Strait of Hormuz is, in the words of the US Department of Energy, "the world's most important oil chokepoint."[10]

Early on, during the Egyptian uprising, the Saudi monarchy warned the Obama administration not to pressure President Hosni Mubarak to step down. The Saudi rulers saw an obvious parallel between their status (and that of the royal family that rules Bahrain) and Mubarak's. They had all served the United States well and were in turn supported by it. When the Obama administration proceeded nevertheless to urge for a transition in Egypt, Saudi fears and concerns were stoked.

In short, two more nations, key to US interests in the region, now face uncertainty. One has been challenged, and the other rests uneasily, fearing it is next in line and consumed by doubts about the extent it can rely on the United States as its main ally.

Jordan

Jordan, which until recently was viewed as a reliable and significant US ally in the region, is also facing challenges to its regime. Here too, a minority group is governing a majority. The majority of Jordanians are of Palestinian descent, while the country is governed by a Hashemite minority. The Jordanian legislature, cabinet, and judiciary are merely "democratic facades . . . subject to control by the Hashemite minority rulers who were placed in charge of the majority Palestinian population by a colonial decision."[11] True, the king is well-respected and so far it looks as if various reforms that are being enacted might satisfy the protestors. However, once such a process starts—especially in the face of high unemployment, a growing educated class, and the availability of modern communication tools—it tends to feed on itself.

In the absence of a strong American presence in the region, Jordan is likely to follow its inclination to accommodate and compromise with the powers that be, even if those powers turn out to be Iran, rather than to push back against them. Thus, when Saddam was riding high, Jordan refrained from condemning Iraq's invasion of Kuwait in 1990. It briefly joined Egypt and Syria in attacking Israel in 1967, but when Israel gained the upper hand, Jordan was quick to cut back its involvement—and before too long, it accepted UN Security Council Resolution 242, worked out in the aftermath of the Six Day War, which represented a de facto transition to peace.[12] In short, Jordan is another US ally that is being undermined and is fearful of being abandoned by the United States.

American Primacy in Retreat

So far, the review has encompassed countries that are holding the line, nervously, although nobody knows what tomorrow's headlines will bring. The United States is doing much less well in the rest of the region.

Iraq

Iraq so far has faced no major new challenges as a result of the 2011 regional uprisings, but it continues to experience ethnic and confessional violent conflicts of its own, especially between a Shi'a-dominated government (which benefits from the fact that Shi'a make up 65 percent of the population) and a small but vocal Sunni minority. Additional conflicts take place among other groups including Kurds, Arabs, and Turkmen. At the same time, it is undergoing a drawdown in American presence and a corresponding increase in Iranian influence.

Pursuant to the Obama administration's commitment, US troops are rapidly leaving Iraq, while those that remain are positioned outside the main population centers and play only a very limited role in securing domestic order and in defending Iraq's borders. The fact that General Ray Odierno, the commander of US forces in Iraq, suggested not long ago that UN peacekeeping might be needed to prevent civil war in Iraq if tensions do not ease is emblematic of America's rapidly diminishing role.[13]

Indeed, Iraq's Prime Minister, Nouri al-Maliki, has already indicated that the Status of Forces Agreement, under which US forces are to remain in the country until the end of 2011, will not be extended once it expires.[14] But significant challenges remain. The Iraqi government is still often unable to provide even such elementary services as electricity for more than a few hours a day.[15] The political system is deadlocked, and violent ethnic strife continues, albeit at a much lower level than in 2005–2006. In short, one may well add Iraq to the list of failing states which the United States is leaving to largely fend for themselves.

Iraq once served as a major counterweight to Iran, which it fought to a stalemate after a grinding eight-year conflict. Today, however, Iraq plays no such role. On the contrary, the influence of Iran over Iraq's Shi'a majority government is significant, although not without ambiguities and difficulties of its own. Iran has provided funding, training, and providing sanctuary to Shi'ite militias.[16] Particularly revealing is the return to Iraq in early 2011 of radical Shi'ite cleric Moqtada al-Sadr from Iran, where he had been living for almost four years in self-imposed exile.[17] Eight months of deadlock following Iraq's 2010 parliamentary elections ended only after Sadr threw his political faction's support behind the unity government of Prime Minister Maliki—in a deal facilitated by Iran in what amounts to a key political victory.[18] Anyway one scores it, Iraq is a place where US influence is diminishing while Iranian influence is rising.

Syria

Syria's reaction to the Middle Eastern uprisings has been to offer some very limited reforms. President Bashar al-Assad has promised to initiate municipal elections, grant more power to nongovernmental organizations, and create a new media law (though no action has been taken yet).[19] He also announced a 17 percent pay raise for the two million Syrians who work for the government.[20] No one can foresee at this stage whether these moves will shore up the regime, whet the appetite of the weakened and oppressed opposition, or lead in some other direction. However, one observation can be made with great assurance: Syria, a nation that the United States once hoped to peel away Iran and bring into the Western fold, is not moving away from Tehran; to the contrary, it is moving much closer.

Under the Bush administration, and especially since the advent of the Obama administration, Washington has actively attempted to court Syria. The United States has done so through a number of steps, including high-ranking diplomatic contacts and the reestablishment of a US embassy in Damascus after years without steady representation. The United States has even been willing to discuss the lifting of sanctions against Syria and pressuring Israel to give up the Golan Heights.[21] Syria not only rebuffed these overtures, but moved in the opposite direction, closer to Iran. With great fanfare, it hosted Iran's President Mahmoud Ahmadinejad in early 2010 in a visit that underscored the strength of the Iranian–Syrian alliance.[22]

Iran has backed its diplomatic support for Syria with concrete action. It has transferred advanced radar to Syria as a means of deterring Israeli military action,[23] and most recently sent two warships to Syria for joint military exercises.[24] Syria likewise serves as a main pipeline through which Iran ships missiles and other arms to Hezbollah in Lebanon, despite UN and other demands to desist.

Lebanon

Like Iraq, Lebanon needs no input from other countries to add to its own convulsions. It was long considered one of the most democratic and pro-Western nations in the region. However, in recent years the role of Hezbollah has gradually increased, first as an opposition to the regime and then—as of 2009—as a major coalition partner whose power is growing. The group recently forced the government to suppress the investigation of the killing of former Prime Minister Rafik Hariri; forced out of office the pro-Western Prime Minister Saad Hariri; and appointed a Prime Minister (Najib Mikati) favored by itself—and by Syria and Iran. A Hariri ally's statement that these developments show that "Hezbollah was trying to 'rule Lebanon' and annex it for Iran"[25] is obviously overblown, but does reflect the way the Lebanese view the shifting political sands.

Hezbollah often acts as an Iranian proxy, one that Tehran finances, inspires, and arms, and one to which it has transferred numerous advanced missiles and other military equipment.[26] Hezbollah, in turn, often follows instructions from Iran about when to employ its arms against Israeli, American, and other targets.

So while Lebanon is often viewed by the American media as a country friendly to the West, in actuality it was and increasingly is more of a client state. Once it was largely controlled by Syria; now it increasingly falls under Iran's sway.

Turkey

Turkey was considered solidly in the Western camp: a secularized state, a staunch member of NATO, a nation keen to join the EU, and one with considerable commercial and even military ties to Israel. However, since the election of Recep Tayyip Erdoğan and the Justice and Development Party (AKP) in 2002, Turkey has become more Islamist, moved away from the West, and moved closer to Iran. In the first five years of AKP rule, trade between Turkey and Iran increased six-fold, as Turkey became Iran's most important regional trading partner.[27] Turkey is also replacing Dubai as Iran's financial conduit, allowing Turkish banks to help Iran circumvent UN sanctions and additional ones imposed by the United States and EU.[28]

This increased economic cooperation has translated into better political ties too. After Iran's highly controversial 2009 elections, President Abdullah Gul and Prime Minister Erdoğan were among the first international leaders to congratulate Mahmoud Ahmadinejad on his victory. Turkey's Foreign Minister, Ahmet Davutoglu, later argued that the election results were an internal Iranian matter and described the elections as "dynamic and well-attended."[29] In June 2010, just before the United States finally succeeded in convincing Russia and even China to support the imposition of additional sanctions against Iran, Turkey (working with Brazil) came up with a deal it had negotiated with Iran regarding the treatment of uranium. Many observers view it as merely a stalling tactic intended to derail the sanction vote. And when the vote did take place, Turkey voted against sanctions. Turkish leaders have criticized the West's "double standard" of allowing Israel to possess nuclear weapons while working to prevent Iran for doing the same.[30]

True, sometimes Turkey sees itself as competing with Iran over who will be a major Middle Eastern power. However, this is a limited rivalry between two nations that have become much closer to one another as Turkey has moved away from the West.

Afghanistan

Afghanistan's course is particularly difficult to chart. However, the United States has announced that as of July 2011, it will start scaling down its forces there and will have withdrawn by 2014, depending on conditions on the ground. America, moreover, is not alone; Switzerland has already removed its troops from the country, while the Dutch and Canadians were gone by the end of 2011. The British have announced they will have all their troops out by 2015. This is not surprising to Afghan elites, who sense that the United States, having already abandoned them once (after they drove out the USSR), may well do so again.[31] They are mindful of the growing opposition to the war in the United States, as well as budgetary difficulties associated with the war effort. All of which makes cozying up to Iran an attractive course. Thus, after President Obama flew to Kabul to publically urge the Karzai government to curb corruption, President Karzai signaled his displeasure by warmly hosting Iranian President Mahmoud Ahmadinejad.[32] Karzai has also admitted to receiving bags of cash from Iran in return for "good relations," among other things.[33]

According to a 2009 State Department report on international terrorism, "Iran's Qods Force provided training to the Taliban in Afghanistan on small unit tactics, small arms, explosives, and indirect fire weapons. Since at least 2006, Iran has arranged arms shipments to select Taliban members, including small arms and associated ammunition, rocket propelled grenades, mortar rounds, 107 mm rockets, and plastic explosives."[34] In March 2011, the British Foreign Ministry announced that it had discovered a shipment of Iranian weapons en route to the Taliban, containing forty-eight long-range rockets.[35] WikiLeaks cables similarly reveal concerns over Iran's attempts to exert influence on the Afghan parliament. One cable reports that "Iranian government officials routinely encourage Parliament to support anti-Coalition policies and to raise anti-American talking points during debates. Pro-Western MPs say colleagues with close Iranian contacts accept money or political support to promote Iran's political agenda."[36] According to another, "Iranian meddling [in Afghanistan] is getting increasingly lethal."[37]

True, many other powers are seeking to influence the future of Afghanistan, including its various ethnic groups, Pakistan, and India. For instance, Pakistan's government has used America's eagerness to pull out of Afghanistan as justification to maintain ties with militant groups for future operations in Afghanistan.[38] Afghanistan therefore may be an unlikely candidate to fall under Iran's sway. However, it is also a nation in which US commitment to the region is severely tested. If the United States withdraws and leaves behind a failing state, many in the region will see this is as proof positive that the United States cannot be trusted as an ally.

Israel

Today, many in Israel are worried by what they see as America's betrayal of a longtime ally, Egyptian President Hosni Mubarak, and by the implications for their country's own relationship with Washington. "American response to uprising in Egypt shows Washington has no qualms about 'dropping' long time ally. Is Israel in danger of receiving similar treatment?" asks an article in the daily *Yediot Ahronot*, voicing a widely held fear.[39]

For Israelis, there is ample reason for concern. Since 2008, both the Israeli government and a majority of its voters have grown suspicious of US support. They have looked critically upon President Obama's viewpoints and acts, chief among them the White House's ill-fated demand for a total freeze on construction in the West Bank and in Jerusalem as a *precondition* for negotiations with the Palestinians—without seeking any such concessions from the Palestinians.

Although there is, of course, no danger that Israel will fall under Iran's hegemony, it seems self evident that the ways it is treated by the United States in the near future will have a profound effect on the issue at hand. The reason is that Israel has been considered for several decades the closest ally of the United States in the Middle East. Hence the way it is treated serves, in effect, as a sort of Rorschach test of the nature of US commitments. The argument, raised by some American Middle East experts that Israel has turned from an American asset to a liability is one signal of a possible change.[40] So is the call on the United States to "lean" more on Israel,[41] or impose the terms of a peace settlement upon it.[42] Much more telling will be the way the question of how to deal with Iran's nuclear program is resolved.

The Coming Test

That the United States is reducing its involvement in the Middle East—and that its influence is reduced by events beyond its control—cannot be contested, especially given the drawdown now underway in Iraq and the similar pullback expected in the near future from Afghanistan. Neither can it be contested that some nations have already moved closer to Iran (Syria, Turkey), that others have been pushed closer (Lebanon), and still others are undergoing regime changes that weaken their ties to the United States.

Where does the United States go from here? What are the options available to the United States if it is not about to abandon the Middle East and let it be subject to increasing Iranian influence and leverage?

Some see hope that the various regimes, led by Egypt, will evolve into stable, pro-Western democracies. Yet this is a course that will take years at best. And the record of many other nations in which people power overthrew the prevailing order is far from reassuring. New military regimes, continued chaos, gridlock (a la Iraq), and Islamic governments are much more likely outcomes. The United States may continue to encourage, cajole, foster, and pressure various nations in the region to support its policies and to stave off Iran. However, as the preceding review suggests, in some nations such efforts are largely spurned; in others, those in power wonder if they can rely on the United States to stay the course; and others still are going to be much too consumed with their internal travails to pay much mind to US wishes.

The key to the future of the Middle East in the near term, therefore, does not lie in dealing with the various nations that are subject to increased Iranian influence or might be subject to it—but with Iran itself. If Iran would cease to be a threat, if it would give up its militaristic nuclear plans and regional ambitions, the United States would have much less reason to be concerned with the regime reforms and transformations taking place throughout the region. In short, the United States can no longer hope to deal with Iran's regional ambitions by dealing with the various nations in the region individually. It must confront Iran itself.

In the best of all worlds, a domestic uprising inside Iran would lead to a regime change, one that would focus on serving Iran's own people and which would cease to meddle in the affairs of other nations. Given the persistent way in which the Iranian regime has been able to suppress the opposition, however, this must be understood as what it is: a very unlikely development. Efforts by the United States to engage Iran diplomatically have clearly failed. Sanctions, for their part, seem to have an effect, albeit one that, at best, will hobble Iran only slowly. Meanwhile, the region is in turmoil and Iran's nuclear program seems to be back on track.

For obvious reasons, the United States is reluctant to consider a military option. The US allies and the UN are exceedingly unlikely to support a strike against Iran; the US military is very leery about opening another military front; and the US public favors scaling back, rather than increasing, US commitments overseas. Yet the question remains: if the United States does not find a way to curb Iran's expansionist and militaristic ambitions, can it live up to its commitments to its allies in the region? Will they trust it to come to their aid? And what conclusions will other US allies—and adversaries—throughout the world draw if the United States gradually abandons the Middle East?

Notes

1. Gonul Tol, "Turkey's Warm Ties with Iran: A Brief History," *InsideIran.org* (March 17, 2010). http://www.insideiran.org/news/turkey%E2%80%99s-warm-ties-with-iran-a-brief-history/ (accessed June 18, 2012).

2. Charles Levinson, "'Brothers' in Egypt Present Two Faces," *Wall Street Journal* (February 15, 2011). http://online.wsj.com/article/SB1000142405 2748704629004576135882819143872.html (accessed June 18, 2012).

3. Lydia Khalil, "Al-Qaeda and the Muslim Brotherhood: United by Strategy, Divided by Tactics," Jamestown Foundation *Terrorism Monitor* 4, no. 6 (March 23, 2006), http://www.jamestown.org/single/?no_cache=1&tx_ttnews[tt_news]=714 (accessed June 18, 2012).

4. Isabel Kershner, "Israel Silent as Iranian Ships Transit Suez Canal," *New York Times* (February 22, 2011), http://www.nytimes.com/2011/02/23/world/middleeast/23suez.html?hp (accessed June 18, 2012).

5. Dina Kraft, "Israel Warns Iran Is 'Taking Advantage' of Middle East Unrest," *Telegraph* (London) (February 20, 2011), http://www.telegraph.co.uk/news/worldnews/middleeast/iran/8336712/Israel-warns-Iran-is-taking-advantage-of-Middle-East-unrest.html (accessed June 18, 2012).

6. Deborah Amos and Robert Siegel, "Saudis Uneasy Amid Arab Unrest," NPR *All Things Considered* (February 21, 2011). http://www.npr.org/2011/02/21/133943624/Arab-Unrest-Makes-Saudi-Arabia-Nervous (accessed June 19, 2012).

7. Ibid.

8. Tom Bowman, "Bahrain: Key U.S. Military Hub," NPR *Weekend Edition Saturday* (February 19, 2011). http://www.npr.org/templates/transcript/transcript.php?storyId=133893941 (accessed June 19, 2012).

9. Department of Energy, U.S. Energy Information Administration, "World Oil Transit Chokepoints" (December 30, 2011). http://www.eia.doe.gov/cabs/world_oil_transit_chokepoints/pdf.pdf (accessed June 19, 2012).

10. Ibid.

11. Alan Dershowitz, "The Case against Jordan," *Jerusalem Post* (October 7, 2003), http://archive.frontpagemag.com/readArticle.aspx?ARTID=15992 (accessed June 19, 2012).

12. King Hussein, "The Jordanian Palestinian Peace Initiative: Mutual Recognition and Territory for Peace" *Journal of Palestine Studies* 14, no. 4 (Summer 1985): 15–22, http://www.jstor.org/stable/2537118 (accessed June 19, 2012).

13. "Odierno: U.S. Might Seek U.N. Peacekeepers in Iraq after 2011," *Fox News* (July 6, 2010). http://www.foxnews.com/world/2010/07/06/general-iraq-ponders-peacekeepers-defuse-kurd-arab-tensions/ (accessed June 19, 2012).

14. Sam Dagher, "Iraq Wants the U.S. Out," *Wall Street Journal* (December 28, 2010). http://online.wsj.com/article/SB10001424052970204685004576045 700275218580.html (accessed June 19, 2012).

15. Charles McDermid and Khalid Waleed, "Dark Days for Iraq as Power Crisis Bites," *Asia Times* (June 26, 2010). http://www.atimes.com/atimes/Middle_East/LF26Ak01.html (accessed June 19, 2012).

16. See note 14.

17. Saad Sarhan and Aaron C. Davis, "Cleric Moqtada al-Sadr Returns to Iraq after Self-Imposed Exile," *Washington Post* (January 6, 2011). http://www.washingtonpost.com/wp-dyn/content/article/2011/01/05/AR2011010500724.html (accessed June 19, 2012).

18. Qassim Abdul-Zahra and Lara Jakes, "Anti-American Cleric Vies for More Power in Iraq," *Washington Post* (October 2, 2010). http://www.washingtonpost.com/wp-dyn/content/article/2010/10/01/AR2010100101360.html (accessed June 19, 2012).

19. Jay Solomon and Bill Spindle, "Syria Strongman: 'Time for Reform,'" *Wall Street Journal* (January 31, 2011). http://online.wsj.com/article/SB10001424052748704832704576114340735033236.html (accessed June 19, 2012).

20. "'Day of Rage' For Syrians Fails to Draw Protesters," *New York Times* (February 4, 2011). http://www.nytimes.com/2011/02/05/world/middleeast/05syria.html (accessed June 19, 2012).

21. "U.S. envoy William Burns Says Syria Talks Were Candid," *BBC* (February 17, 2010), http://news.bbc.co.uk/2/hi/8519506.stm (accessed June 19, 2012).

22. Howard Schneider, "Iran, Syria Mock U.S. Policy; Ahmadinejad Speaks of Israel's 'Annihilation.'" *Washington Post* (February 26, 2010). http://www.washingtonpost.com/wp-dyn/content/article/2010/02/25/AR2010022505089.html (accessed June 19, 2012).

23. Charles Levinson, "Iran Arms Syria with Radar," *Wall Street Journal* (June 30, 2010). http://online.wsj.com/article/SB10001424052748703426004575338923106485984.html (accessed June 19, 2012).

24. Amos Harel, "Iran Is Celebrating Mubarak Downfall with Suez Crossing," *Ha'aretz* (Tel Aviv) (February 23, 2011). http://www.haaretz.com/print-edition/news/iran-is-celebrating-mubarak-downfall-with-suez-crossing-1.345103 (accessed June 19, 2012).

25. Leila Fadel, "After Government Collapse, Hezbollah Works to Get More Power in Lebanon," *Washington Post* (January 13, 2011). http://www.washingtonpost.com/wp-dyn/content/article/2011/01/13/AR2011011306737.html (accessed June 19, 2012).

26. Viola Gienger, "Iran Gives Weapons, $200 Million a Year to Help Lebanese Hezbollah Re-Arm," *Bloomberg* (April 20, 2010). http://www.bloomberg.com/news/2010-04-19/iran-helps-lebanese-hezbollah-rebuild-its-arsenal-pentagon-says-in-report.html (accessed June 19, 2012).

27. Gonul Tol, "Turkey's Warm Ties with Iran: A Brief History," *InsideIran.org* (March 17, 2010). http://www.insideiran.org/news/turkey%E2%80%99s-warm-ties-with-iran-a-brief-history/ (accessed June 19, 2012).

28. Bayram Sinkaya, "Turkey and Iran Relations on the Eve of President Gul's Visit: The Steady Improvement of a Pragmatic Relationship," *ORSAM* (February 10, 2011). http://www.orsam.org.tr/en/showArticle.aspx?ID=408 (accessed June 19, 2012).

29. "Don't Overshadow Dynamic Elections, Turkish FM Advises Iranian People," *Hurriyet Daily News* (June 22, 2009). http://www.hurriyetdaily-news.com/n.php?n=don8217t-overshadow-dynamic-elections-turkish-fm-advises-iranian-people (accessed June 19, 2012).

30. Casey L. Addis, et al., *Iran: Regional Perspectives and U.S. Policy* (Washington, DC: Congressional Research Service, January 13, 2010). http://www.fas.org/sgp/crs/mideast/R40849.pdf (accessed June 19, 2012).

31. Dan De Luce, "Afghans Pose Awkward Questions for U.S. Military Chief." *Agence France Presse* (July 26, 2010). http://www.google.com/hostednews/afp/article/ALeqM5hyyMeTjC4oof3Bg5idtZZuEXLO4Q (accessed June 19, 2012).

32. Dexter Filkins and Mark Landler, "Afghan Leader Is Seen to Flout Influence of U.S.," *New York Times* (March 29, 2010). http://www.ny-times.com/2010/03/30/world/asia/30karzai.html (accessed June 19, 2012).

33. Maria Abi-Habib, Yaroslav Trofimov, and Jay Solomon, "Iran Cash Trail Highlights Battle for Kabul Sway," *The Wall Street Journal* (October 25, 2010). http://online.wsj.com/article/SB100014240527023043883045755740014362056346.html (accessed June 19, 2012).

34. United States Department of State: Office of the Coordinator for Counterterrorism, "Chapter 3: State Sponsors of Terrorism," in *Country Reports on Terrorism 2009* (Washington, DC: U.S. Department of State, August 5, 2010), http://www.state.gov/j/ct/rls/crt/2009/140889.htm (accessed June 19, 2012).

35. Alissa J. Rubin, "British Link Iran to Rockets Found in Afghan Province," *New York Times* (March 9, 2011). http://www.nytimes.com/2011/03/10/world/middleeast/10iran.html (accessed June 19, 2012).

36. "U.S. Embassy Cables: Iranian Influence at Afghanistan Parliament," *Guardian* (London) (December 2, 2010). http://www.guardian.co.uk/world/us-embassy-cables-documents/194913 (accessed June 19, 2012).

37. Jon Boone, "WikiLeaks: Afghan MPs and Religious Scholars 'On Iran Payroll,'" *Guardian* (London) (December 2, 2010). http://www.guardian.co.uk/world/2010/dec/02/afghan-mps-scholars-iran-payroll (accessed June 19, 2012).

38. Mark Mazzetti, "A Shooting in Pakistan Reveals Fraying Alliance," *New York Times* (March 12, 2011). http://www.nytimes.com/2011/03/13/weekinreview/13lashkar.html (accessed June 19, 2012).

39. Aviel Magnezi, "Could U.S. Abandon Israel Too?" *Yediot Ahronot* (Tel Aviv) (January 2, 2011). http://www.ynetnews.com/articles/0,7340,L-4022102,00.html (accessed June 19, 2012).

40. Helene Cooper, "Washington Asks: What to Do About Israel?" *New York Times* (June 5, 2010). http://www.nytimes.com/2010/06/06/weekinreview/06cooper.html (accessed June 19, 2012).

41. Bronwen Maddox, "Will Barack Obama Give Way When He Meets Binyamin Netanyahu in Washington?" *Times of London* (May 13, 2009).

http://thedailyrepublican.com/index.php?option=com_content&task=vie w&id=5978&Itemid=2 (accessed June 19, 2012).

42.　Ari Shavit and Haaretz Correspondent, "Israel Fears Obama Heading for Imposed Mideast Settlement." *Ha'aretz* (Tel Aviv) (March 29, 2010). http://www.haaretz.com/print-edition/news/israel-fears-obama-heading-for-imposed-mideast-settlement-1.265466 (accessed June 19, 2012).

Part III
Pakistan: The Hottest Spot

6

Pakistan: A New,
Geopolitical Approach*

The quest to find a way to transform the deeply troubled relationship between the US and its allies (the West) and Pakistan tends to focus either on Pakistan's role in Afghanistan or on the ways Pakistan itself is governed. This article argues that progress on these two fronts would greatly benefit if the Pakistan–India conflict could be settled. This endeavor, in turn, requires a reassessment of the geopolitical thesis that the West ought to court India in order for it to "balance" China.

The Threats: Intra-Pakistan

The greatest threat to the security of the United States and its allies, it is widely agreed, is the combination of terrorism and nuclear arms. Currently the most likely place for terrorists to acquire such a weapon is Pakistan. Although various measures have been undertaken to improve the security of Pakistan's weapons, the West is concerned about their safety, given that Pakistan, suspicious of the United States, has rejected America's offers to help further secure these arms. Western powers realize that they are unaware of the location of all these weapons. And the 2011 attacks on a highly secure naval base in Karachi—which benefited from Al Qaeda penetration of the Pakistani army—raise concerns that similar attacks on facilities that store nuclear arms might succeed. (The base is located only fifteen miles from a suspected nuclear storage site.)[1]

Pakistan expanded its nuclear arsenal from sixty warheads in 2007 to over hundred in early 2011[2] and accelerated construction at the Khushab nuclear site, which will provide it with a fourth nuclear reactor as early as 2013.[3] It has introduced short-range tactical nuclear weapons, carried by mobile *Nasr* missiles, in response to India's "Cold Start" doctrine (which calls for limited conventional attacks against Pakistan that are designed to stay below Pakistan's strategic nuclear threshold).[4] Such mobile tactical nuclear weapons are particularly difficult to secure.

The West is also concerned that even if terrorists could not acquire nuclear arms by usurping them or gaining them from supporters within the Pakistani forces, insurgents may topple the government. This concern is based on the observation that the government is weak and unstable and that anti-American sentiments in Pakistan are widespread and intense.

Pakistan could also cut off supply routes through which three-quarters of all NATO supplies to troops in Afghanistan currently travel.[5] Twice before, these routes were closed at the Khyber Pass—a vital passageway into Afghanistan—to protest against American operations on Pakistani soil. And in June 2011, after the raid that killed bin Laden, Pakistan cut off the water supply to a CIA base that handles the drones.[6]

A Stable Dysfunctional Relationship

A "stable dysfunctional relationship" is one in which the parties damage each other but maintain the relationship because they also nurture each other. On the one hand, the Pakistani military is helping the United States to fight the Afghan Taliban and Al Qaeda. It has allowed US incursions into Pakistan, and it has provided some of the intelligence on which drone strikes are based. On the other hand, the Afghan Taliban can hide, rest, regroup, rearm, train, and organize in Pakistan, especially in North Waziristan, which greatly hinders the drive to end the insurgency in Afghanistan. Pakistan has publicly criticized the United States for violating Pakistani sovereignty, further inflaming anti-American sentiment in the country. In the spring of 2011, Pakistan demanded that the United States remove most of its military trainers and reduce the number of CIA and Special Operations operatives in the country,[7] but it also asked for more joint operations with the United States against the Taliban and more sharing of information. While the Pakistani military often collaborates with the US military, the Pakistani ISI (Inter-Service Intelligence) is reported to often lend a hand to the Afghan and Pakistani Taliban.

The complicated relationship led to an odd situation in June 2011 when Prime Minister Karzai traveled to Pakistan to seek assurances that Afghan Taliban leaders, who were in negotiations for a peace settlement with his government, would not be killed or detained by Pakistan. Previously, when such negotiations seemed to be succeeding, the Taliban commanders involved would be captured by Pakistan. The opposition by elements of the Pakistani government to the peace process is due, in part, to the fact that the Karzai government is leaving out those Taliban members controlled by the ISI. Shuja Nawaz of the Atlantic Council points out that Pakistan's support for extremists is "leverage in the sense that it allows [the Pakistanis] to have a government in Kabul that is neutral, if not pro-Pakistan. That's why they've always hedged on the Afghan Taliban."[8]

Pakistan is further concerned that, as the United States pulls out of Afghanistan and no longer needs its supply routes, the United States will grow increasingly close to India.[9] Helene Cooper observes in *The New York Times* that Pakistan wants to keep the Taliban in its "good graces" should US forces withdraw and leave the Taliban to reassert control over Afghanistan. "What Pakistan wants most in Afghanistan is an assurance that India cannot use it to threaten Pakistan. For that, a radical Islamic movement like the Taliban, with strong ties to kin in Pakistan, fits the bill."[10]

Pakistan responds that it has taken many military and civilian casualties in fighting both the terrorists and the militants and that it has made progress in South Waziristan and Swat Valley. Major General Nadir Zeb, inspector general of Pakistan's paramilitary Frontier Corps, goes as far as to claim that the tribal areas have been nearly cleared of militants since 2007; only a "very thin belt is left. The rest is all cleared."[11]

Some observers argue that because the Pakistani military wants to ensure the continued flow of billions of US dollars in military aid, the military has a vested interest in not fighting militants and terrorists too vigorously. As Lawrence Wright has noted, "What would happen if the Pakistani military actually captured or killed Al Qaeda's top leaders? The great flow of dollars would stop, just as it had in Afghanistan after the Soviets limped away. I realized that, despite all the suffering the war on terror had brought to Pakistan, the military was addicted to the money it generated. The Pakistani Army and the ISI were in the looking-for-bin-Laden business, and if they found him they'd be out of business."[12]

Pakistanis point out that the United States supported them strongly as long as Pakistan served as the major venue for organizing, arming, and financing the Mujahedeen (the predecessors of the Taliban) to drive out the USSR. However, once this mission was completed, the United States lost interest in Pakistan and the flow of funds dried up.

Pakistan received zero dollars in American aid in 1992, down from $783 million in 1988.[13] Former Pakistani President Pervez Musharraf argues, "The United States 'used' Pakistan and then abandoned it: this was taken as a betrayal. The U.S. nuclear policy of appeasement and strategic co-operation with India against Pakistan is taken by the man in the street in Pakistan as very partisan and an act of animosity against our national interest."[14]

Furthermore, the low ebb of US-Pakistan relations is evident in the recent public expression of anti-American views even by military leaders. In November 2010, a Pakistani newspaper reported that a senior Pakistani military officer stated that his organization views the United States as seeking "controlled chaos" in Pakistan and to "denuclearize" the regime. In a gathering of military officers in May 2011, when a US ambassador asked who constitutes the country's top threat, more chose the United States than the other two choices: India or forces within Pakistan.[15]

In short, the West and Pakistan do not trust one another, mix co-operation with conflict—sometimes helping, sometimes undermining each other—and both hedge against betrayal while drawing on each other's resources. One could characterize the relationship as schizophrenic or byzantine, but hardly as wholesome.

Muscular Diplomacy?

Since the war in Afghanistan started a decade ago, the United States and its allies have sent numerous high-powered representatives to Pakistan to convince, cajole, pressure, and publicly lecture Pakistan to change its ways. These included secretaries of state, foreign ministers, high-ranking military officials, and special representatives (in particular, Richard Holbrooke). Military and civilian aid has been granted, and promises of more and more threats to scale it back have been made in order to compel Pakistan to reform its ways. These efforts have not all been in vain. Pakistan's military did move some of its resources from the border with India and intensified its anti-insurgency drive, especially in North Waziristan. Also, there have reportedly been some improvements in the security of its nuclear facilities, and the A. Q. Khan proliferation network seems to have been deactivated. However, as the preceding overview shows, the total effect of all these moves has been limited. Hence, in 2011, several members of Congress called for "getting tough" with Pakistan and others referred to getting a "divorce."

Such suggestions as to what should be done next to move Pakistan in the direction the West favors ignore that *the United States and its allies are much more dependent on Pakistan than Pakistan is on them.* The nuclear arms of Pakistan pose a very serious threat to the United States and its allies; there is nothing in the West that poses a similar threat to Pakistan. Proliferation is a major Western concern, but not for Pakistan. Closing of the supply routes to Afghanistan would deprive the United States and its allied forces of many of their supplies,[16] while if the West were to cut off help to Pakistan, it would accomplish little; China has shown that it stands by to pick up the slack. Its investment in Pakistan has grown from around $4 billion in 2007 to $25 billion in 2010.[17] (Whether China would be willing to write checks to the Pakistani military, though, the way the United States currently does, remains to be seen.)

Daniel Markey at the Council on Foreign Relations has noted that Pakistani officials talk openly about China as a "strategic alternative to the United States."[18] The government has described China as an "all weather friend" (a pointed contrast to the United States, which is often characterized as only a fair-weather friend).[19] China would benefit from an alliance with Pakistan by gaining an alternate route for China's energy supply (which currently bottlenecks at the Strait of Malacca in the Indian Ocean).[20] On May 20, 2011, China announced the sale of fifty fighter jets to Islamabad. (The fighter, known as the JF-17, was developed jointly between Pakistan and China.)[21] China is a major investor in Pakistan and a primary supplier of its weaponry (70 percent of its tanks are Chinese). China allowed Pakistan to test its first nuclear device on Chinese land and aided in its transportations of missiles purchased from North Korea.[22] The two nations also conducted three joint military exercises.[23] China has made investments in Pakistan's infrastructure, including construction of the deep-sea port of Gwadar and the Karakoram Highway, a roadway that connects China to Pakistan.[24] Pakistan is encouraging Afghanistan to court China as well.[25]

In short, a more muscular Western posture that calls for the United States to divorce itself from Pakistan, or to "get tough," or to condition its aid on Pakistan meeting certain benchmarks in combating militants—is unlikely to achieve its goal. In this stable dysfunctional relationship, the United States is more dependent on Pakistan than Pakistan is on the United States.

Nation-Building?

A rather different approach, and an even less promising one than pressing Pakistan to mend its ways, is to build the civilian government and its societal bases in Pakistan and reduce the role and power of the military, ensuring that it is under the control of elected officials. For example, Aqil Shah, a Postdoctoral Fellow at Harvard, calls for turning Pakistan from a failing state into a viable one with a strong civil society dominated by civilian leaders, rather than one overshadowed by the military, in which corruption is curbed and the economy grows and generates meaningful jobs—in particular, for the large young population. These changes are to be brought about by the United States shifting aid from the military to the civilian sector. Shah argues, "Militant extremism can be fought effectively only through serious governance reforms that ensure the rule of law and accountability."[26] He states that Pakistan's government may need a "multibillion-dollar Marshall Plan," and that "aid should be tightly linked to Pakistan's economic performance, progress in combating corruption, and transparency and responsiveness in government." Shah also argues that Washington should take a tougher approach with the Pakistani military and remind it that "interference in politics will not be tolerated and could have serious repercussions, including a downgrading of military ties, the suspension of nondevelopment aid, and broader diplomatic isolation." The thesis that the United States can build up the civilian elements of Pakistan and scale back the military ones is reflected in the Kerry–Lugar bill, which provides $7.5 billion in aid over five years but demands that Pakistan must cooperate with the United States on nonproliferation, make significant progress in combating terrorist groups, and ensure that the Pakistani military is separated from the country's politics.[27]

This approach disregards the poor record of long-distance nation-building. As William Easterly has shown in his book *The White Man's Burden*, over the last decades, the nations that modernized had a high growth rate and stabilized politically. These countries—South Korea, Taiwan, China, and Singapore—did so on their own, with very little foreign aid. At the same time, the nations that received large amounts of aid, especially in Africa, often did very poorly. A study by the World Bank in 2006 showed that out of twenty-five aid-recipient countries covered by the report, more than half (fourteen) had the *same or declining* rates of per capita income from the mid-1990s to the early 2000s.

The great difficulties the United States and its allies had in transforming Iraq and Afghanistan are well documented.[28] A 2011 report by the Senate Foreign Relations Committee shows that much of the aid to Afghanistan was wasted or has simply not been accounted for, and that the constructive effects it produced were short-lived and distorted the Afghan economy, polity, and society.[29]

Much of the money intended to assist Pakistan's fight against terrorism has been used to purchase weapons to counter India.[30] Much of the rest is lost due to corruption. As Lawrence Wright notes, "The Pakistani military . . . submits expense claims [to be reimbursed for its fight against terrorism] every month to the U.S. Embassy in Islamabad; according to a report in the *Guardian*, receipts are not provided—or requested."[31]

Anticorruption drives are very prone to failure, and there is little reason to believe that civilians are less corrupt than the military. Moreover, the military is one of the few institutions in Pakistan that is widely respected, while the current civilian leadership is considered weak and divided. As Shuja Nawaz puts it, "The Pakistani military is destined to remain an important institution in Pakistan's otherwise dysfunctional polity."[32]

In short, nation-building (or capacity-building, a term preferred since nation-building has acquired a poor reputation) seems even less likely to succeed than muscular diplomacy.

Treating the India "Obsession"

There is widespread agreement that one major reason for the reluctance of the Pakistani army to dismantle the militant groups—for its alliance with the Taliban in Afghanistan, and for the special standing of the Pakistani military in society—is that the Pakistani government and people view India as their first, second, and third enemy. The term "obsession" is often used to describe this preoccupation. India and Pakistan have been arch-enemies ever since the partition in 1947. They have fought three major wars and engaged in several armed clashes, including some that have come close to nuclear war. Both nations have supported terrorist acts against each other. And their sizable armies are trained, equipped, and centered on fighting each other. This conflict seems intractable, and the many attempts that have been made to settle it have failed. The fact that settling the conflict would have major strategic consequences for all the issues at hand does not by itself mean that it now can be suddenly achieved. However, the thesis that a promising way to transform both the Pakistan–Afghanistan relationship and Pakistan itself is to invest much more in trying to settle the India–Pakistan conflict is supported by the observation that progress has been previously made on this front and that the time may now be ripe again for a major conflict-resolution drive.

In 2007, secret negotiations between the two countries were reported to have come close to a wide-ranging and encompassing deal. Confidence-building measures undertaken between the two countries included the easing of visa restrictions between the two[33] and talks to work out the contentious border of Sir Creek.[34] The two governments explored making a preferential trade agreement. Pakistan even considered granting India "most favored nation" status given a few minor changes in Indian policy.[35]

The main point of contention is the fate of Kashmir. When commentators refer to the issue, they often speak of it as intractable. However, in effect there is an emerging consensus between India and Pakistan on how to proceed. Ever since the partition, various approaches to Kashmir were suggested, especially granting it independence or dividing it between Pakistan and India along the Line of Control (LOC), or basing the decision on a referendum of Kashmiris. However, the two countries seem to be moving toward a third way, sometimes referred to as a "soft" border, which would entail giving the two parts of Kashmir considerable autonomy and allowing its citizens free movement and trade between the two. According to a report by an Indian and a Pakistani researcher at the US Institute of Peace, "The governments of India and Pakistan have both repeatedly endorsed the concept." Moreover, an opinion survey on both sides of the LOC reveals public support for peace and soft borders.[36] And there is growing support on both sides for Kashmiri representation in negotiations and for demilitarization of the area.[37]

The 2007 back channel negotiations between representatives of the Musharraf and Singh governments was moving well toward a settlement along the lines already cited, adding a proposal to establish a joint body (comprised of Kashmiris, Indians, and Pakistanis) to oversee issues affecting populations on both sides of the LOC.[38]

Unfortunately, both the Indian and Pakistani governments hesitated to codify the agreement, fearing public reaction, and by 2008 the opportunity to proceed was lost in the aftermath of

Musharraf's resignation and the abandonment of peace talks after the Mumbai attacks. Resistance to a settlement remains strong among select elements in the bureaucratic and military establishments of both countries. However, given the promising resumption of dialogue between India and Pakistan in early 2011[39] and the fact that the deal brokered in 2007 is still on the table, there is reason to suggest that if additional investments (discussed shortly) were made in the settlement of this conflict, significant progress could be made.

Settling the India–Pakistan conflict would remove a major reason Pakistan is keen to control the future government of Afghanistan and ensure that those elements of the Taliban allied with it would be at least a major force in that government. Currently, Pakistan fears that Afghanistan will tilt toward India, and that India will use Afghanistan as a platform for a spy network.[40] Pakistan also fears that because it is such a narrow country, if an Indian attack were launched from the east, it might need to retreat into Afghanistan,[41] and that if India and Afghanistan were allies, Pakistan would be forced to fight on two fronts in the event of a conflict with India. In addition, Pakistan worries about India stirring up ethnic tensions in Afghanistan that could spill over its borders (it has historically supported ethnic minorities, which could create conflict with the Pashtun majorities in Afghanistan and in Pakistan).[42] Pakistan has also accused India of using its presence in Afghanistan to provide funding and training to terrorists groups like the Balochistan Liberation Army in Pakistan's tribal areas with the goal of destabilizing the Pakistani government.[43]

Normalized relations between India and Pakistan would also bring considerable economic benefits to both countries. For example, India needs cement, and Pakistan's factories are close to the border. Currently, bilateral trade is a meager $2 billion a year (compared to India's $60 billion annual trade with China, for example).[44] Normalized relations would raise both nations' incomes per capita significantly, according to Shuja Nawaz.

Visionaries can even see a Pakistan and India that follow France and Germany, who, after they fought each other even longer and caused even more harm to each other than the two Asian nations, reconciled and formed a productive union. If Pakistan and India could one day find their way to such a union, they might even be able to scale back their military nuclear programs and join the NPT, which would do wonders for its weakened state.

103

State Department sources privately confirm that "back channel" negotiations are taking place between India and Pakistan, and that the United States is fostering these negotiations. To significantly increase the likelihood that these negotiations will succeed, the West has to invest in them much more than it currently does. For instance, taking into account that Pakistan is worried about its lack of strategic depth and India's conventional superiority, the West might favor positioning peacekeeping forces on the new borders as they are in the DMZ and were in Berlin. These forces would be positioned only after a settlement was reached and as part of it, rather than imposed on the sides. And they best include forces from nations such as Indonesia and Nigeria, combined with forces from nations such as Canada and Norway, possibly with logistical and intelligence support by the United States, but not American troops. Renegotiation of the US-India Civil Nuclear Agreement seems a particularly good place to start. This deserves some elaboration.

India (and also Pakistan) was for decades barred from nuclear trade with the West because it did not join the NPT.[45] The Bush administration moved in the opposite direction, providing American aid to India's civilian nuclear energy program and expanding US-India cooperation in nuclear technology. This assistance was to be used only for non-military purposes. However, by allowing the sale of uranium to India for its civilian reactors, the United States enabled India to move the limited supply of uranium it had to military use. (Before that, to make more nuclear bombs, Indian power plants were operating at reduced capacity.) The Bush administration rationalized these steps by claiming it would improve relations with India, which it considered the West's best hope to balance China. However, rather than fostering a closer relationship between India and the United States, the treaty was highly controversial in India. It took years of wrangling before it was finally approved by India in August 2010.

In response to the Bush administration's deal with India, Pakistan increased its nuclear program on its own by rapidly expanding its plutonium production, and China granted Pakistan two more reactors as part of an agreement parallel to the US-India one. (Some may argue that the China–Pakistan deal was underway before the US-India one. Although this is true, the China–Pakistan deal was not implemented until after the US-India one.) The result is a case study in how the expansion of nuclear facilities in one country can spur the expansion of nuclear facilities in another—exactly the course that should be avoided. Given the great resistance to the nuclear agreement in India by the opposition and major segments of the public, the United States may find India quite willing to renegotiate the agreement in addition to further reasons to call for reopening an agreement that should not have been made in the first place. Scaling it back seems a very promising way to show that the West is no longer tilting toward India, to try to convince Pakistan that it need not expand its nuclear program, and as part of tension reduction and conflict settlement between the two nations.

This and other such moves are unlikely to take place and, if advanced, to succeed, until the West engages in a major geopolitical reassessment concerning India, which in turn requires examining the West's future relationship with China.

Balancing China?

One major reason the United States has not pressured India more heavily to come to terms with Pakistan, and Pakistan holds—not without reason—that the United States is tilting toward India, is the precept that the United States must court India in order for it to balance China. During much of the Cold War, the West viewed India as leaning toward the communist bloc and Pakistan as a staunch anti-communist ally. Pakistan played a major role in helping the United States drive the USSR out of Afghanistan. Over the decades, Pakistan received considerable amounts of foreign aid, military aid, equipment, and training from the United States, while India was largely spurned.

By 2000, however, the United States was growing increasingly concerned about the rise of China as a superpower and was looking for ways to "balance" it. Washington believed that India could play a key role in this new geopolitical lineup. Additionally, India, as a democratic and economically successful nation, was held up as a counter-model to the Chinese model of state capitalism, which had a growing appeal in the third world. As a result, the United States "tilted" toward India by expanding bilateral cooperation and investment in a number of areas. These overtures were capped by signing a landmark nuclear cooperation deal in 2008.

Thus, just as one is hard-put to see an end to the war in Afghanistan—and more broadly, to the Taliban sanctuaries—without changes in the policies of Pakistan, so one is hard-put to see such changes occur without changes in the Indo–Pakistani relationship. The same holds for "rebalancing" the military–civilian relationships within Pakistan.

In other words, instead of focusing mainly on what the West can get from Pakistan or give to Pakistan, it best pay more mind to what effects changes in the US-India relationship would have on Pakistan's inner balance and Afghanistan policies. Ergo, the place to start is for the United States to reassess the geopolitical role it assigned to India as a China balancer.

This reassessment should encompass the thesis that China needs to be balanced; the timing of such balancing, if it is indeed needed; and the costs of casting India in this role. Much has been made of the rise of China and the decline of the United States. Such commentary tends to overlook that the United States is declining from a very high level of military and economic prowess, while China is rising from a rather low level. True, the size of the Chinese economy is expected to reach that of the US by 2035. However, given that China has four times more people to feed, house, and otherwise service, the more relevant figure is income per capita. China's income per capita is quite low, about $7,400.[46]

Assessments of China's military power vary considerably. However, most experts agree that it would take at least two decades before China could win a major war against the United States.[47] Many of China's latest military acquisitions are either upgraded knock-offs of old Soviet equipment or purchased from the former USSR—hardly state-of-the-art technologies.[48] Others are unlikely to achieve full operational capability for years to come,[49] including the headline-grabbing Chinese stealth fighter, the J-20.[50] And perhaps the greatest perceived Chinese military threat, anti-aircraft—a.k.a. "carrier-killer"—ballistic missiles, have yet to be publicly tested over water against a maneuvering target.[51] China's yet-to-be-deployed first aircraft carrier was purchased from Ukraine in the 1990s.[52] (The United States has eleven.)[53] China's newest attack jet, the J-15, is an updated version of a Soviet one, which carries less fuel than a US one and, as a take-off method, requires flying off a ski-jump-style runway.[54] When Russia refused to sell China nuclear submarines, China attempted to build its own, producing subs that turned out to be noisier than those built by the Soviets thirty years ago.[55]

Some hawks in the United States use the term "China hedge" to argue that the US military ought to prepare for war with China, just in case it turns out to become a major adversary decades from now. However, given that China could not pose a serious threat to the United States for decades, the United States can engage in the opposite kind of

China hedge: an attempt to build peaceful cooperation, a case outlaid in Henry Kissinger's 2001 book on China.

China may well prefer such a course over continuing to increase its investment in the military because it must worry about the large segments of its population that demand the kind of affluence enjoyed, so far, by only a minority, to say nothing of other domestic tensions and major environmental challenges. Additionally, one should note that China does not have an expansionist ideology and has shown no desire to run the world or replace the United States as the global hegemon, although it is keen to play a much greater role in its region and to secure the flow of commodities and energy on which its economic well-being is dependent.

Taking all these factors into account, there seems to be ample time to first try what Henry Kissinger calls "co-evolution," and others have referred to as a China-US partnership.[56] Indeed, defining China as an enemy and moving to balance it could become a factor in making it into an adversary which it otherwise might not be.

Moreover, it is far from obvious what is meant by "balancing" in a twenty-first century context—and if India is well suited as a balancing power, even if there was a need and a way to balance China. Economically, India and China have much to gain from increased trade and cooperation, and from devoting their resources to economic development rather than to accelerated military build up. Politically, India is rather ambivalent about the United States. Above all, the United States tilting toward India, especially the nuclear deal, is generating some rather negative side effects from a balancing viewpoint: they are driving Pakistan to a closer alliance with China, including a military one. And, worst of all, this tilting is a major reason Pakistan is accelerating its build up of nuclear arms. This fact alone justifies the suggested geopolitical reassessment.

In Conclusion

Much attention has been paid to threats posed to major interests of the West by conditions and developments in Pakistan and its role in Afghanistan. Numerous attempts have been made over the last decade to convince Pakistan to close the Afghan Taliban sanctuaries in Pakistan, to cease supporting the insurgency in Afghanistan, to better fight its own insurgency, and to better secure its nuclear arms. They have been only very partially successful. Suggestions for the West to pressure Pakistan to change its behavior in the desired direction by withholding aid ignore that the West at this stage is more dependent on Pakistan than Pakistan is on the West. Suggestions to restructure Pakistan itself, to build up its civil society, and to scale back the military seem rather unrealistic.

The most promising route seems to be the one that at first blush seems the most difficult to negotiate—to help settle the India–Pakistan conflict. Such a settlement would free Pakistani forces to focus on its insurgency, reduce its sense that it best control the course of events in Afghanistan, and possibly scale back its military nuclear program and better secure its nuclear arms. It would also reduce the importance of the military. The fact that there are detailed and rather widely shared ideas about the ways this conflict might be settled and that various tension reduction moves and negotiations between the two nations have taken place indicates that this course is not a road one cannot travel.

For the West to be able to throw its weight behind supporting the conflict settlement, it will need to be viewed by Pakistan as ceasing to tilt toward India. For the West to correct this tilt, a geopolitical reassessment is needed. It would show that China is best treated as a regional power (not a hegemon) with little, if any, global ambitions and one with which the West can partner in dealing with many international affairs matters. This reassessment, moreover, would recognize that balancing is a concept that applies poorly to the twenty-first-century age of WMDs, cyberwarfare, long range missiles, and unconventional forces and terrorism. And thus there is no reason to try to cast India in the role of a China balancer.

In short, the links between Afghanistan and Pakistan (and Pakistan's inner makeup) are affected by the India–Pakistan entanglement. This entanglement, in turn, is affected by the India–China–West relationship. Although at first it may seem farfetched to argue that a promising way to break the persistent morass in Afghanistan and Pakistan is to reexamine Western assumptions about China's course, this paper suggests that this avenue might well be worth exploring in its own right and for the sake of all the parties involved.

Notes

* I am indebted to Julia Milton and Marissa Cramer for research assistance on this article.

1. Ariel Zirulnick, "Pakistani Militants Infiltrate Naval Base Just 15 Miles from Suspected Nuclear Site," *Christian Science Monitor* (May 23, 2011), http://www.csmonitor.com/World/terrorism-security/2011/0523/

Pakistani-militants-infiltrate-naval-base-just-15-miles-from-suspected-nuclear-site (accessed June 19, 2012).

2. Terrence P. Smith, "Pakistan Joins the Nuclear 100 Club," *CSIS* (February 1, 2011), http://csis.org/blog/pakistan-joins-nuclear-100-club (accessed June 19, 2012).

3. Andrew Bast, "Pakistan's Nuclear Surge," *Newsweek* (May 30, 2011).

4. Rodney W. Jones, "Pakistan's Nuclear Poker Bet," *Foreign Policy: AfPak Channel* (May 27, 2011). http://afpak.foreignpolicy.com/posts/2011/05/27/pakistans_nuclear_poker_bet (accessed June 19, 2012).

5. Richard L. Armitage and Samuel R. Berger, "U.S. Strategy for Pakistan and Afghanistan," *Independent Task Fore Report No. 65, Council of Foreign Relations* (2010), 21.

6. Jane Perlez, "Pakistan's Chief of Army Fights to Keep His Job," *New York Times* (June 15, 2011). http://www.nytimes.com/2011/06/16/world/asia/16pakistan.html (accessed June 19, 2012).

7. Jane Perlez and Ismail Khan, "Pakistan Tells U.S. It Must Sharply Cut CIA Activities," *New York Times* (April 11, 2011). http://www.nytimes.com/2011/04/12/world/asia/12pakistan.html (accessed June 19, 2012).

8. Omar Waraich, "Pakistan's Reaction to Obama's Plan: Departure Is Key," *Time* (December 2, 2009). http://www.time.com/time/world/article/0,8599,1945134,00.html (accessed June 19, 2012).

9. Mark Mazzetti, "Should (Could) America and Pakistan's Bond Be Broken?" *New York Times* (June 4, 2011). http://www.nytimes.com/2011/06/05/weekinreview/05pakistan.html?pagewanted=all (accessed June 19, 2012).

10. Helene Cooper, "Allies in War, but the Goals Clash," *The New York Times* (October 9, 2010). http://www.nytimes.com/2010/10/10/weekinreview/10cooper.html (accessed June 19, 2012).

11. Ayaz Gul, "Pakistan Claims Progress against Tribal Area Militants," *Voice of America* (June 9, 2011). http://www.voanews.com/english/news/asia/Pakistan-Claims-Progress-Against-Tribal-Area-Militants-123654394.html (accessed June 19, 2012).

12. Lawrence Wright, "The Double Game," *New Yorker* (May 16, 2011). http://www.newyorker.com/reporting/2011/05/16/110516fa_fact_wright (accessed June 19, 2012).

13. Michael G. Findley, Darren Hawkins, Robert L. Hicks, Daniel L. Nielson, Bradley C. Parks, Ryan M. Powers, J. Timmons Roberts, Michael J. Tierney, and Sven Wilson. "*AidData: Tracking Development Finance*," presented at the PLAID Data Vetting Workshop, Washington, DC (September 2009).

14. Pervez Musharraf, "Pakistan: A Reality Check Amid the Terror and Chaos," *CNN* (June 8, 2011). http://articles.cnn.com/2011-06-08/opinion/pakistan.pervez.musharraf.islamism_1_today-pakistan-religious-militancy-afghanistan?_s=PM:OPINION (accessed June 19, 2012).

15. Fareed Zakaria, "The Radicalization of Pakistan's Military," *The Washington Post* (June. 22). http://www.washingtonpost.com/opinions/the-radicalization-of-pakistans-military/2011/06/22/AGbCBSgH_story.html (accessed June 19, 2012).

16. Jane Perlez and Helene Cooper, "Signaling Tensions, Pakistan Shuts NATO Route," *New York Times* (September 30, 2010). http://www.nytimes.com/2010/10/01/world/asia/01peshawar.html (accessed June 19, 2012).

17. Franz-Stefan Gady, "Pakistan Moves East," *The National Interest* (June 3, 2011). http://nationalinterest.org/commentary/the-china-pakistan-alliance-5400 (accessed June 19, 2012).

18. Mark Mazzetti, "Should (Could) America and Pakistan's Bond Be Broken?" *New York Times* (June 4, 2011).

19. Franz-Stefan Gady, "Pakistan Moves East," *The National Interest* (June 3, 2011). http://nationalinterest.org/commentary/the-china-pakistan-alliance-5400 (accessed June 19, 2012).

20. Ibid.

21. "China to Sell 50 Fighter Jets to Pakistan," *Associated Press* (May 20, 2011). http://www.thenational.ae/news/worldwide/south-asia/china-to-sell-50-fighter-jets-to-pakistan (accessed June 19, 2012).

22. Franz-Stefan Gady, "Pakistan Moves East," *The National Interest* (June 3, 2011). http://nationalinterest.org/commentary/the-china-pakistan-alliance-5400 (accessed June 19, 2012).

23. Ibid.

24. Griff Witte, "Pakistan Courts China as Relations with the U.S. Grow Strained," *Washington Post* (June 22, 2011). http://www.washingtonpost.com/world/asia-pacific/pakistan-courts-china-as-relations-with-us-grow-strained/2011/06/19/AGDCyWfH_story.html (accessed June 19, 2012).

25. Mark Mazzetti, "Should (Could) America and Pakistan's Bond Be Broken?" *New York Times* (June 4, 2011).

26. Aqil Shah, "Getting the Military out of Pakistani Politics," *Foreign Affairs* (May/June 2011). http://www.foreignaffairs.com/articles/67742/aqil-shah/getting-the-military-out-of-pakistani-politics (accessed June 19, 2012).

27. "Conditions in Kerry-Lugar Bill Is Stated Policy of Pak: US," *Indian Express* (October 9, 2009). http://www.indianexpress.com/news/conditions-in-kerrylugar-bill-is-stated-policy-of-pak-us/527107/0 (accessed June 19, 2012).

28. "Evaluating U.S. Foreign Aid to Afghanistan: A Majority Staff Report," *Committee on Foreign Relations, United States Senate* (June 8, 2011); Amitai Etzioni, *Security First* (New Haven, CT: Yale University Press, 2007), 37–85.

29. "Evaluating U.S. Foreign Aid to Afghanistan: A Majority Staff Report," *Committee on Foreign Relations, United States Senate* (June 8, 2011).

30. Lawrence Wright, "The Double Game," *New Yorker* (May 16, 2011). http://www.newyorker.com/reporting/2011/05/16/110516fa_fact_wright (accessed June 19, 2012)

31. Ibid.

32. Shuja Nawaz, "Raging at Rawalpindi," *Foreign Policy* (May 13, 2011). http://www.foreignpolicy.com/articles/2011/05/13/raging_at_rawalpindi?page=full (accessed June 19, 2012).

33. PPI, "India, Pakistan to Ease Visa Restrictions," *The Express Tribune* (June 7, 2011). http://tribune.com.pk/story/184215/india-pakistan-to-ease-visa-restrictions/ (accessed June 19, 2012).

34. Zahid Gishkori, "Indo-Pak Composite Dialogue: No Movement on Sir Creek Talks," *The Express Tribune* (May 22, 2011), http://tribune.com.pk/story/173672/indo-pak-composite-dialogue-no-movement-on-sir-creek-talks/ (accessed June 19, 2012).

35. Mubarak Zeb Khan, "Pakistan Offers MFN Status to India," *Dawn* (April 29, 2011). http://www.dawn.com/2011/04/29/pakistan-offers-mfn-status-to-india.html (accessed June 19, 2012).

36. P. R. Chari and Hasan Askari Rizvi, "Making Borders Irrelevant in Kashmir," United States Institute of Peace, Special Report 210 (September 2008).

37. Moeed Yusuf and Adil Najam, "Kashmir: Ripe for Resolution?" *Third World Quarterly* 30, no. 8 (2009): 1503–28.

38. Steve Coll, "The Back Channel: India and Pakistan's Secret Kashmir Talks," *The New Yorker* (March 2, 2009).

39. Simon Denyer and Karin Brulliard, "India, Pakistan Agree to Resume Peace Talks," *Washington Post* (February 11, 2011). http://www.washingtonpost.com/wp-dyn/content/article/2011/02/10/AR2011021007207.html (accessed June 19, 2012).

40. "Afghanistan and Pakistan: Understanding and Engaging Regional Stakeholders," *Hearing before the House Subcommittee on National Security and Foreign Affairs* (March 31, 2009), 16. https://house.resource.org/111/gov.house.ogr.fa.20090331.pdf (accessed June 19, 2012).

41. Ibid.

42. Ben Arnoldy, "How the Afghanistan War Became Tangled in India vs. Pakistan Rivalry," *Christian Science Monitor* (January 20, 2011). http://www.csmonitor.com/World/Asia-South-Central/2011/0120/How-the-Afghanistan-war-became-tangled-in-India-vs.-Pakistan-rivalry (accessed June 19, 2012).

43. Amin Tarzi, "Afghanistan: Kabul's India Ties Worry Pakistan," *Radio Free Europe/Radio Liberty* (April 16, 2006). http://www.rferl.org/content/article/1067690.html (accessed June 19, 2012).

44. "India and Pakistan: A Willow Branch," *The Economist* (March 31, 2011). http://www.economist.com/node/18485995?story_id=18485995 (accessed June 19, 2012).

45. Mark Hibbs, "Moving Forward on the U.S.-India Nuclear Deal," *Carnegie Endowment for International Peace* (April 5, 2010). http://www.carnegieendowment.org/publications/?fa=view&id=40491 (accessed June 19, 2012).

46. "GDP Per Capita (PPP)," CIA World Factbook. https://www.cia.gov/library/publications/the-world-factbook/rankorder/2004rank.html (accessed June 19, 2012).

47. See Robert D. Kaplan, "How We Would Fight China," *Atlantic* 295, no. 5 (June 2005): 49–64; Kenneth Lieberthal, "Is China Catching Up With the US?" *Ethos* 8 (August 2010): 8; Robert Ross, "The Rise of Chinese Power and the Implications for the Regional Security Order," *Orbis* 54, no. 4 (2010): 525–45.

48. John Pomfret, "Military Strength Eludes China, Which Looks Overseas for Arms," *Washington Post* (December 25, 2010). http://www.washingtonpost.

com/wp-dyn/content/article/2010/12/24/AR2010122402788.html (accessed June 19, 2012)..

49. Ibid.

50. Karen Parrish, "Navy Intel Chief Discusses China's Military Advances," *American Forces Press Service* (January 6, 2011). http://www.defense.gov/news/newsarticle.aspx?id=62346 (accessed June 19, 2012).

51. Ibid. See also Ronald O'Rourke, "China Naval Modernization: Implications for U.S. Navy Capabilities—Background and Issues for Congress," *Congressional Research Service* (April. 22, 2011): 8–14.

52. Michael Wines, "Chinese State Media, in a Show of Openness, Print Jet Photos," *New York Times* (April 25, 2011). http://www.nytimes.com/2011/04/26/world/asia/26fighter.html?_r=1 (accessed June 19, 2012).

53. Robert Ross, "The Rise of Chinese Power and the Implications for the Regional Security Order," *Orbis* 54, no. 4 (2010): 540.

54. See note 52.

55. See note 48.

56. Henry Kissinger, *On China* (New York: Penguin, 2011); David Shambaugh, "Introduction", in *Power Shift* (Berkeley, CA: University of California Press, 2005), 15; C. Fred Bergsten, "Two's Company," *Foreign Affairs* 88, no. 5 (September–October 2009): 169–70; Amitai Etzioni, "Is China a Responsible Stakeholder?" *International Affairs* 87, no. 3 (May 2011): 539–53. (accessed June 19, 2012)

Part IV

Muslims and Arabs: What Makes a Reliable Partner in Peace?

7

Tunisia: The First Arab Islamocracy

Tunisia, famously the first Arab Spring nation to conduct elections, may well be on its way to becoming the first Muslim nation to combine the rule of sharia with elements of democracy. Americans should not seek to stand in the way of such a development. Both American elected officials and the media tend to assume that for a nation to be democratic, it must adopt our kinds of institutions, including the separation of religion and state. (This tendency was very much in evidence when Americans played key roles in writing the new post-liberation Iraqi and Afghan constitutions.) Though Tunisia is a relatively "modern" Arab state and has a sizable secular population, the political struggle is over how much sharia will be implemented, rather than whether the new regime can do without enforcing at least some Islamic rules and traditions.

The new Tunisian government is likely to introduce one form of censorship or another, seeking to ensure that the media does not publish material that disparages Islam. Do not expect to see a rerun of the Danish cartoon of the prophet,[1] a Tunisian edition of *The Satanic Verses*,[2] or even merely a depiction of God as a person. (Recently, when an animated film violated this last taboo, it elicited a firestorm of outrage that included many in the moderate center.) Moreover, it is likely that the new Tunisian constitution will reflect traditional Islamic views of marriage, divorce, and inheritance that strongly favor men over women. At the same time, the new constitution is unlikely to follow the stricter interpretation of sharia that includes the amputation of the hands of thieves, public flogging, and stoning of women who commit adultery—the violent expressions of Islam.

Americans may find it easier to accept Islamocracy if they recall that separation of state and religion is followed by France and the United States, but most other democracies have long had an established religion. Despite the wall said to exist between the government and religious bodies, American taxpayers cover a great deal of the costs of health care and welfare provided by Catholic churches, Jewish religious organizations, and many others, either by direct grants or indirectly via Medicare and Medicaid. Finally, while the United States has a strong commitment to freedom of speech (other democracies impose stricter limits on hate speech and accord their citizens much more leniency to sue critics for defamation), we too impose more limits on speech than it may at first seem. Thus CBS was fined $550,000 for a wardrobe malfunction during the 2004 Super Bowl,[3] and a reporter or anchor who uses the N-word or otherwise shows racial prejudice on the airwaves is likely to lose his job.

As Robert Merry previously put it, we can recognize the exceptionalism of our values without assuming their universality.[4] We should be ready to accept that the Muslim republics will incorporate some moderate elements of sharia into their governments. (For example, polls show that more than 60 percent of Egyptians want sharia to be the sole source of law in their country; an additional 25 percent say that it should be one of several sources.[5]) As long as they avoid the violent parts of sharia, we should hold that those countries have passed the basic litmus test to qualify as regimes with which we can work, even as we hope for and favor further development in the direction of values we hold dear.

Notes

1. "Danish Cartoon Controversy," *New York Times* (August 12, 2009). http://topics.nytimes.com/topics/reference/timestopics/subjects/d/danish_cartoon_controversy/index.html (accessed January 24, 2012).
2. Salman Rushdie, *The Satanic Verses: A Novel* (New York: Picador, 2000).
3. "CBS Hit with $550K Super Bowl Fine," *CNN Money* (September 22, 2004). http://money.cnn.com/2004/09/22/news/fortune500/viacom_fcc/ (accessed January 24, 2012).
4. Robert W. Merry, "American Exceptionalism and the Universality Fallacy," *National Interest* (September 30, 2011). http://nationalinterest.org/commentary/american-exceptionalism-the-universality-fallacy-5956 (accessed January 24, 2012).
5. "Women and the Arab Awakening," *Economist* (October 15, 2011). http://www.economist.com/node/21532256 (accessed January 24, 2012).

8

Illiberal Moderate Muslims Are the Global Swing Vote[*]

Introduction

The fault line that defines the clash of moral cultures and powers in the post–Cold War era does not run between civilizations, but within them. It divides the beliefs of those who hold that they are justified in advancing their values and interests by the use of force (from here on "violent beliefs") and the beliefs held by those who seek to rely on persuasion, education and leadership (persuasive beliefs). True, those who believe in persuasion as the source of legitimacy of their political actions recognize exceptional conditions under which force may be used (for example, in what they consider a just war). And those who believe in force as a major instrument of foreign (and domestic) policy do also use persuasion. However, we shall see that the differences between the two sets of beliefs and their followers are readily discernible and of much moral and political consequence. Above all, I will try to show that the schism between them is the most important fault line in the contemporary world: it is at the heart of the struggle over who will shape the international system and over how it ought to be shaped.

It is empirically wrong, morally faulty, and strategically ill-advised to hold that the pre-eminent global confrontation of our time is between the civilization of the West and all others, especially that of the followers of the Prophet Muhammad, the Muslims—as Samuel Huntington has famously argued in his book *The Clash of Civilizations* and the *Remaking of World Order*.[1] I will shortly point to those who hold violent beliefs—whether they are called Crusaders, Jihadists, or merely terrorists—in all major belief systems, both religious and secular, Eastern and Western. Moreover, I will show that in all these civilizations there are also those who disavow the use of violence to

117

advance their beliefs and instead seek to rely as much as possible on appealing to the values and worldviews of those they seek to convert. In other words, I argue that the true fault line facing the world today runs through civilizations rather than between them, dividing each into two camps—those who see violence as a major and legitimate tool, and those who view the use of force as abhorrent and instead rely largely on normative appeals. In more colloquial terms, the fault line divides those of the sword from those of the word.

As someone who killed and saw many killed long before reaching the age of twenty, I may as well state up front from which camp I hail. I still pain for every life lost, whether it was one of "ours" or "theirs"; I deeply regret every death I helped inflict, even though I was acting to defend those I loved from those who attacked us. Ever since I turned twenty, when I first sat at the feet of Martin Buber, I have been somewhat of a persuader.[2] I am not a pacifist but someone who holds that one is morally obligated to exhaust all other means possible before lifting one's arms, and that force should be applied only when there is a true, imminent, and severe danger. Above all, I maintain that making a compelling case for one's cause is both morally right and much more effective in the long run than the violent alternatives.

Needless to say, I am hardly alone. In effect, it is a main thesis of this essay that those who hold persuasive beliefs currently outnumber those who hold violent beliefs in all major civilizations (some illustrative data follow below). Most importantly, we ought to recognize that the persuaders of the world are the natural allies of anyone who rises against the world of terror and, in effect, all other forms of violence. Though I cannot fully demonstrate this point in the confines of this essay, I suggest that those on the persuasive side of the fault line today include (as distinct from earlier historical periods) the majority of Muslims (especially in nations such as Indonesia, Morocco, Bangladesh, and Turkey, despite some recent increases in radical Islam in these nations), as well as the majority of Hindus, Buddhists, Christians, Jews, socialists, and many other groups. They are all potential members of a "persuasive alliance," a coalition of people who seek first and foremost to draw on normative power[3] rather than on force in forming a new global order and in sustaining domestic regimes.

The Normative Importance of the Fault Line

All societies and groups, whether religious or secular, seek to sustain a measure of social order. However, forcing people to adopt whatever behavior a given belief system extols is—morally speaking—by far the worst option for maintaining order because it degrades their humanity more than any other measure of control. Coercion (the term is used here to mean the exercise of physical force) greatly curtails freedom of choice, if it does not obviate it completely, and thus deprives individuals of their autonomy. Respect for human dignity entails that the actor be free to render decisions, to follow his or her will. The essence of coercion is to nullify this freedom by forcing a course of action on the person at issue. Thus, coercion turns people from sovereign agents of their selves and their communities into automatons driven by those who wield force, or into objects controlled by their violators.[4] Moreover, coercion sharply curtails, if not destroys, the ability of individuals to exercise their individual rights and their ability to discharge their social responsibilities, to contribute to the common good, to love and be loved, to do good and to be virtuous.

In sharp contrast to coercion, persuasion leaves the final say to the actor.[5] Persuaders appeal to people's values, motives or interests, but if at the end of the day those subject to persuasion still choose to follow a different course, they are left to do so, though there may be some cost, say in terms of social popularity, prestige, access to goods in short supply, and so on. Persuasion does not intrude on people's rights, and it thrives on what is considered one of the most important of these: freedom of speech. Nor does persuasion prevent anyone from discharging his or her responsibilities. In the process of persuasion, the persuader may even change his or her views, a point especially stressed by Martin Buber.

Persuaders may well seek to change people's conception of good and evil, and the target of their love, but they do not seek to prevent people from living up to whatever values they choose to follow. Persuasion, as a rule, respects people's humanity by appealing to their values, loyalties, affections, and intellect—even when the contents of the appeal are misguided from the viewpoint of the persuader. Just as coercion reduces people to objects, persuasion respects their agency.

Granted, few, if any, choices are entirely free. There is, however, a continuum of restrictions on choice, from minimal to absolute. When these restrictions are limited, we can still speak of an ability of actors to follow their preferences and still largely be autonomous and treated with respect. In contrast, when restrictions are high, we hold that the freedom of the actors has been greatly curtailed if not eliminated, their autonomy destroyed. This level of restriction is, as a rule, achieved only when violence is employed, as when people are jailed or shot dead.

One may wonder whether my strongly negative view of coercion holds when violence is employed by the state to enforce the law or counteract violent groups. I grant that no social order can rely exclusively on persuasion; some exercise of coercion is found even in the most benign regimes. However, the differences between legal and social orders that are based largely on persuasion versus those that draw extensively on coercion are unmistakable and of enormous human consequence. Regimes that minimize the use of coercion in law enforcement are vastly more effective and legitimate than their opposites. Hence, law enforcement in Norway is superior to that of Singapore, and the current Chinese regime is preferable to that of Mao's—although it is still a long way from being highly persuasive. Legitimacy matters in both domestic and international affairs as never before. As education spreads and the development of communication technologies eases access to information, what people believe matters more now than it did in prior generations. It follows, therefore, that the side of the fault line on which a government, social movement, or religious group falls, and thus the degree to which it is perceived as legitimate, is increasingly critical to its authority.

Not the Liberal/Extremist Fault Line

I cannot stress enough that the fault line this essay points to divides the people of the world along a fundamentally different line than the one often drawn between liberals—in the political theory sense of the term—on the one hand (modern, rational, democratic, and often secular), and extremists on the other (impassioned, radical, authoritarian, and often fiercely religious). The division between liberals and extremists has been highlighted by those who argue that any form of Islam that is incompatible with liberal democratic values is necessarily oppressive and a grave threat to Western societies; they argue that Muslims must limit their faith to personal and otherworldly matters if they are to become good democratic citizens. This position was recently articulated by a group of writers and intellectuals, including Salman Rushdie and Ayaan Hirsi Ali, who declared, "After having overcome fascism, Nazism, and Stalinism, the world now faces a new global totalitarian threat: Islamism . . . Islamism is a reactionary ideology that kills equality, freedom, and secularism wherever it is present."[6]

As a part of this debate, attempts have been made to demonstrate that liberal, democratic Muslims do exist. Some prominent names that have been referenced include Irshad Manji, Reza Aslan, Muqtedar Khan, and Asra Nomani. Most of those cited in this context are found among those who live in the West. Such liberal Muslim leaders and public intellectuals are also found elsewhere but are relatively few and far between.

Liberal Muslims are recognized and celebrated because they serve as a counterpoint to extremists (increasingly referred to as "Islamists") and because they subscribe to liberal values such as mutual tolerance, human rights, free press, and fair elections. In short, they are what liberals in the West consider good citizens, if not also good people. However, this liberal/extremist fault line is not the subject of this paper; it divides the world very differently than the division I see as all-important. For this reason, I also do not use the well-known terms "civility" and "ideology." Though I consider these terms to be valid, I find that they capture a fault line similar to the division between liberals and extremists. I hold that one should not assume, even by implication, that because a Muslim, or an adherent to any other belief system, is a "true" or "strong" believer, does not profess faith in liberal values and does not favor democratic polities or many of the rights enumerated in the Universal Declaration of Human Rights, he or she must therefore be an extremist, an advocate of violence. Millions of people across the world are moderates (those who do not believe that the use of force is justified under most conditions) without being liberals.

Similarly, there is a world of difference between believing in some other form of government than democracy—say, tribal councils or adhering to the rulings of muftis or rabbis—and advocating violence. One can be a strict believer, even a fundamentalist, who reads literally the Bible, the Koran, or some other revered text, closely follows numerous religious or secular injunctions, such as praying five times a day, and vehemently opposes modernization, democracy, and capitalism, and still not believe in imposing one's values on others by the use of force. I readily grant that such true believers (whether religious or secular) are, statistically speaking, more likely than those of little or no faith (religious or secular) to favor violence; some of them are so confident they have seen the light that they are willing to shove it down the throats of non-believers. Nevertheless, there are many millions of strict believers who do not favor coercion.

For example, there are about 55 million evangelicals in the United States but very few of them favor using force to impose their beliefs on others. There are over one billion Catholics worldwide, but only a very small number justify murdering those who perform abortions. In addition, there are hundreds of thousands of Orthodox Jews, but only a minority of them favors the use of force to foster compliance with what they consider the Lord's laws. Among socialists there have been quite a few who have held that if one wants to make an omelette, one must crack eggs (translation: to make a revolution one must inflict violence), especially in Stalin's and Mao's days, but over the last decades more and more socialists have professed faith in the power of ideas and persuasion, not force. To push the point, someone may think homosexuality is a sin, believe with all their heart that God created the universe in six days and rested on the seventh, and hold that women should "graciously submit to their husbands," and still not favor forcing others to hold these beliefs or adhere to the behavior they call for. In short, there are millions upon millions who disavow the use of violence in matters of belief and rely on persuasion to advance their ideals, but who simultaneously do not support the values of a modern, liberal polity.

This has been readily apparent among Muslims during the recent Danish cartoon controversy. While many extremist clerics exhorted their followers to violently retaliate against Western targets, others strongly condemned the cartoons and the free speech that allowed them to be published but were also adamant in their opposition to trashing embassies, threatening Westerners, and committing other acts of violence. For instance, Din Syamsuddin, the conservative head of Indonesia's 30-million-strong Muhammadiyah Muslim association, urged his followers "not to overreact and act in a violent and anarchist way [in protesting the cartoons] because those things are completely against Islamic teachings."[7] The hard-line mufti Sheikh Yusuf al-Qaradawi declared, "We call on Muslims to show their fury in a logical and controlled manner . . . We didn't ask people to burn embassies as some have done in Damascus and Beirut. We don't sanction destruction and torching because this is not in line with morality or Muslim behavior."[8]

Public opinion polls provide further evidence that, though many Muslims do not profess faith in the values of a secular democracy, they also oppose the use of violence. For example, large majorities in Jordan, Pakistan, Morocco, and Indonesia welcome a greater role for Islam in their nations' politics, according to the 2005 Pew Global Attitudes survey; the same is true for a smaller majority in Lebanon.[9] Another poll found that a majority of respondents in Jordan and the United Arab Emirates (55 percent) and a plurality in Morocco (49 percent), Lebanon (44 percent), Saudi Arabia (49 percent), and Egypt (45 percent) believe the clergy play too little a role in their nation's public life and politics, while most others responded that their role is just.[10] Thus, in nearly all the Muslim nations surveyed, a belief in secular government is not dominant.

When it comes to the use of violence in defense of Islam, the Pew survey shows that among the 140 million Muslims in Indonesia, the 69.5 million in Turkey, and the 32.3 million in Morocco, 15 percent or fewer support suicide bombers. Support for suicide bombers has dropped sharply in Pakistan, from 41 percent in March 2004 to 25 percent in May 2005.[11] Other reports have indicated little support for terrorism among Muslims in India, Malaysia, and Bangladesh. In a 2005 poll of Afghans, 81 percent expressed a negative view of Al-Qaeda and 82 percent supported the overthrow of the Taliban.[12] And among Palestinians in 2006, 73 percent favor a peaceful solution to the conflict with Israel and 62 percent believe Hamas should change its position on the destruction of the Israeli state.[13]

Nowhere have I found the violence–persuasion fault line more clearly delineated than when I was a guest in 2002 of the reformers in Iran, at an institution that was aptly called the International Center for the Dialogue of Civilizations. Many of the reformers who strongly opposed the mullahs' theocracy were also not seeking to build a secular civil society. They favored a society in "which people will want to pray (as well as observe many of the other tenets of Islam) but nobody will be coerced to do so." Why should people of such faith not be included on the persuasive side of the civilization fault line? Just because they are illiberal?

Illustrative Evidence in Five Belief Systems

Some highly selective examples from four religious and one secular belief system help highlight the all-important fault line between violent and persuasive beliefs that is found in all major civilizations. In providing these examples, I draw on moral arguments made in different historical periods and articulated in different sources (such as religious texts, major books, and statements by leaders) because, for the purpose at hand, it matters little who said what, or when, but whether or not the statements are considered authoritative by large camps of followers. To illustrate this methodological point, it matters little for the issue at hand whether "an eye for an eye" was recorded 5,000 or 2,000 years ago, or what the reasons are for non-coercive interpretations of this passage becoming more dominant during some periods or circumstances. What matters is that past, current or future extremists have and can use such passages—because they see them as having the authority of the Bible or of a Pope or some other such source—to justify their violent acts. Historians, anthropologists, area studies scholars, and others will be concerned quite correctly about the fact that statements characterizing beliefs are taken out of context. However, it is not the author but the agents under study who engage in such use of texts.

One last word by way of introduction to the following examples: space limitations mandate that I use merely a few illustrative examples from each belief system here examined. There are scores of other examples that could be cited, and many other differences between beliefs that could be explored. The focus here is narrowly limited to illustrate the fault line, which runs through history and belief systems and which is especially prominent in the post–Cold War era.

Christianity

Christian beliefs that are understood to legitimate violence under various conditions, or for particular purposes, draw on passages from the Old Testament such as those commanding that the community stone to death anyone who blasphemes (Leviticus 24:14) and from the New Testament that depict a forceful and angry Jesus. For example, Jesus declares, "Do not think that I have come to bring peace to the earth; I have not come to bring peace, but a sword."[14] Jesus is portrayed as having a "sharp, two-edged sword" (Revelation 1:16) emerging from his mouth with which he strikes down sinners. And Jesus evicts the money changers from the temple: "Making a whip of cords, he drove all of them out of the temple . . . He also poured out the coins of the money changers and overturned their tables" (John 2:15).

When Saint Augustine of Hippo (354–430 CE), a much-celebrated theologian of early Christianity, was faced with the breakaway Christian sect known as Donatism, he advised that they be brought back to the Church through "the stripes of temporal scourging."[15] He references as a scriptural justification, Proverbs 23:14, which says of children that

"If you beat them with a rod, you will save their lives from Sheol [here understood as hell]."

During the early period of the Papal Inquisition (established in 1231 CE), Saint Thomas Aquinas, a much-revered Catholic theologian, drew on the letters of Paul to justify executing heretics (Summa Theologiae II:II, 11:3).[16] Among the early Protestant leaders, John Calvin was adamant in his support of the death penalty for unrepentant heretics, blasphemers, and adulterers. [17] In the case of the proper punishment for adultery, he declared, "The law of God commands adulterers to be stoned."[18]

In recent centuries, condemnation of religious coercion has become increasingly widespread among Catholics and Protestants. This has coincided in part with the separation of ecclesiastical dictates from secular law and in shifts in how scripture is interpreted. Those who have persisted in justifying violence in religious terms, such as abortion clinic bombers, have been denounced and shunned by mainstream Christians.

In contrast to violent Christian beliefs, persuasive Christianity favors education to combat heresy and peaceful evangelization to spread Jesus' message. Use of violence to prevent or punish misdeeds such as heresy, adultery, or blasphemy would deprive the offender of an opportunity to freely repent and require humans to judge what only God can determine. Especially telling is a passage from 2 Timothy, in which the Apostle Paul writes, "The Lord's servant must not be quarrelsome but kindly to everyone, an apt teacher, patient, correcting opponents with gentleness" (2 Timothy, 2:24–25).

During the period of the early Crusades, the influential Saint Bernard of Clairvaux (1090–1153) promoted persuasion over coercion in the case of heretics and preached against the persecution of Jews. He stated in his famous sermon on the Song of Songs, "Heretics are to be caught rather than driven away. They are to be caught . . . not by force of arms but by arguments by which their errors may be refuted."[19] According to Edward Peters of the University of Pennsylvania, the century and a half before the Papal Inquisition (1231) was a time when the Church focused primarily on "persuading dissidents to return to obedience, and launched a great pastoral effort designed to teach religion effectively."[20] In the contemporary period, Dignitatis Humanae, a document released by the Second Vatican Council in 1965, captures the central elements of persuasive Christianity:

No one is to be forced to act in a manner contrary to his own beliefs . . . For He [Jesus] bore witness to the truth, but He refused to impose the truth by force on those who spoke against it. Not by force of blows does His rule assert its claims. It is established by witnessing to the truth and by hearing the truth.[21]

Islam

From the earliest jurists to today's violent extremists, Muslims seeking to justify the use of force have looked to verses in the Koran such as "Slay the idolaters wheresoever you find them, and take them captive or besiege them" (9:5) and "Fight them till sedition comes to end and the law of God [prevails]" (2:193). Such passages have been widely interpreted as commanding Muslims to battle polytheists until they are killed or converted to Islam. This position has been supported by select hadith, the sayings of the Prophet, such as "I have been commanded to fight against people so long as they do not declare that there is no god but Allah" (Muslim 1.9.30). Muhammad Ibn Jarir al-Tabari (ca. 839–923 CE), an influential Persian theologian, argued that even if polytheists surrender militarily, Muslims must continue to fight them until they submit to Islam.[22] Although many scholars have not extended this "convert or die" rule to the People of the Book (Jews and Christians), Hassan al-Banna, a founder of the Muslim Brotherhood argues in his book, *On Jihad*, that "there is a clear indication [in the hadith] of the obligation to fight the People of the Book . . . Jihad is not against polytheists alone, but against all who do not embrace Islam."[23]

Some of the harshest words and strongest punishments in Islamic law have been reserved for apostasy. The Koran states, "Those who turn back on their faith and die disbelieving will have wasted their deeds in this world and the next. They are inmates of Hell and shall abide there forever" (2:217). A hadith records the Prophet as saying, "Whoever changed his Islamic religion, then kill him."[24] In the fourteenth century, Ibn-Taymiya, a theologian whose thought has inspired Islamic extremists such as Osama bin Laden, wrote, "The apostate is more crude in his infidelity than an original unbeliever."[25] Bin Laden himself often invokes the stigma of apostasy when singling out Muslim nations or individuals who conspire with the United States.

In contrast, many Muslim scholars have found texts that, beginning with the Koran itself, condemn coercion and favor religious tolerance. An important passage from the Koran states, "There is no compulsion in matter of faith" (2:256). It is said that when Umar, a companion of the Prophet and second caliph of Islam, asked his slave to convert to Islam and the slave refused, he cited 2:256 and did not persist.[26] The futility of coercion in matters of faith is expanded upon in Koran 10:99–100: "If your Lord had willed, all the people on the earth would have come to believe, one and all. Are you going to compel the people to believe except by God's dispensation?" No human can force a change of heart over which God alone has control.

The Koran also contains clear affirmations of religious diversity and tolerance: "To each of you We have given a law and a way and a pattern of life. If God had pleased He surely could have made you one people (professing one faith)" (5:48) and "O you unbelievers, I do not worship what you worship, nor do you worship who I worship . . . To you your way and to me mine" (109:1–6). These verses do not mean that Muslims should not attempt to convert those of other faiths. The Koran exhorts all Muslims, "Call them [unbelievers] to the path of your Lord with wisdom and words of good advice; and reason with them in the best way possible." Some may never respond to the call, but force must not be brought to bear against them; when Muhammad exclaims, "Oh Lord, these are certainly a people who do not believe," Allah responds to him, "Turn away from them and say: 'Peace'" (Koran 43:88–89).

Since the beginning of Islam many have asked, "How can these condemnations of religious coercion be reconciled with the passages of the Koran and hadith that seem to favor the opposite?" While many classical jurists believe Koran 9:5, the so-called "verse of the sword," supersedes declarations against religious coercion such as 2:256, other scholars disagree. These latter commentators have not found jihad and religious freedom to be inherently contradictory. Some interpret jihad in a strict military sense, whereby "religious freedom could be granted to the non-Muslims after their defeat."[27] Other commentators interpret the violent verses to specifically concern the period of Muhammad's conquests in the Arabian Peninsula and therefore to not have applicability today.[28] Many set violent passages from the Koran alongside those that state, "Permission is granted those [to take up arms] who fight because they are oppressed" (22:39) and "Fight those in the way of God who fight you but do not be aggressive: God does not like aggressors" (2:190). This interpretation of jihad as solely defensive is particularly common among modern commentators. Sheikh Mohamed Sayed Tantawi, Grand Imam of Egypt's Al-Azhar Mosque and one of the most authoritative voices in Sunni Islam, declared in 2003, "Extremism is the enemy of Islam . . . jihad is allowed in Islam to defend one's land, to help the oppressed."[29]

Yusuf al-Qaradawi, the influential conservative mufti, captures the overall nature of non-coercive Islam:

> Moderation, or balance, is not only a general characteristic of Islam, it is a fundamental landmark. The Qur'an says: 'Thus have we made of you an umma [community] justly balanced, that you might be witness over the nations, and the Messenger a witness over yourselves. (2:143)' As such, the Muslim umma is a nation of justice and moderation . . . Islamic texts call upon Muslims to exercise moderation and to reject and oppose all kinds of extremism.[30]

Judaism

Both violent and persuasive sub-systems of belief are reflected in the Old Testament. Legitimating violence can be found in the decrees that anyone who violates the Sabbath or blasphemes be executed (Exodus 31:14–17; Numbers 15:35–36; Leviticus 24:14). Moreover, justifications for expelling non-Jews from the land of Israel have been drawn from passages such as "As for the towns of these people that the Lord your God is giving you as an inheritance, you must not let anything that breathes remain alive. You must annihilate them" (Deuteronomy 20:16–18). Rabbis have been troubled for many generations by these and other such passages and defanged them, for instance, by interpreting the vengeful passage calling for "an eye for an eye" (Exodus 21:24) as referring to monetary compensation.[31]

In other passages in the Old Testament, the Prophets call on the people to do what is right—because God has so commanded. Some of these passages involve threats to those who defy the Lord. The persuasive ones, however, call for doing what ought to be done because the Jews are a holy people (e.g., Deuteronomy 14:2; 14:21). Still others call for special obligations because, as Moses declared to the people of Israel, "the Lord your God has chosen you out of all the people on earth to be his people" (Deuteronomy 7:6).

Reform Jews do not believe in the use of coercion to enforce Jewish law or impose their beliefs on other Jews. Moreover, they have even been reluctant to try to persuade non-Jews in mixed marriages to convert to Judaism.[32] Reform Jews have played an active part in various peace and justice movements, including protests against the

Vietnam War and the Civil Rights Movement, but only in those that have not condoned violence or actively engaged in violent acts. A 1937 document entitled "Guiding Principles of Reform Judaism" captures their basic position:

> Judaism . . . advocates the promotion of harmonious relations between warring classes on the basis of equity and justice . . . Judaism, from the days of the prophets, has proclaimed to mankind the ideal of universal peace. The spiritual and physical disarmament of all nations has been one of its essential teachings. It abhors all violence and relies upon moral education, love, and sympathy to secure human progress.[33]

The leaders of American Reform Jews have actively supported all of the major initiatives for peace with the Palestinians, from the Camp David accords to the Road Map.[34] These positions do not mean that Reform Jews are pacifistic; they strongly support the right of Israel to protect itself from terrorism and to retaliate against its enemies. However, as is the case for persuaders in other traditions, they would only condone the use of violence under exceptional circumstances, and for a narrow set of reasons. It is because of the Reform Jews' reliance on persuasion over coercion, and not their liberal religious and political views, that they fall on the persuasive side of the fault line; illiberal Jewish groups that share a similar aversion to violence and adherence to persuasion fall on the same side of the fault line.

I use the term "extreme religious nationalists" because the names of the groups falling within this category and their positions have often changed over the years. One example of such an extremist group was Gush Emunim (the Bloc of the Faithful), whose members tended to take literally God's promise to the people of Israel in Exodus 21:31: "I will establish your borders from the Red Sea to the Sea of the Philistines [the Mediterranean], and from the desert to the River [the Euphrates]." Hence its members often favored and fought for "Greater Israel," the inclusion of the West Bank, Gaza Strip, and Golan Heights as permanent parts of the Israeli state.

James Hunter found that "Within Gush Emunim, war is a central component to the purgative process that will bring about messianic times. Some within the movement quite literally view Arabs (including women and children civilians) as Amalekites or Canaanites that contemporary Jews, in the tradition of Joshua from biblical times, have a duty to destroy."[35]

129

Even more prone to violence was Rabbi Meir Kahane, and his handful of followers, who stated, "Jewish violence to protect Jewish interests is never bad."[36] In 1971, he moved to Israel from the United States and advocated the complete eviction of Arabs from the land of Israel. Kahane warned that there would be great catastrophes and horrors before the age of redemption if Jews did not reclaim Greater Israel and drive the Arab "cancer" from the land.[37] In his books and speeches, he developed a philosophy of sacred violence that justified slaughtering Arabs as an expression of God's will.[38]

There have also been extensive drives to use the political power of ultra-orthodox Jews (a minority in Israel and often different from religious nationalists such as Gush Emunim and Kahane) to impose their values on Israeli society. These include banning public transportation on the Sabbath and Jewish holidays, closing businesses and entertainment establishments on these occasions, prohibiting the sale of pork, determining who can marry whom (including prohibition on gay marriages), outlawing abortions, regulating who can be buried where, and much else.

Hinduism

Nathuram Godse, the man who assassinated Mohandas Gandhi, condemned Gandhi's faith in nonviolence.[39] Godse contended that if Hindus followed Gandhi they would become weak and vulnerable in the face of "aggressive" Muslims.[40] Godse was a champion of a coercive form of Hindu nationalism, a religio-political movement that believes India has always been the home of the Hindu people and therefore Muslims and Christians living there should be subordinate to them or leave. Madhav Sadashiv Golwalkar, a prominent Hindu nationalist leader, offered a solution for the Muslim and Christian "problem":

> [Nazi] Germany has . . . shown how well-nigh impossible it is for races and cultures, having differences going to the root, to be assimilated into one united whole, a good lesson for us in Hinduism to learn and profit by.[41]

When extremist Hindu nationalists have translated their view of non-Hindus into action, it has often meant mass killings of Muslims and the destruction of mosques.[42] They have also engaged in forcible re-conversion of Hindu converts to Christianity and Islam.[43] Militant Hindu leaders justify violence against non-Hindus in terms of "national honour," "punishment," and "revenge."[44] They claim that conniving

Christian priests and missionaries have "forcibly converted" the lower castes and that Muslim rulers brutally oppressed the Hindus for centuries. Hindu men must therefore now avenge these wrongs and reassert their pride. The writings and speeches of the militant leaders draw heavily on Hindu symbols and deities that support a violent and aggressive ideal of masculinity.[45] The spiritual and moral aspects of Hinduism are eclipsed in Hindu nationalist discourse by the call to reassert Hindu pride and violently reclaim the nation.

In stark contrast, Gandhi's conception of Hinduism focused overwhelmingly on the spiritual elements of the tradition. The scriptural stories of cosmic battles and heroic warriors who fight to restore the order of the universe represented to Gandhi the inner battlefield, where good and evil struggle to gain control over the mind.[46] Gandhi's spiritually oriented religious outlook did not mean, however, that he believed Hinduism was meant only to be a private faith with no political or social expression, and thus no capacity for persuasion.[47] Nonviolence in his view was the means through which religious values could be applied in political and social struggles. At the essence of Gandhi's conception of nonviolence is the notion that persuasion is always superior to coercion. The oppressed have a duty to persuade the perpetrator to atone by refusing to obey or cooperate, not by resorting to violence.[48]

Gandhi derived this position from Hinduism, as he believed it to be "a faith based on the broadest possible toleration," which "enables the followers of that faith not merely to respect all other religions, but also to admire and assimilate whatever is good in them."[49] That is, he believed there are values in all traditions that we can support, and to which we can appeal.

The Beliefs of the Civil Rights Movement

Among the major leaders and organizations of the American civil rights movement, some held that the use of violence to advance social justice was justified. These included leaders such as Malcolm X, Robert Williams, and Huey P Newton and organizations including the Black Panther Party and the Nation of Islam. On the other side of the divide were men such as Martin Luther King, Jr, James Farmer, and James Lawson and organizations that included the Southern Christian Leadership Conference (SCLC), the Student Nonviolent Coordinating Committee (SNCC), and the Congress of Racial Equality (CORE). As in the other cases examined here, it is not suggested that those who favored the persuasive approach never considered striking out in anger, nor that those who held violent beliefs did not also support persuasion. The fundamental differences between the two are, however, clear, even dramatic. As in other cases, we are seeking to illustrate these differences by focusing on a few, select figures from each camp.

Malcolm X's famous phrase—"by any means necessary"—provides an initial cue.[50] By this he meant that if nonviolent means were unsuccessful in gaining greater freedom for blacks, then any other means, including violence, could be legitimately employed. More explicitly, he declared, "If the black man doesn't get the ballot, then you're going to be faced with another man who forgets the ballot and starts using the bullet."[51] X invoked the Koran and the Bible to support his positions:

> There is nothing in our book, the Koran, that teaches us to suffer peacefully . . . That's a good religion. In fact, that's the old-time religion. That's the one that Ma and Pa used to talk about: an eye for an eye, and a tooth for a tooth, a head for a head, and a life for a life. That's a good religion.[52]

In a 1963 speech in Detroit, he argued against those who believed that a revolution in US race relations could be undertaken through nonviolent action:

> You don't have a peaceful revolution. You don't have turn-the-other-cheek revolution. There is no such thing as a nonviolent revolution . . . Revolution is bloody, revolution is hostile, revolution knows no compromise, revolution overturns and destroys everything that gets in its way.[53]

Civil rights movement leaders who championed persuasion argued that violence would increase hatred, hostility, and bitterness between whites and blacks rather than build solidarity. Leaders such as Martin Luther King, Jr. envisioned their movement as leading to greater integration between the races and full recognition of the rights of African Americans. King, for example, writes in *Stride Toward Freedom* that he "does not seek to defeat or humiliate the opponent, but to win his friendship and understanding . . . The aftermath of nonviolence is the creation of the beloved community, while the aftermath of violence is tragic bitterness."[54]

James Lawson, in a speech before the Student Nonviolent Coordinating Committee, stated, "The Christian favors the breaking down of racial barriers because the redeemed community of which he is already a citizen recognizes no barriers dividing humanity. The Kingdom of God, as in heaven so on earth, is the distant goal of the Christian."[55] Many of the civil rights movement's leaders and organizations provided religious justifications for their faith in nonviolence. In biblical passages such as the Sermon on the Mount and the sayings of the Hebrew prophets, they found inspiration for their message of suffering nonviolently to transform the hearts of their opponents. The SNCC's 1962 Statement of Purpose exemplifies the religious character of the nonviolent civil rights struggle:

> We affirm the philosophical or religious ideal of nonviolence as the foundation of our purpose, the presupposition of our faith, and the manner of our action. Nonviolence as it grows from the Judeo-Christian tradition seeks a social order of justice permeated by love . . . Through nonviolence, courage displaces fear; love transforms hate . . . By appealing to conscience and standing on the moral nature of human existence, nonviolence nurtures the atmosphere in which reconciliation and justice become actual possibilities.[56]

In addition to religious and moral justifications for nonviolence, persuasive civil rights leaders also argued that nonviolence was highly effective. The students who initiated the first lunch counter sit-in discovered that nonviolent direct action could be highly persuasive: "We knew that probably the most powerful and potent weapon that people have literally no defence for is love, kindness. That is, whip the enemy with something that he doesn't understand." While strongly preaching the message of love and community, civil rights leaders maintained that they would hold fast to the goal of social change and employ nonviolent direct action as forcefully as necessary to attain social change.[57]

In Conclusion

If we are seeking to engage those who hold beliefs other than our own in a normative dialogue, we had best cease treating all people of a given faith, these days, especially Muslims, as if they were all of one kind, that is, all extremists (as Samuel Huntington effectively does when he writes, "Some Westerners, including Bill Clinton, have argued that the West does not have a problem with Islam but only with violent Islamist extremists. Fourteen hundred years of history demonstrate otherwise."[58]) In the same vein it is also a mistake to view the whole of Islam—or any other belief system—as supportive of peace (as George

W Bush has done when claiming, "Islam is Peace"[59]). The preceding examples illustrate that those who draw on one belief system or another to justify their violence have not "hijacked" their faith, as the former Norwegian prime minister Kjell Magne Bondevik put it.[60] Those who subscribe to violent beliefs do not need to distort the belief systems on which they draw to justify their acts to themselves and to others; they can find in all major systems texts and widely held interpretations that favor violence just as others can draw on the same texts to extol the merit of relying as much as possible on persuasion. Indeed, there is a struggle in all major civilizations between those who adhere to violence and those who hold persuasive beliefs. Hence, the importance of all those who are on one side of the fault line, the persuasive one, to coalesce.

One reason the fault line that separates those who believe in the value of force from those who seek to rely on persuasion is often overlooked is that there are a fair number of contemporary liberals who are suspicious of all religions, and in effect of all strong beliefs, whose adherents are called "true believers." This aversion now blinds many liberals to the opportunities that are to be found in forming alliances with those who hold strong beliefs, many of whom are religious conservatives in the twenty-first century, but are opposed to violence. This approach leaves hundreds of millions of people on the wrong side of a line that separates us (and our allies) from those we must vie with; it leaves out all the true believers who favor persuasion over violence, those with whom we should ally ourselves in the "war against terrorism" and all other forms of violence—whether or not they favor liberal democracy, at least for now. (I join here with those who note that non-democratic states can live in peace with other states and not support terrorism—Singapore, for example.)

My main thesis—that there are many millions of moderate people (albeit many illiberal) in all civilizations, just as there are extremists—has far-reaching implications for the normative foundations of the post–Cold War global order. The argument clashes with the view that Western civilization has a monopoly on legitimate beliefs (especially in its commitment to human rights, democracy, and free markets) and that all other civilizations lack such values, or at least values that undergird political regimes and civil society. Indeed select beliefs found in all major civilizations, East and West, have a place in the amalgam of beliefs that will serve as the source of legitimacy for a new world order.[61]

Notes

*   I am indebted to Derek Mitchell for extensive research assistance and numerous editorial suggestions for this essay and to Kristen Bell for comments on an earlier draft.

1.   Samuel P. Huntington, *The Clash of Civilizations and the Remaking of the World Order* (New York: Touchstone Books, 1996); The "us against them, friend versus foe" characterization of international relations is echoed in the work of the German political theorist Carl Schmitt, particularly in his essay "The Concept of the Political" (1932).

2.   For more discussion of my odyssey, see Amitai Etzioni, *My Brother's Keeper: A Memoir and a Message* (Lanham: Rowman & Littlefield, 2003).

3.   On the concept of normative power, a sub-category of soft power, see Amitai Etzioni, *A Comparative Analysis of Complex Organizations*, revised edn (New York: Free Press, 1975).

4.   See Joan McCord's definition of coercion in "Introduction: Coercion and Punishment in the Fabric of Social Relations," in Joan McCord ed. *Coercion and Punishment in Long-Term Perspectives* (New York: Cambridge University Press, 1995), 1.

5.   Samuel D. Cook, "Coercion and Social Change," in *Coercion*, eds. James R. Pennock and John W. Chapman (Chicago, IL: Aldin, 1972), 116.

6.   "Writers Issue Cartoon Row Warning," *BBC* (March 1, 2006). http://news.bbc.co.uk/2/hi/europe/4763520.stm (accessed April 10, 2006).

7.   Quoted in Karim Raslan, "The Islam Gap," *New York Times* (February 15, 2006). http://www.nytimes.com/2006/02/15/opinion/15raslan.html?th=&emc=th&pagewanted=print (accessed January 20, 2012).

8.   "Muslim Leaders Urge Calm; End of Cartoon Riots," *IslamOnline* (February 8, 2006). http://www.islamonline.com (accessed April 1, 2006).

9.   "Islamic Extremism: Common Concern for Muslim and Western Publics," *Pew Global Attitudes Survey* (July 14, 2005). http://www.pewglobal.org/2005/07/14/islamic-extremism-common-concern-for-muslim-and-western-publics/ (accessed January 24, 2012).

10.   Poll jointly conducted in May 2004 by the Anwar Sadat Chair for Peace and Development at the University of Maryland and Zogby International, http://www.bsos.umd.edu/SADAT/pub/Arab%20Attitudes%20Towards%20Political%20and%20Social%20Issues,%20Foreign%20Policy%20and%20the%20Media.htm (accessed April 18, 2006).

11.   "Islamic Extremism: Common Concern for Muslim and Western Publics."

12.   Survey for WorldPublicOpinion.org conducted by D3 Systems and Afghan Center for Social and Opinion Research from November 27 to December 4, 2005, http://65.109.167.118/pipa/pdf/jan06/Afghanistan_Jan06_quaire.pdf (accessed April 18, 2006).

13.   Poll conducted by the Near East Consulting Group in February 2006, http://www.neareastconsulting.com/ppp/p02.html (accessed April 18, 2006).

14.   All biblical passages are from the New Revised Standard Version.

15. Philip Schaff, ed. *A Select Library of the Nicene and Post-Nicene Fathers of the Christian Church, Vol 4, Augustine: The Writings against the Manicheans and the Donatists* (Buffalo, NY: Christian Literature, 1886), 816.

16. Thomas Aquinas defined heresy as "a species of infidelity in men who, having professed the faith of Christ, corrupt its dogmas" in Summa Theologiae II–II, 11:1.

17. Roland H. Bainton *Hunted Heretic: The Life and Death of Michael Servetus* (Boston, MA: Beacon Press, 1953), 170.

18. Harro Höpfl, *The Christian Polity of John Calvin* (New York: Cambridge University Press, 1982), 183.

19. Bernard Clairvaux, *On the Song of Songs III*; trans. K. Walsh and I. Edmonds (Kalamazoo, MI: Cistercian Publications, 1979), 175.

20. Edward Peters, *Heresy and Authority in Medieval Europe* (Philadelphia, PA: University of Pennsylvania Press, 1980), 165.

21. "Dignitatis Humanae," On the Right of the Person and of Communities to Social and Civil Freedom in Matters Religious Promulgated by His Holiness Pope Paul VI (December 7, 1965), http://www.vatican.va/archive/hist_councils/ii_vatican_council/documents/vat-ii_decl_19651207_dignitatis-humanae_en.html (accessed April 1, 2006).

22. Yohanan Friedmann, *Tolerance and Coercion in Islam: Interfaith Relations in the Muslim Tradition* (New York: Cambridge University Press, 2003), 98.

23. Hassan al-Banna, "On Jihad"; transl. C Wendell, in *Five Tracts of Hasan al-Banna* (Berkeley and Los Angeles: University of California Press, 1978), 142.

24. Bukhari 9.84.57.

25. Quoted in Yohanan Friedmann, *Tolerance and Coercion in Islam: Interfaith Relations in the Muslim Tradition* (New York: Cambridge University Press, 2003), 123.

26. Noted in Friedmann, *Tolerance and Coercion in Islam*, 101.

27. Quoted in Friedmann, *Tolerance and Coercion in Islam*, 103.

28. For example, see the work of Sheikh Muhammad al-Tahir Ibn Ashur (1879–1979 CE), cited in Friedmann, *Tolerance and Coercion in Islam*, 103.

29. "Cleric Condemns Suicide Attacks," *BBC* (July 11, 2003). http://news.bbc.co.uk/1/hi/world/middle_east/3059365.stm. (accessed April 2, 2006).

30. Yusuf al-Qaradawi, *Islamic Awakening between Rejection and Extremism*, transl. AS Al Shaikh-Ali and MBE Wafsy (1991) (Herndon: American Trust Publications and the International Institute of Islamic Thought, 1981), 21, quoted in Charles Kurzman (ed.) *Liberal Islam: A Sourcebook* (New York: Oxford University Press, 1998), 196.

31. The Babylonian Talmud, Baba Kama 83 b: "Does the Divine Law not say 'Eye for eye'? Why not take this literally to mean [putting out] the eye [of the offender]?—Let not this enter your mind, since it has been taught: You might think that where he put out his eye, the offender's eye should be put out, or where he cut off his arm, the offender's arm should be cut off, or again where he broke his leg, the offender's leg should be broken. [Not so,

for] it is laid down, 'He that smiteth any man . . .' 'And he that smiteth a beast . . .' just as in the case of smiting a beast compensation is to be paid, so also in the case of smiting a man compensation is to be paid." (emphasis added).

32. Certain figures within Reform Judaism have recently sought to change this tradition: See Michael Luo, "Reform Jews Hope to Unmix Mixed Marriages," *New York Times* (February 12, 2006): A1.

33. Quoted in Michael A. Meyer, *Response to Modernity: A History of the Reform Jewish Movement* (New York: Oxford University Press, 1998), 390.

34. Union for Reform Jews: Board of Trustees (2004) "Resolution on Unilateral Withdrawals, Security Barriers, and Home Demolitions: Striving for Security and Peace for Israel and the Middle East."

35. James D. Hunter, "Fundamentalism: An Introduction to a General Theory," in *Jewish Fundamentalism in Comparative Perspective*, ed. Laurence J. Silberstein (New York: New York University Press, 1993), 33.

36. Ehud Sprinzak, *The Ascendance of Israel's Radical Right* (New York: Oxford University Press, 1991), 53.

37. Ibid.

38. Ehud Sprinzak, "Extremism and Violence in Israel: The Crisis of Messianic Politics," *Annals of the American Academy of Political and Social Science* 555, no. 1 (January 1998): 120.

39. Godse said during a speech at his trial, "[In the Ramayana] Rama killed Ravana in a tumultuous fight and relieved Sita. [In the Mahabharata], Krishna killed Kansa to end his wickedness; and Arjuna had to fight and slay quite a number of his friends and relations . . . It is my firm belief that in dubbing Rama, Krishna and Arjuna as guilty of violence, the Mahatma betrayed a total ignorance of the springs of human action." For details on Godse's trial see Tapan Ghosh, *The Gandhi Murder Trial* (New York: Asia, 1975).

40. For more on the relationship between Godse and Gandhi, see Ashis Nandy, "Final Encounter: The Politics of the Assassination of Gandhi," in *At the Edge of Psychology: Essays in Politics and Culture* (New Delhi: Oxford University Press), 83.

41. Quoted in Tapan Raychaudhuri, "Shadows of the Swastika: Historical Reflections on the Politics of Hindu Communalism," *Contention* 4, no. 2 (1995): 145.

42. The two largest outbreaks of such violence in recent years were the destruction of the Barbri Mosque in December 1992 and the anti-Muslim riots in the state of Gujarat in March 2002. See Ashis Nandy et al., "Creating a Nationality: The Ramjanmbhumi Movement and Fear of the Self," *Exiled at Home* (New Delhi: Oxford University Press, 2002) and Human Rights Watch, "We Have No Orders to Save You: State Participation and Complicity in Communal Violence in Gujarat," *Human Rights Watch Report* 14, no. 3 (2002): 31.

43. See Human Rights Watch, *Politics by Other Means: Attacks against Christians in India* (New York: Human Rights Watch, 1999).

44. See Nandy, Creating a Nationality, 53.

45. For instance, Hindu nationalists popularly portray Lord Ram with weapons in hand, poised for battle. Their transformation of Ram is examined in Anuradha Kapur, "Deity to Crusader: Changing Iconography of Ram," in *Hindus and Others: The Question of Identity in India Today*, ed. G. Pandey (New Delhi: Viking, 1993), 74–109.

46. For example, Gandhi wrote, "[the Bhagavad Gita] is not a historical work, it is a great religious book, summing up the teachings of all religions. The poet has seized the occasion of the war between the Pandavas and Kauravas . . . for drawing attention to the war going on in our bodies between the forces of Good and the forces of Evil." Quoted in J. T. F. Jordens, *Gandhi's Religion: A Homespun Shawl* (New York: St. Martin's Press, 1998), 130.

47. On Gandhi's religious beliefs see Jordens, *Gandhi's Religion* and Margaret Chatterjee, *Gandhi's Religious Thought* (Notre Dame: University of Notre Dame Press, 1983).

48. On Gandhi's technique of nonviolent resistance, see J. Bondurant, *Conquest of Violence: The Gandhian Philosophy of Conflict* (Princeton, NJ: Princeton University Press, 1988) and M. Juergensmeyer, *Fighting with Gandhi* (San Francisco, CA: Harper & Row, 1984).

49. Mahatma Gandhi, *The Collected Works of Mahatma Gandhi*, vol. 35 (Delhi: Government of India, 1969), 255, 166.

50. Breitman, G., *Malcolm X Speaks: Selected Speeches and Statements* (New York: Merit, 1965), 165.

51. Ibid., 57.

52. Ibid., 12. X's views of Islam and race underwent significant changes after he returned from a pilgrimage to Mecca.

53. Ibid., 9.

54. Martin Luther King, Jr., "Pilgrimage to Nonviolence," *Stride Towards Freedom* (New York: Harper, 1958), 90.

55. Lawson, J. M., "We Are Trying to Raise the Moral Issue," in *Negro Protest Thought in the Twentieth Century*, eds. FL Broderick and A Meier (Indianapolis, IN: Bobbs-Merrill, 1965), 278.

56. Lynd, S., ed. "Student Nonviolent Coordinating Committee, Statement of Purpose," *Nonviolence in America: A Documentary History* (Indianapolis, IN: Bobbs-Merrill, 1966), 399.

57. Howell Raines, *My Soul Is Rested: Movement Days in the Deep South Remembered* (New York: Penguin Books, 1983), 79.

58. Samuel P. Huntington, *The Clash of Civilizations and the Remaking of the World Order* (New York: Touchstone Books, 1996), 209.

59. Remarks by President George W. Bush at the Islamic Center of Washington, DC (September 17, 2001), http://www.whitehouse.gov/news/releases /2001/09/20010917-11.html (accessed March 5, 2006).

60. Kjell Magne Bondevik, Speech at the conference "Europe: A Beautiful Idea?" The Hague (September 7, 2004).

61. For more on legitimacy and a new world order, see Amitai Etzioni, *From Empire to Community* (New York: Palgrave Macmillan, 2004).

9

Should We Support Illiberal Religious Democracies?

The terms on which the United States will agree to settle the conflict in Afghanistan during the on-again off-again negotiations with the Taliban reflect a much greater issue that the United States faces in the Middle East: will it support only those who seek to establish democratic regimes that also respect individual rights (e.g., the nascent coalition of secular parties in Egypt and the Congress for the Republic and similar emerging parties in Tunisia) or—also ally itself with the often much more powerful groups that may be democratic, but are likely to foster regimes based on shari'a law (such as the Muslim Brotherhood associations across the Middle East; the Al-Islah in Yemen; the Ennahda in Tunisia; and the Justice and Development Party and Justice and Spirituality Movement in Morocco).

In Afghanistan, is it enough for the Taliban to lay down their arms? Assume their leaders promise that if they win the majority of votes in the next election—which will be at least as open and fair as those that led to the reinstatement of the Karzai government—they will ensure that Afghanistan will not serve as a haven for terrorists. Moreover, they commit themselves not to support terrorism in other nations (thus not help Pakistan's ISI launch attacks on India or the other way around). However, they insist that at home they are entitled to full self-determination, including the right to pass laws (by parliamentary majority) that impose shari'a law. (They might add, as a dig, that their interpretation of shari'a is neither as strict as that of America's Saudi ally nor as wish-washy as that of Indonesia.) The United States may respond that it assumes the Taliban will abide by its nation's constitution. This scenario in fact reflects what a *Washington Post* source claims are the actual US guidelines for an agreement with the Taliban: it must "renounce violence, reject al-Qaeda and support the Afghan constitution."[1]

Continuing with the hypothetical, the Taliban might smirk and respond, "*Our* constitution?" It was written under heavy pressure from the United States and includes a confused mishmash of clauses. On one hand, it commits to human rights, pluralism, and democracy, but on the other, it declares Afghanistan an "Islamic Republic," in which Islam is the official state religion, stipulating that "no law can be contrary to the beliefs and provisions of the sacred religion of Islam."[2] Should the United States insist at this point that individual rights—at least women's rights and religious freedom—be honored, or let the Afghans make their own laws?

In the numerous articles written recently on what has been called rather optimistically "the Arab Spring," it has often been assumed that the groups rising against the autocratic regimes are democratic forces. "Recent months have brought new surprises as a wave of pro-democracy demonstrations has swept across the Arab world," according to James Taranto, writing in *The Wall Street Journal*.[3] And Joe Nocera remarked in *The New York Times*, "The Arab spring has shown that millions of Muslims have zero interest in the hard-line theocracy favored by Al Qaeda. What they yearn for instead is freedom and democracy."[4]

Autocracy wreckers, however, are not necessarily democracy builders. Indeed, often the wreckers are not the same forces that form the new regimes, as one learns from the French and Russian revolutions. There is, moreover, the concern that even if democratic governments are established, they soon will be perverted into other kinds of regimes, what might be called the Hamas or Weimar Republic conundrum (which also applies to Putin's Russia). Moreover, the military is very likely to play a key role for years to come at least in Egypt, as it did during transitions to democracy in South Korea, Indonesia, and Chile.

The issue in focus here, however, is a different one: assuming that the new regimes *will be* democratic—and not just nominally—can they also be religious? That is, Muslim? And if so, will they respect individual rights? And if not, what should be the position of the United States toward what ought to be called "illiberal democracies?"

Liberal Islam?

Because in popular parlance democracy and liberalism (in the political theory sense of the term) are often conflated, I simply repeat here that democracy refers to a regime in which those in power are changed at institutionalized intervals, in line with the preferences of the majority of voters. Liberalism refers to a regime that respects individual rights, to which all persons are entitled. These rights cannot be denied by acts of a legislator and are enforced by courts. They are, for example, enumerated in the American Bill of Rights and included in the United Nations Universal Declaration of Human Rights. The regime type held dear by Americans and promoted by the US government overseas, is obviously not simply democratic (in which a majority could impose all kinds of restrictions on minorities), but a liberal democracy (in which rights, protected by constitutions and courts, cannot be set aside by legislatures). Hence, when the United States examines the new political forces in the Middle East, it must ask not merely whether they are pro-democracy and will remain so once they gain a majority, but also whether they will respect individual rights.

The Enlightenment spread the idea that reason and rationality would increasingly supplant faith and belief. In the past, the United States often sidestepped the issue in part because it was often simply assumed that democratic governments would be secular. Even today, observers frequently cite both democratic and secular credentials in characterizing the kind of political group the United States should support. For instance the April 6 youth movement and Egyptian Movement for Change were hailed because they were democratic *and* secular. A *New York Times* report from January noted the tepidness of American officials towards the new political forces was eased when renowned dissident Saad Eddin Ibrahim put "a secular, liberal and familiar face on the opposition."[5] Turkish policy expert Fadi Hakura contends, "A crucial piece of the puzzle is missing. Without it, the Arab countries will have the edifice of democracy but not genuine representative institutions. That crucial [missing] piece is secularism, a principle which girds most vibrant democracies; the belief that the state should exist separately from religion or religious beliefs."[6] However, it has become increasingly clear over the last few decades that religion continues to play a major role in many parts of the world, indeed all but North Western Europe. In China, Christianity is blooming. In Israel, Orthodox Judaism plays a major role. And of course, religion is a dominant force in the Muslim world.

Theoretically, religious observance can be completely private and voluntary and the state—secular. People can pray to whom they prefer and follow whatever dos and don'ts their hearts and consciences guide them towards, as long as they are not coercing others. (A diehard libertarian may still worry about social pressure to obey religious authorities, but these kinds of pressure do not violate the separation of church and state.) It could be pointed out, however, that such a combination of a religious society and a secular state is idealized by very few nations (mainly France and the United States) and fully experienced by none. In practice, various religious communities draw on states to enforce commands they hold dear—usually, illiberal ones. Many seek to ban homosexuality, abortion, and divorce; privilege their religion over all others; relegate women to the status of second-class citizens; and so on. True, some religions are more "theological" (spiritual and philosophical) in focus and have fewer behavioral dictates than others, and in all religions, one finds stricter and more moderate versions. This having been said, most contain significant illiberal elements, as is certainly the case with widely held interpretations of Islam.

I write "widely" because some Muslim scholars and a few Muslim activists (most of who live in the West) argue that Islam is "flexible" and compatible with human rights. Muslim law professor Abdullahi An-Na`im holds that, "There is no such thing as the only possible or valid understanding of the Qur'an, or conception of Islam."[7] Others hold that Islam can be made compatible with liberal democracy. For instance, Tariq Ramadan, Professor of Islamic Studies at Oxford University, suggests Islam's core values are fairness, equity and justice, which he argues are also common to the secular law of Western countries.[8]

But the reality is different even in the most moderate and democratic Muslim countries. For example, Indonesia was extolled for some time as a model for the compatibility of Islam and liberal democracy, but it is moving in the opposite direction. Although, Indonesia's constitution prescribes a separation of mosque and state, since the fall of the Suharto dictatorship, a number of local districts have instituted stringent regulations based on shari'a law. These include prohibitions on the sale of alcohol, nighttime curfews on women going out alone, and dress codes particularly geared towards women. Other mandates have included compulsory giving of Islamic alms and Koranic instruction. In Aceh province, the local government introduced public flogging for homosexuality, adultery, pre-marital sex, gambling, and alcohol consumption.[9] The National Legislature passed a strong anti-pornography bill, which mandates steep fines and lengthy prison sentences for the consumption or dissemination of pornography, defined to include poetry and conversations regarded as violating community morality.[10] The nation's top religious body, the Indonesia Ulema Council, issued a fatwa stating that "religious teachings influenced by pluralism, liberalism and secularism are against Islam."[11]

I am not arguing, as Ayaan Hirsi Ali does, that Islam is inherently incompatible with liberalism any more than many other religions.[12] However, there can be no question that its radical version (often associated with Wahhabism) is strongly illiberal. And while it is true that in earlier periods—including in the so called Golden Age of Islam—Islam's dominant interpretations were relatively moderate, the recent trend in many Muslim nations has been to promote more moderate versions.

The West's Choice

The issue the West hence faces, as it sorts out which new political forces to support and ally itself with in the changing Middle East, is in some ways akin to that it faced during the Cold War. In those days, Western leaders debated whether to ally themselves first and foremost with Christian Democratic (conservative) parties that were diehard anti-communists, or also with socialist parties that often shared many beliefs with Communist ones. (Consider that even members of the British Labour party used to salute each other as "comrades," Soviet style, and were committed—until the mid-1990s—to undertake an extensive nationalization campaign if the party came to power.) The West's decision was a challenging one because the socialists had a comparative advantage over the Christian Democrats given they espoused many of the same values and addressed similar concerns the Communists did and hence could appeal to the same people the Communists did—but were they *truly* liberal democrats? Similarly, now moderate, arguably democratic but illiberal Muslim groups, such as the Muslim Brotherhood, may well do much better in gaining support than the secular ones. (During the March referendum in Egypt, 77 percent voted in favor of constitutional amendments that paved the way for quick elections favored by the Muslim Brotherhood and opposed by the nascent secular parties that gained only 23 percent of the vote.)[13]

Polling data show that while many Muslims are pro-democracy and abstractly favor human rights, they reject many specific ones. Substantial majorities of Muslims in all countries polled in a 2006 Gallup study said that if they were drafting a new constitution for their country, it should guarantee freedom of speech.[14] A 2007 Pew poll found similarly that majorities in almost all of the Muslim countries polled held that the courts should treat all equally, citizens should be free to criticize their governments, and honest multi-party elections should be undertaken in their country.[15]

At the same time, a 2010 Pew poll found that more than three-quarters of Egyptians and Pakistanis, a majority of Nigerians and Jordanians, and a sizable minority of Indonesians favored stoning adulterers, sentencing to death those who denounce their Islamic faith, and whipping or cutting off the hands of those who commit theft or robbery—all illiberal punishments based on a fundamentalist interpretation of shari'a.[16]

Moreover, Muslim majorities seek even more influence for religious authorities in their nations' politics, including more than nine in ten in Indonesia, more than three-quarters in Egypt, Nigeria, and Jordan, more than two-thirds in Pakistan, a majority in Lebanon, and a plurality in Turkey, according to a 2010 Pew study.[17] Majorities in eight of nine Muslim countries held that shari'a should be at least a source of legislation in their country, and majorities in four said that it should be the only source, according to the 2006 Gallup study.[18]

This same combination of support for democracy and Islam is evident in a recent, March/April 2011 Pew poll of Egyptians. More than 70 percent held that democracy is always preferable to any other kind of government. However, almost nine in ten said they wanted law to be based on Islam, with 62 percent saying law should strictly follow the Koran.[19]

Illiberalism is particularly evident in all matters concerning gender and sexuality. A Gallup poll found that when asked what they least admire about the West, frequent replies by Muslims concerned personal freedoms involving sexuality, promiscuity, and gender mores.[20] A plurality of Muslims in Jordan and Nigeria and a majority in Egypt (54 percent) and Pakistan (85 percent) said they favor making gender segregation in the workplace the law in their country, according to Pew, 2010.[21] A 2007 Pew study found that in most of the predominantly Muslim countries in Asia and the Middle East, only minorities said a woman alone should have the right to choose her own husband. Substantial majorities in all of those countries said that society should reject homosexuality.[22]

The West hence faces what seems to be a rather difficult choice: either support illiberal forces or ally itself only with liberal ones, often those most likely to lose out in elections, however free and fair, and to be weaker members of the rising coalition governments.

How Illiberal?

To proceed, Western leaders had best look at what their nations were like at similar stages of economic and political development—and how the United States and its most cherished democratic allies actually function. The answer is not only that the United States used to adhere to numerous illiberal practices, a fair number of which were enforced by religious-driven laws, but that it still does. Indeed, no country is completely liberal. Even disregarding that before the Civil War slavery was tolerated and that minorities and women were treated as second-class citizens in the following generations, there were laws on the books in the United States that banned homosexual conduct, abortions, no-fault divorces until quite recently, and—until 1965—selling contraceptives to married couples.

Today commentators scoff about limiting consumer choices in Muslim nations that ban the sale of alcohol as if Americans have never heard the words "dry states." And many in the West are outraged by any limitations on free speech, such as those that prohibit defaming the Prophet, disregarding that Germany and Canada ban hate speech, the United States allows people to be fired on the spot if they use a racial slur, and the FCC fines radio stations and TV networks if they include indecent or profane content. For example, twenty CBS stations were fined $550,000 for airing the Janet Jackson wardrobe malfunction, during the 2004 Super Bowl halftime show.[23] In addition well-known illiberal measures have been enacted since 2001 to enhance homeland security.

One may argue that illiberalism in the West is much more limited and moderate than the current form in many Muslims lands. They execute people for blasphemy and engage in honor killing; the West fines and may jail people who violate its norms. Such statements disregard that Serbian ethnic cleansing and the Protestant and Catholic violent clashes in Ireland took place in the West. However, the point made here is not that Muslim illiberalism is tolerable because the West was, and to some extent still is, illiberal too. Nor that one can sit back and wait for the Muslim lands to go through their violent decades as they mature to become liberal regimes. The point is that one should recognize that historically, and to some extent in this day and age, the West is far from purely liberal, and hence should view some elements of illiberalism elsewhere, in the proper perspective.

One main way to proceed is to treat illiberal laws as if they are of three kinds: beyond the pale (radical illiberalism), illiberal "lite" (moderate illiberalism), and in between. The thesis that not all human rights are created equal has much support in the criminal code of all democratic nations and most others. This is reflected in the fact that societies punish much more severely some violations than others. Violations of the right to life (broadly understood to include freedom from maiming, torture, and starvation) are most punishable, which indicates the high premium society places on their observance. A further basis for the special standing of the right to life can be gleaned from the obvious but nevertheless telling observation that if a person is killed or incapacitated, his other rights mean little; while if he is denied the right to free speech, prayer, or most other rights, he may well recapture these rights another day.

If champions of liberty apply this standard to the issue at hand, it follows that they should only support groups that at minimum reject stoning, amputations, hanging of those who violate one religious dictate or another, refraining from ethnic cleansing and genocide, and other such acts that violate the right to life. Granted, in some cases vital Western national interests will prevent it from fully adhering to this standard, as evident, for instance, in the US dealings with Saudi Arabia. However, the West should make it clear that only special circumstances will force it to deviate from what it holds as the elementary foundation of good government.

One may argue that this is and has long been the Western position. However, the West often does not view respecting the right to life (or the duty to protect) as the basic litmus test for gaining its support. (I write "basic" rather than minimum, because it is far from minimal.) Instead, the West often lists the right to life as one of several rights that it lectures nations about, pressures them to support, or conditions its support on honoring. To highlight the difference between the basic litmus test and the much more elevated one, the following comparison might serve. President Obama stated early in his term, "To those who cling to power through corruption and deceit and the silencing of dissent, know that you are on the wrong side of history, but that we will extend a hand if you are willing to unclench your fist,"[24] and limited the US goal in Afghanistan to "disrupt[ing], dismantle[ing], and defeat[ing] al Qaeda."[25] In contrast, Hillary Clinton stated that for, of making peace in Afghanistan, "It is essential that women's rights and women's opportunities are not sacrificed or trampled on in the reconciliation process."[26] Initially the goal of the intervention in Libya in 2011 was to stop massive killing of civilians—but then went on to demand regime change to one that will provide human rights.

One may ask, why not condition the West's support on adoption of an extensive menu of human rights, on establishing a liberal democracy? There surely is nothing wrong in asking nations to form such regimes and extolling them and supporting them if and when they arise. However, for reasons already indicated, even if most nations in the Middle East democratize, they are unlikely to establish liberal democracies. Hence, the West had best stand ready to work with all those who meet its basic demands, honoring the right to life, and treat other rights as an additional floor that often will not be laid, at the same time as the foundations, however much it is desired.

On the other end of the continuum are rights whose violation should be treated with a grain of salt or two. These include bans on the sale of alcohol and pornography, as well as import limitations on select cultural materials, e.g., those regarded as offensive to the Prophet. Similarly, Westerners ought not to be more up in arms about Muslim dress codes than about their own. And one should be much less troubled if a country's laws mandate sending of girls and boys to separate schools than if they limit education of girls to primary school, while boys continue on to secondary school.

In-between is where the great difficulties lie. They often concern the denial of women and religious minorities rights and limitations on the media. In this case, the West had best determine whether a nation or a political group is moving in the right direction, rather than insisting uncompromisingly on one absolute standard. Thus, the West would support regimes such as those in Jordan, Morocco, and Kuwait, to the extent that they are liberalizing, and express its opposition to regimes that are moving in the opposite direction, such as those of Iran, Syria, and Yemen. The same would apply to various political groups and parties. Thus, the West has strong reasons to favor the less illiberal Fatah over the more illiberal Hamas, moderate parts of the Muslim Brotherhood over the even more illiberal Salafi groups, and the reformers in Iran over the hardliners.

There surely is much room to differ about exactly where to draw the lines among the different kinds of illiberalism and the way one assesses developments in this or that nation or political force. However, one may still agree that the West and the Middle East are both well-served if the former (a) does not limit its support only to secular, liberal democratic groups, demanding that all regimes be transformed accordingly; (b) acknowledges that most of the groups and regimes that are evolving the Middle East—including in Iran, Pakistan, Afghanistan, Bahrain, the United Arab Emirates, Iraq, as well as those now in the headlines—will not be liberal democratic ones in the foreseeable future; (c) affirms that liberalism comes in degrees and that no nation is fully liberal; (d) concedes that there is a need for a liberalism scale.

At the very least, the West should urge all to respect the right to life, call on regimes to negotiate with protesters rather than machine-gunning them, and insist that protesters follow the Egyptian and Tunisian model of peaceful uprising. (Those who hold that such non-violent protests cannot bring down brutal regimes should revisit the way the East German Stasi state was toppled.)

Beyond such liberal basics, it is best to let each nation work out its own regime. Advocates of liberty can always continue to laud much thicker liberal agendas. However, as a matter of policy, in order to support democratic groups and evolving democratic regimes in the Middle East, Western governments had best be prepared to ally themselves with political forces whose liberal credentials, one must recognize, are evolving but not yet particularly high.

Notes

1. David Ignatius, "Signs of an Afghan Deal," *Washington Post* (May 26, 2011): A23.

2. Hannibal Travis, "Freedom or Theocracy? Constitutionalism in Afghanistan and Iraq," *Northwestern University Journal of International Human Rights* 3 (Spring 2005): 1.

3. James Taranto, "The Bin Laden Raid and the 'Virtues of Boldness," *Wall Street Journal* (May 7, 2011). http://online.wsj.com/article/SB1000142405 274870393710457630400202926857.html (accessed January 25, 2012).

4. Joe Nocera, "4 Questions He Leaves Behind," *New York Times* (May 2, 2011). http://www.nytimes.com/2011/05/03/opinion/03nocera.html (accessed January 25, 2012).

5. David D. Kirkpatrick and Michael Slackman, "Egyptian Youths Drive the Revolt against Mubarak," (January 26, 2011), http://www.nytimes.com/2011/01/27/world/middleeast/27opposition.html?pagewanted=all (accessed January 25, 2012).

6. Fadi Hakura, "What Can Rescue the Arab Spring?" *Christian Science Monitor* (May 10, 2011), http://www.csmonitor.com/Commentary/Opinion/2011/0510/What-can-rescue-the-Arab-Spring (accessed January 25, 2012).

7. Abdullahi An-Na'im, "Toward an Islamic Hermeneutics for Human Rights," in *Human Rights and Religious Values: An Uneasy Relationship?* eds.

Abdullahi A. Na'im, Jerald D. Gort, and Henry M. Vroom (Amsterdam: Editions Rodopi; Grand Rapids: William B. Eerdmans Publishing Company, 1995), 233.

8. Tariq Ramadan, *Western Muslims and the Future of Islam* (New York: Oxford University Press, 2005).

9. Dewi Kurniawati, "Shariah in Aceh: Eroding Indonesia's Secular Freedoms," *Jakarta Globe* (August 18, 2010). http://www.thejakartaglobe.com/home/shariah-in-aceh-eroding-indonesias-secular-freedoms/391672 (accessed January 25, 2012).

10. Peter Gelling, "Indonesia Passes Broad Anti-Pornography Bill," *New York Times* (October 30, 2008). http://www.nytimes.com/2008/10/30/world/asia/30iht-indo.1.17378031.html (accessed January 25, 2012).

11. "Workshop on Islam, Freedom, and Democracy in Contemporary Indonesia," Yale University Indonesia Forum. http://www.yale.edu/seas/IslamWorkshop.htm (accessed January 25, 2012).

12. Interview with Ayaan Hirsi Ali, "Is Islam Compatible with Liberal Democracy?" *The Aspen Institute* (July 2007). http://fora.tv/2007/07/06/Is_Islam_Compatible_with_Liberal_Democracy (accessed January 25, 2012).

13. Richard Leiby, "Egyptian Voters Say 'Yes' to Speedy Elections," *Washington Post* (March 20, 2011). http://www.washingtonpost.com/world/egyptian_voters_say_yes_to_speedy_elections (accessed January 25, 2012).

14. Dalia Mogahed, "Islam and Democracy: Muslim World Residents See No Conflict between Religious Principles and Democratic Values," *Gallup Center for Muslim Studies* (2006). http://media.gallup.com/MuslimWest-Facts/PDF/GALLUPMUSLIMSTUDIESIslamandDemocracy030607rev.pdf (accessed January 25, 2012).

15. "World Publics Welcome Global Trade—But Not Immigration," Pew Research Center, Global Attitudes Project, Washington, DC (October 4, 2007), http://www.pewglobal.org/2007/10/04/world-publics-welcome-global-trade-but-not-immigration/ (accessed January 25, 2012).

16. "Most Embrace a Role for Islam in Politics," Pew Research Center (December 2, 2010), http://www.pewglobal.org/2010/12/02/muslims-around-the-world-divided-on-hamas-and-hezbollah/ (accessed January 25, 2012).

17. Ibid.

18. See note 14.

19. "Egyptians Embrace Revolt Leaders, Religious Parties, and Military, As Well," Pew Research Center (April 25, 2011), http://www.pewglobal.org/2011/04/25/egyptians-embrace-revolt-leaders-religious-parties-and-military-as-well/ (accessed January 25, 2012).

20. See note 14.

21. See note 16.

22. See note 15.

23. "CBS Hit with $550K Super Bowl Fine," *CNN Money* (September 22, 2004), http://money.cnn.com/2004/09/22/news/fortune500/viacom_fcc/ (accessed January 24, 2012).

24. "President Barack Obama's Inaugural Address," *White House Blog* (January 21, 2009), http://www.whitehouse.gov/blog/inaugural-address (accessed January 25, 2012).

25. "Obama Unveils Afghanistan Plan," *MSNBC* (March 27, 2009), http://www. msnbc.msn.com/id/29898698/ns/world_news-south_and_central_asia/t/ obama-unveils-afghanistan-plan/#.TyBUY4HpbTo (accessed January 25, 2012).

26. Hillary Clinton, "Remarks With Afghan Women Ministers before Their Meeting," U.S. Department of State (May 13, 2010), http://www.state. gov/secretary/rm/2010/05/141806.htm (accessed January 25, 2012).

10

The Salafi Question[*]

Rana Abdelhai, an Egyptian student, told a *New York Times* columnist, after the Muslim Brotherhood gained 40 percent of the vote and the Salafis 25 percent in the first round of the parliamentary elections,[1] that while she would never vote for a Muslim Brotherhood or Salafi candidate, "This is democracy now. We have to respect who other people choose, even if they make the wrong choice."[2] A few days earlier, Dalia Ziada, a young Egyptian activist, made a similar comment to an NPR reporter, saying, "I'm worried, but you know, as someone who really believes in democracy, I have to respect people's choice."[3] Many others seem to share this view. The much more experienced *New York Times* columnist, Nicholas Kristof considered Abdelhai's observation "wise."

Actually, such observations represent a very basic but surprisingly common misunderstanding about democracy: It assumes that democracy is to be equated with the rule of the majority. Hence, for instance, if a majority ruled that boys can go to schools but girls are not to be educated, one must accept this ruling because it was arrived at in a legitimate way—and to contest it would be to undermine democracy. One may, of course, seek to convince the majority of voters to elect next time those who favor equal rights for women or generally respect individual rights—but for now, whatever the majority enacts is to be considered legitimate.

True, even among those who hold this very truncated view of democracy, there are some who recognize that if a party seeks to use its majority to destroy the democratic process, it may be excluded from participating in the elections and from being represented in the legislature. Thus, some political scientists argue that when the Nazis were on the rise in Germany in the 1920s and clearly sought to establish a tyranny, they should not have been allowed to gain legitimacy by winning elections to the Parliament and, ultimately, having their leader named Chancellor of Germany. Indeed, post–World War II

151

Germany outlawed the Nazi Party, excluding it from participating in elections.[4] And decades later, German interior ministers are attempting to similarly exclude the far-right National Democratic Party.[5] Other countries, like Belgium and Spain, have similarly sought to ban parties that pose threats to their national security, resulting in racist and secessionist parties like Vlaams Blok and Batasuna being forbidden from competing in elections.[6] These nations have banned these select political parties, citing "the need of democratic states to be vigilant and aggressive in defending themselves against antidemocratic threats from within—particularly the threat posed in the electoral arena by antidemocratic parties using democratic elections to assume power."[7]

The Salafis, however, do not hold that they would end the democratic process. They mainly seek to use it to enact laws that will make their Wahhabi interpretation of Islam and Sharia the law of the land.[8] As Ed Husain, a Senior Fellow at the Council on Foreign Relations, put it: "Egypt's Salafis are trying to create the caliphate via the ballot box."[9] Kristof suggests that one should not be too troubled just because "some Salafi leaders have made extremist statements—suggesting that women and Christians are unfit to be leaders, raising questions about the peace treaty with Israel, and denouncing the great Egyptian Nobel laureate in literature, Naguib Mahfouz, for sacrilege."[10] These statements can be viewed as merely symbolic, "a bit like 'In God We Trust' on American coins."[11] Actually, Salafis favor stoning of adulterers and cutting off the hands of thieves.[12] They advocate gender segregation in the workplace, outlawing public displays of affection, and excluding women and non-Muslims from holding executive positions.[13] Moreover, "almost all Salafis believe and constantly remind each other of the need to be loyal only to Muslims, and to hate, be suspicious of, not work in alliance with, and ensure only minimal/necessary interaction with non-Muslims."[14] And Salafis justify violence against Muslims they consider apostates (for example, those who have converted to other religions).[15] If such positions are not deeply troubling, one wonders what is.

One may argue that the Salafis command only about a quarter of the vote. However, policies that violate individual rights on a large scale could be enacted quite readily if the Salafis convinced the Muslim Brotherhood to support key measures they favor in exchange for their support for other agendas of the Muslim Brotherhood. The question hence arises whether the Salafis—and comparable parties in other budding Middle East democracies—should be denied a place in democratically elected legislatures, just as Nazi parties were in Germany, fascist parties in Italy, Norway, and the United Kingdom, and Kurdish separatist parties in Turkey.[16]

One answer lies in a correct understanding of the foundation of democracy, which of course is not only rule by the majority, but also a form of government in which the policies on which the majority can vote are greatly limited by individual and minority rights, by the constitution. (As a reminder, scholars often refer to liberal democracy, although the term "constitutional democracy" might be clearer, especially for those who are not political scientists.) Thus, in a constitutional democracy, the majority cannot act on many of the key elements of the Salafis agenda. The Salafis are, in effect, attacking the foundation of democracy—only they are attacking a different pillar: Not the institutionalized opportunity to change those in power by a majority in the ballot box nor to pass laws on the basis of a majority vote, but individual rights, which are a coequal foundation and an essential element of a true democracy.

There are, however, strong pragmatic reasons for Egypt not to seek to ban the Salafi party and movement, despite their strong anti-democratic nature, as long as they command such a large following. Instead, the writing of the constitution could have been used as an opportunity to share with the Egyptian electorate (and others) the lesson of what democracy entails. Political scientists use the term "constitutional moment" to refer to a phase that often follows the breakdown of an old regime and the laying of the foundation of a new one. People engage in an intense dialogue about the nature of the polity they are forming, the kind reflected famously in the Federalist and Anti-Federalist papers. The importance of these deliberations is that they engage the people—and not merely those represented in the committees that write the new constitution. According to Bruce Ackerman, who popularized the concept (as summarized by Mark Tushnet), "During constitutional moments . . . the general public was deeply engaged in deliberation about the public interest, and the people in the aggregate took a relatively impartial view about developing public policy."[17] It is here that an opportunity to form a new consensus arises—in this case, to decide which rights will be taken as a given, as self-evident, as immune from majority vote. Neil Walker notes, "As well, however, as standing out from what came before and what came after, the constitutional moment is also characterised by its role in altering the framework within which ordinary politics unfolds."[18] Caitria O'Neill describes

153

the cost of failing to take advantage of the constitutional moment as "enormous," pointing out, "The window of opportunity presented by the constitutional moment can easily be lost."[19] Poland had a prolonged and intensive national dialogue about its constitution; this is a reason its transition from communism to a democracy is more accomplished than that of many other former parts of the Soviet realm.

This "constitutional moment" was lost in Iraq after the toppling of Saddam and in Afghanistan after the toppling of the Taliban in part because of heavy-handed American drives to shape the constitutions in ways that the United States favored. In the process, the United States succeeded in getting the new governments of Iraq and Afghanistan to include in their constitutions several Western, liberal principles alongside several Islamic ones—but not to build consensus and wide public support for the framing document.

In Egypt, the writing of the constitution was deferred and elections were rushed. Consequently, the Egyptian electorate was not afforded the opportunity to have a dialogue about what makes a constitutional democracy; the Salafis were elected, and they will play a role in drafting the constitution and in shaping whatever national dialogue will take place. It may hence take much longer for the Egyptian people to realize that the Salafis are antithetical to a true democratic regime and to curtail support for them, let alone consider banning them from participating in elections. Other nations in the Middle East and elsewhere, where political Islam is on the rise, ought to take note.

Notes

*   I am indebted to Julia Milton for research assistance for this article.

1.   David D. Kirkpatrick, "Egypt's Rural Voters Get Their Turn in Elections," *New York Times* (December 14, 2011). http://www.nytimes.com/2011/12/15/world/middleeast/egyption-vote-enters-second-round-in-rural-areas.html?ref=egypt (accessed January 11, 2012).

2.   Nicholas D. Kristof, "Democracy in the Brotherhood's Birthplace," *New York Times* (December 10, 2011). http://www.nytimes.com/2011/12/11/opinion/sunday/kristof-Democracy-in-the-Muslim-Brotherhoods-Birthplace.html (accessed January 11, 2012).

3.   "Egyptian Activist Discusses Recent Elections," *NPR* (December 2, 2011). http://www.npr.org/2011/12/02/143062999/activist-discusses-egyptian-elections (accessed January 11, 2012).

4.   "A Decade of American Foreign Policy 1941–1949 Potsdam Conference," *The Avalon Project*, http://avalon.law.yale.edu/20th_century/decade17.asp (accessed January 11, 2012). See also, "Davis E. Weiss, "Striking a Difficult Balance: Combating the Threat of Neo-Nazism in Germany While Preserving Individual Liberties," *Vanderbilt Journal of Transnational Law* 27 (1994):

899–939.; and Richard S. Cromwell, "Rightist Extremism in Postwar West Germany," *Western Political Quarterly* 17, no. 2 (1964): 284–93.

5. "German Interior Ministers Seek Ban on Far-right NPD," *BBC* (December 9, 2011). http://www.bbc.co.uk/news/world-europe-16113372 (accessed January 11, 2012).

6. Tim Vale, "Are Bans on Political Parties Bound to Turn Out Badly? A Comparative Investigation of Three 'Intolerant' Democracies: Turkey, Spain, and Belgium," *Comparative European Politics* 5 (2010): 141–157.

7. Richard Pildes, "Political Parties and Constitutionalism," *New York University Public Law and Legal Theory Working Papers* Paper 179 (2010): 12.

8. Sarah A. Topol, "Egypt's Salafi Surge," *Foreign Policy* (January 4, 2012), http://www.foreignpolicy.com/articles/2012/01/04/egypt_s_salafi_surge (accessed January 12, 2012).

9. Ed Husain, "Why Egypt's Salafis Are Not the Amish," *Council on Foreign Relations* (December 1, 2011), http://blogs.cfr.org/husain/2011/12/01/why-egypt%E2%80%99s-salafis-are-not-the-amish/ (accessed January 12, 2012).

10. Nicholas D. Kristof, "Democracy in the Brotherhood's Birthplace," *New York Times* (December 10, 2011). http://www.nytimes.com/2011/12/11/opinion/sunday/kristof-Democracy-in-the-Muslim-Brotherhoods-Birthplace.html (accessed January 12, 2012).

11. Ibid.

12. David D. Kirkpatrick, "Egypt's Vote Puts Emphasis on Split Over Religious Rule," *New York Times* (December 3, 2011). http://www.nytimes.com/2011/12/04/world/middleeast/egypts-vote-propels-islamic-law-into-spotlight.html?n=Top/Reference/Times%20Topics/Subjects/I/Islam?ref=islam&pagewanted=all (accessed January 12, 2012); Ben Hubbard and Maggie Michael, "Hard-Line Islamist Gains Surprise In Egypt Vote," *Salon* (December 6, 2011), http://www.salon.com/2011/12/06/hard_line_is-lamist_gains_surprise_in_egypt_vote/singleton/ (accessed January 12, 2012).

13. Tamim Elyan and Muhammad al-Yamani, "Egypt Salafis Want No Pact with Muslim Brotherhood," *Reuters* (December 4, 2011). http://www.reuters.com/article/2011/12/04/us-egypt-salafi-idUSTRE7B30MN20111204 (accessed January 12, 2012).

14. See note 9.

15. Ibid.

16. Angela K. Bourne, "Democratisation and the Illegalisation of Political Parties in Europe," *Working Paper Series on the Legal Regulation of Political Parties* no. 7 (February 2011), http://www.partylaw.leidenuniv.nl/uploads/wp0711.pdf (accessed January 12, 2012).

17. Mark Tushnet, "Potentially Misleading Metaphors in Comparative Constitutionalism: Moments and Enthusiasm," in Weiler and Eisgruber, eds., *Altneuland: The EU Constitution in a Contextual Perspective*, Jean Monnet Working Paper 5/04, http://centers.law.nyu.edu/jeanmonnet/papers/04/040501-04.pdf (accessed January 12, 2012).

18. Neil Walker, "After the Constitutional Moment," *The Federal Trust Constitutional Online Paper Series* 32 (November 2003), http://papers.ssrn.com/sol3/papers.cfm?abstract_id=516783 (accessed January 12, 2012).

19. Caitria O'Neill, "Revolution and Democracy," *Harvard Political Review* (May 19, 2011), http://hpronline.org/covers/revolution/revolution-and-democracy/ (accessed January 12, 2012).

11

Why There Cannot Be a Marshall Plan for the Middle East

At first blush, the idea that the United States, working with other nations, should initiate, guide, and finance economic development, and the introduction of democratic regimes to the nations of the Middle East—just as it did in post–World War II Germany and Japan—is very appealing. From a humanitarian viewpoint, one cannot help but be moved by the idealism of helping scores of millions of people who are currently unemployed and poor, including many children and young people, and who live under oppressive regimes, to gain the kind of life Americans so rightly cherish. From a *realpolitik* viewpoint, one can readily see that to end terrorism that threatens the United States and its allies and insurgencies that destabilize the Middle East, military means will not suffice.

General James Jones, who served as the Security Adviser to President Obama, summarized the viewpoint held by many other military leaders. He stated that there are three things needed to attain peace: "One is the security pillar, and you've got to have that. But accompanying that, you have to have an economic package that gives people who don't have any hope, hope for a better future. That's the answer to the terrorist threat, really . . . And the third one is governance and rule of law, and I include corruption and all of those other things."[1] Secretary of Defense Robert Gates agrees. He holds that "economic development, institution-building and the rule of law, promoting internal reconciliation, good governance, providing basic services to the people, training and equipping indigenous military and police forces, strategic communications, and more—these, along with security, are essential ingredients for long-term success."[2]

Moreover, one cannot help but note, with great satisfaction, the different ways the defeated nations were treated after World War I and World War II. After World War I, the nations that lost the war were given a very raw deal, which is widely believed to be one reason Fascism rose, which in turn lead to World War II. After World War II, the defeated nations were treated, the way General Jones put it, "generously"; they were helped to rebuild their economies and reform their polities. They have since become stable, peaceful nations, and allies of the United States.

One would have to have ice water in one's veins, a heart of stone, and be politically unwise not to wish the same for the Middle East. Indeed, several major public voices have called for such a Marshall plan for the region. General Jones has explained, "We learned that lesson after World War II—you know we rebuilt Europe, we rebuilt Japan. That was an example of an enlightened view of things. The Marshall Plan, I am told, wasn't very popular in this country, but we went ahead and did it."[3] Secretary of State Hillary Clinton believes "as the Arab Spring unfolds across the Middle East and North Africa, some principles of the [Marshall] plan apply again, especially in Egypt and Tunisia. As Marshall did in 1947, we must understand that the roots of the revolution and the problems that it sought to address are not just political but profoundly economic as well."[4] Two professors at Columbia Business School, Glenn Hubbard (who was also Chairman of the Council of Economic Advisors under George W. Bush) and Bill Duggan, argued that a Middle East Marshall Plan would "limit the spread of Islamic extremism" in the region.[5] Senator John Kerry argued that "we are again in desperate need of a Marshall Plan for the Middle East."[6] Senator John McCain also expressed support for such a plan.[7]

A Bridge Too Far

Regrettably, there is no way to bring anything remotely resembling the Marshall Plan to the Middle East, and trying to launch one is likely to have some undesirable side effects. Before the reasons for this dire thesis are outlined, one should note that to realize that it is not possible for the West to transform the economics and polities of the Middle East, or help them to transform themselves in the desired ways in the foreseeable future, does not mean that terrorism and insurgency can be dealt with only by military means. It only means that the non-military means will have to be rather different from those that were used at the end of World War II.

Different Sociologies

Many conditions that contributed to the success of the Marshall Plan (which was applied to Germany, Italy, and select other European nations) and a similar approach to post–World War II Japan are missing in the Middle East. Arguably, the most important difference concerns *security*. The nations reconstructed after World War II were countries that had surrendered after defeat in a war and fully submitted to occupation, had been neutral during the war, or were on the US side and at were at peace at home to begin with (such as the United Kingdom, France, and Turkey). That is, development occurred only after hostilities completely ceased and a high level of domestic security was established. There were no terrorists, no insurgencies, no car bombs, and no rocket attacks. Moreover, the forces that took over the management of these nations could fully focus their resources on rebuilding; security needs were minimal compared to those in Afghanistan and Iraq, and those faced by Western forces if they sought to play a similar role say in Libya, Sudan, or Yemen.

Indeed, given the experience in Iraq and Afghanistan, few, if any, even consider the proposition that the West will occupy more lands in the Middle East and manage their transformation. Defense Secretary Robert Gates made this very clear when he testified "there will be no American boots on the ground in Libya. Deposing the Qadhafi regime, as welcome as that eventuality would be, is not part of the military mission."[8] Gates reaffirmed the United States "will provide the capabilities that others cannot provide either in kind or in scale," but "the removal of Colonel Qadhafi will likely be achieved over time through political and economic measures and by his own people."[9] In other words, while the German and Japanese reconstructions were very much hands-on projects, those now considered amount to long-distance social engineering with the West providing funds and advice, but the execution is to be largely done by locals. That is, no boots on the ground—and no managers.

While transforming regimes in the Middle East are quite eager to receive financial aid and economic resources from the West, they oppose the strings attached to these funds. The Pakistani government, and especially the powerful and influential military, greatly resented that conditions of building civil society that are part of the 2009 Kerry–Lugar Bill, which provides $7.5 billion in aid over five years.[10] This resistance is one major reason the funds have largely not been dispersed. In post-Mubarak Egypt, the government complained about Western interference when USAID "published ads in Egyptian newspapers asking for grant proposals on a $100 million program to support 'job creation, economic development and poverty alleviation' and a $65 million program for 'democratic development,' including elections, civic activism and human rights."[11] The Egyptian newspaper *al Akhbar* argued that USAID "dealt with Egypt as a humiliated country."[12] Fayza Aboul Naga, Egypt's minister for planning and international cooperation, has stated "I am not sure at this stage we still need somebody to tell us what is or is not good for us—or worse, to force it on us."[13] US assistance in Egypt is often seen as an infringement on sovereignty as expressed by Hafiz Salama, an influential Muslim cleric, when he stated: "We tell America and its allies lurking in Egypt: end your evil interference in Egypt's internal affairs, interference that we condemn as a conspiracy against the future of Egypt."[14] Others argue that Western models of development are not appropriate for their countries and that they should follow the Chinese or some other model.

One further notes that Germany and Japan were very strong nation-states before World War II in the sense that citizens strongly identified with the nation and showed their willingness to make major sacrifices for the "father land." And they continued to so act during the reconstruction period. The first loyalty of many citizens of Middle Eastern nations, which are tribal societies cobbled together by Western countries, is to their ethnic or confessional group. They tend to look at the nation as a source of spoils for their tribe and fight for their share rather than make sacrifices for the national whole. Deep ethnic and confessional hostilities, such as those between the Shi'a and the Sunnis, the Pashtun and the Tajik, the Hazara and the Kochi, and various tribes in other nations either gridlock the national polities (e.g., in Iraq and Afghanistan), lead to large scale violence (e.g., in Yemen, Bahrain, and Sudan), result in massive oppression and armed conflicts (e.g., in Libya and Syria), or hinder economic development.

Cultural Differences

Max Weber, a sociological giant, established the importance of culture (in the sense of shared normative values) when he demonstrated that Protestants were more imbued than Catholics with the values that lead to hard work and high levels of saving, both essential for the rise of modern capitalist economies. For decades, developments in Catholic countries (such as those in Southern Europe and Latin America) lagged behind the Protestant Anglo-Saxon nations and those in Northwest Europe. Similar differences have been recorded between Quebec and other provinces of Canada. These differences declined, however, only after Catholics became more like Protestants.[15]

Weber also pointed to the difference between Confucian and Muslim values,[16] thus, in effect, predicting the striking difference between the very high rates of development of the South Asian "tigers"—China, Hong Kong, Taiwan, Singapore, and South Korea—and low rates of Muslim states, especially those that adhere more strictly to Sharia than others. The thesis is *not* that Muslim states cannot be developed because of some genetically innate characteristics of the people, but because their cultures stresses other values, especially traditional religious values and communal and tribal bonds. These cultures can change, but, as the record shows, only slowly, and the changes involved cannot be rushed by outsiders.

Pre-conditions

One also must take into account that Germany and Japan were developed nations before World War II with strong industrial bases, strong infrastructure, educated populations, and strong support for science and technology, corporations, business and commerce. Hence, they had mainly to be reconstructed. In contrast, many Middle Eastern states that lack many if not all of these assets, institutions, and traditions cannot be reconstructed because they were not constructed in the first place. This is most obvious in Afghanistan, Yemen, Sudan, and Libya. It is also a major issue in nations that have drawn on one commodity, oil, to keep their economy going, but do not develop the bases for a modern economy, especially Saudi Arabia and Bahrain. Other nations, such as Tunisia, Pakistan, Morocco, Syria, and Egypt, have better prepared populations and resources, but still score very poorly on all these grounds compared to Germany and Japan.

Given that Western powers are extremely unlikely to carefully occupy and manage the transformation in the Middle East, the help they can give basically amounts to one form or other of foreign aid—that is, working with the existing institutions in the countries at issue while trying to encourage them to reform.

Germany and Japan had competent government personnel and relatively low levels of corruption. In many nations in the Middle East, corruption is endemic, pervasive, and very difficult to scale back to tolerable levels. In 2010, it was discovered that over $3 billion in cash had been openly flown out of Kabul over the course of three years. The number is particularly startling because Afghanistan's GDP was only $13.5 billion in 2009, and more declared cash flies out of Kabul each year than the Afghan government collects in tax and customs revenue nationwide. The large sum is believed to have mostly come from stolen foreign assistance.[17] Thus, one must take into account that a significant proportion of whatever resources are made available to Middle Eastern nations will be siphoned off to private overseas bank accounts, allocated on irrelevant bases to cronies and supporters, and that a good part of the funds will be wasted and not accounted for.[18] Steve Knack of the World Bank showed that, "huge aid revenues may even spur further bureaucratization and worsen corruption."[19] Others found that mismanagement, sheer incompetence, and weak government were almost as debilitating.

One way to highlight this point is to examine the annual corruption perception ranking issued since 1995 by Transparency International.[20] Transparency International stresses that because of the ways the rankings are constructed, they cannot be used for the kind of quantitative social science analysis one wishes to carry out. However, given that these rankings parallel information from other sources, they provide a preliminary way of assessing changes. Thus, one finds that most of the nations that had the lowest rankings in 1995 continue to rank low some fifteen years later, for instance, New Zealand and Denmark have ranked among the top four least corrupt countries in all these years. Likewise, many countries that ranked high still maintain their troubled status, such as Nigeria and Venezuela. Indeed, very few countries have improved their scores more than a few points in the half-generation that has passed since the rankings began.

One should add that not all the waste and corruption is local. Large portions of the aid budgeted for Afghanistan and other such countries are handed over to non-governmental organizations subject to little accountability, or spent on extraordinary profits to Western contractors and corporations for high-fee Western consultants. (American law requires that 100 percent of food for American foreign aid be purchased from US farmers, and that US freight carriers ship 75 percent of it.)[21]

A 2008 study by *The Economist* found that one of the main reasons that Afghanistan's development is proceeding so poorly is widespread corruption, cronyism and tribalism, lack of accountability, and gross mismanagement.[22]

Champions of reconstruction also ignore the bitter lessons of foreign aid in general. An extensive 2006 report on the scores of billions of dollars that the World Bank invested since the mid-1990s in economic development shows that despite the bank's best efforts, the "achievement of sustained increases in per capita income, essential for poverty reduction, continues to elude a considerable number of countries."[23] Out of twenty-five aid-recipient countries covered by the report, more than half (fourteen) had the same or worsening rates of per capita income from the mid-1990s to the early 2000s.[24] Moreover, the nations that received most of the aid (especially in Africa) developed least, while the nations that received very little aid grew very fast (especially China, Singapore, South Korea, and Taiwan). Other nations found foreign aid to be a "poisoned gift" because it promoted dependency on foreigners, undermined indigenous endeavors, and disproportionately benefited those gifted at proposal writing and courting foundation and foreign aid representatives, rather than local entrepreneurs and businessmen.[25]

The Marshall Plan entailed much larger outlays than have been dedicated in recent decades to foreign aid that seeks to help economic development (not to be conflated with military aid). In 1948, the first year of the Marshall Plan, aid to the sixteen European countries involved totaled 13 percent of the US budget.[26] In comparison, the United States currently spends less than 1 percent of its budget on foreign aid, and not all of it is dedicated to economic development.[27] Some of these appropriations are so small that they seem more to indicate that the West is supportive rather than trying to make a serious difference. However, as long as they are framed and perceived as transforming aid, they will not generate the PR, now often called Public Diplomacy, advocates hope for.

Moreover, the United States and its allies are entering a protracted period of budget retrenchments in which many domestic programs will be scaled back—including aid for the unemployed and poor, and for education and health care—as well as military outlays. It is a context in which the kinds of funds a Marshall Plan would require are extremely unlikely to be available. Amounts recently dedicated to help the new regimes in Egypt and Tunisia illustrate the points. The United States has pledged a mere $1 billion in debt relief and $1 billion in loan guarantees for Egypt, and the G8 pledged a total of $20 billion in aid for both Egypt and Tunisia. However, a timeframe for delivering these funds was not set "and the Group of 8 countries have in the past made commitments that they did not ultimately fulfill."[28] If the aid package is delivered, it is unclear how big an effect it will have on an Egyptian economy losing $1 billion each month in the tourism sector (40 percent loss).[29]

Suggestions have been made that the West could provide only part of a massive aid package and that rich Middle Eastern nations, especially Saudi Arabia, could provide large-scale funds. Indeed, oil-producing nations may contribute to the costs involved. However, note should be taken that they are basically opposed to the new regimes, which threaten their own, and above all that they face economic and social challenges of their own, which result in lower revenues and increased outlays at home. Multilateral help is richer than a unilateral approach; however, it is very unlikely to suffice.

What Can Be Done?

1. Scale ambitions and rhetoric to reality

The repeated suggestions that the West ought to launch a Marshall Plan for the Middle East—which is widely understood to mean that the West could turn the nations involved into stable democratic regimes and Western-style economies "just as we did in Germany and Japan," and in relatively short order—backfire. These promises raise expectations that cannot be met and lead to disappointment in the new regimes and in the West. In 2011, only months after the autocrats in Tunisia and Egypt were forced to quit, millions were already disappointed because they still did not have jobs. And, as already indicated, the precept that the West will provide what the transformation requires delays the point at which local populations realize that they will have to make major efforts, including changing their work, consumption, and governing habits. Instead, the West should stress that most of the transformation will have to be done by the people who seek it and who will benefit from it, and that they will have to find ways to proceed that are suitable to their conditions. The West should be ready to help, if asked, but this help should be by necessity and limited and conditioned on locals taking the lead and carrying most of the load.

2. Focus should be on security and not regime change

Western interventions to stop genocides discourage nations from invading others, and peacekeeping operations—while far from universally successful—have achieved their goals much more often than attempts to usher in new political and economic regimes. And these achievements have been made with much lower levels of Western and local loss of human life and economic outlays. Compare the Western intervention in Kosovo, the 1991 pushback of Saddam's forces in Kuwait, the 1989 intervention in Panama to oust military dictator General Manuel Noriega to Vietnam, the occupation of Afghanistan and Iraq, and the 2011 intervention in Libya to see the point.

Local authorities are also best advised to focus on restoring basic security. The reverse argument, that development is essential for security and hence must precede it, is erroneous because without basic security, development cannot take place. If oil pipelines laid during the day are blown up at night, oil will not flow very far. If electricity stations are constructed at great costs but not secured, they are merely another place resources are wasted. If professionals fear terrorists, they will leave the country to work elsewhere, and so on.[30]

3. Trade is better than aid

Dissatisfaction with the lack of progress made by foreign aid has led several leading economists and world leaders to conclude that aid may not be the most effective tool for promoting development. Proponents of "trade over aid" point to the drawbacks of aid discussed above (corruption, mismanagement) and argue that aid can create a culture of dependency in recipient countries. Rwanda's president, Paul Kagame, argues, "As long as poor nations are focused on receiving aid they will not work to improve their economies."[31] Aid critics often compare the effect of aid on developing nations' economies to the "resource curse" experienced by countries that discover oil or mineral wealth. The influx of funds eliminates the need for governments to be accountable to either private lenders or to voters.[32] Analysts also point out that the infusion of cash can negatively impact a country's exchange rate and can actually "inflict an economic loss even when there is no counterpart reverse transfer of resources."[33] According to the President of Uganda, Yoweri Museveni, "Aid is a recipe for permanent poverty."[34]

The alternative to problematic foreign aid is trade, in the form of reducing barriers and tariffs as well as eliminating agricultural subsidies in wealthy countries and encouraging local entrepreneurs. Trade proponents argue that "developing economies are shackled by an array of internally imposed trade barriers, tariffs and regulations that hamper business."[35] Dambisa Moyo, the author of an influential book on the subject, *Dead Aid*, argues that removing these impediments and increasing trade will improve governance in developing nations; governments that wish to borrow money must demonstrate prudence and accountability.[36] Timothy Cox and Alec van Gelder of the International Policy Network, a non-profit think tank, cite the economic growth of business-friendly Asian nations like Hong Kong, Singapore, and China as evidence that "trade is the surest known route out of poverty." And Kagame credits Rwanda's improved trade with an 11 percent increase in growth in 2008 (in the face of the global recession).[37] There is also evidence to indicate that moves to improve trade would have much greater public support in the West than increases in aid. A 2004 survey of people in France, Germany, Great Britain, and the United States found that 64 percent of all respondents (and a majority in all countries) believe that trade was better for developing countries than aid.[38]

4. Focus aid

Whatever foreign aid can be granted is best delivered directly to those involved in the projects to be aided rather than channeled through the government. Projects that have a high multiplier effect are to be preferred over those that have low multiplier effect, those that are labor-intensive and not capital-intensive over those that have the opposite profile, and those that use little energy or renewable energy over those that have the opposite profile. In each area, strong preference should be accorded to the completion of a small number of projects over starting a large number. (This is the opposite of the way development has been approached in Afghanistan and Iraq.) As a rule, old elements should be left in place and fixed or reformed gradually rather than replaced. This holds true for equipment and for institutions and their staffs. For instance, tribal chiefs (in Afghanistan) and members of the governing party in public service (the Ba'ath in Iraq) should have been allowed to continue their leadership roles, as the United States did at the end of World War II by leaving the emperor in place in Japan.

5. Humanitarian aid is justified

Large-scale foreign aid, the kind of amounts a Marshall like plan would entail for the Middle East, cannot be provided given the austere regimes in the West. However, if as a result of the regime transformations there are massive numbers of refugees (on a larger scale than those who escaped Libya to Tunisia or Syria to Turkey in 2011) or other forms of massive human suffering, one can make a case on moral grounds that West should grant the kind of aid it provided after the 2010 earthquake in Haiti and the 2004 tsunami in Southeast Asia. However, one should realize that such funds aim to alleviate immediate suffering; the reconstruction that follows will have to be carried out largely by the local population.

Notes

1. Comment of General James Jones, Stimson Center Chairman's Forum on international security issues (June 14, 2011).
2. Comment of Defense Secretary Robert Gates, Kansas State University "Landon Lecture," (November 26, 2007).
3. See note 1.
4. Hillary Clinton, "Secretary of State Hillary Rodham Clinton's Remarks on Receiving the George C. Marshall Foundation Award," http://www.marshallfoundation.org/SecretaryClintonremarksJune22011.htm (June 2, 2011).
5. Glenn Hubbard and Bill Duggan, "A Marshall Plan for the Middle East?" *The Huffington Post* (February 28, 2011). http://www.huffingtonpost.com/glenn-hubbard/marshall_plan_mid_east_b_829411.html.
6. "Senator John Kerry Addresses the Fletcher School Graduating Class of 2011," *The Fletcher School* (May 21, 2011), http://fletcher.tufts.edu/news/2011/05/news-update/Kerry-May26.shtml.
7. Ibid.
8. Defense Secretary Robert Gates, Testimony on Libya to House Armed Services Committee (March 31, 2011).
9. Ibid.
10. Christoph Bangert, "Pakistanis View U.S. Aid Warily," *The New York Times* (October 7, 2009).
11. Yaroslav Trofimov, "Egypt Opposes U.S.'s Democracy Funding," *Wall Street Journal* (June 14, 2011).
12. Ibid.
13. Ibid.
14. Ibid.
15. Sam Huntington, *Who Are We? The Challenges to America's National Identity* (New York: Simon & Schuster, 2004), 92–98.
16. Max Weber, "The Social Psychology of the World Religions," in *Essays in Sociology* (London: Psychology Press, 1991). For analyses on Weber's work see Mark Thompson, "Whatever Happened to Asian Values?" *Journal of Democracy* 12, no. 4 (October 2001): 155. and Syed Anwar Husain, "Max Weber's Sociology of Islam: A Critique," http://www.bangladeshsociology.org/Max%20Weber-Anwar%20Hosain.htm.
17. Matthew Rosenberg, "Corruption Suspected in Airlift of Billions in Cash from Kabul," *Wall Street Journal* (June 25, 2010).
18. Dana Hedgpeth, "Spending on Iraq Poorly Tracked," *Washington Post* (May 23, 2008); "Section 4 Official Corruption and Government Transparency," in *2009 Human Rights Report: Afghanistan*, U.S. Department of State Bureau of Democracy, Human Rights, and Labor (March 11, 2010).

19. William Easterly, *The White Man's Burden: Why the West's Efforts to Aid the Rest Have Done so Much Ill and So Little Good* (New York: Penguin Press, 2006), 136.

20. "Corruption Perception Index," *Transparency International* (October 26, 2010), http://www.transparency.org/policy_research/surveys_indices/cpi.

21. John Norris and Connie Veillette, "Five Steps to Make Our Aid More Effective and Save More Than $2 Billion," brief for *Center for American Progress* (April 2011).

22. "A War of Money as well as Bullets," *The Economist* (May 22, 2008).

23. Peter Goodman, "The Persistently Poor: An Internal Report Criticizes World Bank's Efforts on Poverty," *The Washington Post* (December 8, 2006).

24. Ibid.

25. "Annual Review of Development Effectiveness 2006: Getting Results," World Bank Independent Evaluation Group, Washington, DC (2006).

26. Representative Keith Ellison, H.Res.157.IH, 112th Congress (March 9, 2011).

27. Office of Management and Budget, "The President's Budget for Fiscal Year 2012," http://www.whitehouse.gov/omb/budget (accessed June 24, 2011).

28. Liz Alderman, "Aid Pledge by Group of 8 Seeks to Bolster Arab Democracy," *New York Times* (May 27, 2011).

29. "International Support for Egypt's Plan of Bridging Budget Deficit," Egyptian State Information Service, http://www.sis.gov.eg/en/Story.aspx?sid=54900 (April 17, 2011).

30. Amitai Etzioni, *Security First: For a Muscular, Moral Foreign Policy* (New Haven, CT: Yale University Press, 2007).

31. Paul Kagame, "Africa Has to Find Its Own Road to Prosperity," *Financial Times* (May 7, 2009). http://www.ft.com/intl/cms/s/0/0d1218c8-3b35-11de-ba91-00144feabdc0.html#axzz1QsyTnIdk (accessed June 19, 2012).

32. Paul Collier, "Dead Aid, by Dambisa Moyo," *The Independent* (January 30, 2009). http://www.independent.co.uk/arts-entertainment/books/reviews/dead-aid-by-dambisa-moyo-1519875.html (accessed June 19, 2012).

33. Oxford Analytica, "Aid vs. Trade," *Forbes* (March 30, 2005), http://www.forbes.com/2005/03/30/cz_0330oxan_aid.html (accessed June 19, 2012).

34. Yoweri K. Museveni, "We Want Trade, Not Aid," *The Wall Street Journal* (November 6, 2003).

35. Timothy Cox and Alex van Gelder, "Trade, Not Aid, Is the Best Way out of Poverty," *South China Morning Post* (June 29, 2010). http://www.policynetwork.net/development/media/trade-not-aid-best-way-out-poverty (accessed June 19, 2012).

36. Dambisa Moyo, *Dead Aid: Why Aid Is Not Working and How There Is a Better Way for Africa* (New York: Farrar, Straus, and Giroux, 2009).

37. See note 31.

38. John J. Audley and Hans Anker, "Reconciling Trade and Poverty Reduction," *The German Marshall Fund of the United States* (2004), http://www.gmfus.org/galleries/ct_publication_attachments/TAAudlyTrade_and_Poverty.pdf (accessed June 19, 2012)

Part V

Nuclear Arms: Wrong Priorities

12

Zero Is the Wrong Number

President Barack Obama has so far made only one strategic mistake, but it is a major one. It concerns the greatest security threat to the United States, other free nations, and world peace—nuclear arms in the hands of terrorists, as well as rogue and failing regimes. President Obama's strategy calls for leading by example in dealing with these weapons of mass destruction (WMD). It assumes that after the United States and Russia re-commit themselves to nuclear disarmament, other nations will be inspired either to give up their nuclear arms or refrain from acquiring them. This goal, referred to in short as the "zero strategy" (for zero nuclear weapons), is dangerous if implemented, distracts the international community from more certain and pressing goals, and is extremely unlikely to move those who do need to be inspired, cajoled, or otherwise made to forgo nuclear arms.

How did this usually sure-footed president slip on such a vital issue? The strategy that calls for the United States and Russia to lead the parade to nuclear disarmament was formed and then run up the flagpole by four highly regarded statesmen: two Republicans, Henry Kissinger and George Shultz; and two Democrats, Sam Nunn and William Perry. In January 2007, they issued a collective proclamation, subsequently endorsed by a number of leading American specialists in nuclear weapons policy, calling for a world free of nuclear arms.[1] The Quad, as the four authors of the zero strategy are often called, are all senior veterans of the Cold War. But perhaps this anachronistic experience is a hindrance. (Indeed, one critic called them "dinosaurs.")

To move their strategy forward, the Quad outlined their view in a position paper endorsed by thirty-six experts in the nuclear weapons field. The Quad focused largely on Russia and the United States, and mainly on their strategic nuclear weapons, calling for reductions in the number of warheads arming the two powers' strategic bombers and missiles. Such a move would effectively extend the principal US-Russian treaty that covers these weapons and that is about to expire. The Quad also favors an increase in the warning and decision time before either country could launch their nuclear warheads. Currently, American and Russian missiles remain on alert at levels equaling the Cold War. This means that large parts of their nuclear arsenals are armed and pre-targeted, and that either country could launch their nuclear weapons within minutes of detecting an attack.

The foundations of the Quad's position date back to a much earlier period in the nuclear age. On March 5, 1970, the Nuclear Non-Proliferation Treaty (NPT) entered into force, effectively creating two groups of nations: those that already had nuclear weapons and agreed to give them up, and those that did not have them and promised not to seek them. Many countries comprising the second class ended their nascent military nuclear programs in the years that followed, including South Africa, Argentina, Brazil, and Egypt. But the members of the first class—the "nuclear club" of China, Russia, Britain, France, and the United States—did not live up to their obligations. Moreover, three nations—India, Pakistan, and Israel—refused to sign the NPT and developed nuclear arsenals, while North Korea, which signed on in 1985, quit the NPT in January 2003 after developing the means to produce nuclear bombs. These failures and inconsistencies in the non-proliferation regime are often cited by nations, such as Iran, when they express irritation with being cajoled or pressured by the United States and other nuclear states to be good citizens and not acquire nuclear weapons.

Given this background, it is not surprising that the Quad's statement generated considerable excitement among advocates of nuclear disarmament, especially among those who have long hoped that the United States and Russia would lead other nations to a world free from The Bomb. Such voices had been barely heard in the years since the groundbreaking arms agreements of the Carter and Reagan years. The first of these agreements arose from the Strategic Arms Limitations Talks (SALT II), a treaty signed by Jimmy Carter and Leonid Brezhnev in June 1979.[2] In 1987, Ronald Reagan and Mikhail Gorbachev struck a major deal that led to a considerable reduction in the levels of US and Russian strategic arms. The agreement resulted in the Intermediate Range Nuclear Forces Treaty.[3] A subsequent pact, the Strategic Arms Reduction Treaty (START I) was signed in July 1991 and limited both nations to 6,000 warheads each, deployed on no more than 1,600 strategic delivery vehicles.[4] These levels were to be reached by December 2001. A second arms reduction treaty, START II, was signed by George H. W. Bush and Boris Yeltsin in January 1993 and envisioned more extensive cuts in warheads and strategic delivery vehicles.[5] However, it never officially entered into force, with the Russians officially declaring that they would no longer be bound by the agreement following the US withdrawal from the Anti-Ballistic Missile Treaty in 2002. Despite the problems with START II, Russia and the United States continued to make cuts as required under START I. They announced in December 2001 that they had completed those reductions long before the treaty's planned expiration.

In 2002, George W. Bush and Vladimir Putin made their contribution to strategic arms control with the signing of the Strategic Offensive Reductions Treaty (SORT).[6] The countries pledged to reduce their total number of deployed strategic nuclear warheads beyond START I levels to between 1,700 and 2,200 each by December 31, 2012. As of early 2009, the United States has already reached the 2,200 limit, while Russia reportedly has about 2,800 warheads and is on track to fulfill its obligations by the 2012 deadline. But, there is much less here than meets the eye. The figures deal only with the number of deployed warheads, many of which have not been destroyed and can be readily re-deployed.[7] The number of these is not known because destroying the warheads was not part of the deal and not subject to verification measures. Also, while there are fewer missiles, many have been modified to be able to carry more warheads.

While there have been deals aplenty, recent action toward these goals has been wanting, and over the past decade the dreams of disarmament advocates have been tinged with cynicism. The hope that nuclear abolition would follow the original Reagan–Gorbachev arrangement lost much of its appeal after the collapse of the Soviet Union. Though reductions in arsenals continued on both sides, including during the George W. Bush administration, dealing with American and Russian weapons lost any sense of urgency. Challenges to the non-proliferation regime, such as the rise of India, Pakistan, and North Korea as nuclear states, dimmed the possibility of global disarmament even further. Pakistan is expanding its nuclear bomb-making facilities and India is responding in kind. North Korea is adding to its stockpile of nuclear bombs, leading Japan and South Korea to consider developing their own nuclear arms. In short, the nuclear contagion, far from contained, is spreading like the swine flu.

Moreover, the 2002 US Nuclear Posture Review suggested that nuclear weapons have a role to play in America's security for the fore-seeable future.[8] In effect, in the decades following the first Reagan–Gorbachev pact, much of the interest in nuclear abolition was replaced in favor of arms control and non-proliferation. Thus, when the Quad unveiled its zero strategy, it was warmly received by those advocates of nuclear disarmament who have spent decades frustrated, waiting for a new beginning.

The Zero Mirage

Earlier this year, as the Obama administration was looking to develop its position on nuclear arms, it seems to have found it convenient to buy into this attractive vision of zero. During his first major speech about nuclear arms, in Prague on April 5, the new president promised that "the United States will take concrete steps towards a world without nuclear weapons . . . we will reduce the role of nuclear weapons in our national security strategy, and urge others to do the same."[9] It is important to note that President Obama was careful to acknowledge that "this goal will not be reached quickly—perhaps not in my lifetime."[10]

So far, these are just words. There have been no new cuts in either the Russian or American nuclear arsenals. But is this the direction the Obama administration is headed—toward full and complete nuclear disarmament, however gradually? And should we trust that this heart-warming goal will actually inspire others to do the right thing? In a word, no.

Zero is the wrong number. Indeed, if zero is really the goal, it is an extremely hazardous one. Though the Obama administration basked in international goodwill in the aftermath of the Prague speech, this public diplomacy victory is unlikely to last long. Indeed, there were few signs of its after-glow during Obama's July visit to Russia. Obama's major speech at Moscow's New Economic School was not broadcast live on any major Russian television channel. During Obama's meeting with Russian Prime Minister Vladimir Putin, the latter spent most of the time griping about US foreign policy. By the end of the trip, the Obama administration had little to show for its efforts at diplomacy. An agreement to seek further reductions in strategic nuclear arms favors Russia, which finds it difficult for financial reasons to keep up with the United States. Finally, Washington gained no ground in convincing Moscow to pressure Iran to give up its nuclear program—a major US priority.

Unfortunately, so far the dream has produced just a series of potentially catastrophic distractions—particularly in relations with Russia. But even more problematically, we must not allow day-dreaming about zero to divert our attention from rogue states, such as North Korea and Iran, and failing states such as Pakistan. Virtually every expert who has examined the matter agrees that the two greatest dangers to our security emanate from the threat of terrorists getting their hands on nuclear weapons and from those devices that rogue states have or may acquire. It is critical to note, however, that neither of these threats involves the strategic nuclear arms of the United States and Russia, the relatively well-guarded and secured high-yield weapons, which terrorists would find extremely difficult to operate even if they somehow got their hands on them.

Currently, the United States and Russia are discussing a reduction of their strategic nuclear arsenals beyond the level negotiated in SORT in 2002.[11] The new target—discussed in Moscow this July in preparation for an agreement not yet worked out—is between 1,500 and 1,675 deployed warheads, a reduction that will take place over seven years. However, as yet it is unclear if the warheads removed through such an agreement will be merely stored away or disabled. Indeed, this has been a problem with the two earlier treaties as well. Washington has always wanted to count only deployed warheads. Reports suggest it will continue this stance even though Moscow would prefer the reverse.[12] (The United States has dismantled some of the warheads it no longer deploys despite a lack of provisions in the arms control treaties requiring it to do so. It is thought that Russia has done the same, though there is no way of telling.)

More critically, the reductions desired do not include tactical nuclear weapons. Russia has several thousand such arms (estimates vary between 5,000 and 14,000, though it has never disclosed a precise count) while the United States has about 1,000. Such weapons are numerous, less well-protected, and much more user-friendly for terrorists than strategic weapons. They lack safeguards such as "permissive action links"—complex electronic locks that prevent the use of strategic warheads without high-level authorization from at least two sources. Moreover, it is worth remembering that the yield of an average tactical nuclear weapon is still roughly 200 kilotons, approximately ten times the destructive force of the bomb dropped on Hiroshima.

The Ultimate Risk

If zero is indeed the goal of the Obama administration, even if it is only over the very long term, it is a dangerous notion—unless it is preceded by radical changes in the ways the world is governed. (The same holds for reducing nuclear weapons stockpiles substantially en route to zero.) The reason is quite clear: if either Russia or the United States conceals ten such weapons, above the levels permitted by some current or future treaty, so long as each country has hundreds of them, it matters little. However, if one of the superpowers gives up its entire nuclear arsenal and the other stashes away ten warheads, it would pose a major threat to international stability. The whole concept of Mutually Assured Destruction, which secured the stability and ensured the restive peace of the Cold War and continues to this day, albeit in a modified fashion, would go out the window.

Moreover, this concern extends far beyond the two major nuclear powers. Even were both Russia and the United States to move to a true and verified zero, any other nation that failed to do so would have a significant strategic advantage. Imagine if North Korea were to somehow remain the only nuclear player, blackmailing the superpowers and menacing East Asia, merely by threatening to use its stockpile of nuclear weapons. True, this is an extremely unlikely development. Still, it serves to highlight that a US-Russia zero is unthinkable—unless all other nations also give up their nuclear arms. However, it is not only rogue states that are reluctant to line up. There are precious few signs that France, Britain, and China are interested in joining the zero nukes club. Even the most ardent supporters of zero recognize that, at best, the process will be long and difficult, and that moving to a world without "The Bomb" requires a very extensive system of verification and a global implementation of policies dedicated to the end of nuclear weapons—quite appealing but, at the same time, very elusive ideals.

One may suggest (a bit cynically, perhaps, but international relations can lead one to cynical thoughts) that nuclear disarmament is simply an inspiring but harmless vision. However, the Quad strategy explicitly makes this a goal—that American and Russian disarmament will lead, indeed inspire, the rest of the world to relinquish their nuclear arsenals as well. Last year, the Quad noted: "The U.S. and Russia . . . have a special responsibility, obligation and experience to demonstrate leadership."[13] Likewise, during his July trip to Moscow, Obama stressed that the United States and Russia should "lead by example."[14] Certainly, nonproliferation and disarmament advocates see the Quad's pronouncements through rose-tinted glasses, but where in the Obama administration are the realists? Do they really believe that one can inspire Iran and North Korea to jettison their nuclear programs?

To better understand how these nations will view the disarmament pronouncements, we must try to put ourselves in their shoes. For years, nations such as India, Iran, and North Korea have faulted the members of the nuclear club for not living up to their obligations under the NPT, while pressuring others to abide by the same agreement. Indeed, the treaty mandates that the declared nuclear powers must "pursue negotiations in good faith on effective measures relating to cessation of the nuclear arms race at an early date and to nuclear disarmament."[15]

The Carrot Myth

"Disarmament," in this context, is understood to mean zero bombs, not fewer bombs. But the realists in Pyongyang and Tehran know full well that zero is not coming anytime soon. Rather, the proposed negotiations between the United States and Russia are akin to informing someone who is to be executed by firing squad that the number of riflemen will be reduced to fifteen from twenty. It matters not. Even a handful of strategic nuclear weapons would suffice to obliterate the major population centers of North Korea and Iran, killing millions of people and rendering those lands unsuitable for human habitation for centuries. Faced with the reality of this existential threat, it is obvious to see why these nations so desperately seek the deterrent of having their own weapons. The inducement for Pyongyang or Tehran to give up nuclear weapons in lock step with Russia and Washington is nil. Indeed, as Stephen Rademaker, a former assistant secretary of state, notes, North Korea's "Kim [Jong Il] would be even more interested in having nuclear weapons if he thought he could be the only leader on Earth to possess them."[16]

Beyond the threats posed to lesser nations by the two major nuclear states, there are regional factors that compel nations to keep a nuclear arsenal. Pakistan, for example, maintains its arms due to the persistent fear of going to war with its much larger neighbor, India. A nuclear capability thus serves, from the viewpoint of Islamabad, as the main deterrent against being overrun. Moreover, New Delhi has nuclear weapons of its own as a counterbalance to both Pakistan and China.

Beijing (which virtually ignored the Quad's call for zero) maintains a nuclear arsenal to impress India and as the definitive marker of being a major strategic power. And so, on and on are threats—real and imagined—woven in a delicate and tangled nuclear web.

The nuclear club is also a ticket to the front row, a "look-at-me-now" demand for international prestige, if not necessarily respect. While Iran certainly seeks to counterbalance Israel's significant (though undeclared) nuclear arms, the ayatollahs know well that nuclear weapons and delivery capability could make them the leading regional power in the Middle East. And though Pyongyang claims it needs nuclear weapons to deter an imminent attack from the United States or its East Asian enemies, in the near-term it has used its nuclear arsenal as a bargaining chip, shuttering then restarting its processing plants again and again to bully the West and to gain international aid. Israel committed itself to join a Middle Eastern zone free of weapons of mass destruction, but only if a stable regional peace and an effective verification system is established. Meanwhile, the tiny nation continues to box far above its weight due, in part, to its nuclear arsenal.

Given these compelling reasons, it is hard to imagine that any further US-Russian arms reduction deal would sway governments in Pyongyang, Tehran, or Tel Aviv. Indeed, following Obama's Prague speech and the announcement of planned reductions in nuclear arms during the president's July visit to Moscow, North Korea continued to test its missiles, which potentially could be used one day to deliver nuclear bombs. Meanwhile, there has been not even a hint that Iran plans to yield an inch in its nuclear ambitions.

The Fissile Material Folly

There is certainly a healthy dose of idealism in the zero strategy, but beyond the daydreaming lies danger. Zero distracts attention and uses up political capital needed for major, urgent problems concerning nuclear arms. Paramount among these issues is the lack of oversight of tactical nuclear weapons. Currently, the negotiations between Washington and Moscow have neglected this major worry. An existing treaty that deals only with Cold War era issues such as a reduction in the number of strategic nuclear warheads and missiles is all but useless given the real threats we face today.

Regarding fissile material, especially highly enriched uranium, from which terrorists could fashion nuclear devices, the United States has been a major player in securing the stockpiles and controlling the illegal sale of such material. Considerable progress has been made in safeguarding these materials and blending them down so that they are no longer useful for making nuclear bombs. This has occurred largely as part of the Cooperative Threat Reduction Program, also known as Nunn–Lugar (named for the two American senators who initiated the program), through which the United States has contributed hundreds of millions of dollars a year over the last decade to help secure these fissile materials. Some of its greatest early successes came in Kazakhstan, which was left with large stockpiles of dangerous materials following the collapse of the Soviet Union. Washington paid the Kazakh government for the materials, which were then sent to the United States and blended down into nuclear fuel to be sold for use in nuclear reactors used to generate electricity. Beyond these successful actions, there is still much work to be done. Accelerating the implementation of these safeguards deserves much higher priority than it is now granted.

On several recent occasions, some of this material found its way onto the transnational black market. For example, in 2007, officials from Georgia noted that they had twice in the past four years arrested men attempting to cross their borders, each with over four ounces of weapons-grade uranium.[17] An official in the body that manages Russia's nuclear-powered icebreakers was arrested in 2003 when he tried to sell two pounds of yellowcake, a raw form of uranium.[18] And, in 2001, Russian authorities stopped the sale of over two pounds of highly enriched uranium to a criminal gang from a group that included a man later found to be an agent of the Federal Security Service of the Russian Federation (FSB).[19] The uranium's ultimate destination was not known.

To be fair, the Quad has mentioned the matter of loose fissile materials. Their plan is to create an international "nuclear fuel bank" that would provide enriched uranium to non-nuclear nations for fueling nuclear reactors to generate electricity. The idea is to discourage nations from developing their own facilities for enriching uranium, instead securing access to ready-made fuel from the international bank. Hand in hand with greater monitoring, it would also supposedly ensure that client nations not siphon off material for making weapons. The United States agreed to provide nuclear know-how and material to the United Arab Emirates, although they do not currently have nuclear facilities. It does the same for other nations—such as Japan and India—whose governments the United States considers "safe." However, there is no sign that Iran, North Korea, India, and Pakistan would agree to such a plan. They seem to feel, not without reason, that if they gave up their own uranium processing facilities, they would be at the mercy of the nations that own and run the international fissile fuel bank.

Zero as a Distraction

To be fair, the real hot issue—nuclear arsenals, real or anticipated, of rogue states and failing states—is not being ignored by President Obama. His new administration seems first to be building bridges of diplomacy and engagement before threatening sanctions. But it is far from clear that Iran and North Korea will prove remotely amenable to negotiations. Even convincing Pakistan and India to give up their nuclear arms is a very long shot.

Although various suggestions have been made in previous years to encourage India and Pakistan to join the NPT and dial down their nuclear arms programs, the opposite has been happening. Obama so far has focused on inspiring all nations with his rhetoric about zero, but has not moved to deal with this particular hot spot. On the contrary, his administration continued the steps taken by the Bush administration to expand the materials and know-how available to India's nuclear industry. And in dealing with Pakistan, other issues—such as fighting the Taliban—have absorbed whatever leverage the United States has over this unstable regime.

There is room for considerable differences of opinion about what can be done with these nuclear states. But there is no sign, no hint, and no reason to believe that these nations will be moved to give up their status as nuclear powers because Russia and the United States are cutting their arsenals by, at most, 25 percent over seven years, under the plan agreed to in principle by Obama and Medvedev in July 2009, or that the non-core members of or aspirants to the nuclear club envision a day the whole world will move to zero.

Yet dealing with these hot spots is urgent because of the danger that they may lead to nuclear confrontations, thereby undermining the whole non-proliferation regime. Of immediate concern is the instability of the government in Pakistan—where there is real fear that terrorists might usurp nuclear arms. There seems to be no way directly to tackle this issue. In the longer run, one might hope to deal with it only if the conflict between India and Pakistan, especially their disagreement about Kashmir, is resolved. But there is no reason to believe that talking about zero will affect the Kashmir issue—in any shape or form.

If North Korea continues to develop its delivery systems and add more nuclear bombs to its arsenal, Japan and South Korea are likely to seek nuclear arms. They are unlikely to trust vague American talk about a nuclear umbrella, especially if the United States claims that it seeks to abolish its nuclear arms.

Most experts agree that if (Shiite) Iran develops nuclear arms, other Middle Eastern nations—especially the Sunni ones, such as Saudi Arabia and Egypt—will seek their own. Meanwhile, there exists the very real possibility that Israel may attack Iran in order to slow down Tehran's development of nuclear bombs. Iran is sure to retaliate.

One may say that it makes no sense trying to keep nations such as Japan and Saudi Arabia from acquiring nuclear weapons while simultaneously arguing that zero for the United States is both a dangerous and distracting specter—at least until we have an effective global verification system. However, this is like saying that because two people have lung cancer, and there is no way of curing it given the current state of medicine, we should not urge other people to stop smoking. Russia and the United States have shown that they can deter each other, but it is far from obvious that if more and more nations become nuclear states, all their leaders will stay rational all the time. This should, in no sense, be construed as denying that a world without nuclear bombs might be a safer one, but only to suggest that if the United States and Russia do not disarm, it does not follow that there are no strong reasons to stop other nations from going down the same road.

What Can Be Done Now

Moscow and Beijing have important roles to play in dealing with two of the three hottest hot spots—Iran and North Korea (but not Pakistan). Still, talking about zero, the record shows, is not moving Moscow and Beijing in the needed direction. To get Russia to use its leverage over Iran—without which the United States and its allies may not be able to compel the mullahs to reconsider their course—it is essential to determine what Moscow most wants.

High on the Kremlin's list is stopping the eastward expansion of the North Atlantic Treaty Organization (NATO) and ditching plans for an American missile defense system in Poland and the Czech Republic. Indeed, President Obama indicated that if Iran abandons its pursuit of a nuclear military program, there would be no need for the United States to set up a missile defense system in Central Europe. But, Moscow's immediate concerns and the imminent threat of a nuclear

Iran will not quickly be solved if the goal is a long and slow march to zero. So far, however, those exploring the reduction of strategic arms have not been authorized to offer deals on other fronts—such as supporting Russia's membership in the World Trade Organization, granting greater access to American markets, and promising at least to delay pushing NATO eastward. It is less clear what Beijing wants in exchange for using its leverage with North Korea to move it off its nuclear course, but zero nuclear weapons is surely not what China is planning for its arsenal.

Now that the dream of a world free of nuclear arms has been invoked by the president of the United States, it seems heartless to call it a risky business and a distracting dream—but that is exactly what it is. Rather, this idealistic vision should be seen as a shining city on the far horizon, which merely retreats as one seeks to rush toward it. Instead, the nuclear powers and concerned nations would do best to keep their sights on the hot spots and what might be done to douse these flames—lest major conflagrations are to follow.

Washington should entice, cajole, and if all else fails, compel North Korea and Iran to give up their nuclear ambitions. The United States and Russia should agree to accelerate the Cooperative Threat Reduction Initiative, which entails ensuring that tactical nuclear arms are well guarded and fissile materials secured. And the international community should make arrangements to stabilize the regime in Pakistan, meanwhile preparing for what can be done if it collapses. We are better served in addressing these burning issues with the attention they deserve than trying to grasp the mirage of zero.

Notes

1. Henry Kissinger, George Shultz, Sam Nunn, and William Perry, "A World Free of Nuclear Weapons" *Hoover Digest* 1 (January 2007), http://www.hoover.org/publications/hoover-digest/article/6109 (accessed January 25, 2012).

2. "Strategic Arms Limitation Talks (SALT II)," *The Nuclear Threat Initiative.* http://www.nti.org/treaties-and-regimes/strategic-arms-limitation-talks-salt-ii/ (accessed January 26, 2012).

3. "Intermediate Range Nuclear Forces Treaty," *Arms Control Association.* http://www.armscontrol.org/documents/inf (accessed January 26, 2012).

4. "Strategic Arms Reduction Treaty (START I)," *Council on Foreign Relations.* http://www.cfr.org/proliferation/strategic-arms-reduction-treaty-start-/p15097 (accessed January 26, 2012).

5. "Strategic Arms Reduction Treaty II (START II)," *Council on Foreign Relations*. http://www.cfr.org/proliferation/strategic-arms-reduction-treaty-ii-start-ii/p15099 (accessed January 26, 2012).

6. "Strategic Offensive Reductions Treaty (SORT)," *Arms Control Association*. http://www.armscontrol.org/documents/sort (accessed January 26, 2012).

7. Amy Woolf, "The Nuclear Posture Review: Overview and Emerging Issues," CRS Report for Congress (January 31, 2002), http://www.iwar.org.uk/news-archive/crs/8039.pdf (accessed January 26, 2012).

8. Ibid.

9. Barack Obama, "Remarks By President Barack Obama, Hradcany Square, Prague, Czech Republic," (April 5, 2009), http://www.whitehouse.gov/the_press_office/Remarks-By-President-Barack-Obama-In-Prague-As-Delivered (accessed January 26, 2012).

10. Ibid.

11. Peter Baker and Helene Cooper, "U.S. and Russia to Consider Reductions of Nuclear Arsenals in Talks for New Treaty" (March 31, 2009), http://www.nytimes.com/2009/04/01/washington/01arms.html?scp=1&sq=Strategic+Offensive+Reductions+Treaty&st=nyt# (accessed January 26, 2012).

12. "Nuclear Weapons Counting Rules Under START I, the Moscow Treaty, and New START," *The Center for Arms Control and Non-Proliferation*. http://armscontrolcenter.org/policy/nuclearweapons/articles/031009_counting_rules_start_sort/ (accessed January 26, 2012).

13. Henry Kissinger, George Shultz, Sam Nunn, and William Perry, "Toward a Nuclear-Free World," *The Nuclear Threat Initiative* (January 15, 2008), http://www.nti.org/analysis/opinions/toward-nuclear-free-world/ (accessed January 26, 2012).

14. Luke Harding, "Obama and Medvedev Offer to Cut Nuclear Arsenals," *Guardian* (July 6, 2009). http://www.guardian.co.uk/world/2009/jul/06/obama-russia-nuclear-medvedev (accessed January 26, 2012).

15. "The Nuclear Nonproliferation Treaty (NPT) at a Glance," *Arms Control Association*. http://www.armscontrol.org/factsheets/nptfact (accessed January 26, 2012).

16. Stephen Rademaker, "Blame America First," *Wall Street Journal* (May 7, 2007): A15.

17. Lawrence Scott Sheets and William J. Broad, "Smuggler's Plot Highlights Fear over Uranium," *New York Times* (January 25, 2007). http://www.nytimes.com/2007/01/25/world/europe/25nuke.html?pagewanted=all (accessed January 26, 2012).

18. Graham T. Allison, *Nuclear Terrorism: The Ultimate Preventable Catastrophe* (New York: Owl Books, 2005): 73.

19. "Balashikha organized crime group members arrested for attempted sale of uranium-235," *The Nuclear Threat Initiative* (December 7, 2001), http://www.nti.org/analysis/articles/balashikha-organized-crime-group-members-arrested-attempted-sale-uranium-235/ (accessed January 26, 2012).

13

A Deeply Flawed
Fuel Bank*

There is a new idea afloat in the world of nuclear proliferation. To ensure nations will not enrich uranium—a key element in making nuclear bombs—they will be provided with already-enriched uranium. The providers will include nations that already have significant enrichment capabilities, including France, Germany, the Netherlands, Russia, the United Kingdom, and the United States.[1] And, to ensure the recipient nations that they will not be dependent on the good (or not so good) will of any one nation, countries would contribute to an international nuclear fuel bank, regulated by the International Atomic Energy Agency (IAEA), from which recipient nations could obtain enriched uranium. Call it a "fallback bank."

Most important, the uranium that will be provided will be low-enriched uranium (LEU, usually defined as enriched to 20 percent or less in the fissile isotope uranium-235) and not highly enriched uranium (HEU, usually defined as 90 percent enriched or more in U-235), the kind needed to make nuclear bombs. Hence, there is supposed to be no danger that the recipient nations will use the readymade uranium they receive to make bombs. In short, nations will be able to build nuclear reactors and use them for peaceful purposes without enriching uranium, and the world will rest assured that no nuclear proliferation is in the offing.

Sounds good, but as is so often true, there is a great distance between the lip and the cup. As several steps have been taken to actually implement this idea—it turns out that the outsourced enrichment precept has one major merit, but also has a significant flaw in its very design and a substantial catch in the way it is implemented. Both pitfalls make it likely that the outsourcing will actually propel proliferation rather than slow it.

Correcting for a Major NPT Flaw

The main merit of outsourcing of uranium enrichment is that it serves to correct a gaping hole in the Nuclear Non-Proliferation Treaty (NPT)—a flaw that is acknowledged by a considerable consensus of those who have studied nuclear security for years on end (my first books on the subject were published in 1962 and 1964).[2] The treaty allows a nation to build nuclear facilities, including those needed to produce enriched uranium, as long as these facilities are said to be used for non-military purposes. But the treaty further allows a nation to give three months' notice to the other parties and the United Nations Security Council, basically by postcard, that it is opting out of the treaty—and taking with it the fully developed nuclear facilities so it can merrily proceed to make bombs.[3] That is exactly what North Korea did.

Given that there are 189 parties to the NPT, including countries such as Iran, Venezuela, and Burma, reaching consensus on modifying the treaty is about as likely as getting all of the oil that has spilled into the Gulf of Mexico to flow back into the BP Deepwater Horizon well. Indeed, when the signatories do meet—once every five years—they have a very hard time agreeing even on the agenda of the meeting. Typically, their efforts produce very little.[4]

Instead of vainly seeking to correct this very detrimental flaw in the treaty, the community of experts who lose sleep over these matters came up with the idea that if nations could be cajoled, enticed, and pressured not to build facilities that enable them to enrich uranium themselves, but instead would purchase enriched uranium from other nations, the NPT could work without correcting its core loophole. In this way, if a nation stuck to its commitments to avoid enriching uranium and to use its reactors merely for non-military purposes, would have all the readymade fuel it needed—and if it strayed, the supply could be cut off. Moreover, if a nation quit the NPT, it would not have the enrichment facilities from the get-go. So far so good.

Rod Possession and the Substitution Effect

The fuel bank idea, which for years was mainly the subject of position papers and theoretical discussions among experts, has been implemented as of 2009 in the United Arab Emirates, and is being offered to others. In the process, the fuel bank idea faces two major challenges that are almost never mentioned, and there are no indications that they are about to be successfully confronted.

One concerns the used rods that are left in reactors as the fuel (the uranium) is used up. These rods can be reprocessed to make plutonium-239, to make bombs. Plutonium warheads are smaller than HEU ones. By some estimates it takes fifteen kilograms of uranium, but only four kilograms or even less of plutonium to make bombs. Hence they can more readily be fitted into missiles and do not require bombers to deliver them on target, or be put on heads of missiles with a longer range.[5] For instance, the reactor-grade plutonium that can be derived from used rods in the nuclear reactors in Bushehr, Iran—now fueled by Russia—could be used to make thirty bombs a year, according to Paul Leventhal, former president of the Nuclear Control Institute.[6] This is not some kind of theoretical notion, some outlier "possible" but unlikely development. It is precisely what North Korea did to develop part of its stockpile of nuclear bombs.[7]

Supporters of the fuel bank are likely to argue that the basic deal entails that the recipient nation will turn over the spent fuel rods to the supplier nation or nations. Indeed, many reports on the subject simply take it for granted that this will be the case, as if picking up these rods is akin to picking up a package at the post office. Thus, Gerald Seib writes in the *Wall Street Journal*, "By providing the fuel, and taking away spent fuel, the Russians have undercut Iran's argument that it has to do its own enrichment."[8] Likewise, a State Department spokesman tried to assure observers by saying that Bushehr was "under IAEA safeguards and Russia is providing the needed fuel and taking back the spent nuclear fuel, which would be the principal source of proliferation concerns."[9] One can also imagine that the uranium suppliers would cut off future supplies of enriched uranium if the recipient nation did not cough up the used rods. However, such a nation still could use the rods to make a hefty batch of plutonium-based bombs, before the readymade uranium supplies it has on hand run out. True, such a nation would need a reprocessing plant. And the emissions of krypton-85 from reprocessing might give away where the plant is located. Iran though has such plants. And, there is not much the world can do to prevent it from making plutonium. Nor can one rule out that such a nation would be unable to purchase these supplies from some other source (say, South Africa) or meanwhile build enrichment facilities of its own.

In addition, a major catch arises in the ways the fuel bank idea is implemented. It lies in the observation that when enriched uranium is provided to nations that already have enrichment facilities, but are short of the ore from which uranium is extracted or have only limited enrichment facilities and skills—providing them with enriched uranium frees them to use what they already have—for military purposes. We shall see shortly that this substitution effect is an all too true risk.

There follows a brief review of recent developments on the uranium outsourcing front.

The "Trusted" Governments

The United Arab Emirates signed a deal with the United States in January 2009 based on the outsourcing model. The pact, called a "123 agreement," obligates the United States to supply uranium for use in power plants, but the government of the UAE agreed in exchange to forgo any enrichment or reprocessing activities at risk of having its fuel supply cut off. This agreement also freed the UAE to conclude a $20 billion agreement with South Korea in December 2009 to build four nuclear reactors, with the first to become operational by 2017.

Bahrain and Saudi Arabia are reported to be next in line. Together with the UAE, these three nations have no uranium enrichment facilities of their own and hence the substitution effect is of no concern here. But while the UAE and Bahrain seem not to have the wherewithal to make bombs out of the used rods, even if they so desired, the same cannot be said about Saudi Arabia. Indeed, several observers expect Saudi Arabia to seek to develop nuclear arms if Iran turns out to have some.

The United States and its allies though consider these governments as trustworthy, and hence are not concerned that they will abuse their enriched uranium supplies. This notion came up before, in reference to Brazil, when Colin Powell excused friction between the Brazilian government and the IAEA by declaring that he was "sure" that the Brazilian government was not pursuing nuclear weapons.[10]

However, this approach has two defects. First, governments change. One can readily imagine that the authoritarian and oppressive Saudi regime will come to a sudden end. Moreover, the idea that there are "good" governments that can be trusted with nuclear weapons and bad governments that cannot is by itself a dangerous concept. Pakistan could fall to the Taliban before you finish reading this text—and even before that, Jordan, which has abundant sources of uranium and is seeking nuclear power plants, could fall to the Palestinians. Even Brazil, which General Colin Powell considered a reliable partner, has taken a rather sharp left turn in recent years.

Second, to some extent the effort to limit proliferation is based on international norms, what Brown University professor Nina Tannenwald called the "nuclear taboo," the notion that good citizens of the international community develop neither nuclear arms nor the facilities that can be used to make them.[11] Once "exceptions" are allowed, it becomes more difficult to encourage still other nations not to go down this road.

Once one major power holds that it can make exceptions for its allies, other major powers can hardly be expected to be far behind. Thus, China followed the US deal with India with its own deal with Pakistan, and still other governments feel fewer inhibitions in helping Syria and Burma.

Vietnam

Another "exception" for a "trusted" government (also favored because it is considered a counter-weight to China) is the communist government of Vietnam. The United States is negotiating an agreement with Vietnam to provide it with nuclear fuel and technology—without the usual constraints on enriching uranium to prevent proliferation. The deal has been under discussion for several months following Hanoi's announcement of plans to build fourteen nuclear power stations over the next twenty years.[12] Vietnam signed an initial memorandum of understanding on nuclear power with the Bush administration in 2001. The Obama administration has accelerated these talks. Indeed, the United States and Vietnam signed a new memorandum of understanding in April 2010 over broad cooperation on nuclear power including access to "reliable sources of nuclear fuel," such as enriched uranium.[13] In addition, Hanoi signed nuclear co-operation agreements with several other countries including China, France, and Russia—as sources for fuel.

Henry Sokolski, director of the Nonproliferation Education Center in Washington, said the United States agreeing to allow Hanoi to produce its own nuclear fuel would undermine anti-proliferation efforts. "After the U.S. set such a good example with the UAE, the Vietnam deal not only sticks out, it could drive a stake through the heart of the general effort to rein in the spread of nuclear fuel-making," he told the *Wall Street Journal*.[14]

Iran

On August 13, 2010, Russia announced that it would supply low-enriched uranium fuel rods into the 1,000 megawatt nuclear reactor, which has been constructed at Bushehr on Iran's southern coast.[15] The reactor was fueled eight days later, though it will take six months or more before the plant operates at full capacity. Russia says that it will retrieve the used rods from Iran, but it is far from clear how such an understanding will be enforced. Moreover, because Iran is short of both yellowcake and enrichment facilities, providing it at this stage with enriched uranium frees the uranium it already had and is enriching to be used for military programs. (True, Western powers offered to enrich uranium for Iran—but only if it stopped enriching it on its own, thus not increasing the total enriched amount.)

Providing Iran with enriched uranium at this point in time is like pouring gasoline on fire. After years of protracted negotiations, the international community—at least as it expressed itself via the UN—agreed that Iran is not living up to the international obligations it assumed by signing the NPT. Iran did not allow the kind of inspections needed to vet its claim that it plans to use the nuclear facilities it is constructing exclusively for peaceful purposes. Indeed the IAEA, whose board members number thirty-five nations, including non-Western nations such as Russia, Malaysia, and Cameroon, has implied that Iran is moving to build nuclear arms. Other observers hold that some of the facilities, for instance, the one at Qom that Iran tried to conceal, are suited only for bomb-making purposes. And after much give and take, even Russia and China agreed to impose some additional sanctions on Iran, albeit not the crippling ones the United States sought.

In this context, Russia's recent move has strong consequences. Iran has difficulties in enriching uranium and was reported in April 2010 to be nearly out of uranium yellowcake to enrich.[16] By Russia providing it with uranium for some facilities, this difficulty is greatly alleviated. Whatever remaining yellowcake Iran possesses or is able to acquire, it can enrich for its weapons program instead of for power generation.

Reference was already made to the question of how and who will process the spent rods. The rods Russia is providing to Bushehr can be processed to yield enough plutonium-239 to make about thirty nuclear weapons a year (assuming the reactor is fully fuel loaded). Plutonium-239 allows for making much smaller bombs than HEU ones, making them especially suited for Iran's evolving offensive missile program.

Russia announced that part of the deal is that it will remove these rods. However, there is no realistic way to enforce this part of the deal, especially considering that Iran never adopted the voluntary additional protocol to the NPT that mandates more extensive inspections and verification procedures than the NPT alone. If Iran refuses to release these rods, the most that Russia can do is to refuse to provide Iran with more uranium in the future. This of course will not prevent Iran from using those it has for making bombs or getting uranium elsewhere, say from Jordan.

Indeed, until recently, the United States strongly opposed Russia's completion of the project. Thus, as recently as March 2010, Hillary Clinton stated that to do so would be premature given suspicions of Tehran's nuclear intentions. However, in August 2010 the Obama administration gave a green light to Russia's move, apparently in exchange for Russian support for additional sanctions against Iran, albeit it not the crippling ones the United States sought. This is like allowing someone to deliver an ocean liner full of heroin as long as he pays customs. The loss is huge and the gain—slight.

Trying to provide a positive framing to this deal, Robert Gibbs, the White House spokesman, stated that the reactor "proves to the world that if the Iranians are sincere in a peaceful program, their needs can be met without undertaking its own enrichment program."[17] The UK Foreign Office took the same position, stating that the "announcement underlines the fact that Iran does not need to pursue these other activities to enjoy the benefits of nuclear power."[18] However, one wonders if "the world" needed such evidence and whether it is worthwhile to enable Iran to divert its limited uranium assets to a military program—in order to gain a public relations point. Also, Iranian nuclear engineers at Bushehr will be trained by Russia in the skills and knowledge required to operate a nuclear reactor. This is no small matter, because Iranian engineers are reported to have difficulties in making fuel rods out of the enriched uranium they have.

India

India is one of the two nations that acknowledged having nuclear bombs and the facilities to make them, but has refused to join the NPT. (The other nation is Pakistan. Israel is also commonly believed to have nuclear bombs, but has not acknowledged this fact.) This alone should suffice for the nations of the world to do what they can to pressure India to give up its nuclear arms. (The same pressure of course would have to be applied to Pakistan, a country which already came perilously close to exchanging nuclear blows with India, and one that has a highly unstable government and is a home to many terrorists. There are those who envision a Middle East free of weapons of mass destruction, to include Israel and Iran, as well as Jordan.)

Instead, the Bush administration moved in the opposite direction by providing American aid to India's civilian nuclear energy program and expanding US-India cooperation in nuclear technology, as India negotiated its own 123 deal. Ostensibly, this assistance was to be used only for non-military purposes. But, by allowing the sale of uranium to India for its civilian reactors, the United States is enabling India to move the limited supply of uranium it already has to military use. In plain English: to make more nuclear bombs, Indian power plants were operating at reduced capacity, because they were short of uranium.[19]

The Bush administration's rationale for these steps was that the United States had to improve its relations with India, considered the West's best hope to "balance" China. I leave it for another day to wonder whether the whole idea of balancing can be applied to the post-modern world—and whether India can, should, or is inclined to balance China. Moreover, rather than moving India closer to the United States, the deal was and is very controversial in India. It took years of wrangling before it was finally approved by India in August 2010.

Above all, the agreement damages the deproliferation strategy. In direct response to the Bush administration's deal with India, Pakistan increased its nuclear program on its own by rapidly expanding its plutonium production, and China granted Pakistan two more reactors as part of an agreement parallel to the US-India one. The result is a case study in how the expansion of nuclear facilities in one country leads to the expansion of nuclear facilities in other countries—exactly the course most experts agree should be avoided.

Far from winning US political support in India, Indian opposition to the deal was loud, swift, and widespread. Opposition politicians maintained that American assurances of steady fuel supply were not legally binding.[20] Leftist members of Parliament held that the accord violates Indian sovereignty and that the government was hiding details of the agreement regarding Indian obligations. Others claimed that the deal submits Indian foreign policy to an effective American veto.

The Indian opposition to the deal grew gradually as Indian politicians came to believe they were misled by the government about the details of the accord.

In short, the developments in India highlight the diversion risks and the mistaken notion that political gains can begin to make up for the losses to the deproliferation agenda, when uranium is supplied with the hope of wining friends and influence among the nations of the world.

Jordan

The next chapter of the outsourcing saga will be written in Jordan. Unlike India and Iran, which are short of uranium, Jordan discovered recently that it has sizable deposits of uranium. It has sought to sign a 123 agreement with the United States as way to gain the nuclear reactors and knowhow. However, so far Jordan has refused to submit to the same demands that the UAE agreed to in its 123 agreement: no domestic enrichment and no reprocessing of the used rods. With the newly discovered uranium, Jordan insists it has a right under the NPT to enrich on its own as much uranium as it wants.[21] Moreover, the King believes that only pressure from Israel prevents Washington, so far, from acceding to its nuclear ambitions. Stay tuned.

The Diversion Risk

Enriching uranium is a tricky business. Iran, for instance, which has considerable resources, thousands of trained engineers (many trained in the United States), and a considerable industrial base, nevertheless has run into many difficulties in proceeding. Often ignored, however, is that the greatest difficulties in enriching uranium are in the first stage. To get weapons-grade uranium (WGU), one must separate the rare and highly fissile U-235 isotope from the much more common and heavier, non-fissile U-238. When the ore is found in nature it contains only a small amount of the uranium-235, always below 1 percent. Hence, large amounts of uranium need to be enriched to increase the concentration of the fissile U-235. The enrichment process becomes progressively much easier and requires ever fewer centrifuges as more U-238 is removed over time. The uranium ore has about 140 atoms of the heavy isotope (U-238) for every light one (U-235), and separating the two requires a great deal of spinning in centrifuges. However, by the time the enrichment process reaches 4 percent, it has successfully removed some 115 of the heavy atoms. To get to 20 percent—the spinning centrifuges need remove only twenty more of the heavy atoms. And from there it is even easier to jump to 90 percent WGU. One must remove only four or so additional heavy atoms.[22] (Another way to highlight the same point is to note that it takes 24 cascades of 164 centrifuges to enrich natural uranium to 3.5 percent; 8 cascades of 164 to bring it to 20 percent; but only 4 cascades of 114 centrifuges to bring it to 60 percent, and a mere 2 cascades of 64 centrifuges to bring it to WGU.)

Inspection supposedly is the way to ensure no uranium enrichment takes place and that the LEU provided is not converted into HEU, but inspections have a rather sorry record.[23] Iraq, Iran, Libya, and North Korea all managed at one point (or still today) to make considerable progress toward a clandestine nuclear stockpile even while being subject to one kind of inspection or another.

The problem is that there is an "information asymmetry": inspectors can only visit sites that host nations choose to declare to the IAEA. It was only once Western intelligence sources discovered the planned Qom nuclear facility that Iran even informed the IAEA of its existence. It also bears mention that even though Iran is an NPT signatory, it has not done all it can to ensure IAEA access to its *declared* facilities, either. Iran signed an "Additional Protocol" with the IAEA in 2003, an agreement allowing more intrusive inspections with shorter notice time but withdrew its assent in 2005. (Over a hundred countries have adopted such agreements.)[24]

In Conclusion

The idea of providing nations with enriched uranium works best if the nation has neither enrichment facilities of its own nor the ores from which uranium can be extracted, and assuming such conditions can be vetted. This may be true, for instance, in the case of the UAE. Even then the question of who will control the spent fuel rods is a very serious consideration for all other nations. There is a considerable risk that the provided uranium will enable the recipient country to divert uranium from peaceful programs to military ones or that it will reprocess the spent fuel rods to produce plutonium to make nuclear weapons. Hence, from a proliferation viewpoint, the fuel bank idea is troubling. At best conditions, nations will have neither nuclear facilities nor ambitions. Granted those concerned with green power or selling nuclear reactors and uranium ore will not see it this way.

Notes

*   I am indebted to Charles Ferguson, President of the Federation of American Scientists, and to Benn Tannenbaum, Program Director of the Center for Science, Technology and Security Policy at the American Association for the Advancement of Science, for comments on an early draft.

1. While Russia and the United States have relatively large reserves of uranium, nations with enrichment capabilities typically import relatively inexpensive natural uranium from countries such as Australia, Canada, and Kazakhstan to feed into the enrichment plants.

2. See Amitai Etzioni, *The Hard Way to Peace: A New Strategy* (New York: Collier, 1962); *Winning Without War* (Garden City, NY: Doubleday, 1964).

3. "Scheinman: Iran, North Korea, and the NPT's Loopholes," Council on Foreign Relations. http://www.cfr.org/publication/7661/scheinman.html.

4. Nikola Krastev, "NPT Review Conference Struggles To Find Common Ground," *Radio Free Europe* (May 28, 2010). http://www.rferl.org/content/NPT_Review_Conference_Struggles_To_Find_Common_Ground/2055636.html (accessed June 19, 2012).

5. Tad O'Farroll, "T Minus Bushehr," *Nukes of Hazard blog* (August 18, 2010), http://nukesofhazardblog.com/story/2010/8/18/164241/897 (accessed June 19, 2012).

6. "Bushehr," Globalsecurity.org, http://www.globalsecurity.org/wmd/world/iran/bushehr-opp.htm (accessed June 19, 2012).

7. Thom Shanker and David Sanger, "North Korean Fuel Identified as Plutonium," *New York Times* (October 17, 2006). http://www.nytimes.com/2006/10/17/world/asia/17diplo.html?_r=1 (accessed June 19, 2012).

8. Gerald Seib, "An Exit off Iran's Atom Highway," *Wall Street Journal* (August 24, 2010): A2.

9. "No 'Risk' from Iran's Russian-Built Nuclear Plant: US," *AFP* (August 22, 2010), http://www.spacewar.com/afp/100822000307.4fud8zcj.html (accessed June 19, 2012).

10. "US 'Sure' of Brazil Nuclear Plans," *BBC* (October 5, 2004), http://news.bbc.co.uk/2/hi/americas/3715556.stm (accessed June 19, 2012).

11. Nina Tannenwald, *The Nuclear Taboo: The United States and the Non-Use of Nuclear Weapons Since 1945*, Cambridge Studies in International Relations 87 (Cambridge: Cambridge University Press, 2007).

12. Chris McGreal, "US and Vietnam in Controversial Nuclear Negotiations," *Guardian* (August 5, 2010), http://www.guardian.co.uk/world/2010/aug/05/us-vietnam-nuclear-negotiations (accessed June 19, 2012).

13. "U.S.-Vietnam Cooperation on Civil Nuclear Power and Nuclear Security," U.S. Department of State (March 30, 2010), http://www.state.gov/r/pa/prs/ps/2010/03/139255.htm (accessed June 19, 2012).

14. Jay Solomon, "U.S., Hanoi in Nuclear Talks," *Wall Street Journal* (August 3, 2010). http://online.wsj.com/article/SB10001424052748704741904575409261840078780.html (accessed June 19, 2012).

15. Mark Tran, "Iran to Gain Nuclear Power as Russia Loads Fuel into Bushehr Reactor," *Guardian* (August 13, 2010). http://www.guardian.co.uk/world/2010/aug/13/iran-nuclear-power-plant-russia (accessed June 19, 2012).

16. Yitzhak Benhorin, "Report: Iran's Uranium Supply Nearly Out," *Ynetnews* (April 28, 2010), http://www.ynetnews.com/articles/0,7340,L-3881821,00.html (accessed June 19, 2012).
17. Talea Miller, "Russia to Deliver Uranium Fuel for Iran Plant, Raising New Nukes Concerns," *PBS* (August 13, 2010), http://www.pbs.org/newshour/rundown/2010/08/russia-to-deliver-nuclear-fuel-for-iran-plant.html (accessed June 19, 2012).
18. See note 15.
19. Sanil Raghu, "India's 11 Nuclear Power Units Short of Local Uranium," *Wall Street Journal* (December 9, 2009). http://online.wsj.com/article/NA_WSJ_PUB:SB126034438674983263.html (accessed June 19, 2012).
20. Parrull, "BJP Sees Red after Bush's Fuel Supply Comment," *CNN-IBN* (September 13, 2008), http://ibnlive.in.com/news/bjp-sees-red-after-bushs-comment-on-fuel-supply/73462-3.html (accessed June 19, 2012).
21. Jay Solomon, Jordan's Nuclear Ambitions Pose Quandary for the U.S.," *Wall Street Journal* (June 12, 2010). http://online.wsj.com/article/NA_WSJ_PUB:SB10001424052748704414504575244712375657640.html (accessed June 19, 2012).
22. David Albright and Jacqueline Shire, "Misconceptions about Iran's Nuclear Program," Institute for Science and International Security (July 8, 2009), http://www.isisnucleariran.org/static/297/.
23. See Amitai Etzioni, *Security First: For a Muscular, Moral Foreign Policy* (New Haven, CT: Yale University Press, 2007), 236–37.
24. "Safeguards and Verification," IAEA, http://www.iaea.org/OurWork/SV/Safeguards/sv.html (accessed June 19, 2012).

Part VI
EU: How to Save the Union?

14

Nationalism: The Communitarian Block*

The difficulties experienced by the EU, and in particular the seventeen members of the eurozone, highlight a major challenge faced by many nations that are not members of the EU. These nations face a communitarian paradox: On the one hand, they need a significantly higher level of transnational governance, which—I shall attempt to show—can be provided only if the expansion of such governance is paralleled by a considerable measure of transnational community building. On the other hand, this communal expansion is encountering nationalism, which acts as an overpowering communitarian block by standing in the way of building more encompassing communities, ones comprised of nations.

The article finds that nations must either find ways to overcome this block (a very challenging undertaking)—or limit the level of transnational governance (and in the case of the EU, scale it back!). The article closes by reviewing measures that have been undertaken in the pursuit of communities that encompass nations and points to some that might be tried.

The Communitarian March

A popular narrative sees the course of human history as a movement from numerous small communities (traditional villages) to more encompassing social groupings (city-states and feudal fiefdoms) to still more encompassing groups (nation-states), leading next to regional communities (such as the EU), and ultimately, some argue, to global governance and community.

Theodore Lowi illustrated this narrative using Europe as an example:

There were approximately 500 political, state-like units [in 1500]. By 1800 there were 'a few dozen' . . . After World War I, the census of states was 23, having been reduced significantly by the absorption of many states into the Union of Soviet Socialist Republics (USSR) and others by the new Yugoslavia. By 1994 there were 50 states, arising out of the collapse of the Soviet Union and Yugoslavia. There is now a movement to reduce that number by 27, in a new megastate called the European Union (EU).[1]

In *Bounding Power*, Daniel Deudney finds, "Over this period [the past 500 years], all human political communities, initially isolated or loosely connected, have become more densely and tightly interconnected and subject to various mutual vulnerabilities in a manner previously experienced only on much smaller spatial scales."[2]

Deudney sees "security-from-violence" as the primary driver behind this trend.[3] People were safe in small units in the days of bows and arrows but needed increasingly more encompassing entities once gunpowder was invented until finally intercontinental missiles and WMD pushed them toward a global community.[4] Other scholars point to different motivators, including irrigation and access to water, trade, and population growth.[5] A 2008 analysis by Jürgen Klüver predicts that "the social future of mankind is probably a global society based on the traditions of Western societies with local adaptations."[6]

Actually, very few attempts have been made to form communities using nations as building stones—and they have all collapsed. These included the United Arab Republic (1958–1961) and the West Indies Federation (1958–1962). (It is not clear if the social entities that were combined to make the USSR and Yugoslavia were full-fledged nations by the definition presented below. In any case, they too disintegrated.) The EU is by far the most advanced attempt to form a community made up of a large number of well-formed nations. Its difficulties are hence particularly illuminating for those who seek to study the communitarian march toward ever more encompassing social groupings.

Matters of Terminology

For the purposes of the discussion at hand, it is essential to distinguish between states and nations. In defining nations, I follow others who have defined them as communities invested in states; that is, nations have the attributes of communities, albeit imagined ones.[7] People in well-formed nations see themselves not merely as citizens (who pay taxes, are entitled to services, follow public affairs, and vote) but also as members of a national community. They have a strong sense of affinity for and loyalty to one another and to the good of their nation, and their identities are deeply invested in the nation. On major (albeit select) issues, loyalty to the nation trumps other loyalties. They tend to have a shared moral culture (although not one necessarily shared by all citizens), a sense of a shared history, and often one of shared destiny, or at least of a joint future. For the sake of brevity, I shall refer to these beliefs as the ethos.

Some scholars distinguish between "nations" and "nation-states" (where the former may exist within or beyond the boundaries of a state and may precede it, while the latter describes cases in which the boundaries of the nation and state are congruent). This valid distinction can be set aside here because it does not directly affect the issue under consideration—the factors which prevent the communitarian march from moving to the next supra- or post-national level.

Enter Nationalism

If one employs the terms just laid out to re-examine the communitarian march, one finds that in earlier ages, there was indeed a very strong overlap between the state and the community, namely, in the days people when lived in small tribes, clans, and villages.[8] However, in the following stages, during much of history, the state grew in scope—both in terms of people and the territory it encompassed—but the community remained localized. For instance, during the Middle Ages in Europe, most citizens lived in pre-nation-states, in the sense that they had a parochial (or local) rather than cosmopolitan viewpoint.[9] Their cognitive maps of the world were largely limited to their immediate environment, often to their village. They had little information about the world beyond their local one, and to the extent that such information penetrated their insularity—they typically had no gestalt in which to integrate it, and the information did not affect their sense of self or their relationships to others. This localism was enforced by the rigidity of divisions of the estates, such as the aristocracy, the bourgeoisie, and the peasantry, which stifled identification with those outside one's immediate social sphere, regardless of citizenship.

As a result, state realignments engendered by the various monarchies—even those that resulted in territorial reallocations (either through treaty or conquest) and thus a change of states' boundaries—mattered little to the peasantry. Thus, when in 1806 the Prussian army was defeated, its fate was met with apathy by the populace, so detached were they from "the personal instrument of the crown."[10] Similarly, the French peasantry frequently demonstrated the "self-absorbed indifference . . . on which two Napoleonic dictatorships had rested."[11]

In sharp contrast, with the rise of nationalism in Europe in the nineteenth century, the great community lag was overcome; state and community overlapped again in well-formed nations. The citizens of nations personally followed national developments or were linked to peers, leaders, or opinion makers who did. Most citizens became deeply invested in the nation and hence, for example, the mere suggestion of making territorial concessions to other nations often resulted in sharp emotional responses. The bitter contests between Israelis and Palestinians and between Serbs and Kosovars are two cases in point. Perceived or actual humiliation of the nation—or achievements (say, in soccer matches)—were experienced as individual insults or gains.

Several historical developments enabled the transformation of the state into an imagined community—into a nation. These include the spread of education, the expansion of the mass media, and increased geographical and even status mobility. Economic factors also played a role. In the pre-nation era, those in power could secure the military they needed by hiring mercenaries or drawing on the aristocracy. Local politicians (say, Chicago aldermen or New York City pols) could gain the votes they needed by doing material favors for their constituents, sometimes as crude as handing out money or jobs.[12] However, as the escalating demands of warfare came to require the mobilization of millions—and the same held true for winning elections—those in power found that appealing to peoples' sentiments and ideals was much more economical than providing them with material goods. National values and sentiments thus became a major asset for those who sought to win wars and elections.

I keep referring to well-formed nations as a reminder that the depth and scope of the communal commitment to the state that nationalism entails are contiguous and not dichotomous variables. Some national communities are weak, some are growing, and others have reached a high level of integration. Thus, many of the states initially forged by colonial powers, often by imposing arbitrary geographical lines that cut across tribal and confessional communities, resulted in weak nations. For instance, Afghanistan still has a particularly weak national community, and its citizens have strong allegiances to tribes such as the Pashtun, Tajik, and Hazara. Iraq is similarly divided among confessional (Shia and Sunni) and ethnic groups (Arabs, Kurds, and Turkmen), although they do have some sense of a shared nation. Indeed, both the United States and France are often cited to highlight that several states were formed well before their national communities developed. In the case of the United States, this development occurred mainly after the Civil War.

However, the closing of the communitarian gap following nationalism is evident in very large segments of the world; as of the nineteenth century, empires (a form of a state without a strong community) were torn apart to form national states. The process manifested itself first in Latin America, as Portugal lost Brazil, and Spain hemorrhaged colonies during a tide of independence movements. It then showed itself in Europe, with the dismembering of the Austro-Hungarian Empire after World War I, and in the Middle East, with the parceling out of the Ottoman Empire. It was followed after World War II by the collapse of the remaining European colonial powers and the rise of scores of nations in Asia and Africa.

The point of all these observations is to note that once community caught up with the state, under nationalism, a qualitative change occurred in the relationship between the citizens and the state. Once a nation was well formed, the people, and not just the ruling classes, strenuously resisted forming more encompassing communities and jealously guarded the rights, privileges, boundaries, identity, and culture—the ethos—of their nation. Thus, nationalism is standing in the way of what is considered the "natural" or "much needed" next step in the development of the transnational order.[13]

The End of Nationalism?

The preceding thesis differs from the argument that, far from presenting a formidable, potentially immutable block, the nation-state has ceased to be an effective form of social organization and is being steadily and inexorably eroded. This erosion is said to be both external (due to globalization) and internal (due to pluralization).[14] Adherents to this view—sometimes referred to as post-nationalists—maintain that economic globalization has created markets that are beyond the capabilities of traditional nation-states to regulate.[15] And immigration is said to have led to heterogeneous nations in which ethnic minorities maintain transnational diaspora cultures,[16] divide national self-identities, and further weaken a vital source of social cohesion undergirding the nation-state.

Moreover, post-nationalists view this erosion of the nation-state as heralding a liberation of sorts from a "barbaric nationalism," and point to an international political successor. Jürgen Habermas, for instance, holds that major functions must be transferred to supranational institutions.[17] This is not to suggest that the post-nationalists expect states to simply disappear.[18] Rather, they hold, we must actively construct a post-national democracy oriented around civic solidarity. Gaining the citizens of nation-states as voluntary partners in the construction of a post-national system would enable state actors to cede power to supranational authorities.

Skeptics of this approach dismiss it as chimerical, doubting the possibility of constructing a "post-national polity through deliberation and attachment to civic values."[19] They are dubious about the viability of an EU-wide citizenry, arguing that nation-states are "the largest communities within which the identitarian (membership, belongingness) aspect of citizenship still makes sense."[20]

True, nations are buffeted by forces beyond their borders that they often cannot control. The list of challenges that cannot be handled by the nations on their own is all too well known (spread of WMD, economic contagions, pandemics, global warming).[21] However, so far no bodies have emerged that have proven capable of handling major problems nations cannot—or at least that can match the nations in this regard. Nations continue to be the relevant decision makers in all matters concerning war. For instance, although the 2011 campaign in Libya was labeled a NATO operation, the key decisions—and commitment of resources—were made by France, the United Kingdom, and the United States and were opposed by Germany and Turkey. Nations also continue to be the main players in the global economy, as was evident most recently during negotiations regarding the financial crisis in the eurozone. The main actors were Germany and France, on one side, and Greece (as well as Italy, Ireland, Spain, and Portugal), on the other, although the European Central Bank did play a role, as well.

Transnationalism with Limited Community Building

Faced with both the need for more transnational governance and the communitarian block that stands in the way of forming more encompassing social groupings, nations developed various adaptations that seek more transnational governance—without building a parallel community. In a previous publication, I reviewed such attempts on a global level, including the roles played by civil society bodies, networks of government officials from different countries, and a few supranational bodies (e.g., the ICC and ICANN). I showed that these bodies do not and cannot provide more than a fraction of the needed additional global governance.[22]

The following analysis is focused on the EU. Although it is but a regional body, it is by far the most advanced attempt to generate a major transnational source of governance without building a supranational ethos (or demos)—without building a European community that has the kind of attributes nations now command.

The EU: The Test Case

The EU is by far the most advanced attempt to forge a major regional source of governance that has many of the features of a state, including a parliament, an executive branch, courts, and select reinforcement mechanisms (albeit mainly non-coercive ones). The European Commission, the main driver of the EU, has issued thousands of directives and forged a very large number of regulations, it sets standards and harmonizes policy, and it collects revenues and subsidizes projects—all across national borders.[23]

Moreover, the EU is a particularly important "natural experiment" for the thesis of this article: that there are steep limits to the extent one can advance the development of transnational administrative, legal, and economic integration—with little community building.[24]

The Commission's progress was made possible with rather little community building (as the term is used here) by drawing on several political and sociological mechanisms.

(a) The Commission introduced measures that benefit the various EU members (even if not equally) and hence gained their support, most clearly in removing barriers to the movement of goods.[25] The Commission standardized technical specifications for technology and products such as railroads, medical devices, and toys.[26]

(b) Instead of seeking to make all members adhere to the same standards and rules, the Commission qualified nations and their industries and services, colleges, hospitals, and much else on the basis of minimum compliance. That is, although the various national providers could vary a great deal in their level of competence, achievements, and reliability, they qualified as long as they met basic standards. This is much less sociologically taxing than if the Commission insisted that they all meet the same exact standards.

(c) Numerous small measures were introduced "under the radar"; for instance, by being buried in complex legal documents and treaties.[27]

(d) The Commission tolerated a high level of violation of its rules and policies (sometimes referred to as the "compliance gap"). Even before eastern enlargement, implementation of EU policy within the fifteen original member states was inconsistent and weak. Gerda Falkner and Oliver Treib analyzed over ninety implementation cases of six EU labor law directives and found that, for most member states, "domestic concerns frequently prevail if there is a conflict of interests, and each single act of transposing an EU Directive tends to happen on the basis of a fresh cost-benefit analysis."[28] Christoph Knill examined the implementation of four environmental initiatives passed by the Commission between 1980 and 1993 in Germany, the United Kingdom, and France. He found that implementation of these policies was, at best, inconsistent, and in some cases he found a "dominant pattern of ineffective implementation."[29] One of the gravest examples of this disregard for EU authority is Greece's falsified budget data in its application to join the eurozone. The European Commission's statistical agency failed to alert officials to the suspicious data, which should have prevented Greece's admission to the eurozone.[30] The admission of the eastern European states, which were considerably less developed and more corrupt, led to even more violations.[31]

The net result of proceeding in these ways was a considerable increase in alienation among the electorate of many EU members. The alienation intensified as the EU policies entered areas of great normative, emotive, and political import. A case in point is the Schengen Agreement, which removed border controls for the movement of people between twenty-five EU member countries. This led to large numbers of immigrants who entered Europe from the south (where nations were more open to them) moving to northern countries, whose citizens resented them. And it led to large movements of cheap labor from nations such as Poland and the Baltic countries to nations such as France and Ireland, generating more resentment still.

Why Is Regional Community Needed?

There are major differences of opinion among scholars about the way in which polities work. Some see them as the coming together of special interest groups, which work out policies that serve their respective constituencies. The legislature, and more generally the government, serves as a clearing house of sorts. There is no need for shared values or consensus building with the public at large. The policies reflect specific interests. Indeed, when these cannot be made to converge—gridlock ensues. If polities could be made to work this way, one could build transnational regional administrative semi-states, based on negotiations among various national and transnational interest groups, with little need for community building.[32]

In contrast, my analysis relies on Durkheim, and assumes that (a) members of communities are bonded with one another in affective ways; (b) they share values and not just interests; and (c) they are willing to make sacrifices for one another and the common good of their community—sacrifices they would be unwilling to make for others outside the community. The fact that this holds true for members of nations, but only to a rather limited extent for members of the EU, is next highlighted.

The West Germans gave the equivalent of a trillion dollars to the East Germans during the decade that followed reunification with little hesitation. "They are fellow Germans" was about all the explanation that was needed. However, the same Germans have a very hard time granting much smaller amounts to Greece and other EU nations that are in trouble. They are not members of "the tribe." As Alan Bance writes, "Before there can be federalism, it is necessary to create a set of European 'myths' (no doubt as selective as those out of which nineteenth-century nationalism was constructed) to supply 'symbolic justification' for the sacrifice of immediate interests in favour of the collective European enterprise."[33] In short, if Greece were one of the *neu länder*, the former East German states, it would be bailed out without particular difficulty.

Americans can readily gain insight into this same phenomenon. Once every few years, some reporter will call attention to the fact that, in the United States, Southern and Midwestern states pay substantially fewer taxes but gain a disproportionately larger share of federal outlays than do the northern states. However, such stories have very short legs; these are fellow Americans, case closed. In contrast, when Americans are asked to extend to other nations much smaller amounts than the wealthier states (say, Connecticut and New York) give to the poorer states (such as Mississippi and Alabama) in the union (in the form of foreign aid), it is widely opposed. In other words, if Greece had been the fifty-first American state, its troubles would be over (although it would have to buy into those hardships that plague the United States).

The clearest demonstration of the powerful communal bonds at the national level is that people are willing to die for their nation; no one is even thinking about dying for the EU, not to mention less advanced transnational unions.

Finally, public policies—in which (since nationalism) the "masses," not just interest groups, are involved—reflect in part values, not just interests. This is most obvious in policies that concern so-called cultural issues such as gay marriage, abortion, separation of church and state, attitudes toward minorities and immigrants, and—in the United States—gun control. However, values play a key role in practically all policies, from whether larger estates or the rich ought to be taxed more than others, to how much we should scale back economic growth to protect the environment, to the scope and kind of foreign aid, and so on. When there is no normative consensus, forming such policies—and above all, implementing them—becomes much more arduous.

Indeed, studies show that movement toward building a European community has led to stronger alienation among millions of European citizens.[34] According to an analysis of Eurobarometer surveys,[35] from 1973 to 2004, net public support[36] for the EU grew steadily in the 1980s (averaging about 42 percent) and reached an apex of 62 percent in 1991.[37] However, support then declined. By 1997, net support for integration had fallen to 39 percent. Since 2004, it has fluctuated within a 10 percentage point range of roughly 30 to 40 percent.[38] In 2010, net support was only 31 percent. Moreover, the supporters of the EU are concentrated in countries in which people consider their own government to be particularly inept and corrupt (e.g., Italy), while the critics are in the major European powers, especially Germany and the United Kingdom. The disaffection with the EU further intensified following the financial crisis triggered by Greece.[39]

In response, the EU is actively considering various institutional measures that would increase the power of the EU over the member nations—without any new community building measures. For instance, Jean-Claude Trichet, outgoing president of the European Central Bank, suggested a eurozone-wide Ministry of Finance that would ensure member states' adherence to fiscal and competitiveness policies, control the region's financial sector, and centralize representation of the currency bloc in international financial institutions like the International Monetary Fund.[40] The ministry would also monitor whether countries were pursuing the right policies[41] to be competitive.[42] If the analysis presented here is valid, these measures would increase the tensions and difficulties of the EU, rather than help members to cope with them—because they entail more transnational decision making in matters of great import, without consensus building and the communal foundations on which it must rest.

Legitimacy without Consensus?

A political science response to the communitarian block is to point to the movement toward increasing democratization of the EU. Originally, member nations had veto power on practically all matters. However, over time, various changes have been introduced (which are referred to as "deepening") that allow various EU bodies to make decisions based on majority votes of the member states and do not require unanimity. These changes allow the EU to make more progress in state building without community building because no single member can hold up policies (if they are covered under the democracy rule). Furthermore, the changes presumably provide a source of legitimacy, given that democracy is an accepted way to resolve policy differences.[43] (Legitimacy is widely defined as acting in line with established norms.)[44]

Democracy, however, presumes community—or at least a measure of community—and a value consensus. As Jean-Marc Ferry puts it, any legal community must overlap with a "moral community" which would be based on "a common political culture and . . . a shared historical memory."[45] First of all, those subject to the votes must recognize the legitimacy of the institution, which in turn would reflect their core values. Thus, most Americans would not view policies passed by the UN General Assembly as binding—because the United States never recognized this body as expressing a community to which the United States belongs and whose basic values it shares. The governments of the EU members agreed to yield a measure of their sovereignty to the EU; however, large segments of their citizens did not. Hence, the fact that a democratic vote takes place often does not build legitimacy, and certainly not consensus. In other words, consensus on basic values and the legitimacy of institutions must be built before or at the least at the same time as democratic power is increased.[46] This largely has yet to take place in the EU.[47]

Of those who agree that the EU needs community building in the sense of the terms used here—not more top-down introduction of institutions, but the formation of a shared ethos—a considerable number hold, in effect, that this observation is irrelevant, because no such ethos can be formed. For instance, Richard Bellamy and Dario Castiglione dispute that a public culture founded on common values can be formed from as diverse (culturally, politically, and not least economically) a body as Europe: "Despite the member states sharing a loose set of liberal-democratic values, they often interpret them in different and conflicting ways. For example, they differ over the interpretation of the right to privacy, the ways they tolerate religious differences, their view of human dignity and so on, all of which reflect their very distinct political cultures . . . Thus far, what the ECJ [European Court of Justice] and member states have achieved is not so much a consensus as a series of different sorts of compromise."[48]

EU Community Building: Past and Future

The EU has sought to engage in community building not in the sense of introducing more top-down institutions, but in the sense of building bonds of affinity among its citizens and promoting shared values. These efforts have taken place mainly in four areas that are widely considered places community building can happen: education, language, media, and "symbols." It would take an army of social scientists years to review and evaluate all of the attempts made. Here, a few select examples are given to point to the reasons these measures have not been very effective. One may well contest these assessments individually, but there can be no doubt about the final outcome: There is no EU ethos in the making, and the sense of affinity and shared values among EU citizens is weak and possibly declining.

(a) Education: Currently, education is a national concern and often excludes European history (or it examines it from a nation-specific perspective). The movement to "Europeanize" aspects of national curricula has existed since the 1970s but met resistance from member states. The Commission strove to reach young audiences with "The Raspberry Ice Cream War," a comic book released in 1997 that strove to promote the idea of "a peaceful Europe without frontiers" among the children of member nations.[49]

One notes that the suggested changes concern changing some textbooks and the content of some curricula but not a sweeping Europeanization of the way history, literature, and social sciences are taught. Removing hostile and prejudicial comments is of course of merit, but education continues to be largely national and does not contribute to building a shared ethos. Furthermore, one cannot but question how much schools can contribute to transmitting a shared ethos and implanting it in future citizens, if no such EU ethos exists in the first place. Any serious attempt to move in this direction faces the fact that integrated education has received the lowest support of all policy initiatives on the Eurobarometer.[50]

(b) Language: Historically, the promotion of a shared language (and in very few cases, more than one) has served as a major ethos-building measure. Nation building often meant that people who spoke different tongues were strongly encouraged to use the newly promoted national language as their primary language, at least in public. Laws were enacted allowing only the use of the national language in court hearings, public documents, street signs, voting ballots, and so on.

For the EU to choose one language as its supranational tongue is neither possible nor desired. The various members have very rich cultures that are deeply associated with their particular languages and access to these cultures would be largely lost if all nations chose to speak, say, French from here on out. However, the EU could have chosen for all member nations to lock in on the same second language. (This would be in line with the idea that the supranational community does not seek to replace nations but rather to add a layer on top of them.) In effect, English does serve as such in many EU proceedings, mainly for the elites and professionals. However, the Barcelona European Council in 2002 simply established the goal of teaching at least two foreign languages,[51]—but which particular languages was left to each individual nation to choose.[52] English is the only serious candidate to become a shared second language, but so far France, Germany, and Italy have strongly opposed this development, thus slowing down the agreement upon a shared European tongue—a major element of community building.

(c) Media: Various attempts to fashion a European newspaper have not truly taken off. The same holds for other media, such as television and radio. One major reason is that the citizens do not share one language. The EU should consider establishing a European Broadcasting Agency, modeled after the BBC, which draws on public funds but has autonomous control of the content of its broadcasts. Its mandate would be to provide news and interpret it from a European perspective.

Europe-wide media, such as the *Financial Times*, are limited to an exclusive group of elites or have expanded to become global publications, as opposed to merely Euro-centric. In the 1980s, an experiment with a European television channel (Eurikon) was conducted

211

by an international consortium of public broadcasters, who rotated responsibility for programming each week (e.g., the United Kingdom programmed the first week, Italy the second, and so on). This failed due to inconsistent programming, cultural barriers, and the lack of a need for or interest in transnational advertising (and therefore, a lack of funds). One observer noted, "While viewers from different countries were united in their dislike for Eurikon's programs, the precise reasons for their dislike tended to diverge along national lines."[53] While the Internet has made mass transnational communication much easier, developments have been mainly confined to the private sector. Furthermore, the Internet promotes communications with non-EU members just as readily as it does with members and, thus does little for EU community building in particular.

(d) Symbols: In 2008, the European Parliament passed a proposal to display the European flag (a circle of gold stars on a dark blue background) in every meeting room and at official events; to play the European national anthem, based on Beethoven's *Ode to Joy*, at the start of each new Parliament; and to print the European motto—Unity in Diversity—on all Parliament documents. Additionally, Europe Day was formally recognized as a holiday.[54] The EU emblem has been imprinted on license plates, passports, and in numerous other places.

These and other such measures have done little for EU community building. Some efforts do not capture any particular normative or affective content (e.g., the emblem). Others speak to universal values and neither reflect nor promote EU-specific values (e.g., Ode to Joy as the EU anthem). Above all, symbols can express and even help promote shared values—when they exist—but cannot serve instead of values or be created out of whole cloth.

In short, so far the EU community building efforts, to the extent that they sought to build a shared ethos, have been particularly ineffectual.

What Can Be Done?

(a) EU megalogues: Societies, even large ones, engage in dialogues about public policies that link many local dialogues into one national give-and-take—a "megalogue." Typically, just one or two topics top the megalogue's agenda; for instance, whether or not to legalize gay marriage, engage in war, introduce austerity measures during an economic slowdown, or join the eurozone. These dialogues mainly concern values and are not dominated by considerations of facts. They often

212

seem endless and impassionate, but actually frequently lead to new, widely shared public understandings. Such understandings, in turn, often provide a well-grounded normative basis for changes in public policy and institutions; they generate new sources of legitimacy.[55] In the United States, for instance, public dialogues paved the way for new legislation to protect the environment and for the creation of the Environmental Protection Agency and preceded the abolition of legal segregation and the formation of the Equal Employment Opportunity Commission.

The fact that the majority of EU citizens feel ill-informed about the EU and the actions of its various institutions and that their views are not considered when policies are changed suggests the merit of seeking to engender EU-wide megalogues.

Launching EU-wide referendums is one way to launch a megalogue, as long as ample time is allowed before the referendums are taken, that is, a period during which people can consult with one another and their leaders before voting. Megalogues dialogues and some referendums do take place in Europe, but they are, as a rule, conducted within each nation. This is in part because people still see themselves primarily as citizens of this or that nation rather than of the EU, and in part because the points of closure—the endpoints or changes in public policy that these dialogues lead to or support—are often on the national level rather than EU-wide. To enhance the formation of a core of share values associated with the EU, megalogues and referendums had best take place in all member nations at the same time and be tied to decisions to be made on the EU, and not the internal, national, level.

The issues to be discussed and voted on at an EU-wide level need to be salient enough to draw people into participating. Suggested changes in immigration policy are an obvious example. Finally, to succeed, participating citizens must be able to trust that the results of these referendums will be binding—that the EU officials will be required to heed them, rather than view them as merely advisory.

(b) EU-wide voting: As EU consensus solidifies, the EU should move toward EU-wide voting on EU candidates, rather than the current system in which votes for the EU Parliament are conducted largely for national candidates, on a national basis. Currently, most candidates running for a seat in the European Parliament are put up by national parties and campaign only in their home country. In the European Parliament, most "European parties" are largely comprised of alliances between existing national parties; they function less like political parties and more like international coalitions.

A switch to European parties and candidates raises numerous issues concerning whether different weight should be assigned to the voters of various countries and how to protect minorities.[56] These are concerns that cannot be handled within the confines of this essay but clearly must be resolved before major progress on this front can be anticipated.

Standing between Two Stairs

The arguments laid out above suggest that if the EU is unable to engage in much stronger community-building—if there is no significant transfer of commitment and loyalty from the citizens of the member nations to the evolving supranational community—the EU will be unable to sustain the kind of encompassing state-like shared governance endeavor it attempts to advance. The EU needs either to move up to a higher level of community or to retreat to being only a free trade zone enriched by numerous legal and administrative shared arrangements. It will be unable to sustain a shared currency and will be forced to restore national veto power on numerous important policies, in particular those that have a significant normative and emotive content. One the one hand, the EU needs to be able to overcome the nationalism that blocks progress on the communitarian march toward more encompassing social groupings—to parallel the need for more encompassing and effective transnational governance. On the other hand, it seems unable to meet this challenge. Hence, as much as one may favor its communitarian advancement, one must acknowledge that the EU is more likely to scale back, as it is already doing with regard to the freedom of movement[57] of people with the EU.[58]

The world is watching, both because of the importance of the EU per se and because several other regional bodies (such as the African Union, the Central American Integration System, and the Association of Southeast Asian Nations) in much earlier stages of development seek ways to engage in community building, with nations as the members of the community. I learned long ago that few things irritate people more than hearing, "I told you so." So let me just say that one criterion that those who make policy recommendations should be judged by is how well their previous suggestions have stood the test of time.

Notes

*   I am indebted for research assistance on this article to Julia Milton, Courtney Kennedy, and Aviva Shen.

1.   Theodore J. Lowi, "Globalization, War, and the Withering Away of the State," *Brown Journal of World Affairs* 17, no. 2 (Spring/Summer 2011): 243.

2.   Daniel H. Deudney, *Bounding Power* (Princeton, NJ: Princeton University Press, 2007), 1.

3.   Ibid, 3.

4.   Daniel H. Deudney, personal communication with the author.

5.   Kent V. Flannery, "The Cultural Evolution of Civilizations," *Annual Review of Ecology and Systematics* 3 (1972): 399–426.

6.   Jürgen Klüver, "The Socio-Cultural Evolution of Human Societies and Civilizations," *EMBO Reports* 9 (2008): S55–S58.

7.   Benedict Anderson. *Imagined Communities: Reflections on the Origin and Spread of Nationalism* (New York: Verso, 1983).

8.   The state function, of keeping order, was carried out by members of the community who were so designated by the leaders of the community—or by ad hoc forces put together when the occasion arose.

9.   Daniel Lerner, *The Passing of Traditional Society: Modernizing the Middle East* (New York: Macmillan, 1958).

10. Michael E. Howard, *The Franco-Prussian War: The German Invasion of France, 1870–1871* (New York: Routledge, 2001), 11.

11. Ibid, 235.

12. Allison R. Hayward, "Revisiting the Fable of Reform," *Harvard Journal on Legislation* 45 (2008): 429.

13. For further analysis of this phenomenon, see Sean Carey, "Undivided Loyalties: Is National Identity an Obstacle to European Integration?" *European Union Politics* 3 no. 4 (2002): 387–413 and Adam Luedke, "European Integration, Public Opinion and Immigration Policy: Testing the Impact of National Identity," *European Union Politics* 6, no. 1 (2005): 83–112.

14. Ruud Koopmans and Paul Statham, "Challenging the Liberal Nation-State? Postnationalism, Multiculturalism, and the Collective Claims Making of Migrants and Ethnic Minorities in Britain and Germany," *American Journal of Sociology* 105, no. 3 (November 1999): 652–96.

15. Jürgen Habermas, *The Postnational Constellation: Political Essays* (Cambridge: MIT Press, 2001), 49.

16. Mark Juergensmeyer, "Religious Nationalism and Transnationalism in a Global World."

17. Jürgen Habermas, *The Postnational Constellation: Political Essays* (Cambridge: MIT Press, 2001), 54.

18. Ibid, 81.

19. Pablo Jiménez Lobeira, "Exploring Cosmopolitan Communitarianist: EU Citizenship – An Analogical Reading," *Open Insight: Revista de Filosofía* 2, no. 2 (June 2011): 145.

20. Ibid.

21. For more, see Amitai Etizoni, *From Empire to Community* (New York: Palgrave Macmillan, 2004).

22. Ibid.
23. For the various approaches to EU governance, see James Caporaso, "The European Union and Forms of State: Westphalian, Regulatory or Post-Modern?: A Logical and Empirical Assessment" *Journal of Common Market Studies* 34, no. 1 (1996): 29–52.
24. For extensive analysis of the evolution of the EU community experiment, see Willem Maas, *Creating European Citizens* (Lanham MD: Rowman & Littlefield, 2007).
25. Council Resolution, "On a New Approach to Technical Harmonization and Standards," (May 7, 1985), http://eur-lex.europa.eu/LexUriServ/LexUriServ.do?uri=CELEX:31985Y0604(01):EN:HTML (accessed June 19, 2012).
26. "European Standards" *European Commission: Enterprise and Industry*, http://ec.europa.eu/enterprise/policies/european-standards/documents/harmonised-standards-legislation/list-references/index_en.htm (accessed June 19, 2012).
27. Business Green Staff, "Green Groups Take EU to Court over Biofuels—Again," *The Guardian* (May 26, 2011), http://www.guardian.co.uk/environment/2011/may/26/biofuels-energy (accessed June 19, 2012).
28. Gerda Falkner and Oliver Treib, "Three Worlds of Compliance or Four? The EU-15 Compared to New Member States." *Journal of Common Market Studies* 46, no. 2: 293–313 (March 2008): 297.
29. Christoph Knill, "European Politics: Impact of National Administrative Traditions," *Journal of Public Policy* 18, no. 1 (January–April 1998): 11.
30. Manuela Saragosa, "Greece Warned on False Euro Data," *BBC News* (December 1, 2004), http://news.bbc.co.uk/2/hi/business/4058327.stm (accessed June 19, 2012).
31. See note 28.
32. For an example of this argument, see Andrew Moravcsik, "In Defense of the 'Democratic Deficit': Reassessing Legitimacy in the EU," *Journal of Common Market Studies* 40, no. 4 (November 2002): 603–24.
33. Alan Bance, "The Idea of Europe: From Erasmus to ERASMUS," *Journal of European Studies* 22, no. 1 (March 1992): 1–19.
34. For additional studies of patterns in public support for the EU not discussed here, see Matthew Gabel, "Public Support for European Integration: An Empirical Test of Five Theories," *The Journal of Politics* 60, no. 2 (May 1998): 333–54 and Liesbet Hooghe and Gary Marks, "A Postfunctionalist Theory of European Integration: From Permissive Consensus to Constraining Dissensus," *British Journal of Political Science* 39 (2009): 1–23.
35. The Eurobarometer is a bi-yearly survey of public opinion by the European Commission. http://ec.europa.eu/public_opinion/index_en.htm.
36. Net public support refers to the percentage of those who say their country's membership in the EU is a good thing minus those who say it is a bad thing.
37. Richard C. Eichenberg and Russell J. Dalton, "Post-Maastricht Blues: The Transformation of Citizen Support for European Integration, 1973–2004," *Acta Politica* 42 (2007): 128–52, Figure 1.

38. Eurobarometer surveys, 2004–2010, *European Commission: Public Opinion.* http://ec.europa.eu/public_opinion/index_en.htm.

39. For a study of the financial crisis' impact on public opinion, see Felix Roth, D. Felicitas Nowak-Lehmann, and Thomas Otter, "Has the Financial Crisis Shattered Citizens' Trust in National and European Governmental Institutions? Evidence from the EU Member States, 1999–2010" *Center for European Policy Studies* no. 343 (June 2011).

40. "Speech by Jean-Claude Trichet, President of the ECB on receiving the Karlspreis 2011," delivered in Aachen, Germany (June 2, 2011), http://www.ecb.int/press/key/date/2011/html/sp110602.en.html (accessed June 19, 2012).

41. Jack Ewing and Niki Kitsantonis, "Trichet Urges Creation of Euro Oversight Panel," *The New York Times* (June 2, 2011). http://www.nytimes.com/2011/06/03/business/global/03euro.html?_r=1 (accessed June 19, 2012).

42. For additional discussion of efforts to centralize fiscal policy in the eurozone, see Emiliano Grossman and Patrick LeBlond, "European Financial Integration: Finally the Great Leap Forward?" *Journal of Common Market Studies* 49, no. 2 (2011): 413–35.

43. For further arguments that the democratic process creates legitimacy, see Renaud DeHousse, "Constitutional Reform in the European Community: Are There Alternatives to the Majoritarian Avenue?" in *The Crisis of Representation in Europe*, Jack Ernest and Shalom Hayward (1995) and Jurgen Habermas, "Why Europe Needs a Constitution," *New Left Review* 11 (September–October 2001).

44. Seymour Martin Lipset, *Political Man: The Social Basis of Politics* (New York: Doubleday, 1960), 77.

45. Jean-Marc Ferry, "Ten Normative Theses on the European Union," *Ethical Perspectives* 15 no. 4 (2008): 527–44.

46. For different approaches to the problem of consensus-building, see Justine Lacroix, "For a European Constitutional Patriotism," *Political Studies* 50 (2002): 944–58 and Joschka Fischer, "From Confederacy to Federation: Thoughts on the Finality of European Integration," delivered at the Humboldt University, Berlin, Germany (May 12, 2000).

47. Claus Offe, "Is There, or Can There Be, a 'European Society?'" in *Civil Society: Berlin Perspectives*, ed. John Keane (New York: Berhahn Books, 2007), 169–88.

48. Richard Bellamy and Dario Castiglione, "Lacroix's European Constitutional Patriotism: A Response," *Political Studies* 52 (2004): 190.

49. "General publications: young people," *European Commission website*, http://ec.europa.eu/publications/archives/young/01/index_en.htm (accessed September 30, 2011).

50. Lars-Erik Cederman, "Nationalism and Bounded Integration: What It Would Take to Construct a European Demos," *European Journal of International Relations* 7 (2001): 139–74.

51. "Presidency Conclusions," *Barcelona European Council*, in Barcelona, Spain, March 15 and 16, 2002, http://ec.europa.eu/research/era/docs/en/council-eu-30.pdf.

52. Commissioners Leonard Orban and Jan Figel, "Key Data on Teaching Languages at School in Europe," *Eurydice Network* (2008 edition).

53. Tobias Theiler, "Viewers into Europeans? How the European Union Tried to Europeanize the Audiovisual Sector, and Why It Failed," *Canadian Journal of Communication* 24, no. 4 (1999), http://www.cjc-online.ca/index. php/journal/article/view/1126/1035 (accessed June 20, 2012).

54. "Symbols of the Union to be adopted by Parliament," press release, *Committee on Constitutional Affairs,* European Parliament, http://www.europarl. europa.eu/sides/getDoc.do?language=en&type=IM-PRESS&reference=2 0080909IPR36656 (accessed September 11, 2008).

55. For proposals on how to create a climate of discourse, see Claudia Schrag, "The Quest for EU Legitimacy: How to Study a Never-Ending Crisis," *Perspectives on Europe* 40, no. 2 (Autumn 2010): 27–34.

56. For more detailed discussion of these issues, see J. H. H. Weiler, "A Constitution for Europe? Some Hard Choices," *Journal for Common Market Studies* 40, no. 4 (2002): 563–80.

57. Dean Carroll, "Strengthened Schengen to 'Europeanise' Borders," *Public Service Europe* (September 16, 2011), http://www.publicserviceeurope. com/article/864/strengthened-schengen-to-europeanise-borders (accessed June 20, 2012).

58. Martin Banks, "Mixed response to EU plans for shake-up of Schengen area," *The Parliament* (September 19, 2011), http://www.theparliament. com/latest-news/article/newsarticle/mixed-response-to-eu-plans-for-shake-up-of-schengen-area (accessed June 20, 2012).

15

The Good Life in an Austere Age

There is no way to prevent massive public anger from boiling over unless we change what we consider the good life. The West has entered an age of austerity that will extend at least until 2020. As a result, the overwhelming majority of the citizens of Europe and the United States will be highly frustrated. There is no way to restore, in the foreseeable future, the Western economies to a level at which they could again provide the kind of rising affluence most Americans and many Europeans have long learned to expect.

To prevent the mounting disenchantment that the disappointed expectations will generate from undermining civil society and possibly the democratic regime, we need a dialogue about what a good life makes, a life not centered around consumerism, the provisions for which will be in short supply. Such a recharacterization of the good life will allow people to make—to use a rather archaic turn of phrase—a silk purse out of a sow's ear; in plain English, to turn their misery into an opportunity. Public intellectuals and think tanks can launch such a dialogue. Only after it takes off and a sort of renewed, albeit much more moderate, counterculture gains in following can one expect political leaders to embrace the new characterization of the good life.

Austerity: The "Lost" Decade

There are many reasons the West must expect an age of austerity. One is the projected low growth rate of the economies involved. Another is the global shift of investments and natural resources to the East, in particular to China and India. Above all, paying down the debt will put a heavy damper on peoples' lifestyles. While once millions in the West (especially in the United States) could float a lifestyle that cost, say, 120 percent of what they earned, accumulating a debt that paid for the 20 percent "extras," now these millions will have to do with lifestyles that cost, say, 80 percent of their income, that is, live with a 33 percent cut! The rest their earnings will have to be dedicated to paying down what they owe individually and collectively. And given the size of the debt, it will take years to bring it down to sustainable levels. Thus, according to a US Congressional Budget Office projection, even if the politicians get the "grand bargain" and reduce the deficit by $2 to $4 trillion, the deficit ten years down the road is still expected to range from $9 to $11 trillion. Dedicating trillions to paying down the debt means, by definition, that there will be less money for all other pursuits. Hence, at least for the next decade, citizens of the West will have to do with less in all aspects, from buying new clothes to going on vacation. Those who hoped to buy a large house will have to make do with a smaller one (kids bunking together, rather than each commanding his own room); many will unable to buy a house but be forced to rent or stay with their folks, even after they've married. Numerous youngsters will be forced to go to nearby, less costly colleges, rather than to the universities of their choice. Many will be even forced to cut back on medication and health care interventions, especially for elder care.

Not Greece

One of the new clichés of the day is that more and more Western societies will look like Greece. Reference is not to the crushing debt and the imposed austerity that followed, but to the massive violence in the streets. However, this assumption is based on the disproven SR (stimulus/response) theory, namely, that a particular challenge will engender a predictable response. If you slap someone, he will hit you; actually, he may run or sob. Societies, too, respond to massive frustration in rather different ways. Such frustrations may engender voter support for right wing, racist, and xenophobic political parties; to wanton vandalism of the kind Paris witnessed during the 2005 riots and the recent torching of cars in Berlin; or to mass withdrawal into alcohol abuse, as we have seen in Russia. In short, in direct contrast to the SR theory, the specific response to massive frustration is unpredictable—other than that they tend to be antisocial and highly disruptive. One hence had better ask: What can be done to avoid massive frustration in the age of austerity?

Good Life in a Historical Perspective

People immersed in Western civilization find it difficult to imagine a good life that is based on profoundly different values than those they live by. However, throughout history, different conceptions of what makes a good life have arisen. For instance, for centuries the literati of imperial China came to prominence not through acquisition of wealth, but through pursuit of knowledge and cultivation of the arts. This group of scholar-bureaucrats dedicated their early lives to rigorous study, in preparation for the exams required for government service. They spent years memorizing the Confucian classics.

The literati, having passed the imperial exams, were qualified for government service, but instead elected to dedicate their lives to the arts, or retired early in order to follow artistic pursuits. They played music and composed poetry, learned calligraphy, and gathered with like-minded friends to share ideas and discuss great works of the past.

Sociologist Reinhard Bendix writes that in keeping with Confucian teachings, "the educated man must stay away from the pursuit of wealth . . . because acquisitiveness is a source of social and personal unrest. To be sure, this would not be the case if the success of economic pursuits was guaranteed, but in the absence of such a guarantee the pose and harmony of the soul are jeopardized by the risks involved . . . The cultured man strives for the perfection of the self, whereas all occupations that involve the pursuit of riches require a one-sided specialization that acts against the universality of the gentleman."[1]

During the Middle Ages, knights were expected to adhere to an exacting code of chivalry. The tenets they were expected to live by are well captured in Song of Roland, an eleventh-century poem. Throughout the poem, the worthy knight is shown to gladly and faithfully serve his liege lord, to protect the weak and the defenseless, to show proper reverence for God, to respect and honor women, to be truthful and steadfast, and to view financial reward with revulsion and disdain. In traditional Jewish communities, studying to Torah was considered the preferred way of life.

Even in recent Western history, there were significant changes in what was viewed as the good life. One such major change occurred after the end of World War II. At the time, economists held that human beings had fixed needs and that once these were satisfied, people would consume no more. Moreover, economists noted that during

World War II, the American productive capacity greatly expanded. They feared that with the end of the war, the idling of the assembly lines that produced thousands of tanks, planes, and many war-related materials would lead to massive unemployment—because there was nothing that the assembly lines could produce that people needed, given that their fixed needs were sated.

In this context, John Kenneth Galbraith came up with a solution. In his book *The Affluent Society*, he conceded that private needs were satisfied, but he pointed out that the public sector could absorb the "excess" capacity. It could be invested in public schools, parks, museums, and such.

Sociologist David Riesman published an influential essay "Affluence for what?" in which he suggested that the "surplus" be used for projects such as paying the people of New Orleans to continue to maintain their 1955 lifestyle so future generations of children could come and visit this sociological Disneyland to see what life was like in earlier ages, as they do in Williamsburg.

Instead, in the years that followed World War II, industrial corporations discovered that they could produce needs for the products they were marketing. For instance, first women and then men were taught that they smelled poor and needed to purchase deodorants. Men, who used to wear white shirts and grey flannel suits like a uniform, learned that they "had to" purchase a variety of shirts and suits, and that last year's wear was not proper in the year that followed. The same was done for cars, ties, handbags, towels and sheets, sunglasses, watches, and numerous other products. Vance Packard laid all this out in his best selling book, *The Hidden Persuaders*.

More generally, the good life was defined as having a high and rising level of consumption, in the sense that a person could never consume enough. There was always a new smartphone, flat-screen TV, or this year's fashionable towels and sheets that the person "needed."

Less often noted, probably because it is so self evident, is that paying for the high level of consumption requires hard work. Initially, mainly the husbands worked to provide for the family, leaving little time and energy for other pursuits, including being with their family, a life depicted in Arthur Miller's *Death of a Salesman*. In later decades, as more and more women joined the labor force, the incomes from husband and wife combined went to paying for the high-consumption lifestyle. More and more people began to take their work home with them, even on holidays, courtesy of Blackberries and their equivalents.

In short, there is nothing natural or unavoidable about what is considered the affluent life. It entails the kind of lifestyle that was considered worthy of contempt by previous societies and in early historical periods of the West.

Replacing versus Capping

Criticisms of consumerism, materialism, and hedonism are at least as old as capitalism. Numerous social movements and communities have pursued other forms of the good life within capitalist societies. The Shakers, who left Manchester for America in the 1770s, founded religious communities characterized by a simple ascetic lifestyle.[2] Other such communities (some secular, some religious) include the Brook Farm Institute, the Harmony Society, the Amana Colonies, and the Amish. In Britain, John Ruskin founded the Guild of St. George in the 1870s, which he intended to guide the formation of agrarian communities that would lead a simple and modest life. Jewish refugees who emigrated to Palestine starting early in the twentieth century established kibbutzim, in which the austere life was considered virtuous, consumption was held down, communal life promoted, and advancing a socialist and Zionist agenda was a primary goal of life. Numerous religious orders also started with an ascetic life.

In the 1960s, a counterculture (hippie) movement rose on both sides of the Atlantic Ocean. Its core values were anti-consumerism, communal living, equality, environmentalism, free love, and pacifism. Timothy Leary encapsulated the hippie ethos when he advised a crowd to "turn on, tune in, drop out."[3] The British iteration of the hippie movement manifested itself in London's underground culture, a "community of like-minded anti-establishment, anti-war, pro-rock 'n' roll individuals, most of whom had a common interest in recreational drugs," and many who opted out of mainstream consumerist culture.[4]

Many of these movements and communities sought to buy out of both the consumption and work system of capitalism and to form an alternative universe committed to ascetic life, while dedicating themselves to transcendental activities, including spiritual, religious, political, or social elements. They sought to replace capitalism rather than to cap it and graft on it a different society.

Most important: practically all these movements and communities failed to lay a foundation for a new contemporary society, and practically all of them either disintegrated, shriveled, or lost their main alternative features. It seems that there is something in ascetic life

223

that most people cannot abide for the longer run. It hence seems that if the current environment calls for a new attempt to form a society less centered around consumption, the endeavor will have to graft the new conception of a good life onto the old one. That is, not seek to replace consumption but to cap it and channel the resources and energy thus freed to other pursuits.

Once one approaches the subject at hand through this lens, one finds millions of people who already have moved in this direction, although they hardly are following a vision of a new good society or come together to promote it. These millions include a large number of senior citizens who retired before they had to, to allow more time for alternative pursuits. These seniors typically lead what might be called a comfortable life from a materialistic viewpoint, but spend more of their time socializing and engaged in politically active, spiritual, and cultural pursuits, rather than continuing to be employed and consume full throttle. (Note: by definition those who retire early earn less than those who continue to work, and hence either consume less or leave less of a bequest, which limits the consumption of their families.) The same holds for the millions of women who decide not to return to work after they have children, at least until they reach school age, and many for much longer, although this means that they will have to consume less.

As these two large groups, as well as those who drop out of high-earning pursuits to follow a more "meaningful" life—say, as teachers for those less privileged—illustrate, one need not lead a life of sack cloth and ashes, of deprivation and sacrifice. One can work enough to ensure one's basic creature comforts but dedicate the rest of one's resources, energy, and aspirations to goods other than consuming more, and one can find more satisfaction in alternative pursuits to working long and hard to pay for consumption above and beyond what is needed for a comfortable life. The fact that millions have long persisted in capping their consumption and finding other sources of contentment suggests that such capping is much more sustainable than the ascetic life of the social movements and communities that sought to replace capitalism altogether.

The Main Alternatives

Consumerism has long been shown to not provide contentment (or happiness). The data, as most social science data, are complex. Not all the correlations point to the same results.[5] However, overviews of the data have repeatedly concluded that after income rises above a given level, additional income buys little happiness. Japan is an often-cited example. Between 1962 and 1987, Japan's economy more than tripled its GNP per capita. Yet Japan's overall happiness remained constant over that period.[6] In 1970, Americans' average income could buy over 60 percent more than it could in the 1940s, yet the average happiness had not increased.[7]

At high income and consumption levels, additional consumption (and the work required to afford it) lead people to deny themselves alternative pursuits. It seems a form of fixation. It has been referred to as a hedonic treadmill.

These data ought now to be reexamined, as many middle and working class people face not so much giving up additional income (and obsessive consumption) in order to free time and resources for alternative pursuits—but are forced to give up the dream of an affluent life based on high and rising levels of consumption. Can they come to see such capping not as a source of frustration but as an opportunity to reexamine their priorities? The analogue is to a worker who finds that he is furloughed one day each week and hence works only four days, but finds that the extra day offers a welcome opportunity to spend more time with the kids or going fishing—not to someone who lost his job.

Not Status Acceptance

I must digress to stress that the thesis that people will be better off if they cap their consumption and dedicate the freed energy and resources to alternative pursuits should not be interpreted as suggesting that people should engage in what sociologists call status acceptance. Status acceptance is the argument that whatever your position in society is, you should accept it as your place in life and not seek upward mobility. Such precepts find their roots in the philosopher who dealt most explicitly with the subject at hand, what a good life makes, and gave us the felicitous term "flourishing," Aristotle. He did not mean by it, as modern thought might, that people live up to their fullest human potential—but that people will find their basic contentment if they labor to carry out best whatever social role they find has been cast their way. The servant serves well, the lord leads well, and so on. (Aristotelian philosophy is much more nuanced and complex than the preceding lines suggest, but this need not detain us here.) The Catholic Church made this precept one of its central tenants during the Middle Ages. And status acceptance is built into the Indian caste system.

The precept here advanced is that those whose basic needs are not well sated are indeed fully entitled to higher levels of consumption. Capping is called for only once these needs are satisfied. To highlight the point, it is useful to draw on Abraham Maslow's hierarchy of human needs. At the bottom of this hierarchy are basic creature comforts; once these are sated, more satisfaction is drawn from affection, self-esteem, and beyond that, from self-actualization. When the acquisition of goods and services is used to satisfy the higher needs, consumption turns into consumerism—a social disease. The transition is empirically indicated by the level at which additional income generates little or no additional contentment. In short, the thesis here outlined is not a suggestion that unemployment or low wages are legitimate, but that working fewer hours and hence consuming less can be viewed—at relatively high level of income—as an opening for reexamining one's lifestyle and the beginning of a quest for alternative sources of contentment.

The Alternatives

The main alternative pursuits that generate much more contentment than consumerism are very familiar and hence visited next very briefly.

Social activities: Individuals who spend more time with their families, friends, in social clubs, and in communal activities—those who do not bowl alone—are more content than those less socially active. An analysis of nearly 150 studies found that individuals with stronger social relationships exhibited a 50 percent increased likelihood of survival.[8] Robert E. Lane writes, "Most studies agree that a satisfying family life is the most important contributor to well-being . . . The joys of friendship often rank second."[9] Robert Putnam presents a mountain of data to the same effect.

Spiritual and religious activities: Individuals who spend more time living up to the commands of their religion (attending church, praying, fasting, making pilgrimages, and doing charity work), studying for studying's sake rather than as a vocation, or engaged in cultural activities such as painting or making music, not to serve a market but for the intrinsic enjoyment, are more content than those less so engaged. For example, studies have demonstrated that people with a deep religious faith are healthier, live longer, and have lower rates of divorce, crime, and suicide.[10] To cite but one study, Robert Putnam and David Campbell found that the difference in happiness between an American who goes to church once a week and someone who does not attend church was "slightly larger than the difference between someone who earns $10,000 a year and his demographic twin who earns $100,000 a year."[11]

Community involvement: Researchers who examined the effect of community involvement found a strong correlation with happiness. One study, which evaluated survey data from forty-nine countries, found that membership in (non-church) organizations has a significant positive correlation with happiness.[12] Derek Bok notes, "Some researchers have found that merely attending monthly club meetings or volunteering once a month is associated with a change in well-being equivalent to a doubling of income."[13] Other studies have found that individuals who devote substantial amounts of time to volunteer work have greater life satisfaction.[14]

There is no need for more documentation here as these studies are familiar and readily accessible. They suggest that capped consumption combined with greater involvement in one alternative pursuit or another (or a combination of several) leads to more contentment than consumerism. The challenge we face is to share these findings and their implications for those dragged into an age of austerity.

Two Bonuses

A society in which capping consumption is the norm and majorities find much of their contentment in transcendental pursuits will gain two bonuses of much import. One is obvious, and one much less so.

Obviously, a good life that combines a cap on consumption and work with dedication to transcendental pursuits is much less taxing on the environment than consumerism and the level of work that paying for it requires. This is the case because transcendental activities require relatively few scarce resources, fossil fuels, or other sources of physical energy. Social activities (such as spending more time with one's children) require time and personal energy but not large material or financial outlays. (Often those who spend large amounts of money on their kids' toys or entertainment bond less with them than those whose relations are much less mediated by objects.) The same holds for cultural and spiritual activities such as prayer, meditation, enjoying and making music, art, sports, and adult education. True, consumerism has turned many of these pursuits into expensive endeavors. However, one can break out of this mentality and find that it is possible to engage in most transcendental activities quite profoundly using a moderate amount of goods and services. One does not need designer clothes to enjoy the sunset or shoes with fancy labels to benefit from a hike. Chess played with plastic pieces is the same game as the one played with carved mahogany or marble pieces. And the Lord does not listen better to prayers read from a leather-bound Bible than those read from a plain one, printed on recycled paper. In short, the transcendental society is much more sustainable than consumeristic capitalism.

Much less obvious are the ways the transcendental society serves social justice. Social justice entails transferring wealth from those disproportionally endowed to those who are underprivileged. A major reason such reallocation of wealth has been surprisingly limited in free societies is that those who command the "extra" assets tend also to be those who are politically powerful. Promoting social justice by organizing those with less and forcing those in power to yield has had limited success in democratic countries and led to massive bloodshed in others. Hence the question: Are there ways to reduce the resistance of the elites to the reallocation of wealth?

Recharacterization of the good life along the lines here indicated helps, because it leads those with high income to derive a major source of contentment not from acquiring additional goods and services but from transcendental activities, activities that are neither labor- nor capital-intensive and, hence, do not require great amounts of assets. There are numerous accounts of rich people who have given substantial parts of their wealth to what they consider good causes. More generally, those who have strong religious beliefs (note that all major religions make giving to the poor a major commandment) and those who subscribe to social liberalism or democratic socialist ideals of social justice and opposition to inequality tend to share willingly with those less endowed. Hence, the more transcendental ideals are accepted, the greater the number of affluent and powerful people who will have less reason to oppose reallocation of wealth, and the more who may even find some source of contentment in supporting it.

One surely can envision other characterizations of a good life. However, the dialogue about what such a society will look like and what its norms and projects can be should not be delayed. The West would greatly benefit if the coming austerity were viewed not as frustrating the affluent life but as an opportunity to reexamine life's priorities, and to see if we can do so without seeking to deny that we all seek basic creature comforts. Such recharacterization of the good life will not only spare Western societies major social and political upheaval but also make them into societies whose members can flourish.

Notes

1. Reinhard Bendix, "Max Weber: An Intellectual Portrait," 124.
2. "The Shakers," *National Park Service*, http://www.nps.gov/nr/travel/shaker/shakers.htm.
3. "Summer of Love Program Transcript," *PBS*, http://www.pbs.org/wgbh/amex/love/filmmore/pt.html (accessed January 26, 2012).
4. Barry Miles, "Spirit of the Underground: the 60s rebel," *Guardian* (January 30, 2011). http://www.guardian.co.uk/culture/2011/jan/30/underground-arts-60s-rebel-counterculture (accessed January 26, 2012).
5. See Ruut Veenhoven and Michael Hagerty, "Rising Happiness in Nations 1946–2004," *Social Indicators Research* 79, no. 3 (2006): 421–36; Betsey Stevenson and Justin Wolfers, "Economic Growth and Subjective Well-Being: Reassessing the Easterlin Paradox," *Brookings Papers on Economic Activity* 69 (Spring 2008): 1–87.
6. Richard Easterlin, "Diminishing Marginal Utility of Income? Caveat Emptor," *Social Indicators Research* (2005).
7. Richard Easterlin, "Does Money Buy Happiness," *The Public Interest* 30 (Winter 1973).
8. Julianne Holt-Lunstad, Timothy B. Smith, and J. Bradley Layton, "Social Relationships and Mortality Risk: A Meta-analytic Review," *PLoS Medicine* 7, no. 7 (July 2010): 1–20.
9. Robert E. Lane, "Does Money Buy Happiness?" *Public Interest* (Fall 1993): 58.
10. Derek Bok, *The Politics of Happiness: What Government Can Learn from the New Research on Well Being* (Princeton, NJ: Princeton University Press, 2010): 21–22.
11. Robert D. Putnam and David E. Campbell, *American Grace: How Religion Divides and Unites Us* (New York: Simon and Schuster, 2010), 491.
12. John F. Helliwell, "Well-Being, Social Capital and Public Policy: What's New?" *Economic Modelling* 20, no. 2 (March 2003): 331–60.
13. Bok, *The Politics of Happiness*, 20.
14. Ibid., 22.

Part VII

When Are Armed Humanitarian Interventions Justified?

16

The Lessons of Libya

What a difference six months makes. Early in 2011, an overwhelming majority of American policymakers, opinion makers, and the public were strongly opposed to more military entanglements overseas, particularly a third war in a Muslim country. And there was a strong sense that given our overstretched position due to the war in Afghanistan, continued exposure in Iraq, and—above all—severe economic challenges at home, the time had come to reduce US commitments overseas. In June 2011, when announcing the withdrawal of troops from Afghanistan, President Obama put it as follows: "America, it is time to focus on nation-building here at home."[1] Regarding involvement in Libya, then-Secretary of Defense Robert Gates stated in March 2011: "My view would be, if there is going to be that kind of assistance [providing arms] to the opposition, there are plenty of sources for it other than the United States."[2] Admiral Mike Mullen raised questions about a Libyan involvement, stating in a March 2011 Senate hearing that a no-flight zone would be "an extraordinarily complex operation to set up."[3]

Six months later, in September 2011, as the military campaign in Libya was winding down, it was widely hailed as a great success. As Helene Cooper and Steven Lee Myers wrote in *The New York Times*, while "it would be premature to call the war in Libya a complete success for United States interests . . . the arrival of victorious rebels on the shores of Tripoli last week gave President Obama's senior advisers a chance to claim a key victory."[4] NATO Secretary General Anders Fogh Rasmussen stated in early September, "We can already draw the first lessons from the operation, and most of them are positive."[5] In a meeting on September 20 with Libya's new interim leader, Mustafa Abdul-Jalil, President Obama said, "Today, the Libyan people are writing a new chapter in the life of their nation. After four decades of darkness, they can walk the streets, free from a tyrant."[6]

Moreover, Libya was held as model for more such interventions. Cooper and Myers wrote, "The conflict may, in some important ways, become a model for how the United States wields force in other countries where its interests are threatened."[7] Philip Gordon, Assistant Secretary of State for European Affairs, opined that the Libyan operation was "in many ways a model on how the United States can lead the way that allows allies to support."[8] Leon Panetta, current Secretary of Defense, said that the campaign was "a good indication of the kind of partnership and alliances that we need to have for the future if we are going to deal with the threats that we confront in today's world."[9]

As international attention turned to the massacres in Syria, the application of the "Libyan model" was discussed. French President Nicolas Sarkozy pointedly said on his visit to post-Qaddafi Libya, "I hope that one day young Syrians can be given the opportunity that young Libyans are now being given."[10] Syrian activists called for the creation of a no-fly zone over Syria, similar to that imposed over Libya.[11] An August *New York Times* article noted, "The very fact that the administration has joined with the same allies that it banded with on Libya to call for Mr. Assad to go and to impose penalties on his regime could take the United States one step closer to applying the Libya model toward Syria."[12]

There is little doubt in my mind that as time passes, the assessment of the Libya campaign will be recast—and more than once. Nevertheless, one can draw already several rather important lessons from the campaign.

Lesson 1: Advantage, Boots off the Ground

The Libya campaign showed that a strategy previously advocated for in other countries, particularly Afghanistan, can work effectively. The strategy, advocated by Vice President Biden and John Mearsheimer, a political scientist at the University of Chicago,[13] entails using airpower, drones, Special Forces, the CIA, and, crucially, working with native forces rather than committing American and allied conventional ground forces. It is sometimes referred to as offshoring, although calling it Boots off the Ground (BOG) may better capture its essence.

BOG was the way in which the campaign was carried out in Kosovo, which was won with no allied combat fatalities and at low costs. It was also the way the Taliban were overthrown in Afghanistan in 2001, in a campaign that relied largely on the forces of local tribes, such as the Northern Alliance of Tajiks, Pashtuns, Hazaras, and Uzbeks, among others—although some conventional backup was committed. The United States "[took] full advantage of their air superiority and the [Taliban's] lack of sophisticated air defenses . . . using a wide and deadly repertoire: B-52's, B-1's, Navy jets, Predator drones, and AC-130 Special Operations gunships."[14] And it worked in Libya, with minimal casualties for NATO, at relatively low costs, and with fighting mainly carried out by Libyans seeking a new life for themselves.

Aside from the very important but obvious advantages of low casualties and low costs, BOG has one major merit that does not immediately jump out. It is much less alienating to the population and makes disengagement—the exit strategy—much easier to achieve.

People of most nations (and certainly many in the Middle East) resent the presence of foreign troops within their borders. Thus, even many of the Iraqis and Afghans who view the American military presence as beneficial to their security (or pocketbook) often seem troubled both by US combat methods (which they see as yielding too many civilian casualties) and by what they deem freewheeling personal conduct (including the presence of female soldiers). Above all, native people consider foreign troops a violation of their sovereignty and a sign of their underlying weakness. They cannot wait for the day when these troops can be sent home.

The Libyan rebels made it clear from the beginning that although they sought NATO support, they did not want foreign boots on the ground. By avoiding such an engagement, this whole issue of a perceived threat to sovereignty was largely mitigated.

Similarly avoided were the political traps that await an administration seeking to disengage from a military campaign but forever fearing that the opposition will criticize it for being weak on defense if it leaves prematurely, as we have seen in Iraq and Afghanistan. This whole issue is avoided in Libya; as the military campaign ends—disengagement is not much of a problem.

Can BOG be applied elsewhere? Is it the new model for armed interventions overseas? One should be leery of generalizations. Obviously, what can be made to work in Libya cannot be employed against North Korea. Arguably, it is already being employed in Yemen, but it would not work against a well-entrenched Hezbollah.

Also, questions have been raised whether BOG can be made to work in land-locked nations like Afghanistan. Because there is no shoreline, when local forces or our Special Forces need, say, airpower backup, the planes have to come from aircraft carriers a thousand miles away—which will hinder the BOG effort. The same holds for collecting human intelligence when one has no local bases. Whether these weaknesses are sufficient to nullify the merits of the strategy, especially in view of the high casualties and costs of a long war that draws on conventional forces, is a question on which reasonable people can differ. One lesson, though, stands out: when BOG can be employed, it seems to compare rather favorably to conventional invasions and occupations.

Lesson 2: Avoid Mission Creep

Assessments of various military campaigns obviously depend on what one assumes their goals were. Thus, if one looks at Operation Desert Storm that pushed Saddam out of Kuwait in 1991, one will rank it as very successful if one assumes its goal was to reaffirm that the Westphalian norm that it lies at the very foundation of the prevailing world order that no nation may use its armed forces to invade another nation, and—that nations in violation of this long-established norm will be pushed back and "punished." However, one would rank Desert Storm less well if one assumes its goal was to force a regime change in Iraq, to topple Saddam, and to protect the Shi'a who were rising up against him.

The American tendency is to allow campaigns with originally limited goals to morph into campaigns that have more expansive goals—turning successful drives into questionable and contested operations. Soon campaigns that might well be judged as successful by their original purpose are found to be lacking by the expanded mission statement. The failures or defects are thus as much a consequence of mission creep as of inherent difficulties.

A key example is the war in Afghanistan. In March 2009, President Obama narrowly defined the goals of the war in Afghanistan as to "disrupt, dismantle and defeat al-Qaeda."[15] Later, in October 2009, the Obama administration reiterated the plan to "destroy [al-Qaeda's] leadership, its infrastructure, and its capability."[16] This definition reflected a scaling back of a much more ambitious goal set by President Bush, who sought "to build a flourishing democracy as an alternative to a hateful ideology."[17] However, over time, a variety of forces led the Obama administration to re-expand the goals of the war in Afghanistan to include defeating the Taliban (even after very few al-Qaeda were left in Afghanistan, and much larger numbers were threatening

US interests in other places) and helping to establish a stable Afghan government.

This added goal of nation-building was outlined by Obama in May 2010, which included the intent to: "strengthen Afghanistan's capacity to provide for their own security" and "a civilian effort to promote good governance and development; and regional cooperation."[18] Secretary of State Clinton offered a more expansive view: "I would imagine, if things go well [under President Karzai], that we would be helping with the education and health systems and agriculture productivity long after the military presence had either diminished or disappeared."[19]

The forces that push for this mission creep deserve a brief review, because we shall see them in play in Libya and elsewhere. In part, they are idealistic and normative. Americans hold that all people, if free to choose, would "naturally" prefer a free society—one based on the rule of law, respecting rights, and the democratic form of government. Indeed, the neo-conservatives argued after the collapse of the Soviet Union that the whole world is marching toward "the end of history," a state in which all governments would be democratic. They held—and President Bush is reported to have agreed with them —that in the few situations in which nations were held back, the United States had a duty to help them "catch up with history." Or, in plain English: to force a regime change. This is one of the reasons given for US armed intervention in Iraq in 2003. At the same time, liberals strongly hold that the United States should use its power to protect people from humanitarian abuse and thus support more armed interventions on this ground. For instance, Special Assistant to the President Samantha Power, who was reported to have played a key role in convincing President Obama to engage in Libya, authored an influential book, *The Problem from Hell*, in which she chastised the West for not using force to stop genocide in places such as Cambodia, the Congo, and Rwanda.

In addition, a military doctrine was developed that held that one cannot achieve the narrow security goals (e.g., defeating al-Qaeda) without also engaging in nation-building. It was suggested that one cannot win wars against insurgencies merely by use of military force, but that we had to win the hearts and minds of the population by doing good for them (e.g., building roads, clinics, schools, etc.) and by shoring up our local partner; to show that to support, say, the Karzai administration would lead to a stable, democratic government and at least a reasonable level of integrity. The record of this doctrine (referred to as counterinsurgency or COIN in contrast to counterterrorism or CT), which entailed a very considerable mission expansion, is subject to considerable difference of opinion. However, there is no denying that while the military victories in Iraq and Afghanistan came swiftly, at low human and economic costs, the main casualties and difficulties are still being faced in the nation-building phase, where the outcomes are far from clear.

All these considerations have played and continue to play a role in Libya. Initially, the goal of the operation was strictly delineated as a humanitarian one: to prevent Qaddafi from carrying out his threat, issued in February 2011, to "attack [the rebels] in their lairs" and "cleanse Libya house by house."[20] He repeated his intent by saying, "The moment of truth has come. There will be no mercy. Our troops will be coming to Benghazi tonight."[21] In March, President Obama stated, "We are not going to use force to go beyond a well-defined goal—specifically, the protection of civilians in Libya."[22] True, even at that point, the need to also achieve a regime change was mentioned, but it was explicitly ruled out as a goal of the military operation. It was going to go by other means; as Obama put it, "In the coming weeks, we will continue to help the Libyan people with humanitarian and economic assistance so that they can fulfill their aspirations peacefully."[23]

Very quickly, the goal of the Libyan mission expanded. In April 2011, Obama, French President Nicolas Sarkozy, and British Prime Minister David Cameron published a joint pledge asserting that, in order to achieve the humanitarian goal, regime change must take place. They stated, "Qaddafi must go, and go for good" so that "a genuine transition from dictatorship to an inclusive constitutional process can really begin, led by a new generation of leaders."[24] Moreover, they added that NATO would use its force to promote these goals: "So long as Qaddafi is in power, NATO must maintain its operations so that civilians remain protected and the pressure on the regime builds."[25]

The issue came to a head when, in May, Qaddafi offered a ceasefire with the rebels that would have ended the humanitarian crisis and would have led to negotiations between the rebels and the Qaddafi regime. (The ceasefire could have been enforced either by the threat to resume NATO bombing if it was not honored or by putting UN peacekeeping forces between the parties.) NATO, however, rejected the offer out of hand; Qaddafi—and his regime—had to go. NATO proceeded to then bomb not only military targets but also Qaddafi's residential compound in Tripoli,[26] reportedly killing his son and three grandchildren.[27]

As of September 2011, both goals of averting a humanitarian crisis and toppling the Qaddafi regime had been achieved, and hence one might conclude that, at least in this case, the mission creep had no deleterious effects; on the contrary, two goals were served for the price of one.

It is here that the question of what follows becomes crucial for a fuller assessment of the Libya campaign. There are strong sociological reasons to expect that it is unlikely that a stable democratic government will emerge in Libya. These include the absence of most institutions of a civil society after a decade of tyranny, the thin middle class, and the lack of democratic tradition. (For more indicators, see below discussion of a Marshall Plan.) Hence if, over the next years, we witness in Libya some kind of a new military authoritarian government—whether or not it has a democratic façade and holds doctored elections—we shall reevaluate the mission expansion rather differently than if a stable democratic regime arises.

The same holds for the level of civil strife and number of casualties that will follow. Libya, like many other societies, is a tribal amalgam. If these tribes hold together to support a new government and solve their differences through negotiations, the 2011 NATO involvement will be deemed a great success. If what we witness next involves the kind of massive civilian casualties we have seen in Iraq, where more than 100,000 are estimated to have died between 2004 and 2009[28] and inter-group violence continues, the assessments will be less rosy. Indeed, despite assurances by Libyan rebel leader Abdel Hakim Belhaj that the new leadership is "building a democratic and modern civil state with rules, governed with justice and equality,"[29] there is room for concern. An Amnesty International report[30] released in September found that the Libyan rebels have committed war crimes ranging from torture to revenge killings of Qaddafi loyalists. Furthermore, they have stirred up racism against many sub-Saharan Africans, who have been attacked, jailed, and abused under the new government.

As early as July, Human Rights Watch reported that rebel forces had "burned some homes, looted from hospitals, homes and shops, and beaten some individuals alleged to have supported government forces."[31] An Amnesty International report[32] released in September found evidence that the Libyan rebels have committed extensive war crimes ranging from torture to revenge killings of Qaddafi loyalists.

The report finds that, since February, "hundreds of people have been taken from their homes, at work, at checkpoints, or simply from the streets."[33] These detainees were beaten, tortured with electric shocks, and sometimes shot or lynched immediately. Furthermore, the rebels have stirred up racism against many sub-Saharan Africans, who have been attacked, jailed, and abused under the new government. Entire villages of black Libyans have been emptied and deemed "closed military areas" by rebel forces.[34] Black African women have also alleged mass rape by rebel forces in the refugee camps outside of Tripoli.[35]

Reports of internal conflicts and lawlessness are also cause for concern; in July, the rebel military chief, Abdel Fattah Younes, was assassinated by allied militia, who had been sent to arrest him for possible contact with Qaddafi.[36] These militias have also looted ammunition warehouses abandoned by Qaddafi's forces and are amassing weapons that are reported to have gone to al-Qaeda factions in North Africa and other terrorist groups outside the Libyan borders.[37]

Lesson 3: Nation-Building Is a Bridge Too Far

The ink has hardly dried on September's rosy assessments of the Libyan NATO operation, and we already hear a chorus of voices that hold that "we" (the West, the United States, or the UN) should help the Libyan people build what we consider the right kind of government, economy, and society. Moreover, the nation builders seem to seek to repeat the mistakes the United States made in Iraq in trying to recast everything, which resulted in scores of unfinished and failed projects. Thus, in a "Friends of Libya" session at the UN on September 20, more than sixty government representatives "offered assistance in areas including the judiciary, education, and constitutional law."[38] President Obama promised to build new partnerships with Libya to encourage the country's "extraordinary potential" for democratic reform, claiming that "we all know what's needed . . . New laws and a constitution that uphold the rule of law . . . And, for the first time in Libyan history, free and fair elections."[39]

Others seek to include all the Arab Spring nations, or better yet—the entire Middle East. MP and former Foreign Office Minister David Davis calls for a British Marshall Plan in the Middle East, arguing that such a plan is "one of the best ways to consolidate and support the Arab Spring as it stands, [and] could spark reform in other Arab and Gulf countries too."[40] Secretary of State Hillary Clinton believes that "as the Arab Spring unfolds across the Middle East and North Africa, some principles of the [Marshall] plan apply again, especially in Egypt and Tunisia."[41] Senator John Kerry argues that "we are again in desperate need of a Marshall Plan for the Middle East."[42] Senator John McCain also favors such a plan.[43]

Although the Marshall Plan did not cover Japan, the great success of the United States and its allies in introducing democracy and a free economy into it and Germany are usually cited as proof of what can be done. In effect, the opposite is true. What was possible in these countries at the end of World War II in fact highlights what cannot be done now in the Middle East, and particularly not in Libya.

The most important difference concerns security. Germany and Japan had surrendered after defeat in a war. Political and economic developments took place only after hostilities ceased. There were no terrorists, no insurgencies, no car bombs—things which Western forces are now sure to encounter if they sought to play a similar role in, say, Libya, Sudan, Somalia, or Yemen.

Moreover, following the experiences in Iraq and Afghanistan, few would even consider the proposition that the West should occupy more lands in the Middle East and manage their transformations. Thus, while the German and Japanese reconstructions were very much hands-on projects, those now being considered amount to long-distance social engineering, with the West providing funds and advice while the execution is left largely to the less prepared locals.

One further notes that Germany and Japan were strong nation-states before World War II. Citizens strongly identified with the nation and were willing to make major sacrifices for the "fatherland." In contrast, the first loyalty of many citizens of Middle Eastern nations, which are tribal societies cobbled together by Western countries, is to their individual ethnic or confessional group. They tend to look at the nation as a source of spoils for their tribe and fight for their share, rather than make sacrifices for the national whole. Deep hostilities, such as those between the Shi'a and the Sunnis, among the Pashtun, Tajik, Hazara, and Kochi, and among various tribes in other nations, either gridlock the national polities (e.g., in Iraq and Afghanistan), lead to large-scale violence (e.g., in Yemen and Sudan), result in massive oppression and armed conflicts (e.g., in Libya and Syria), or otherwise hinder political and economic development.

Max Weber established the importance of values when he demonstrated that Protestants were more imbued than Catholics with the values that lead to hard work and high levels of saving, essential for

241

the rise of modern capitalist economies. For decades, development in Catholic countries (such as those in Southern Europe and Latin America) lagged behind the Protestant Anglo-Saxon nations and those in Northwest Europe. Similarly, Weber pointed to the difference between Confucian and Muslim values, in effect predicting the striking difference between the very high rates of development of the South Asian "tigers"—China, Hong Kong, Taiwan, Singapore, and South Korea—and low rates of Muslim states, especially those that adhere strictly to Sharia. The argument is not that Muslim countries cannot develop into Western-like nations, but merely that it will entail considerable cultural transformation.

One must also take into account that Germany and Japan were developed nations before World War II, with strong industrial bases, strong infrastructures, educated populations, and strong support for science and technology, corporations, business, and commerce. Hence, they had mainly to be reconstructed. In contrast, many Middle Eastern states lack many of these assets, institutions, and traditions, and therefore cannot be reconstructed but must be constructed in the first place—a much taller order. This is most obvious in Afghanistan, Yemen, Sudan, and Libya. Other nations, such as Tunisia, Pakistan, Morocco, Syria, and Egypt have better prepared populations and resources, but still score poorly compared to Germany and Japan.

Finally, the advocates of a Marshall Plan for the Middle East disregard the small matter of costs. During the Marshall Plan's first year, it demanded 13 percent of the US budget. Today foreign aid commands less than 1 percent, and given the currently grave budgetary concerns, America and its NATO allies are much more inclined to cut such overseas expenditure than to increase them.

Both the West and the Middle East—in particular, countries that have the sociological makeup of Libya—will be better off if we make it clear that the nations of the region will have to rely primarily on themselves (and maybe on their oil-rich brethren) to modernize their economies and build their polities. Arguing otherwise merely leads to disappointment and disillusion—on both sides of the ocean.

Lesson 4: Leading from Behind—But Who Is on First?

The campaign in Libya was structured differently from most, if not all, of its predecessors in which NATO (or NATO members) was involved, in that the United States deliberately did not play the main role.

French President Sarkozy was the first head of state to demand armed intervention in Libya, initially in the form of imposing a no-fly zone. He was soon joined by British Prime Minister David Cameron,[44] and only then did the United States add its support. Although the United States did launch 97 percent of the Tomahawk cruise missiles against Qaddafi's air forces at the beginning of the mission,[45] NATO forces took over relatively quickly. NATO Secretary General Rasmussen pointed out that "European powers carried out the vast majority of the air strikes and only one of the 18 ships enforcing the arms embargo was American."[46] France was the largest contributor, with French planes flying about a third of all sorties.[47]

This approach reflected President Obama's longstanding position that the United States should consult and cooperate with allies to share the burden of such operations and not act unilaterally or even as the leader of the pack (in contrast to President Bush's approach). As David Rothkopf, a former national security official under Clinton, put it: "We need to give the Obama administration credit for finding a way, taking the long view, resisting the pressure to do too much too soon, resisting the old approaches which would have had the U.S. far more involved than it could have or should have . . ."[48] Critics of this approach considered it a reflection of weakness. "Leading from behind" became a much-mocked phrase. In March 2011, Mitt Romney stated: "In the past, America has been feared sometimes, has been respected, but today, that America is seen as being weak," offering as evidence the fact that "we're following France into Libya."[49] Even in the more recent wake of praise for the operation, Senators John McCain and Lindsey Graham expressed "regret that this success was so long in coming due to the failure of the United States to employ the full weight of our air power."[50]

As I see it, there is room for legitimate disagreement about the best ways to organize such campaigns and what the US role in them should be—however, both those who favor leading from behind and those who oppose it should realize that the Libya campaign does not favor either of these positions. The main reason it revealed for the whole world to see that there was no there there. NATO—the grand military machine that was initially designed to able to thwart the attacks of the USSR—turned out to be a very weak body.

NATO has always had some difficulty in acting in unison, as there are often considerable differences among the members about who to fight, how to fight, and for what to fight. Thus, many nations have in the past introduced caveats restricting how and where their troops may be deployed, essentially allowing nations to opt out of NATO operations. This is the case in Afghanistan, where German, French, and Italian troops have been restricted to non-combat areas.[51] Caveats also hindered the KFOR response in Kosovo in 2004, when German troops refused orders to join other elements in controlling the riots.[52] An article in *The Economist* observes in Libya a "worrying trend of member countries taking an increasingly a la carte approach to their alliance responsibilities."[53] It elaborates:

> The initial ambivalence of Muslim Turkey was to a degree understandable. But Germany marked a new low when it followed its refusal to back Resolution 1973 with a withdrawal of all practical support for NATO's mission, even jeopardising the early stages of the campaign by pulling its crews out of the alliance's airborne warning and control aircraft. . . . Poland also declined to join the mission, adding insult to injury by describing NATO's intervention as motivated by oil.
>
> Out of 28 NATO members, 14 committed military assets, but just eight were prepared to fly ground-attack sorties. They were France, Britain, America (albeit on a very limited scale after the opening onslaught on the regime's air defences), Belgium, Denmark, Norway, Italy and Canada. Only France and Britain deployed attack helicopters.[54]

Moreover, "NATO's European members were highly dependent on American military help to keep going. The U.S. provided about three-quarters of the aerial tankers without which the strike fighters, mostly flying from bases in Italy, could not have reached their targets. America also provided most of the cruise missiles that degraded Colonel Qaddafi's air defenses sufficiently for the no-fly zone to be established. When stocks of precision-guided weapons held by European forces ran low after only a couple of months, the U.S. had to provide fresh supplies. And, few attack missions were flown without American electronic warfare aircraft operating above as 'guardian angels.'"[55]

Rasmussen admitted, "The operation has made visible that the Europeans lack a number of essential military capabilities."[56] In June, Former Defense Secretary Gates criticized the lack of investment by European members in "intelligence, surveillance and reconnaissance assets" which he believes hindered the Libya campaign. He warned,

"The most advanced fighter aircraft are little use if allies do not have the means to identify, process and strike targets as part of an integrated campaign." In short, he concluded, NATO European allies are so weak they face "collective military irrelevance."[57]

In Conclusion

The military success of the 2011 NATO-led camping in Libya indicates that even in the current context of economic challenges, calls for re-entrenchment, and concerns that US forces are overstretched overseas, humanitarian missions can be effectively carried out. The strategy of Boots off the Ground has many advantages—when it can be employed. It results not only in comparatively low casualties and low costs but it is also less alienating to the local population and makes disengagement much easier. While the United States succeeded in the Libya to let the European members of NATO carry a good part of the burden, the European nations' low level of resources and disagreements with one another makes one wonder if such "leading from behind" could work in dealing with more demanding challenges, say, with Iran.

One must guard against the strong tendency of humanitarian missions (which set out to protect civilians) to turn into missions that seek forced regime change, which lead to much higher levels of casualties. Moreover, it is far from clear what will be the nature of the new regime in Libya, for which NATO has opened the door by destroying the old leadership structure. Wrecking a tyranny does not automatically make for a democratic government. Above all, those who seek to engage in nation-building should carefully examine the conditions under which it succeeds, and avoid nation-building or minimize their involvement when the conditions are as unfavorable as they are in Libya and several other parts of the Middle East.

Notes

1. Barack Obama, "Remarks by the President on the Way Forward in Afghanistan," Washington, DC (June 22, 2011), http://www.whitehouse.gov/the-press-office/2011/06/22/remarks-president-way-forward-afghanistan.
2. Donna Cassata and Lolita Baldor, "Gates Calls For Limited Role Aiding Libyan Rebels," *Associated Press* (March 31, 2011), http://abcnews.go.com/US/wireStory?id=13264595.
3. Elisabeth Bumiller, "Gates Plays Down Idea of U.S. Force in Libya," *The New York Times* (March 1, 2011): A11. http://www.nytimes.com/2011/03/02/world/africa/02military.html.

4.   Helene Cooper and Steven Lee Myers, "U.S. Tactics in Libya May Be a Model for Use of Force," *The New York Times* (August 28, 2011): A9. http://www.nytimes.com/2011/08/29/world/africa/29diplo.html.

5.   Anders Fogh, "Libya Operation Coming to an End," *Secretary General's Video Blog* (September 5, 2011). http://andersfogh.info/2011/09/05/libya-operation-coming-to-an-end.

6.   Michele Kelemen, "President Obama Praises Libya's Political Transition," *NPR* (September 20, 2011), http://www.npr.org/2011/09/20/140642290/president-obama-praises-libyas-political-transition.

7.   See note 4.

8.   "NATO in Libya a 'model' for Euro-US cooperation: US official," *The Telegraph* (September 15, 2011). http://www.telegraph.co.uk/news/worldnews/africaandindianocean/libya/8764812/NATO-in-Libya-a-model-for-Euro-US-cooperation-US-official.html.

9.   Robert Marquand, "Could NATO's Libya Mission Be Its Last Hurrah?" *The Christian Science Monitor* (August 24, 2011). http://www.csmonitor.com/World/Europe/2011/0824/Could-NATO-s-Libya-mission-be-its-last-hurrah.

10. Patrick McDonnell, "David Cameron, Nicolas Sarkozy Visit Post-Kadafi Libya," *Los Angeles Times* (September 15, 2011). http://articles.latimes.com/2011/sep/15/world/la-fg-libya-cameron-sarkozy-20110916.

11. Liz Sly, "Calls in Syria for Weapons, NATO Intervention," *The Washington Post* (August 28, 2011), http://www.washingtonpost.com/world/middle-east/calls-in-syria-for-weapons-nato-intervention/2011/08/26/gIQA-3WAslJ_story.html.

12. See note 4.

13. John Mearsheimer, "Pull Those Boots Off the Ground," *Newsweek* (December 30, 2008). http://www.newsweek.com/id/177380.

14. Michael Gordon, "A Nation Challenged: Military; Tora Bora Attack Advances Slowly in Tough Fighting," *The New York Times* (December 16, 2001): B2. http://www.nytimes.com/2001/12/16/world/a-nation-challenged-military-tora-bora-attack-advances-slowly-in-tough-fighting.html.

15. Barack Obama, "President Obama's Remarks on New Strategy for Afghanistan and Pakistan," Washington, DC (March 27, 2009), http://www.nytimes.com/2009/03/27/us/politics/27obama-text.html.

16. Peter Baker and Eric Schmitt, "Afghan War Debate Now Leans to Focus on Al Qaeda," *The New York Times* (October 7, 2009): A1, http://www.nytimes.com/2009/10/08/world/asia/08prexy.html.

17. Tom Bowman, "Obama Sets More Modest Goals for Afghanistan," *NPR* (February 6, 2009), Available at http://www.npr.org/templates/story/story.php?storyId=100279589.

18. Barack Obama, "Remarks by President Obama and President Karzai of Afghanistan in Joint Press Availability," Washington, DC (May 12, 2010), http://www.whitehouse.gov/the-press-office/remarks-president-obama-and-president-karzai-afghanistan-joint-press-availability.

19. Mark Landler, "Hillary Clinton Is Obama's Key Link to Afghan Leader," *The New York Times* (November 19, 2009): A12. http://www.nytimes.com/2009/11/20/world/asia/20clinton.html.

20. "Qaddafi: I Will Fight Protests, Die a Martyr," *CBS News* (February 22, 2011). http://www.cbsnews.com/stories/2011/02/22/501364/main20034785.shtml.

21. Dan Murphy, "Qaddafi Threatens Libya Rebels as UN No-Fly Vote Nears," *Christian Science Monitor* (March 17, 2011). http://www.csmonitor.com/World/Middle-East/2011/0317/Qaddafi-threatens-Libya-rebels-as-UN-no-fly-vote-nears.

22. Barack Obama, "Remarks by the President on the Situation in Libya," Washington, DC (March 18, 2011), http://www.whitehouse.gov/the-press-office/2011/03/18/remarks-president-situation-libya.

23. Ibid.

24. Barack Obama, David Cameron, and Nicolas Sarkozy, "Libya's Pathway to Peace," *International Herald Tribune* (April 14, 2011). http://www.nytimes.com/2011/04/15/opinion/15iht-edlibya15.html.

25. Ibid.

26. Thom Shanker and David E. Sanger, "NATO Plans to Take Libya War to Qaddafi's Doorstep," *The New York Times* (April 26, 2011). http://www.nytimes.com/2011/04/27/world/middleeast/27strategy.html.

27. Hill, Tim. "Muammar Gaddafi Son Killed by NATO Air Strike—Libyan Government." *The Guardian* (April 30, 2011). http://www.guardian.co.uk/world/2011/may/01/libya-muammar-gaddafi-son-nato.

28. Tavernise, Sabrina and Lehren, Andrew W. "A Grim Portrait of Civilian Deaths in Iraq." *The New York Times* (October 22, 2009), http://www.nytimes.com/2010/10/23/world/middleeast/23casualties.html.

29. William Maclean, "Libya Islamist Takes Inclusive Stance," *Reuters* (September 19, 2011), http://in.reuters.com/article/2011/09/19/idINIndia-59413620110919.

30. "The Battle for Libya: Killings, Disappearances, and Torture," *Amnesty International Report* (September 13, 2011), http://www.amnesty.org/en/library/info/MDE19/025/2011/en.

31. "Libya: Opposition Forces Should Protect Civilians and Hospitals," *Human Rights Watch* (July 13, 2011), http://www.hrw.org/news/2011/07/13/libya-opposition-forces-should-protect-civilians-and-hospitals.

32. See note 30.

33. Ibid.

34. David Enders, "Empty Village Raises Concerns about Fate of Black Libyans," *McClatchy* (September 13, 2011), http://www.mcclatchydc.com/2011/09/13/123999/empty-village-raises-concerns.html.

35. David Enders, "African Women Say Rebels Raped Them in Libyan Camp," *McClatchy* (September 7, 2011), http://www.mcclatchydc.com/2011/09/07/123403/african-women-say-rebels-raped.html.

36. Rania El Gamal, "Libyan Rebel Commander Killed by Allied Militia," *Reuters* (July 30, 2011), http://www.reuters.com/article/2011/07/30/us-libya-idUSTRE76Q76620110730.

37. Tom Miles and Tim Pearce, "Niger Asks Help Fighting Terrorism after Libya Conflict," *Reuters* (September 19, 2011), http://old.news.yahoo.com/s/nm/20110919/wl_nm/us_niger_libya_security.

38. Christopher Rhoads and Laura Meckler, "International Leaders Pledge to Back New Libya," *Wall Street Journal* (September 21, 2011): A9.

39. Matt Spetalnick and Laura MacInnis, "Obama Urges Gaddafi Forces to Give Up, Vows Libya Aid," *Reuters* (September 20, 2011), http://www.reuters.com/article/2011/09/20/us-libya-obama-idUSTRE78J31H20110920.

40. David Davis, "A 21st-Century Marshall Plan," *Prospect* (July 2011): 12–13.

41. Hillary Clinton, "Secretary of State Hillary Rodham Clinton's Remarks on Receiving the George C. Marshall Foundation Award," http://www.marshallfoundation.org/SecretaryClintonremarksJune22011.htm (June 2, 2011).

42. "Senator John Kerry Addresses the Fletcher School Graduating Class of 2011," *The Fletcher School* (May 21, 2011), http://fletcher.tufts.edu/news/2011/05/news-update/Kerry-May26.shtml.

43. Ibid.

44. Nicolas Sarkozy and David Cameron, "Letter from David Cameron and Nicolas Sarkozy to Herman Van Rompuy," (March 10, 2011), http://www.guardian.co.uk/world/2011/mar/10/libya-middleeast.

45. Eric Westerwelt, "NATO's Intervention in Libya: A New Model?" *NPR* (September 12, 2011), http://www.npr.org/2011/09/12/140292920/natos-intervention-in-libya-a-new-model.

46. Ibid.

47. Ben Smith, "A Victory for 'Leading from Behind?" *POLITICO* (August 22, 2011), http://www.politico.com/news/stories/0811/61849.html.

48. Ibid.

49. "Mitt Romney's Analysis of Barack Obama's Libyan Policy," *The Hugh Hewitt Show* (March 21, 2011), http://www.hughhewitt.com/transcripts.aspx?id=e3bf5a59-b9c6-4a10-846b-f573a9a9d74d.

50. Ben Smith, "A Victory for 'Leading from Behind?" *POLITICO* (August 22, 2011), http://www.politico.com/news/stories/0811/61849.html.

51. Caroline Wyatt, "Afghan Burden Tasks NATO Allies," *BBC News* (October 27, 2007), http://news.bbc.co.uk/2/hi/south_asia/7061061.stm.

52. Kristin Archik and Paul Gallis, "NATO and the European Union," Report by *Congressional Research Services* (January 29, 2008), http://www.fas.org/sgp/crs/row/RL32342.pdf.

53. "NATO after Libya: A Troubling Victory," *The Economist* (September 3, 2011), http://www.economist.com/node/21528248.

54. Ibid.

55. Ibid.

56. See note 45.

57. See note 53.

17

The Case for Decoupled Armed Interventions*

The difficulties the 2011 NATO intervention encountered in Libya and that the United States continues to encounter in Afghanistan are but two recent developments that reinforce the argument against armed intervention. The economic austerity regimes the United States and many of its allies are facing, as they seek to draw down their debt and reinvigorate their economies, further agitate against the expenditures involved in such interventions. As President Obama put it in the middle of 2011: "America, it is time to focus on nation-building here at home."[1]

This article suggests that if the humanitarian goals of these interventions are decoupled from coerced regime change and nation-building, they can be carried out effectively and at rather low costs. In addition, the standard for justifying a humanitarian intervention must be set on a high level (to be specified below). We shall see that this high level is justified by strong normative reasons and not merely prudential ones.

The thesis for narrowly crafted armed humanitarian intervention is supported in the following pages by showing that a mixture of idealism and hubris drives the West to assume that it can achieve much more, and that its repeated failure to accomplish these expansive goals is leading to calls to avoid armed humanitarian intervention—including those missions whose normative standing is strong and which can be carried out effectively. (The following examination focuses on the United States, because it played a leading role in the matters at hand; however, the points made also apply to other NATO members, as well as other democracies such as Australia, South Korea, and Japan.)

The Idealism: Right and Left

Several armed interventions in the recent past sought much more than the Responsibility to Protect calls for, or interpreted it in a very expansive way. They often started with relatively narrowly crafted goals but soon expanded these goals to include regime change and nation-building, both because the United States and its allies held that their values call for such expanded missions and because they believed that they could successfully transform other nations in the region in a relatively short time and without undue outlays.

President Bush entered office in 2001 after strongly criticizing, indeed mocking, nation-building. In the second presidential debate against Al Gore, Bush argued, "I just don't think it's the role of the United States to walk into a country and say, we do it this way, so should you."[2] The reasons he decided to invade Iraq in 2003 are reported to include intelligence reports that Iraq was amassing weapons of mass destruction, claims that it had links to al-Qaeda, and—according to some—a response to alleged attempts by Iraq to kill his father. While all these attributed motives have been contested, there is no question that neo-conservative beliefs that called for coerced regime change played a key role in justifying the intervention in Iraq. Following the collapse of the Soviet Union in 1990, neoconservatives championed "The Freedom Agenda," which assumed that the nations of the world were moving toward liberal democratic regimes and that the lagging nations ought to be made to catch up with history. In this vein, Iraq was not to be liberated merely for its own sake, but also to "flip" other autocratic regimes throughout the Middle East.[3]

President Obama entered office in 2009, committing to avoid such coerced regime change interventions. The Obama's position was first laid out during his inaugural speech, in which he stated: "To those who cling to power through corruption and deceit and the silencing of dissent, know that you are on the wrong side of history; but that we will extend a hand if you are willing to unclench your fist."[4] This short quote deserves a careful reading. The first half of the sentence, in effect, announces that the United States will not seek to change regimes that violate human rights. The second half lays out a condition: such intervention will be avoided as long as these illiberal nations will not use force. This is in a sharp break from the Fukuyama-neoconservative-Bush position that, in order to secure peace, nations must have democratic regimes.[5]

Obama elaborated his position in what was framed as a major foreign policy speech in Cairo. He explicitly tied US military intervention to security and to no other goals:

> We do not want to keep our troops in Afghanistan. We see no military—we seek no military bases there. [. . .] We would gladly bring every single one of our troops home if we could be confident that there were not violent extremists in Afghanistan and now Pakistan determined to kill as many Americans as they possibly can. But that is not yet the case.[6]

Late in the speech, when Obama did turn to discuss democracy, he stated: "I know there has been controversy about the promotion of democracy in recent years, and much of this controversy is connected to the war in Iraq. So let me be clear: no system of government can or should be imposed upon one nation by any other."[7]

And he stated, "Each nation gives life to this principle in its own way, grounded in the traditions of its own people. America does not presume to know what is best for everyone, just as we would not presume to pick the outcome of a peaceful election."[8]

As time passed, President Obama came under withering criticism from both the right and the left for not more actively promoting human rights and democracy. Of Obama's trip to China, Phelim Kine, a spokesman for Human Rights Watch, said, "It was a missed opportunity. He failed to address some of the most specific and visceral human rights abuses going on in China."[9] Larry Cox, Executive Director of Amnesty International United States, stated that Obama "has created a false choice between having to speak out forcefully on human rights or being pragmatic and getting results on other issues."[10] Bret Stephens, a columnist at the *Wall Street Journal*, wrote that Obama's time in office has "[treated] human rights as something that 'interferes' with America's purposes in the world . . ."[11]

In the second half of 2009, millions of Iranian citizens rose in protest against their government, beginning with what was considered the fraudulent reelection of Mahmoud Ahmadinejad. Initially, the government reaction was rather muted. Over time, however, the government's reaction turned much more violent, resulting in torture, the massive beating of protestors, and the deaths of several demonstrators. Obama's reactions were initially subdued—as long as the Iranian government violated mainly the political rights of demonstrators—and Obama faced considerable criticism as a result. True to his doctrine, Obama's

251

criticisms of Iran grew much stronger once the Iranian government turned to the use of force. On June 14, 2009, Iranians took to the streets to protest the results of Iran's presidential election and continued to demonstrate in the days that followed. The government's initial reaction was largely limited to the use of tear gas and batons. In response, Obama stated only that he was "deeply troubled by the violence that [he'd] been seeing on television," but that the United States would continue to seek to dialogue with Iran. Obama's reaction was widely observed to be subdued. "Obama's posture has been very equivocal, without a clear message," said Representative Eric Cantor, House minority whip. "Now is the time for us to show our support with the Iranian people. I would like to see a strong statement from him that has moral clarity."[12] Steven Clemons, director of the American Strategy Program at the New America Foundation, said, "For Barack Obama, this was a serious misstep . . . It's right for the administration to be cautious, but it's extremely bad for him to narrow the peephole into an area in which we're looking at what's happening just through the lens of the nuclear program."[13]

In the weeks that followed, the Iranian government's reaction to continued demonstration became much more violent. Demonstrators were shot, arrested, and tortured. During this period, Obama gradually increased his censure of the regime, stating: "The United States and the international community have been appalled and outraged by the threats, the beatings, and imprisonments of the last few days. I strongly condemn these unjust actions . . . [Iran] must govern through consent and not coercion."[14] This statement emphasizes force as the reason for outrage. The same was the focus of the following statement: "For months, the Iranian people have sought nothing more than to exercise their universal rights. Each time they have done so, they have been met with the iron fist of brutality . . ."[15] Thus, Obama's responses were governed by his primary human rights concern: the protection of the right to life.

The same pattern unfolded in the first weeks of the 2011 uprising in the Middle East. President Obama was at first rather circumspect in his comments but, under criticism from both the right and the left, spoke out more strongly in support of democratic forces in Tunisia and Egypt. And in 2011, he ordered an armed intervention in Libya that started as a humanitarian intervention but quickly morphed into a forced regime change drive. And before too long, several leading voices called for massive nation-building by introducing a Marshall

Plan for the Middle East. General Jones has explained, "We learned that lesson after World War II—you know, we rebuilt Europe, we rebuilt Japan. That was an example of an enlightened view of things. The Marshall Plan, I am told, wasn't very popular in this country, but we went ahead and did it."[16] Secretary of State Hillary Clinton believes "as the Arab Spring unfolds across the Middle East and North Africa, some principles of the [Marshall] Plan apply again, especially in Egypt and Tunisia. As Marshall did in 1947, we must understand that the roots of the revolution and the problems that it sought to address are not just political but profoundly economic as well."[17] Two professors at Columbia Business School, Glenn Hubbard (who was also Chairman of the Council of Economic Advisors under George W. Bush) and Bill Duggan, argued that a Middle East Marshall Plan would "limit the spread of Islamic extremism" in the region.[18] Senator John Kerry argued that "we are again in desperate need of a Marshall Plan for the Middle East."[19] Senator John McCain also expressed support for such a plan. In a recent issue of *Prospect*, MP and former foreign office minister David Davis calls for a British Marshall Plan in the Middle East, arguing that such a plan "is one of the best ways to consolidate and support the Arab Spring as it stands, [and] could spark reform in other Arab Gulf countries too."[20]

Some realists and conspiracy theorists may well deconstruct these normative appeals and the reactions to them and point to other motives instead (access to oil being one often cited). However, I suggest that analysis of these deconstructions (not carried out in the confines of this article) would show that normative considerations, which had "real" effects because they resonate with opinion makers and voters in the United States and in other nations, did play a significant role in the repeated transformation of foreign policy from a position that was antagonistic to forced regime change and nation-building—to one that sought to carry it out.

Lack of Consistency

One serious difficulty the expansive approach to armed intervention encounters, as a normative principle, is that it has not (and we shall see cannot) be consistently applied.

In earlier ages, nations could act with limited concern for public opinion. However, as the masses gained in education, attention to public affairs, and access to information via media, governments realized the need to justify their actions, to provide a normative rationale for them. Making such a brief in turn requires a measure of consistency. This is of course what is meant when one states that the goddess of justice is blind; she treats all comers in the same way. Inconsistency is associated with arbitrariness, which has dogged US foreign policy in the matters at hand.

Throughout the Cold War, the United States positioned itself as the champion of freedom, yet it supported military dictatorships in South America, Asia, and elsewhere. During the recent uprisings in the Middle East, the United States fought to oust Qaddafi, urged Mubarak to step down in Egypt, and cheered the departure of Ben Ali in Tunisia, while at the same time making few, delayed, and muted pleas for Saleh to step down in Yemen, waffling on Syria and the Green Movement in Iran, and in effect supporting the autocrats of Saudi Arabia and Bahrain. Even as Bahrain was violently suppressing protests, and just before Saudi Arabia sent its troops to help, Secretary Clinton commended King Hamad for engaging in "meaningful outreach and efforts to try to bring about the change that will be in line with the needs of the people."[21]

American leaders tried to explain away these gross inconsistencies. Most notably, Secretary Clinton, in a speech asserting a US commitment to "sustained democracies" in the region, argued that diverse approaches were called for given such a "fluid" situation and that "a one-size-fits-all approach doesn't make sense."[22] In his speech at the National Defense University justifying the Libyan intervention, President Obama took pains to emphasize that it is geared only toward this particular country, rather than representing than a broader doctrine.[23] These arguments, however, have not persuaded critics abroad and at home, because they are inconsistent. Critics point out that the United States lectures Russia and China about human rights but provides equipment and training to the secret police of Saudi Arabia, Egypt, Yemen, and did previously to the dictators of Argentina, Chile, and Indonesia, among others. It pressured Mubarak to leave but not Assad; it interfered in Libya but not in Syria, where there were more casualties and the rising groups were composed of peaceful civilians rather than armed rebels.

Consistency does not require relying only on one criterion. As President Obama pointed out, if US vital interests are directly affected—say, a foreign power is blocking the shipment of oil through the Strait of Hormuz—the United States will act, based on interest considerations and not necessarily what other nations consider the right foreign policy. There will be other grounds for differential treatment of nations that seem to engage in similar violations of human rights, but these must be articulated. Otherwise, instead of adding to the legitimacy of one's action, the rationale provided raises doubts and opposition, as has been the case often in the past. Indeed, when a nation cannot provide a consistent rationale for its armed interventions in the internal affairs of other nations, this ought to be one reason such acts are avoided.

The Hubris

Coerced regime changes, as well as long-distance nation-building (that is, nation-building by one country in some other country, often on the other side of the ocean), are undergirded not merely by the precept that it is the role of the West to bring its light to those who have not found it, but also by the assumption that the West can transform other nations into liberal democracies, or at least help stabilize their government, prevent civil war, shape law and order (what is called state-building, which is less demanding than nation-building), and develop modern economies (which key advocates hold requires mainly freeing the nations from the old regimes that rely heavy on government interventions in the marketplace). That is, these transformations are not merely worthy ideals but ideals that can be advanced and in relatively short order, without undue taxing of the involved Western nations. This attitude reflects a mixture of a Western sense of exceptionality, superiority, positive thinking, and faith in social engineering. The result is what Peter Beinart calls "the beautiful lie": a hubristic sense that the United States can accomplish anything and thus needs no limits, and that US interests are wedded to international military domination.[24]

Actually, the record of such interventions is very poor. The United States, for instance, engaged in coerced regime changes in sixteen nations, eleven of which failed to establish a functioning democracy. Germany and Japan are the exceptions.[25] However, even a cursory examination of the conditions that existed in these nations shows that these conditions do not exist in the Middle East, which is the reason a Marshall Plan here cannot be effectively introduced.

Germany and Japan had surrendered after defeat in a war and fully submitted to occupation. That is, new regimes were installed only after hostilities had completely ceased. There were no terrorists and no insurgencies.

While the German and Japanese reconstructions were very much hands-on projects, following the experience in Iraq and Afghanistan, few, if any, even consider the proposition that the West will occupy more lands in the Middle East and manage their transformation. Regime change and nation-building, following the Arab Spring, amount to long-distance social engineering, with the West providing funds and advice, but the execution to be largely done by locals. However, such engineering is much more difficult to carry out.

One further notes that even before World War II, German and Japanese citizens strongly identified with their nations and were willing to make major sacrifices on their behalf. And they continued to so act during the reconstruction period. The first loyalty of many citizens of Middle Eastern nations (many of which are tribal societies cobbled together by Western countries) is to their ethnic or confessional group. They tend to look at the nation as a source of spoils for their tribe and fight for their share rather than make sacrifices for the national whole. Deep ethnic and confessional hostilities, such as those between the Shi'a and the Sunnis, among the Pashtun and the Tajik, the Hazara and the Kochi, and various tribes in other nations either gridlock the national polities (e.g., in Iraq and Afghanistan), lead to large-scale violence (e.g., in Yemen, Bahrain, and Sudan), result in massive oppression and armed conflicts (e.g., in Libya and Syria), or otherwise hinder political and economic development.

Max Weber established the importance of differences in core values when he demonstrated that Protestants were more imbued than Catholics with the values essential for modern open economies. Indeed, developments in Catholic countries (such as those in Southern Europe and Latin America) lagged behind the Protestant Anglo-Saxon nations and those in Northwest Europe. Weber also pointed to the difference between Confucian and Muslim values, thus, in effect, predicting the striking difference between the very high rates of development of the South Asian "tigers"—China, Hong Kong, Taiwan, Singapore, and South Korea—and the low rates of Muslim states, especially those that adhere strictly to Sharia.

One also must take into account that Germany and Japan were developed nations before World War II, with strong industrial bases, strong infrastructure, educated populations, and strong support for science and technology, corporations, business and commerce. Hence, they had mainly to be reconstructed. In contrast, many Middle Eastern states that lack many of these assets, institutions, and traditions cannot be reconstructed but must be constructed in the first place—a much taller order. This is most obvious in Afghanistan, Yemen, Sudan, and Libya. It is also a major issue in nations that have drawn on one commodity, oil, to keep their economy going, but do not develop the bases for a modern economy—especially Saudi Arabia and Bahrain. Other nations, such as Tunisia, Pakistan, Morocco, Syria, and Egypt, have better prepared populations and resources, but still score poorly on all these grounds compared to Germany and Japan.

Germany and Japan had competent government personnel and relatively low levels of corruption. In many nations in the Middle East, corruption is endemic, pervasive, and very difficult to scale back to tolerable levels. Thus, one must take into account that a significant proportion of whatever resources are made available to Middle Eastern nations will be siphoned off to private overseas bank accounts, allocated on irrelevant bases to cronies and supporters, and that a good part of the funds will be wasted and not accounted for.

Also often overlooked is the fact that the Marshall Plan entailed much larger outlays than have been dedicated in recent decades to foreign aid that seek to help economic development (not to be conflated with military aid). In 1948, the first year of the Marshall Plan, it consumed 13 percent of the US budget. In comparison, the United States currently spends less than one percent of its budget on foreign aid.

Moreover, the United States and its allies are entering a protracted period of budget retrenchments in which many domestic programs will be scaled back—including aid for the unemployed and poor, and for education and health care—as well as military outlays. It is a context in which the kinds of funds a Marshall Plan would require are extremely unlikely to be available.

In short, even if there were no normative reasons to question the value of most armed interventions in other nations, there are prudential reasons to minimize them, namely, that they tend not to yield the hoped-for results. Moreover, they squander scarce resources (both economic and political capital) and backfire, because the disappointing outcomes agitate against future interventions, even those that are normatively compelling and can be accomplished.

Criteria for Interventions

The quest for finding criteria for interventions that can be justified and that can be carried out effectively may start with the R2P (Responsibility to Protect). There has been considerable difference of opinion as to what it entails. Francis Deng and his associates, who were the first to write about "Sovereignty as Responsibility," defined nations in which outside powers should intervene by defining the opposite: nations in which intervention would be impermissible. These are nations whose governments ". . . strive to ensure for their people an effective governance that guarantees a just system of law and order, democratic freedoms, respect for fundamental rights, and general welfare."[26] With the bar set so low and defined so vaguely, there are few nations that would not be vulnerable to intervention.

Substantially more limiting criteria were proposed by The Evans–Sahnoun Commission. It proposed that intervention require: "(a) large-scale loss of life, actual or apprehended, with genocidal intent or not, which is the product either of deliberate state action, or state neglect or inability to act, or a failed state situation; or (b) large-scale 'ethnic cleansing,' actual or apprehended, whether carried out by killing, forced expulsion, acts of terror or rape." Moreover, both the Commission and the High-Level Panel assert that any intervention must be based on exclusively humanitarian intentions, be taken as a last resort, use only the minimum force necessary to complete the mission, and have reasonable prospects of success. That is to achieve the large-scale saving of lives, not to force regime change and most assuredly not for nation-building.

Setting the bar for interventions along the lines the Commission suggested is supported by the tragic but inescapable fact that the political capital and economic resources needed for advancing human rights on the international level by the use of force are in very short supply. This is evidenced by the observation that many rights are often violated, and no actions are taken by foreign powers. Even stopping genocides has been, so far, beyond the international community's abilities, and so has stopping the bloodshed in numerous civil and international conflicts still smoldering across the world. This harsh reality is in sharp contrast to the vision that, following economic development and toppling of the old regimes, rights will flourish in one country after another. These great difficulties point to the need to set a high bar and to the importance of examining which rights should be promoted first and foremost.

A major reason it is morally appropriate to recognize the paramount standing of the right to life is that all other rights are contingent on this one, while the right to life is not contingent on the others. It seems all too simple to state that dead people cannot exercise their rights, yet it bears repeating because the implications of this observation are often ignored: When the right to life is violated because basic security is not provided, all other rights are undermined—but not vice versa.

The supreme standing of the right to life is also supported by the finding that when basic security is provided, the public support for non-security (e.g., civil and political) rights increases, but not the other way around. A review of public opinion polls concerning attitudes toward civil liberties after 9/11 revealed that shortly after the attacks, nearly 70 percent of Americans were strongly inclined to give up various constitutionally protected rights in order to prevent more attacks. However, as no new attacks occurred on the American homeland and the sense of security returned (as measured by the return of passengers to air travel), support for rights was restored. By 2004–2005, about 70 percent of Americans were more concerned with protecting rights than with enhancing security.[27] Hence the principle reasons for employing the limited intervention capital to save lives, along the lines specified by the commission, should be considered before armed intervention in order to promote other goals.

A Mental Experiment

To highlight the issue, the following minor mental experiment may serve. Assume that the Taliban in Afghanistan offers the United States the following deal: The Taliban will commit itself to preventing Afghanistan from being used as base for terrorists. Indeed, it offers to chase the remaining al-Qaeda members out of Afghanistan or turn them over to the United States and its allies if caught. In turn, it expects that the coalition forces will allow the Taliban to contend with other Afghan groups, and if it prevails, to govern Afghanistan the way it prefers, namely, by imposing Sharia. The Taliban would close schools for girls; require women to stay home unless accompanied by a husband or relative; force religious observances; eliminate the rights to vote, free speech, assembly; and so on. (The Taliban further suggests that the United States could keep troops on some military bases out of populated areas for years to come so they would be readily available if the Taliban did not live up to its commitments, and the Taliban also understands that it would be severely bombed under such circumstances.)

The United States would thus face a stark choice between narrowly crafted security goals and the promotion of human rights beyond the right to life. Strong human rights advocates would reject such a deal.

If the preceding analysis is valid, the United States should accept it, on the grounds that even if many more lives of Americans, of other NATO members, and of Afghans are sacrificed, the Afghan people will still have to work out their own form of government and economy.

Which Means?

To argue that force—armed interventions—should be employed rarely, when the rationale that support them can clear the high bar outlined above, does not suggest that other means cannot be employed more liberally in the support of a much more extensive array of human rights. Following the tri-power classification of the means, the use of normative and economic means is briefly reviewed, given that limiting the exercise of coercive power has already been carried.

Regarding normative means, national leaders can often chastise other nations for not respecting human rights and express their approval when such nations improve their human rights record. There are many instances where the lives of dissenters were spared, or they were released from prisons or house arrest, because of drumbeats of criticisms by international community—without armed interventions. Even general changes in policy have taken place. For instance, after the firestorm of criticisms of China following the Tiananmen Square massacre, China has been acting in a more restrained way in dealing with opposition. Indeed, while China used to maintain that human rights are Western bourgeois values, it now holds that it respects them but merely is delaying the implementation of political rights until socio-economic ones are better advanced. Other Southeast Asian nations—Singapore, for instance—have similarly learned to at least pay homage to these rights and have moved to violate them less often. Critics argue that by publically exhorting other nations, one merely insults their sensibilities and stiffens their rejection. Indeed, in some cases private presentations by one national leader to another may be the preferred way to proceed. However, by and large, other nations have shown little reluctance to voice their criticism of the West, and the West should as a rule articulate in normative terms the case not just of the right to life but for all the others.

The imposition of economic sanctions to advance human rights has a much more mixed record. They often result in imposing more suffering on the people than on the regime, as has been the case in Saddam's Iraq. They rarely have brought down a regime, as one notes after a generation of sanctions on Cuba. "Smart" sanctions, focused on leaders and specific industries may be more effective, but unless these are very widely supported by other nations, they rarely produce significant concessions.[28]

The observation that nations can employ non-lethal (normative and economic) means to promote human rights and democracy further supports the thesis that the use of force should be reserved to large scale saving of life and not to be allowed to morph into coerced regime change, not to mention to futile attempts at nation-building.

Notes

* I am indebted to Julia Milton for research assistance on this essay.

1. Obama, B., "Remarks by the President on the Way Forward in Afghanistan." (2011), http://www.whitehouse.gov/the-press-office/2011/06/22/remarks-president-way-forward-afghanistan (retrieved July 13, 2011).

2. Bush, G. W., "Second Presidential Debate," (October 11, 2000), http://www.fas.org/news/usa/2000/usa-001011.htm (retrieved July 14, 2011).

3. Tanenhaus, S., "The World: From Vietnam to Iraq: The Rise and Fall and Rise of the Domino Theory," *New York Times* (March 23, 2003).

4. Obama, B., "Inaugural Address," (2009) http://www.whitehouse.gov/blog/inaugural-address/ (retrieved January 10, 2010).

5. Kristol, W., "The Long War," *The Weekly Standard* 11, no. 24 (2006): 9; see also Fukuyama, F. *End of History and the Last Man* (New York: Free Press, 1992).

6. Obama, B., "Remarks by the President on a New Beginning," (2009), http://www.whitehouse.gov/the_press_office/Remarks-by-the-President-at-Cairo-University-6-04-09/ (retrieved January 10, 2010).

7. Ibid.

8. Ibid.

9. Mosk, M., 2009. "Obama Too Polite in Shanghai for Some Rights Defenders See Forum as a Key 'Missed Opportunity," *Washington Times* (17 November): A3.

10. Colvin, R., "Obama rights record questioned ahead of Nobel prize," (2009): Available at http://www.reuters.com/article/idUSTRE5B82TM20091209 (retrieved January 10, 2010).

11. Stephens, B., "Does Obama Believe in Human Rights?" *Wall Street Journal* (October 20, 2009): A19.

12. Cooper, H. and Landler, M., "For Obama, Pressure To Strike Firmer Tone," *New York Times* (June 18, 2009): A16.

13. Ibid.

14. Obama, B., "The President's Opening Remarks on Iran," (2009) http://www.whitehouse.gov/blog/The-Presidents-Opening-Remarks-on-Iran-with-Persian-Translation/ (retrieved January 10, 2010).

15. Obama, B., "Statement by the President on the Attempted Attack on Christmas Day and Recent Violence in Iran," (2009), http://www.whitehouse.gov/the-press-office/statement-president-attempted-attack-christmas-day-and-recent-violence-iran (retrieved January 10, 2010).

16. Jones, J., "Comment of General James Jones" at Stimson Center Chairman's Forum on international security issues (June 14, 2011).

17. Clinton, H. "Secretary of State Hillary Rodham Clinton's Remarks on Receiving the George C. Marshall Foundation Award," (2011), http://www.marshallfoundation.org/SecretaryClintonremarksJune22011.htm (retrieved July 14, 2011).

18. Hubbard, G. and Duggan, B., "A Marshall Plan for the Middle East?" *The Huffington Post* (February 28, 2011). http://www.huffingtonpost.com/glenn-hubbard/marshall_plan_mid_east_b_829411.html.

19. Kerry, J. "Senator John Kerry Addresses The Fletcher School Graduating Class of 2011," *The Fletcher School* (May 21, 2011), http://fletcher.tufts.edu/news/2011/05/news-update/Kerry-May26.shtml.

20. Davis, D., "A 21st Century Marshall Plan," *Prospect* (July 2011): 12–13.

21. Clinton, H., "Secretary Clinton on Libya," at Andrews Air Force Base (February 27, 2011).

22. Clinton, H., "Senator Clinton's Remarks at the U.S. Islamic World Forum," (April 12, 2011).

23. See note 1.

24. Beinart, P., *The Icarus Syndrome: A History of American Hubris* (New York: HarperCollins, 2010).

25. Pei, M. and Kasper, S., "Lessons from the Past: The American Record on Nation-building," Carnegie Endowment Policy Brief No. 24 (2003).

26. Deng, F., *Sovereignty as Responsibility: Conflict Management in Africa* (Washington, DC: Brookings Institution, 1996).

27. Etzioni, A., *How Patriotic Is the Patriot Act?* (New York: Routledge, 2004): 38–39.

28. Pape, R., "Why Economic Sanctions Do Not Work," *International Security* 22, no. 2 (1997): 90–136.

Part VIII
Human Rights Post 2000

18

Life: The Most Basic Right[*]

Not all rights have been created equal. This essay contends that the right to life—broadly understood as a right to be free from deadly violence, maiming, torture, and starvation—is paramount and argues that the unique standing of the right to life has significant implications for public policy, in general, and for foreign policy, in particular.

The Implications of Moral and Political Scarcity

In numerous discussions of human rights, both scholars and activists treat these rights as a unitary concept. A typical statement follows: "All human rights are universal, indivisible, and interdependent and interrelated. The international community must treat human rights globally in a fair and equal manner, on the same footing, and with the same emphasis."[1] Indeed, for such declaratory purposes there may not be an immediate reason to differentiate among various individual rights or to examine their relative standing vis-à-vis one another. However, often, in order to address specific constitutional, legal, and public policy questions, such ranking is required—if only because different rights come into conflict, and hence criteria must be found to determine which right will prevail under a given set of circumstances. Their relative normativity is one such criterion. Another major reason for the ranking of rights is that due to the scarcity of moral and political capital that are needed to promote and implement human rights, some rights will be under-served. Ranking them is one way to determine which rights we ought to promote more than others, if choose we must.

Scarcity is a term used by economists to denote the observation that wants exceed the availability of the resources needed to satisfy these wants. (Prices are one major way this discrepancy is bridged.) I suggest that those who seek to advance human rights face a similar situation. Human rights are not self-implementing; they need to be promoted through educational means, moral suasion, incentives, and the coercive powers of the state, all of which command resources. Given that the resources needed to promote human rights are limited and substantially short of that which full implementation requires, various rights must be ranked so that we may effectively allocate these resources. These include not merely economic assets but also moral and political capital. Moral capital is the capacity to persuade. Moral authorities, such as religious and public leaders, have a limited capacity to win the support of their followers for particular lines of action. Taking on particular moral issues inevitably means that there will be other issues with which they will be unable to engage. Political capital is the ability to garner the support of individual legislators, voters, and various factions or lobbies. It also falls chronically short of that which is needed by those who seek to promote human rights. It follows that not all rights can be fully served, and that hence one ought not avoid the question: which right, if any, commands a higher standing than the others?

Examples of Ranking

An implicit ranking of rights is fairly common.[2] East Asian societies tend to claim that socio-economic rights outrank civil and political rights, which they advance as one justification for their neglect of civil and political freedoms,[3] at least while they are focusing on socio-economic development. In contrast, Americans tend to question the status of socio-economic rights much more than the standing of civil and political rights, while the German constitution and the United Nations Universal Declaration of Human Rights treat these two categories of rights as if they have similar standing.

Rankings can also be found among civil and political rights. For instance, Americans tend to rank the First Amendment as higher, or more absolute, than the others. This is evidenced when freedom of speech clashes with other rights or the common good. In those situations, American constitutional and legal traditions and political lore tend to favor allowing the First Amendment to trump these other considerations. Examples include the absence of state secret acts in the United States (which allows the freedom of the press to take precedent over national security)[4]; the ways American libel laws are written compared to the British ones, which rank freedom of the press higher than the violation of privacy under many circumstances[5]; and the absence of hate speech clauses in federal and state constitutions of the United

States, as compared to Brazil, for instance.[6] More generally, even a cursory examination of the criminal codes of many nations reveals that they rank rights by exacting much higher penalties for violations of some rights than for violations of others. This is particularly true with regard to the right to life. Taking someone else's life—murder—is punished more severely in the criminal codes of all democratic nations than practically all other crimes, including the violation of property rights, discrimination, and harassment. Also, torture is considered a more egregious violation than the violation of most other rights. The special status of life is reflected in the Ten Commandments. The Koran teaches that "if anyone saves a life, it shall be as though he had saved the lives of all mankind."[7] In the Jewish tradition, "He who saves one soul, it's as if he saved the entire world."[8] Jews are commanded to violate the Sabbath and even the holiest of Jewish holidays, Atonement Day, if this is required to save a life. The Catholic Church extends this right to the unborn.[9] The primacy of the right to life is well recognized in the following comments on the Universal Declaration of Human Rights: "The right to life, liberty and personal security, recognized in Article 3, sets the base for all following political rights and civil liberties, including freedom from slavery, torture and arbitrary arrest, as well as the rights to a fair trial, free speech and free movement and privacy."[10]

Self-Evident? Implicit Ranking

A critic may argue that the concept that the right to life trumps all others is so self-evident and widely accepted that it is a trivial claim. However, there are several ways to show that this is not the case. First of all, many lists of rights do not list the right to life first or show in any other way that it has a special status. I note that the order in a list is not necessarily a deliberate and explicit form of ranking. One can list an important item second or even last. However, it often reflects at least implicitly a sense of value.

Probably the best known example of a list in which the respect for life does not command top billing is the Ten Commandments, although it is of course a list of duties and not rights.

The Human Rights Watch, a highly regarded human rights advocacy group, was founded in 1978 as the Helsinki Watch in order to support Soviet bloc groups promoting human rights. The Helsinki Watch mission statement enumerates the rights it promotes, including protection from discrimination, loss of political freedom, and inhumane conduct during war, and justice for human rights violators. However, protecting the right to life is not even mentioned.[11]

Human Rights First is a group founded in 1978 to promote laws and policies that protect human rights. In its charter, the group lists freedom and equality of thought, expression, and religion as the primary rights to be protected. The right of security for individuals and protection against arbitrary power comes almost as an afterthought, after the charter asserts its methods for promoting its conception of human rights.[12]

In 2003, high-level delegates from each country of the EU produced the European Union Charter of Fundamental Rights. The Charter places human dignity first, followed by the right to life and freedom from the death penalty, and the integrity of the person, which concerns the ethical boundaries of science.

According to German Basic Law, all basic rights, including the right to life, have to be balanced with other basic rights with the sole exception of the right to human dignity—the right to be free of torture is thus placed above the right to life. "Article 1 [of the German Basic Law] is the Basic Law's crown. The concept of human dignity is this crown's jewel: an interest so precious that the state must affirmatively protect and foster its inviolability. This uniquely important status is evident from human dignity's prominence in the constitution,[13] the early Federal Republic's pressing need to repudiate the Third Reich, the many judicial and scholarly exegeses of Article 1, and human dignity's unique claim to absolute protection."[14]

The contrast between these documents and ones that do list the right to life first stands out when one examines the UN Universal Declaration of Human Rights.[15] The first substantive right enumerated is unequivocally the right to life: "Everyone has the right to life, liberty and security of person."[16]

The third one is closely related: "No one shall be subjected to torture or to cruel, inhuman or degrading treatment or punishment."[17] In between is sandwiched one that concerns freedom: "No one shall be held in slavery or servitude; slavery and the slave trade shall be prohibited in all their forms."[18]

Eckart Klein studied of the Convention for the Protection of Human Rights and Fundamental Freedoms and found that the European Court of Human Rights characterized the right to life not only as 'one of the most fundamental provisions in the Convention,' but has elevated it to the 'supreme value in the hierarchy of human rights'... While the term 'supreme value' remains reserved for the right to life, the prohibitions of torture has attained 'the status of a peremptory norm or *jus cogens* meaning that the norm 'enjoys a higher rank in the international hierarchy than treaty law and even ordinary customary rules.'[19]

Explicit Ranking

Several scholars have explicitly studied the ways rights are or ought to be ranked. However, far from agreeing that the right to life should rank supreme, they differ in terms of which right they rank as paramount.

R. J. Vincent defined the right to life as the right to sustenance and security and argued that it must always be protected first. He noted, though, that this is not necessarily always recognized. He writes,

> it is true that basic needs doctrine has a programmatic appeal that is not obvious in the lists of human rights. The idea of a hierarchy of basic needs, from physiological to psychological, with each level in the hierarchy requiring to be met before progress to the next level, seems to provide the starting-place for a detailed development strategy: first provide food and water, then security, and so on ... If the right to life becomes the need for food, then a society has some notion of what is to be done.[20]

Charles Brocket has proposed a hierarchy of rights that is topped with the right to life, which he defines as freedom from murder. This right fits into what he calls physiological rights, which also include the right to be free of severe malnutrition, the right to food, water, and air, which life requires.

Safety rights—protection from physical or psychic injury, which includes freedom from torture as well as the right to basic health care—come next, while the last range of protected rights are "gratifications such as love, esteem, and self-actualization."[21] In my terms, he breaks the right to life into two, both of which he calls physiological rights. Brockett makes it clear that these physiological rights must be met before other rights can be sufficiently protected. He writes "The instrumental nature of security does set it apart from the other two dimensions and the other sets of needs. .... its inclusion is redundant since its instrumental relation to the other needs means that it is already taken into account by those needs . . ."[22]

Others do rank rights, however, in different ways. Some single out a piece of the right to life, and put it at the top of the list. The Irish Human Rights Commission places freedom from torture as its most fundamental human right.[23] Food and Agricultural Organization Director-General Dr. Jacques Diouf believes the most fundamental right is the right to food, as he expressed at the plenary session of the European Assembly in 2007.[24] Mohamad Mova Al 'Afghani believes the right to water is the most essential human right.[25]

Others lead with other rights. Privacy International, an advocacy group for privacy rights, ranks the right to privacy as a fundamental right that underpins basic conceptions of human dignity and other human rights.[26] Basil Fernando of the Asia Human Rights Commission believes that human dignity is the foundation of human rights "and the worst form of negation of it [is] poverty."[27] Margaret Somerville, a professor at McGill University, holds that "the most fundamental human right of every person is the right to be born from natural human origins that have not been tampered with by anyone else."[28] The organization "Creating a Sustainable Future" is based on the premise that a sustainable future is the most fundamental human right.[29] Walter Williams, a professor at George Mason University, asserts that property rights are the most important human rights, and he believes that false distinctions have been made between human rights and property rights.[30]

In short, although ranking of rights is hardly a new step, moving toward an agreement that the right to life ought to top the hierarchy of human rights, the key thesis of this article, is far from agreed upon.

In a More Popular Lingo

To the American mind, discussing the standing of the right to life brings to mind the very popular line "give me liberty or give me death." This normative claim is often imbedded in the calls to soldiers and anti-terrorist agents to fight for the freedom of their country or that of others, even if it entails endangering their lives. (The opposite claim, "better red than dead," was considered a position embraced only by outliers such as pacifists and the extreme left.) Thus, at least in this context, liberty outranks life.

While it is much more legally permissible to deny people liberty (by incarcerating them) than to legally take their lives (the death penalty), and many civilized nations have banned the death penalty, the United States still allows it to stand. And there are a fair number of jurists who justify it. In 1976, the Supreme Court ruled in *Gregg v. Georgia* that the death penalty, meeting certain criteria of fairness, was a constitutionally acceptable form of punishment in the United States.[31] Here a concept of public order (or the safety of others) takes priority over the right of life of the individual involved.

In Conclusion

One cannot but conclude that the thesis that the right to life trumps all others is far from self-evident, incorporated in all declarations and charters enumerating human rights, or agreed upon among scholars. Furthermore, one notes that like other rights, even the right to life is not completely absolute. Exceptions are incorporated, for instance, into American law and the normative precepts that constitute patriotism. One may suggest that one should place a heavy burden on those who seek to trump the right to life, as so frequently the call to sacrifice one's life for this or that common good (or right) is found on closer examination to be with little foundation. Many would agree that this was the case when the call to arms was made in the context of invading Iraq in 2003. In other words, granting the right to life a special status—the most respected of them all, even if not an absolute one—serves as a normative hedge against spurious claims by governments that our rights are endangered or that the death penalty is called for. The default position, the right to life implies, is that such claims are not justified and that the burden of proof rests with those who make such claims. However, one cannot presume that claims that the right to life should be set aside can never clear this bar.

The High Level of Scarcity

Before I can point to the key implications of the ranking of rights and the particularly high ranking accorded to the right of life, one more step is needed: one must determine the level of scarcity of moral and political capital available to those who promote human rights. The more severe the scarcity, the more crucial ranking becomes, and the greater the damage caused in situations in which ranking is neglected or obscured, causing a poor allocation of moral and political capital. The tragic fact is that the moral and political capital needed for advancing human rights in general, and in particular on the international level, is in very short supply; scarcity is very high. This is evidenced by the observation that many rights are often violated both within a wide range of societies and in international relations. Even stopping genocides has been so far beyond the international community's abilities,[32] as so has stopping the bloodshed in numerous civil and international conflicts still smoldering across the world.[33] This harsh reality is in sharp contrast to the vision that following economic development and toppling of the old regimes, rights will flourish in one country after another. It especially flies in the face of the hope that such developments can be advanced relatively quickly by foreign powers and international bodies such as the UNFDP, World Bank, IMF, and I-NGOs using means such as foreign aid, loans at favorable terms, trade, and forced regime change.[34]

The great difficulties in promoting rights and the scarcity of moral and political capital point to the importance of examining which rights should be promoted first and foremost.

The Morality of Scarcity

There seems to be a reluctance to rank rights during public policy formulation that arises out of concerns that such ranking will lead to neglect of those rights that are accorded a low rank. For instance, in a country like Afghanistan, the issue arises as to whether the United States and its allies can and should simultaneously promote women's rights, children's rights, and animal rights while seeking to advance freedoms of speech, assembly, and religious expression. This issue came into sharp relief when the Afghan parliament enacted a law in 2009 that allowed Shia men to rape their wives if they did not provide sex at least once every two weeks. Some hold that the United States and its allies should lean heavily on the Afghan government to set aside this law, while others believe that the United States should invest what limited political capital it has in other matters—for instance, in pressuring the Afghan government to curb corruption. For those who may respond that both matters should be taken up, one must note that at the same time numerous other rights are regularly violated in Afghanistan.[35] In short, it is clear beyond a reasonable doubt that there is a high level of scarcity of moral and political capital available to promote human rights.

As I see it, a major implication of this high level of scarcity is that the ethic of triage, applied in medical emergencies and natural disasters, should be applied here. If one refuses to choose which rights to promote first and, instead, spreads widely whatever limited moral and political capital is available, the advance of all rights will be greatly hindered. This is especially the case in situations in which the observation of some rights is a prerequisite for the observation of others. These considerations point to the conclusion that in situations in which scarcity of moral and political capital cannot be overcome, moral considerations command a triage of rights. Avoiding it because one considers such choices abhorrent results in doing less good than could be achieved.

Life Is the Most Basic Right

I already tried to show earlier that the right to life is very often ranked higher than other rights. A major reason I suggest this ranking is morally appropriate, to recognize the paramount standing of the right to life (broadly understood to include freedom from torture, maiming, and starvation), is that all other rights are contingent on this one, while the right to life is not contingent on the others. It seems all too simple to state that dead people cannot exercise their rights, yet it bears repeating because the extensive implications of this observation are often ignored: When the right to life is violated because basic security is not provided, all other rights are undermined—but not vice versa. (This statement refers, of course, only to true threats to life, not to the politics of fear.)

The primacy of the right to life, and hence the duty to provide for security, refers to basic and not complete security. By "basic security" I mean conditions under which people can feel secure in their lives and in their homes, and feel safe enough so they can freely use public spaces, go to work, let their children go to school, and exercise their other rights, such as attending religious and political events—but not an environment in which they are risk-free. One reason for this difference is that a risk-free environment is not needed for the exercise of other rights—a major reason, we have seen, the right to life is granted its special standing. Second, reducing risk to very low levels tends to involve high violation of many other rights, especially privacy. And thirdly, a risk-free society is unattainable. None of these difficulties are faced when one seeks merely to establish basic security. It was restored in major American cities after violence reached high levels in the 1970s; in Moscow after violence reached high levels in the 1990s; and in several major Iraqi cities after 2004–2006.

The supreme standing of the right to life is also supported by the finding that when basic security is provided, the public support for non-security (e.g., civil and political) rights increases, but not the other way around. This stands in contrast to the assumption that "regime change" (i.e., forced democratization, including the introduction of the institutional arrangements required for the implementation of civil and political rights) is essential to turning nations into peaceful members of the international community, that is, to further global and domestic security. Only democracies, this argument holds, do not wage war with other democracies.[36] However, recent experience shows that democratization is not a guarantee for security,[37] and that it is extremely difficult to forcefully democratize nations.[38]

And to reiterate, basic security is needed to promote other rights. In a review of public opinion polls concerning attitudes towards civil liberties after 9/11, I found that shortly after the attacks, nearly 70 percent of Americans were strongly inclined to give up various constitutionally protected rights in order to prevent more attacks. However, as no new attacks occurred on the American homeland and the sense of security returned (a sense I measured by the return of passengers to air traffic), support for rights was restored. By 2004–2005, about 70 percent of Americans were more concerned with protecting rights than with enhancing security.[39]

While I am unaware of an empirical study proving this point, it seems obvious that the criticism of policies introduced by the Bush Administration after 9/11, including harsh interrogation techniques, detention without trial or term in Guantanamo Bay, and massive increases in surveillance, rose as years passed without new attacks on the American homeland. They were relatively weak in the first Bush Administration and grew stronger during the second one. A case in point: the Patriot Act was passed by a wide margin in 2001 but faced considerable opposition and was re-approved with substantial changes only after considerable debate and opposition in 2006.

Another case in point is Russia. Although Russia has never met the standards of a liberal democracy, a good part of what it had achieved on that front after the Cold War was gradually lost as Russians began to experience very high levels of violent crime. Vladimir Putin, who has been moving the regime in an authoritarian direction, is widely regarded in Russia as not being strong enough on crime, rather than too strong, because many still feel that basic security is lacking.

In short, these observations support the thesis that as security is provided, the road is paved for the promotion of civil and political rights.

Implications for Public Policy

In the following lines I point to several implications of the preceding discussion for domestic and foreign policies. I cannot stress enough that these short lines do not provide an analysis of the various policies, let alone an evaluation of normative and prudential standings. I merely try to illustrate one point: that the primacy of the right to life has significant policy implications.

On the domestic front, the preceding analysis favors the kind of policies introduced in New York City when it faced high levels of violent crime. These policies involved reactivating various communities to enforce their norms against those who violated them by treating minor transgressions as if they were serious offenses. (The core idea behind these policies is often associated with the term "Broken Windows." It was championed by George Kelling and James Q. Wilson in 1982 in the *Atlantic Monthly*.[40]) While this policy is not free from criticism,[41] it has been widely credited with achieving its expected results: restoring basic security and opening the door to greater promotion of other rights aside from the protection of life.[42] The same might be said about community policing, although it too is far from free from criticism.

With regard to foreign policy, one must take into account that it is implemented in an environment that is often particularly taxing, and hence ranking rights is particularly necessary in this realm. I already suggested that primacy of the right to life implies that basic security must be provided before democratization and a general promotion of human rights can take off, in direct opposition to the forced regime change hypothesis. (President Barack Obama articulated this position when he stated: "To those who cling to power through corruption and deceit and the silencing of dissent, know that you are on the wrong side of history, but that we will extend a hand if you are willing to unclench your fist.")

With regard to the promotion of various security goals, the primacy of life clearly indicates that de-proliferation and the prevention of the spread of WMDs should trump all other considerations, as these are means through which the lives of very large numbers of people can be annihilated and through which they are currently threatened. This may seem obvious, but on numerous occasions this issue has not been given the first priority; for instance, in dealing with Russia, for years promotion of democracy and human rights was given priority over accelerating the implementation of the Cooperative Threat Reduction

Initiative which seeks to enhance the safe-guarding of nuclear weapons and fissile materials.[43]

Also, the primacy of life favors policies that seek to stop genocides, civil wars, pandemics, and mass starvation. One cannot rely on the primacy of life as the leading normative principle to guide and legitimate the foreign policy of a nation—or the policies of a group of nations or international institutions—if the life to be protected is only of the citizens of a given nation. Even a modicum of consistency, a major foundation of robust ethnical judgments, requires that all lives be respected. True, it is beyond the reach of current human capacity to stop all killing, maiming, torture, and starvation. However, it is not impossible to stop them when they occur on a large scale. (Those who may argue that the definition of "large" scale is a subjective concept, depending upon the eyes of the beholder, may note that the United Nations has developed a fairly clear set of definitions that allow one to determine whether or not a genocide is occurring.)[44]

The high regard for life also indicates that as moral and political capital is available for the promotion of democracy and human rights by the people of one country on behalf of those living under some other regime—this promotion should be limited to non-lethal means. Military interventions for these goals are not in line with the stated principle.

One may ask whether the high priority accorded to security, broadly understood, implies that organizations devoted to other purposes—say, Doctors Without Borders—should seek to change their charter or turn over their resources to organizations dedicated to security. Arguably, in some abstract world, all organizations dedicated to the common good would follow the same overarching strategy. However, given that these organizations have different funding sources, political structures and even legal foundations, they cannot and should not all focus on security. However, these organizations best engage in triage within their own realm of service. For instance, Doctors Without Borders might focus more on saving lives than on, say, repairing cleft palates, or those who provide food might concentrate on curbing starvation before providing diet supplements to prevent malnutrition. Such ranking examples may at first seem heartless; their normativity stands out only when one recognizes that there are not enough resources to cover all the numerous purposes that deserve to be promoted, and hence avoiding triage results in consequences that offend values the promoters of human rights, at least, hold dear.

Notes

*   I am indebted to Radhika Bhat and S. Riane Harper for research assistance and editorial comments.

1.   The United Nations, *Vienna Declaration and Programme of Action at the World Conference on Human Rights* (1993), http://www.unhchr.ch/ huridocda/huridoca.nsf/(Symbol)/A.CONF.157.23.En?OpenDocument (accessed June 11, 2009); Other sources articulating this view of human rights are The United Nations Population Fund, *Human Rights Principles*, http://www.unfpa.org/rights/principles.htm (accessed June 11, 2009); Atty. Rene V. Sarmiento, "Human Rights: Universal? Individisble? Interdependent?" (speech, PAHRA-Sponsored Forum on Human Rights, Quezon City, Philippines, June 20, 1995), http://www.hrsolidarity.net/mainfile. php/1995vol05no02/92/; Morton Winston, "On the Indivisibility and Interdependence of Human Rights," (Twentieth World Congress of Philosophy, Boston, MA, August 10–15, 1998), http://www.bu.edu/wcp/Papers/Huma/ HumaWins.htm.

2.   See Bryan Turner, "Rights and Communities: Prolegomenon to a Sociology of Rights," *Australian and New Zealand Journal of Sociology* 31, no. 2 (1995): 1–8; Koji Teraya, "Emerging Hierarchy in International Human Rights and Beyond: From the Perspective of Non-derogable Rights," *European Journal of International Law* 12, no. 5 (2001): 917–41.

3.   Civil and political rights, also known as "first-generation rights," have a direct relationship with the state, and include such rights as the right to justice and the rights to information and expression. Darren J. O'Byrne, *Human Rights: An Introduction* (New York: Pearson Education, 2003), 11.

4.   "Secrecy in government is fundamentally anti-democratic, perpetuating bureaucratic errors. Open debate and discussion of public issues are vital to our national health.": Justice Brennan's concurrence in New York Times v. United States, 403 U.S. 713 (1971).

5.   New York Times Co. v. Sullivan, 376 U.S. 254 (1964).

6.   Brazilian Constitution, art. 2, sec. XLIII, http://www.v-brazil.com/government/laws/constitution.html (accessed June 11, 2009); Norman Fischer, "The Moral Core of U.S. Constitutional Ban on Hate Speech Codes," (Twentieth World Congress of Philosophy, Boston, MA, August 10–15, 1998), http://www.bu.edu/wcp/Papers/Law/LawFisc.htm (accessed June 11, 2009).

7.   Koran (5:32).

8.   Babylonian Talmud, Sanhedrin 4:8 (37a).

9.   For the articulation of this standard by the United States Conference of Catholic Bishops, see their website: United States Conference of Catholic Bishops, "Respect for Unborn Human Life: The Church's Constant Teaching," http://www.usccb.org/prolife/constantchurchteaching.shtml (accessed June 11, 2009).

10.   The United Nations, "A United Nations Priority: Universal Declaration of Human Rights," http://www.un.org/rights/HRToday/declar.htm (accessed June 11, 2009); For additional discussion see Rhona Smith, *Textbook*

on *International Human Rights* (Oxford: Blackstone Press, 2003); B. G. Ramcharan, *The Right to Life in International Law* (Leiden, The Netherlands: Martinus Nijhoff Publishers, 1985).

11. Human Rights Watch, "About Us," http://www.hrw.org/en/about (accessed July 22, 2009).

12. Human Rights First, "Charter," http://www.humanrightsfirst.org/about_us/charter.aspx.

13. Craig Smith, "More Disagreement over Human Dignity: Federal Constitutional Court's Most Recent Benetton Advertising Decision," *German Law Journal* 4, no. 6 (June 2003).

14. Eckart Klein, "Establishing a Hierarchy of Human Rights: Ideal Solution or Fallacy?" *Israel Law Review* 41 (2008): 477–88.

15. The United Nations, "The Universal Declaration of Human Rights," (December 10, 1948), http://www.un.org/en/documents/udhr/ (accessed July 22, 2009).

16. Ibid.

17. Ibid.

18. Ibid.

19. Klein, Establishing a Hierarchy of Human Rights, 486.

20. Vincent, R.J., *Human Rights and International Relations* (New York: Cambridge University Press, 1986), 87.

21. Charles Brockett, "A Hierarchy of Human Rights," Paper presented at Annual Meeting of the American Political Science Association (New York, August 31–September 3, 1978).

22. Ibid.

23. Irish Human Rights Commission, "Press Release: Urgent Action Needed to Address Unsafe and Degrading Nature of Irish Prisons," http://www.ihrc.ie/press_releases/newsarticle.asp?NID=221&NCID=12&T=N (accessed July 24, 2009).

24. FAO Newsroom, "The Most Fundamental Human Right Is the Right to Food," (June 26, 2007), http://www.fao.org/newsroom/EN/news/2007/1000610/index.html (accessed July 24, 2009).

25. Mohamad Mova Al 'Afghani, "Access to Water Is a Fundamental Human Right," *The Jakarta Post* (July 10, 2007).

26. Privacy International, "About Privacy International," http://www.privacy-international.org/article.shtml?cmd[347]=x-347-65428 (accessed July 24, 2009).

27. Philip Matthew, "Thailand: 'Freedom of Poverty Is a Fundamental Human Right,' Says Consultation," *Human Rights Solidarity* (September 1996), http://www.hrsolidarity.net/mainfile.php/1996vol06no03/184/ (accessed July 24, 2009).

28. Margaret Somerville, "Children's Human Rights and Unlinking Child-Parent Biological Bonds with Adoption, Same-Sex Marriage and New Reproductive Technologies," *Journal of Family Studies* (November–December 2007), http://findarticles.com/p/articles/mi_6968/is_2_13/ai_n28469751/ (accessed July 24, 2009).

29. CASF, "About Us," http://rtsf.wordpress.com/about/ (accessed July 24, 2009).

30. Walter Williams, "Property Rights Are a Fundamental Right," *Capitalism Magazine* (August 3, 2005), http://www.capmag.com/article.asp?ID=4341 (accessed July 24, 2009).

31. Gregg v. Georgia, 428 U.S. 153 (1976).

32. Samantha Power, *The Problem From Hell* (New York: Basic Books, 2002).

33. According to BIPPI, as of February 2008, there were thirty-one ongoing conflicts worldwide. B's Independent Pro-Peace Initiative, "Wars, Conflicts, International and Intra-national Crises," (February 2008), http://www.bippi.org/bippi/menu_left/conflicts.htm (accessed June 11, 2009).

34. For an argument discounting these views, see: William Easterly, *The White Man's Burden* (New York: Penguin Press, 2006); World Bank, "Assessing Aid—What Works, What Doesn't, and Why," Policy Research Report (1998).

35. Ann Jones, *Kabul in Winter: Life without Peace in Afghanistan* (New York: Metropolitan Books, 2006).

36. For more readings that support the "Democracies don't fight Democracies premise," see R.J. Rummel, "Democracies Don't Fight Democracies," *Peace Magazine* (May–June 1999): 10; Alex Mintz and Nehemia Geva, "Why Don't Democracies Fight Each Other?" *The Journal of Conflict* Resolution 37, no. 3 (September 1993): 484–503; Solomon W. Polachek, "Why Democracies Cooperate More and Fight Less: The Relationship between International Trade and Cooperation," *Review of International Economics* 5, no. 3 (December 2002): 295–309. A strong argument against the "Democracies Don't Fight Democracies" argument can be found in Thomas Schwartz and Kiron K. Skinner's piece, "The Myth of Democratic Pacifism," *Hoover Digest* no. 2 (April 1999). Also see Fareed Zakaria, *The Future of Freedom: Illiberal Democracy at Home and Abroad* (New York: W. W. Norton & Company, 2003) and Robert D. Kaplan, *The Coming Anarchy: Shattering the Dreams of the Post Cold War* (New York: Random House, 2000).

37. "There is much evidence from many parts of the world that . . . in fact, such 'reforms as the installation . . . of 'multi-party democracy' actually exacerbate or even create ethnic, religious, or tribal differences, which then create unrest . . ." N. J. Rengger, "Toward a Culture of Democracy? Democratic Theory and Democratization in Eastern and Central Europe," in *Building Democracy? The International Dimension of Democratization in Eastern Europe*, ed Geoffrey Pridham, Eric Herring, and George Sanford (London: Continuum International Publishing Group, 1997), 63.

38. Amitai Etzioni, *Security First* (New Haven, CT: Yale University Press, 2007), 44.

39. Amitai Etzioni, *How Patriotic Is the Patriot Act?: Freedom versus Security in the Age of Terrorism* (New York: Routledge, 2004), 38–39.

40. George Kelling and James Q. Wilson, "Broken Windows," *Atlantic Monthly* (March 1982); George Kelling, *Fixing Broken Windows* (New York: Free Press, 1996).

41. Bernard E. Harcourt, *Illusion of Order: The False Promises of Broken Windows Policing* (Cambridge, MA: Harvard University Press, 2001).

42. Benjamin Chesluk, "Community Policing in New York City," *Cultural Anthropology* 19, no. 2 (2004): 250–74.

43. Amitai Etzioni, *Security First* (New Haven, CT: Yale University Press, 2007), 15–19.

44. Ibid., 31.

19

Terrorists: Neither Soldiers nor Criminals

In current hostilities in Iraq, Afghanistan, parts of Pakistan, and elsewhere, from Colombia to the Horn of Africa, non-state actors—in particular, terrorists and insurgents who behave like terrorists—play a much greater role than they did during World War I, World War II, and the Korean War. In those wars between states, the accepted rules of war, embodied in documents such as the Geneva Conventions, applied much more readily than in contemporary conflicts. Currently, conventional armies that seek to adhere to the rules of war are disadvantaged when they confront terrorists, which suggests that the rules of war need to be updated.

Changes to the rules of war would hardly be unprecedented. The First Geneva Convention dealing with the treatment of battlefield casualties did not exist until 1864, and since then, additional conventions have been agreed upon and other rules of war have been modified. The same holds for "international law," which some people invoke as if it were cast in stone and unambiguous—though it is actually neither. Indeed, even in well-established democratic societies, laws are constantly recast; for instance, there was no constitutional "right to privacy" in the United States until 1965,[1] and the way we now understand the 1st Amendment and the right to free speech was formed in the 1920s.[2] In both cases, no changes were made in the text of the US Constitution, but new interpretations were employed to bring the Constitution—as a living document—in line with the normative precepts of changing times. Hence, it stands to reason that the new threats to security now posed by non-state actors—several of whom have a global reach, are supported by massive religious radical movements, and have potential access to weapons of mass destruction—require modifications in the interpretations, if not the texts, of the rules of war.

New Conditions

Advocates of two major approaches to counterterrorism present strong opposition to the needed adaptations. On the one side are those who speak of a "war on terror," which implies that terrorists ought to be treated like soldiers who, under the current rules of war, can be detained without being charged or tried until the end of the war. Such was the position of the Bush administration. In the words of former Bush Administration Attorney General Michael Mukasey:

> The United States has every right to capture and detain enemy combatants in this conflict, and need not simply release them to return to the battlefield . . . And although wars traditionally have come to an end that is easy to identify, no one can predict when this one will end or even how we'll know it's over . . . . those differences do not make it any less important, or any less fair, for us to detain those who take up arms against us.[3]

On the other side are those who favor treating terrorists like criminals, endowed with the rights and privileges accorded to citizens of democratic societies who have been accused but not yet convicted of having committed a crime. This view is held by prominent figures like Harvard professor and Obama advisor Samantha Power. She criticized the Bush administration for "branding the cause a war and calling the enemy terror" and "[lumping] like with unlike foes and [elevating] hostile elements from the ranks of the criminal (stigmatized in all societies) to the ranks of soldiers of war (a status that carries connotations of sacrifice and courage)."[4] General Wesley Clark stated that terrorists "are merely criminals, albeit criminals of an especially heinous type, and that label suggests the appropriate venue for dealing with the threats they pose."[5] This position was also held by former United Kingdom Prime Minister Gordon Brown's administration. Brown's Home Secretary, Jacqui Smith, stated: "Let us be clear, terrorists are criminals, whose victims come from all walks of life, communities and religions."[6]

The difficulties in characterizing terrorists as criminals are highlighted by the difficulties in trying them. The few cases brought before American judges, even conservative ones, were decided against the government. As Benjamin Wittes and Zaahira Wyne of the Brookings Institution note, the US District Court for the District of Columbia has thus far issued rulings in habeas cases for thirty-eight Guantánamo detainees—thirty of which it held to be unlawfully detained.[7] Bring them to military tribunals? The evidence against them—often obtained on the battlefield—frequently does not satisfy even these less demanding tribunals. Benjamin Wittes reports that military prosecutors have estimated that even under the Military Commissions Act they have enough evidence to be able to bring to trial at best only eighty Guantanamo detainees.[8]

Terrorists Do Not Fit Old Categories

Terrorists are defined individuals who seek to drive fear into a population by acts of violence in order to advance their goals in a sub-rosa manner.[9] Terrorists, as a rule, wear no insignia that identifies them as combatants, engage in a large variety of other means to make themselves indistinguishable from noncombatant civilians, and often use civilians' vehicles, homes, and public facilities, such as schools and places of worship, for their terrorist acts.

One aspect of this definition needs further elaboration. Several scholars hold that the individuals at issue qualify as terrorists only if they attack noncombatants[10]; if they limit themselves to openly attacking combatants, they do not qualify as terrorists. An open attack on combatants may qualify one as an enemy combatant (as in insurgency) but not as a terrorist. I suggest that one should rely much more on the observation that terrorists pass themselves off as noncombatant civilians, which is a cardinal factor affording them considerable advantages over conventional armies that turns confronting them into a highly asymmetric armed conflict and is a major reason for the collateral damage and the ethical and tactical difficulties they raise.

In contrast to terrorists, soldiers are agents of a state, which can be held responsible for their conduct; states can be deterred from violating the rules of war by cajoling, incentives, and threats of retaliation. In contrast, most terrorists and insurgents are not agents of a state, nor are they necessarily members of a group currently qualifying for POW status under international law. They often act in parts of the world that lack effective government, or are supported by foreign governments, but only indirectly, and hence one often cannot determine whether they fight for a government or on their own. Even when they are affiliated with a state or are part of a government, as Hezbollah is in Lebanon, the national government often is unable to control their actions.

That terrorists are typically not agents of an identifiable state is particularly an issue as we face what is widely considered the greatest threat to world security—the use of weapons of mass destruction

(WMD) by terrorists.[11] Although nuclear forensics has made some progress, there is considerable likelihood that in the event of a terrorist nuclear attack, we would be unable to ascertain promptly and accurately from whom the terrorists acquired their weapons and how.[12] This absence of a "return address" and the resulting inability to deter nuclear attacks with the threat of retaliation alone ought to lead one to recognize that terrorists cannot be treated like soldiers.

Furthermore, the notion that terrorists are akin to soldiers wrongly presumes that there is a clear line that separates them from civilians who—it is widely agreed although not always honored—ought to be spared hostilities as much as possible. In World War II, it was considered highly troubling when civilians were deliberately targeted (as distinct from injured as "collateral damage"), for instance, in London, Dresden, Tokyo, Hiroshima, and Nagasaki—given that here the difference between civilians and military targets was clear and well-understood, but ignored. In contemporary conflicts, in which non-state actors play a large and increasing role, such distinctions often cannot be readily made.

Terrorists capitalize on the blurring of the line between soldiers and civilians by acting like civilians as long as it suits their purpose, then deploying their arms and attacking before quickly slipping back into their civilian status. To the extent that state militaries adhere to the old rules, they are often expected to wait until the civilians reveal themselves as combatants before engaging them, and even then they cannot respond with full force because both terrorists and insurgents often hide in civilian homes and public facilities as they launch their attacks.[13]

The media reports with great regularity that American soldiers, bombers, or drones killed "X" number fighters and "Y" number civilians in Afghanistan, Pakistan, or in Iraq. One wonders how the media can determine who is who even after the fact. In any case, this clarity is often missing during the conflict. Ergo, such a line cannot serve as the basis for dealing with fighters who act like and locate themselves among civilians.

In short, characterizing terrorists as soldiers greatly hampers the security of those who abide by the rules of war, and casts doubt on the legitimacy of their actions if they do not.

As I showed in detail elsewhere,[14] without first establishing basic security, development cannot proceed. Regimes that do not provide for elementary safety lose not only their legitimacy but also their credibility. Second, there are strong limitations on what one can achieve through development.[15] To reduce corruption to tolerable levels, to elevate national commitments to a level in which they supersede tribal ones, to modernize an economy, and to build a civil society takes decades and a very large monetary investment, at best. Winning the hearts and minds of the population (to the extent that it can be achieved) supplements measures that enforce safety, but safety cannot be based on it alone in areas in which terrorists maintain a strong presence and in which significant elements of the civilian population are combatants.

Above all, to demand that civilians who raise their arms against us be treated like noncombatants until they choose to reveal themselves, and to allow them to slip back into this status whenever it helps advance their goals, imposes several costs. The most obvious one is casualties among the conventional force under attack. This approach also generates perverse incentives for nations with conventional armies, already explored above: to circumvent the rules, to find some sub-rosa way to deal with combatant civilians. Redefining the rules of armed conflicts is not only a more effective but also a more legitimate method of dealing with violent non-state actors.

The reasons terrorists cannot be treated as criminals are equally strong. By far the most important of these is that security requires that the primary goal of counterterrorism be *preventing* attacks rather than prosecuting the perpetrators after the attack has occurred. This is particularly evident when we concern ourselves with terrorists who may acquire WMDs. It also holds for many terrorists who are willing to commit suicide during their attack and hence cannot be tried, and who are not going to pay mind to the personal consequences of their assault. Finally, even terrorists with no intention of committing suicide attacks are often "true believers" who are willing to proceed despite whatever punishment the legal system may prescribe. All these individuals—those who may use WMDs, the suicide bombers, and others who are merely fanatics—are best prevented from proceeding rather than vainly trying to prosecute them after the fact, and most cannot be effectively deterred by the criminal justice system.

In contrast to the need for prevention, law enforcement often takes action after a criminal has acted—when a body is found, a bank is robbed, or a child is kidnapped. Thus, while "criminal justice also has a preventive component . . . criminal law is generally retrospective in focus, in that it addresses past acts."[16] Law enforcement assumes that punishment after the fact serves to deter future crimes (not to eliminate them, but to keep them at a socially acceptable level). Furthermore, as Ruth Wedgwood writes, "The purpose of domestic criminal law is to inflict stigma and punishment, and so it must be applied cautiously. Such reticence is proper for civil government in peacetime, but it is not always appropriate in war."[17] True, to some extent law enforcement can be modified to adapt to the challenge of terrorism. For instance, greater use can be made of statutes already enacted against those who engage in conspiracy to commit a crime. However, significant kinds of preventive action cannot be accommodated within the law enforcement paradigm. For instance, as "criminal law is concerned with punishment, it sets a high bar for detention."[18] Acts that subject a considerable number of people to administrative detention, or even simply surveillance or interrogation—without any individualized suspicion—would not be allowed. The aim in such cases is to disrupt *possible* planning of attacks without necessarily charging anybody with anything, or to pry loose some information through what under criminal law would be considered fishing expeditions. For example, in 2002–2003, the FBI invited 10,000 Iraqi-Americans to be interviewed, without claiming that any of them were terrorists or supported terrorists.[19]

Following normal criminal procedures also makes the prevention of terrorist attacks and the prosecution of captured terrorists more difficult. First, collecting evidence that meets the standards of a criminal court while in the combat zones and ungoverned regions in which many terrorists are captured is often not practical. And, to quote Matthew Waxman, a professor of law at Columbia University, the criminal justice system "is deliberately tilted in favor of defendants so that few if any innocents will be punished, but the higher stakes of terrorism cannot allow the same likelihood that some guilty persons will go free."[20] In one 2009 case, Ali Saleh Kahlah al-Marri, who had admitted to being a sleeper agent for Al Qaeda, was granted a plea bargain which cut his maximum sentence in half, the Justice Department in effect acknowledging that it may have had a hard time prosecuting Mr. Marri in the criminal justice system.[21]

Additionally, most violent criminals act as individuals while most terrorists act in groups. Hence, the criminal procedures of open arrest records, charging suspects within forty-eight hours or so, and speedy trials in open court all undermine the fight against terrorism. Counterterrorism requires time to capture other members of the cell before they realize that one of their members has been apprehended, to decipher their records, and to prevent other attacks that might be under way. Also, security demands that authorities do not reveal their means and methods, and often it does not allow terrorists to face their accusers. As stated by Robert Chesney and Jack Goldsmith

> Neither [the criminal justice or the military detention] model in its traditional guise can easily meet the central legal challenge of modern terrorism: the legitimate preventive incapacitation of uniformless terrorists who have the capacity to inflict mass casualties and enormous economic harms and who thus must be stopped before they act.[22]

In short, terrorists are a distinct breed that requires a distinct treatment.

A Distinct Species

Distinct rules for engaging terrorists have not been developed, in part because the two camps are each locked into their soldiers/civilians and criminal/innocent legal and normative precepts. We need a group of leading legal minds *combined with people who have extensive combat experience* to create these rules. This essay turns next to outline select preliminary guidelines concerning the ways to deal with terrorists during armed conflicts and in future counterterrorism campaigns, as well as with those individuals already detained. Important work on this issue has already been carried out by Matthew Waxman,[23] Tung Yin,[24] Jack Goldsmith,[25] Robert Chesney,[26] and Amos Guiora,[27] among others. In addition, Columbia University's Phillip Bobbitt makes such a case in his valuable *Terror and Consent: The Wars for the Twenty-First Century*, in which he implores policymakers to stop relying on outdated legal and strategic thinking in dealing with terrorism. Much more detailed work is carried out in *Law and the Long War* by Benjamin Wittes. Both agree that there is a need for distinct legal and normative precepts for dealing with terrorists.[28]

For each of the following suggested guidelines, much remains to be developed and surely additional criteria are called for. These guidelines principally serve to illustrate the third approach:

Terrorists Are Entitled to Select Basic Human Rights

Terrorists are entitled to select basic human rights by virtue of being human. Although terrorists should be treated as civilians who have forfeited much, certain basic rights should be considered inviolate. They should not be killed when they can be safely detained and held, nor should they be subjected to torture.[29] Other basic rights are implied in the examination that follows; for instance, concerning their rights not to be detained indefinitely and to an institutionalized review of their status. As Amos N. Guiora states, "The dilemma is in determining and implementing the appropriate balance between legitimate national security rights and equally legitimate rights of the individual. Democratic States cannot afford the luxury of refusing all rights for suspected terrorist detainees."[30]

Special Detention Authority

Terrorists cannot be held until the end of the war (as a POW may be) because the armed conflict with terrorists may continue indefinitely or fade without any clear endpoint. Furthermore, holding an individual without review for an indefinite period is a gross violation of basic human rights, and one that can be readily remedied. Detained terrorists should be subject to periodic review by a special authority (see below), to determine if they can be safely released or if their history warrants further detention. Note that while much attention has been paid by the media to the plight of those detained, little attention has been paid to those that have been released and proceeded to commit acts of terror, particularly, killing civilians. For instance, Abdallah Saleh al-Ajmi, a former Guantanamo Bay detainee, was repatriated to Kuwait as per a prisoner transfer agreement with the United States. In his trial in Kuwait, al-Ajmi was acquitted and then released. About two years after his release from Guantanamo, al-Ajmi killed thirteen Iraqi soldiers in a suicide bombing.[31]

At the same time, terrorists should not be incarcerated for a set period of time depending on the gravity of their attack, the way criminals are. The main purpose of detention is to *prevent* them from attacking again rather than to punish them for their crime. Thus, if the conflict between Israel and Palestine is finally settled and the settlement is faithfully implemented, those terrorists jailed by Israel and by the Palestinian Authority can be released.

Additionally, holding terrorists merely for forty-eight hours or so before they must be charged, as criminals are in the United States, does not allow enough time for essential counterterrorism measures already listed. Various extended detainment periods, but not unlimited ones, that have been set in law in other democratic societies provide a precedent of sorts. For instance, in the United Kingdom, criminal suspects are usually held only forty-eight hours without being charged, but that can now be extended by a court to up to twenty-eight days.[32]

Many related issues remain to be developed, including how to ensure that preventive detention is not used too widely and which procedures should be used to determine who can be released.[33]

A National Security Court

Neal Katyal, a highly respected legal scholar and the Principal Deputy Solicitor General of the United States, favors a separate judicial authority for dealing with terrorists: a congressionally created national security court.[34] Unlike a military commission, this court would be overseen by federal judges with life tenure, and detainees would have the right to appeal decisions—appeals which would then be reviewed by a second set of federal judges.[35] But unlike a civilian court, detainees would not receive the full plethora of criminal protections (for instance, they would not be allowed to face all their accusers, if these include, for example, CIA agents working covertly), and the national security court would also have different evidentiary standards than civilian courts[36] (such as allowing the introduction of certain kinds of hearsay as evidence).

Similarly, Wittes writes that, thus far, the main steps in the United States to develop a systematic position on the treatment of captured terrorists have been taken by the executive branch (various presidential declarations, orders, and "findings") and the courts (including decisions such as *Rasul v. Bush* and *Hamdan v. Rumsfeld*).[37] He criticizes this approach, and suggests that Congress should formulate a distinct legal architecture to deal with terrorists by authorizing the creation of a national security court, with rules and practices less exacting than those that govern domestic criminal courts, but in which terrorists are granted more legal rights and protections than in the current Combatant Status Review Tribunals (CSRT).[38]

Wittes also favors that the standards for admissible evidence be lower than for domestic criminal cases; the court should bar the admission of evidence gleaned from torture, but, aside from that, "probative material—even hearsay or physical evidence whose chain of custody or handling would not be adequate in a criminal trial—ought to be fair game.[39]

Terrorists cannot gain full access to all the evidence against them, which criminals are entitled to, without creating significant security risks. Even for the evidence that can be revealed, I favor allowing terrorists to choose only among lawyers who have security clearances. (This also greatly curtails the possibility that the lawyers will serve as go-betweens for terrorists and their compatriots, as was the case with lawyer Lynne Stewart.[40])

There is room for differences about the specific nature and workings of the national security court. For instance, it might be best called a national security review board to stress that it is not a typical court. However, the main point is that terrorists must be tried in different ways than criminals are.[41] Even "tried" may be the wrong term; granted a hearing might be more accurate.

Surveillance of Civilians

An essential element of counterterrorism is identifying the attackers before they strike. Surveillance has a key role to play in such efforts. This entails allowing computers (which do not "read" messages and hence cannot violate privacy) to screen the billions of messages transmitted through cyberspace as well as over phone lines. It is a highly obsolescent notion to suggest that in order to conduct this kind of surveillance the government must first submit evidence to a court that there is individualized probable cause for suspicion—as is typically done with criminals. All messages that pass through public spaces (as distinct from, for instance, within one's home) might be screened to identify likely terrorism suspects who then may be submitted to closer scrutiny.

Second, the notion that one can and should deal differently with Americans versus others is also highly anachronistic. Generally, there is no way of determining the nationality of those who communicate through modern technology. The rule of thumb used in the past by American authorities—that if the message originates in American territory or is sent to someone who is in American territory, it is presumed to involve an American—leads to results favorable to terrorists. For instance, numerous messages (such as emails, phone calls, or text messages) sent between those in foreign countries pass digitally through the United States; these messages cannot be legally scrutinized as long as the said rule is followed. It is quite possible terrorists will be among the over 50 million visitors who come to the United States each year, and that before they strike, these terrorists will contact their superiors overseas, as the 9/11 attackers did, as well as did those who attacked other nations, such as the United Kingdom and Spain. Monitoring for this entails that all messages should be initially screened, in the limited sense that computers would determine whether they actually should be read or their patterns further examined.

One effective way to ensure that mass surveillance is not abused is to set up a review board that will examine regularly the ways in which data are collected and used, and that will issue annual reports to the public on its findings. That both the US Department of Homeland Security and the Office of the Director of National Intelligence have privacy officers is also a step in the desired direction. This kind of oversight works largely after the fact, rather than slowing the collection of information to a crawl, which would be the case if each act of surveillance faced review by a special court before it was undertaken, and points to the right balance between allowing the government to advance security and subjecting these efforts to public scrutiny.[42]

Tomorrow's Freedom Fighters?

There are some who say that those we consider terrorists today will be considered freedom fighters tomorrow—and that some already view them in this way. As I see it, deliberately killing or terrorizing a human being is a morally flawed act. There are conditions under which this act is justified, as in self-defense, or legal, as when a court orders an execution or a head of state orders an army to defend the nation. However, this does not make killing and terror "good"; we are always commanded to see whether we can achieve the same purpose without killing or terror—for example, by taking the enemy soldiers as POWs rather than killing them once they no longer endanger us.

While killing and terrorism are always morally flawed means, there is no moral equivalency in terms of the purposes for which they are applied. Those who use these means to overthrow a tyrannical government (for instance, members of the underground in France who fought the Nazis during WWII) may deserve support, while those who use them to undermine a democracy (for instance, those who attacked the United States on 9/11, and those who attacked Spain and Britain in the following years)—deserve special condemnation. *However, the fact that some purposes are noble and others foul does not make the means used good.* Hence, while combatant civilians are not all created equal, while some may indeed be today's or tomorrow's freedom fighters—none of them are engaged in regime change in ways that one should consider morally superior to non-lethal means.

In Conclusion

Up to a point, these and other such counterterrorism measures might be viewed as merely modifications of the criminal justice system or as a hybrid of that system and the laws of war. However, given the scope and number of differences involved, together they amount to a distinct approach. This is most evident when one acknowledges that the prevention of terrorism requires questioning and even detaining some people who have not yet violated any law when there are reasons to fear that they may be mounting an attack insufficient to convince a criminal court.

The preceding suggestions are merely ways to launch and foster the explorations of the third approach. They do not constitute an elaborated model that could be implemented as public policy without considerable additional deliberations and modifications. Moreover, for the distinct treatment of terrorists to be fully embraced, it must gain acceptance by the American public, while also being viewed as legitimate by other people. It hence requires transnational dialogues and the development of new norms and agreements—for instance, a new Geneva Convention—which, to reiterate, would be hardly the first time these conventions have been significantly altered.

One might differ about the proper actions that may be taken to prevent terrorism and about how to best contend with terrorists, but still agree that it makes little sense to treat terrorists either as criminals or as soldiers. At issue is not a matter of neat classifications, but ways to maintain the institutions of a free society while also protecting it from devastating attacks.

Underlying many of the discussions of the issue at hand is a sub-text, a quest for a clean war, one in which no bystanders are hurt, collateral damage is minimized if not avoided all together, and in which strikes are "surgical." Thus, for instance, various observers objected to the use of airpower in Kosovo—and recently of bombers and drones in Afghanistan and Pakistan—and urged greater reliance on land troops, because they hoped that these troops might be able to better separate civilians from fighters.

As I see it, the same respect for human life and for human rights takes one elsewhere. One must recognize that, although some measures can be taken to protect noncombatant civilians, at the end of the day some such civilians are very likely to be hurt. Hence, the best way to minimize innocent civilian casualties is to exhaust all other means possible to manage conflict short of armed interventions—to go the extra mile, to ignore provocations, to invite intermediaries, to turn the other cheek, and to avoid, if at all possible, an armed clash. Combat is by nature bloody. Although it can be tidied up to some extent, at the end of the day it is tragic and best avoided if at all possible. However, when an armed conflict is forced on a people, for example, by those who bomb their heartland, killing thousands of innocent civilians working at their desks—an appropriate response requires dealing with the attackers as terrorists, and not being hobbled by precepts and rules concerning criminals and soldiers. The time has come to recognize that those who abuse their civilian status, by pretending to be civilians but acting like terrorists, forfeit many of the rights of true civilians without acquiring the privileges due to soldiers.[43]

Notes

1. Griswold v. Connecticut, 381 U.S. 479 (1965).
2. Whitney v. California, 274 U.S. 357 (1927).
3. Michael B. Mukasey, "Remarks Prepared for Delivery by Attorney General Michael B. Mukasey at the American Enterprise Institute for Public Policy Research," (remarks, American Enterprise Institute, Washington, DC, July 21, 2008).
4. Samantha Power, "Our War on Terror," *New York Times* (July 29, 2007), http://www.nytimes.com/2007/07/29/books/review/Power-t.html?_r=1 (accessed April 23, 2010).
5. Wesley K. Clark and Kal Raustiala, "Why Terrorists Aren't Soldiers," *The New York Times* (August 8, 2007), http://www.nytimes.com/2007/08/08/opinion/08clark.html (accessed April 23, 2010).
6. David Rieff, "Policing Terrorism," *The New York Times* (July 22, 2007), late edition, sec. 6.
7. Benjamin Wittes and Zaahira Wyne. "The Current Detainee Population of Guantánamo: An Empirical Study." The Brookings Institution. (October 21, 2009), 1, http://www.brookings.edu/reports/2008/~/media/Files/rc/reports/2008/1216_detainees_wittes/1216_detainees_wittes_supplement.pdf.
8. Senate Committee on the Judiciary, *Improving Detainee Policy: Handling Terrorism Detainees within the American Justice System*, 110th Cong., 2nd sess., 2008, testimony of Benjamin Wittes.
9. This basic definition is derived from that which is common to most definitions, as there is no accepted single definition of terrorism or terrorists. Bruce Hoffman defines terrorism briefly as "the deliberate creation and exploitation of fear through violence or threat of violence in the pursuit of political change" (Bruce Hoffman. *Inside Terrorism* [New York: Columbia University Press, 1998], 43). Tamar Meisels defines it as "the intentional

random murder of defenseless non-combatants, with the intent of instilling fear of mortal danger amidst a civilian population as a strategy designed to advance political ends" (Tamar Meisels, "The Trouble with Terror: The Apologetics of Terrorism—a Refutation," *Terrorism and Political Violence* 18 [2006]: 480). Boaz Ganor defines it more simply as "the deliberate use of violence aimed against civilians in order to achieve political ends" (Boaz Ganor, "The Relationship between International and Localized Terrorism," Jerusalem Center for Public Affairs Jerusalem Issue Brief, 4:26 [2005], http://www.jcpa.org/brief/brief004-26.htm). Title 18, Section 2331 of the US Code defines international terrorism as activities that "involve violent acts or acts dangerous to human life that are a violation of criminal laws . . . appear to be intended—(i) to intimidate or coerce a civilian population; (ii) to influence the policy of a government by intimidation or coercion; or (iii) to affect the conduct of a government by mass destruction, assassination, or kidnapping; and . . . occur primarily outside the territorial jurisdiction of the United States . . ."

10. Caleb Carr, *The Lessons of Terror: A History of Warfare against Civilians*, revised edn. (New York: Random House, 2003), 6; Boaz Ganor, "Defining Terrorism: Is One Man's Terrorist Another Man's Freedom Fighter?" International Policy Institute for Counter-Terrorism, Herzlia, Israel. (September 24, 1998), http://www.ict.org.il/ResearchPublications/tabid/64/Articlsid/432/currentpage/1/Default.aspx; Albert J. Bergesen and Omar Lizardo, "International Terrorism and the World-System," *Sociological Theory* 22 (2004): 50.

11. Department of Defense, *Nuclear Posture Review Report* (April 2010), 10, http://www.defense.gov/npr/docs/2010%20Nuclear%20Posture%20 Review%20Report.pdf.

12. Sharon Begley, "Deterring a 'Dirty Bomb'," *Newsweek* (April 26, 2010); Joint Working Group of the American Physical Society and the American Association for the Advancement of Science, *Nuclear Forensics Role, State of the Art, Program Needs* (2008), 23, http://www.aps.org/policy/reports/upload/Nuclear-Forensics-Report-FINAL.pdf.

13. For more see "Unmanned Aircraft Systems: The Moral and Legal Case," *Joint Force Quarterly* 57, no. 2 (2010): 66–71.

14. Amitai Etzioni, *Security First: For a Muscular, Moral Foreign Policy* (New Haven, CT: Yale University Press, 2007); Amitai Etzioni, *The Moral Dimension: Toward a New Economics* (New York: Free Press, 1988).

15. Amitai Etzioni, "Reconstruction: An Agenda," *in Statebuilding and Intervention: Policies, Practices, and Paradigms*, ed. David Chandler (New York: Routledge Press, 2009), 101–21.

16. Matthew Waxman, "Administrative Detention of Terrorists: *Why* Detain, and Detain *Whom*?" *Journal of National Security Law and Policy*, 3 (2009): 12–13.

17. Ruth Wedgwood and Kenneth Roth, "Combatants or Criminals? How Washington Should Handle Terrorists" *Foreign Affairs* (May/June 2004), http://www.foreignaffairs.com/articles/59902/ruth-wedgwood-kenneth-roth/combatants-or-criminals-how-washington-should-handle-terrorists.

18. Tung Yin, "Ending the War on Terrorism One Terrorist at a Time: A Noncriminal Detention Model for Holding and Releasing Guantanamo Bay Detainees," *Harvard Journal of Law and Public Policy* 29 (2005): 155.
19. John Ashcroft, "Success and Strategies in the Effort to Liberate Iraq" (April 17, 2003), http://www.usdoj.gov/archive/ag/speeches/2003/041703effortsliberateIraq.htm (accessed April 23, 2010).
20. See note 16, 11.
21. John Schwartz, "Path to Justice, but Bumpy, for Terrorists," *The New York Times* (May 1, 2009).
22. Robert Chesney and Jack Goldsmith, "Terrorism and the Convergence of Criminal and Military Detention Models," *Stanford Law Review* 60 (2008): 1081.
23. See note 16.
24. See note 18.
25. See note 21.
26. Ibid.
27. Amos N. Guiora, "Quirin to Hamdan: Creating a Hybrid Paradigm for the Detention of Terrorists," *Florida Journal of International Law* 19 (2007): 529.
28. One may ask why I hold that this third approach is very unpopular despite the fact that both books received rave reviews, as did my much more limited attempt to deal with this issue in *The Financial Times* on August 22, 2007. I reached this conclusion by noting that despite the warm welcome to these texts, so far they have been almost completely ignored by policy makers, most legal scholars, and most assuredly by advocates of human and individual rights.
29. It remains to be worked out what should be considered torture. It can be defined so broadly that it would block most interrogation techniques—for instance, if it encompasses a ban on humiliating the detainees and it leaves up to them to define what is humiliating—or so narrowly that waterboarding and many other cruel measures would be allowed as long as they do not lead to organ failure. It goes without saying that the suggested guidelines' use would be much hampered unless the definition is worked out, presumably somewhere in between these two extremes.
30. See note 27, 521.
31. Rajiv Chandrasekaran, "From Captive to Suicide Bomber" *Washington Post* (February 28, 2009).
32. Terrorism Act 2006, 2006, c. 11, §25 (U.K.)
33. For such a discussion see Matthew Waxman's article in the *Journal of National Security Law and Policy*, "Administrative Detention of Terrorists: *Why* Detain, and Detain *Whom*?"
34. Jack Goldsmith and Neal Katyal, "The Terrorist' Court," *The New York Times* (July 11, 2007).
35. Ibid.
36. Ibid.
37. Benjamin Wittes, *Law and the Long War* (New York: The Penguin Press, 2008), 11–16.

38. Ibid, 164–78.
39. Ibid, 165.
40. Phil Hirschkorn, "Civil Rights Attorney Convicted in Terror Trial," *CNN.com* (February 14, 2005), http://www.cnn.com/2005/LAW/02/10/terror.trial.lawyer/.
41. Nor can they be tried as soldiers, as much of the evidence is not admissible in military commissions either. On May 15, 2009, President Obama announced his intentions to continue to use military commissions to try suspected terrorists, among other venues. According to his announcement, these commissions will be different from the Bush Administration Commissions. The outline of changes he provided, however, was vague:

    a. First, statements that have been obtained from detainees using cruel, inhuman and degrading interrogation methods will no longer be admitted as evidence at trial. Second, the use of hearsay will be limited, so that the burden will no longer be on the party who objects to hearsay to disprove its reliability. Third, the accused will have greater latitude in selecting their counsel. Fourth, basic protections will be provided for those who refuse to testify. And fifth, military commission judges may establish the jurisdiction of their own courts. Office of the Press Secretary, The White House, *Statement of President Barack Obama on Military Commissions*, May 15, 2009, http://www.whitehouse.gov/the_press_office/Statement-of-President-Barack-Obama-on-Military-Commissions/ (accessed April 23, 2010).

42. For more discussion, see Amitai Etzioni, *How Patriotic Is the Patriot Act?* (New York, NY: Routledge, 2004).
43. For more discussion, see Amitai Etzioni, "Unmanned Aircraft Systems: The Moral and Legal Case," *Joint Force Quarterly* 57, no. 2 (2010): 66–71.

20

Drones: Moral and Legal?

The substantial increase in the employment of Unmanned Aircraft Systems (UAS) in Afghanistan, Pakistan, and other arenas has intensified the debate about the moral and legal nature of the targeted killing of people who are said to be civilians. As I see it, the United States and its allies can make a strong case that the main source of the problem are those who abuse their civilian status to attack truly innocent civilians and to prevent our military and other security forces from discharging their duties. In the longer run, we should work toward a new Geneva Convention, one that will define the status of those now called unlawful combatants. These people should be viewed as having forfeited most of their rights as civilians by acting in gross violation of the rights of others and of the rules of war.

To support my thesis, we must go back to the period in which the precept that currently still dominates much of the public discourse on the issue at hand was forged. For generations, growing efforts had been made to limit wars to confrontations among conventional armies, sparing civilians. That is, a sharp line was drawn between soldiers (who were considered fair targets during war) and civilians (whose killing was taboo). True, these shared understandings were not always observed. Thus during World War II, the Nazis tried to break Britain by blitzing London, and their dive bombers attacked many other civilian centers. The Allied Forces bombed Dresden, set a firestorm in Tokyo, and leveled Nagasaki and Hiroshima. However, these attacks were condemned, or at least ethically questioned, precisely on the grounds that they eroded the line that ought to separate armed forces from civilians and protect the latter.

Over the last decade, however, we have witnessed a rise in terrorism with a global reach and potential access to weapons of mass destruction—the gravest threat to our security, that of our allies, and of many others. These terrorists systematically and repeatedly use their civilian status to their advantage, both to enhance their operations and to mobilize public opinion. Thus, they have used ambulances to transport suicide bombers and their bombs—and have had their allies complain when security forces started checking ambulances, causing some delays in their services. Terrorists disguised themselves as civilian passengers in order to hijack airplanes full of innocent people, turning the planes into missiles in order to kill thousands working peacefully at their desks—and afterwards found people who complained vociferously about the security measures that were introduced to prevent such attacks. They stored their ammunition in mosques, mounted anti-aircraft guns on top of schools and hospitals, set their command-and-control centers in private homes and made them into bivouacs—and then screamed bloody murder when any of these installations were hit by our bombers, artillery, or drones. In short, we must make it much clearer that those who abuse their civilian status are the main reason for the use of UAS and targeted killing.

Another way to illustrate this key point is to conduct the following mental experiment. Take any fighting force, say the Japanese military in World War II. If that force is abiding by the rules of war—wearing clear insignia identifying the troops and their encampments, and thus the government that is accountable for their actions—they can be (and were) legitimately targeted, bombed, and killed. No one raises moral or legal issues—beyond a few pacifists who would rather surrender than fight at all—even if the particular unit is not engaged in battle: it might be resting in its camp, being resupplied, or in training somewhere in the hinterland. Now imagine the same troops take off their uniforms, put on civilians' clothing, and move into civilians' homes, community centers, and shrines. Now, are they no longer legitimate targets?

Unlike armchair ethicists, who write about this matter and never come closer to combat than watching a movie in a nearby downtown theater—I have some first hand experience in the matter. In 1946, I was a member of the Palmach, a Jewish underground commando unit that pressured the British to allow Jews who escaped Nazi-ravaged Europe to settle into what would become Israel. (I say "pressured" because unlike our competitor, the Irgun, we fought a largely public relations war. We did so by alerting the British military to leave before we blew up the buildings that housed them—to grab headlines not bodies.) One day we attacked a British radar station near Haifa. A girl and I, in civilian clothes and looking as if we were on a date, casually walked up to the radar station's fence, cut the fence, and placed a bomb. Before it exploded, we disappeared into the crowd milling around in an adjacent street. All the British could do was either indiscriminately machine gun the crowd—or let us get away. Indeed, their inability to cope with abusive civilians was one reason the British retreated from Palestine and scores of other colonial territories, the French ultimately lost the war in Algeria, the Soviet Union in Afghanistan, and the United States in Vietnam (although here the North Vietnamese regular forces also played a key role).

Does all this mean that we should attack masses of civilians, merely because some of them have—or may be about—to attack us? Certainly not. It does mean that in order to negate the tactical advantages abusive civilians have and to minimize our casualties, we must attack abusive civilians whenever we can find them, before they attack us. As we shall see shortly, UAS are a particularly well-suited means to serve this goal.

Hence instead of apologizing each time the wrong individual is targeted or collateral damage is caused, we should stress that the issue would be largely resolved in very short order if the abusive civilians would stop their abusive practices and fight—if they must—according to established rules of war. That they cannot have it both ways—violate these rules repeatedly and seek to be shielded by them. And while in-vestigations after each incident have their place, to determine whether we received wrong intelligence or to further refine the decision-making matrix involved (more about this shortly), they should not be construed as an indication that the main source of the problem is our response to abusive civilians who attacked us.

To suggest that we need a new shared understanding, for which we must first make the moral case and then move to ensconce it in a new Geneva-like convention, is far from implausible. After all, the Geneva Conventions have been extended, revised, and augmented several times.

Smaller Print

In examining the arguments about the moral and legal status of using UAS (and other forms of targeted killing), I am using as my text an October 2009 article in *The New Yorker* by Jane Mayer.[1] The article touches on all the major issues involved, albeit with a dose of liberal coloring. (The article is called "The Predator War," a name which is both accurate and revealing. Mayer has previously written critically about the treatment of terror suspects in her 2008 book, whose title again speaks volumes: *The Dark Side.*[2])

Mayer opens her reportage with a case in point: a man is lounging on the rooftop somewhere in Pakistan. He has a bunch of visitors. He is not well: he has diabetes and a kidney disease. We even can see—thanks to a drone that is hovering above—his IV drip. Suddenly, poof, two missiles strike, and all we have left is a torso. Several of the visitors are also dead.

The picture changes though, as Mayer reports that Baitullah Mesud was the man on the roof top, a man responsible for the assassination of Benazir Bhutto, the September 2008 bombing of the Islamabad Marriott, and numerous attacks on American and coalition forces in Afghanistan. Another case Mayer points to is a 2002 killing by a UAV of a few people driving in a car, somewhere on a road deep inside Yemen. This, Mayer tells us, was Qaed Salim Sinan al-Harethi, an Al Qaeda operative who is reported to have played a key role in the bombing of the USS Cole. It is helpful to keep such cases in mind when one faces the questions Mayer, speaking in effect for other skeptics of the program, raises about the use of UAS.

Can Abusive Civilians Be Treated like Criminals?

Some suggest that we would be better off if we with dealt with abusive civilians like criminals; that is—instead of killing them—haul them into a court of law. Of course in numerous situations, including the two Mayer describes, such capture could not be executed or only at very great risk to our forces and to the local civilian population.

Moreover, often—say when dealing with Al Qaeda leaders and foot soldiers and others like them—security requires *preventing* attacks rather than prosecuting the perpetrators after the attack has occurred. This is particularly evident when we concern ourselves with terrorists who may acquire weapons of mass destruction. It also holds for terrorists who are willing to commit suicide during their attack and hence either cannot be tried, or will pay no mind to what might be done to them after their assault. Finally, even terrorists not bent on committing suicide attacks are often "true believers" who are willing to proceed despite whatever punishments the legal system may throw at them. All these kinds of terrorists are best prevented from proceeding rather than vainly trying to prosecute them after the fact, and most cannot be effectively deterred by the criminal justice system.

In contrast to the need for prevention, law enforcement often springs into action after a criminal has acted—when a body is found, after bank is robbed, or a child is kidnapped. By and large, the criminal law approach is retrospective rather than prospective. Law enforcement assumes that punishment after the fact serves to deter future crimes (not to eliminate them, but to keep them at a socially acceptable level). This will not do for the likes of Osama bin Laden.

This is not to say that if captured, terrorists should not be granted basic human rights. They should not be killed when they can be safely detained and held, nor should they be subjected to torture or detained indefinitely without an institutionalized review of their status. However, they are not entitled to the full plethora of rights our citizens are entitled to because they choose to fight in a way that abuses the rules on which these rights are based.

I leave it for another day to examine the argument implied in the rules of war that both parties have the same basic moral status, and hence both must abide equally by the rules, and to examine the notion of fair play—which suggests that when we kill many of the enemy but have only few casualties of our own, that there "must be" something foul in the way we fight. Suffice it to say here, that those who attack us in the disguise of being civilians and who act brutally, not only toward our civilians, but even toward their compatriots (e.g., if they heed a different version of the same religion, happen to be women, minors, or of a different color)—do not have the same moral standing as our troops.

Is There Enough Accountability?

The preceding analysis does not suggest that UAS should be used indiscriminately against anybody who may threaten our security or that of others. The statement Mayer quotes that "no tall man with a beard [i.e. similar to bin Laden] is safe anywhere in Southwest Asia" is obviously false. Indeed, the use of UAS is subject to close review. The US military developed a set of criteria that must be met before a strike is authorized. The details are not publicized, but during a visit with officers of a brigade before it shipped out to Afghanistan, I was told that they include the reliability of the intelligence that identified the target (in some cases, verification from two independent sources is required) and the number and status of other people in the area. The less reliable the information and the greater the potential collateral damage, the more people review the information and the higher the rank of those in the military who must approve the strike—all the way up to the Commander-in-Chief. Strikes also are reexamined after they occur in cases in which we erred. Thus, in effect, abusive civilians benefit from an extensive review before targeted killing takes place.

One should, though, note that just as the matrix (the decision-making apparatus used by the military) can be too accommodating—it can also be too restrictive. In several cases, the delay in decision involved, or the strictness of the criteria employed, allowed abusive civilians of considerable rank and power to escape. (Bin Laden was given the time to escape to a new location when the Pakistani government delayed giving permission for an attack on its soil in 2004.)

And at least according to one source, after General McChrystal decided to cut back on bombing and targeted killing, because of what was considered excessive collateral damage—our casualties increased. The *Washington Post* reported on September 23, 2009 that there has been "a sharp increase in U.S. troop deaths in Afghanistan at a time when senior military officials acknowledge that American service members are facing greater risks under a new strategy that emphasizes protecting Afghan civilians."[3] The moral ground for this approach is far from self-evident. I turn below to the prudential argument that such sacrifices will win over the population, and hence will save lives—ours and theirs—in the longer run.

What about Collateral Damage?

Even if one fully accepts that targeted killing of the leaders and maybe foot soldiers of groups like Al Qaeda is justified, one still must be concerned, for moral and prudential reasons, about collateral damage—which involves by definition innocent civilians. Here, too, one must first of all reiterate that the main fault lies with the abusive citizens, who refuse to separate themselves from the local population. Second, to some extent collateral damage can be reduced by enabling the general population to leave an area before an attack, as the Pakistani army did in Swat Valley, or by encouraging the general population to separate itself from abusive citizens, as Israel did during the 2009 operation in Gaza.

Thirdly, the extent of potential collateral damage is and should continue to be one criterion in the matrix of decision-making that is used by the US military when UAS strikes are authorized. That is, consideration is given not only to the "values" of the target and to the reliability of information about the target, but also the number and kind of innocent civilians surrounding the target (children in particular).

Additionally, one should note that some of the population acts like part-time spies, intelligence agents, lookouts, and providers of services like accommodations and medical care to the terrorists. To the extent that these services are provided voluntarily rather than coerced, the population must be warned that they will be treated the same ways as combat service support personnel that provide such services.

Last but not least, there is no reason to hold that UAS cause more collateral damage than bombing or even attacks with Special Forces or regular ones.

Are UAS Legal?

Are UAS strikes legal by our own laws? Congress has authorized the President "to use all necessary and appropriate force" against "persons he determines planned, authorized, committed, or aided" in 9/11 or who harbored such persons.[4] Both the Obama and Bush Administrations have stated that this act of Congress grants them the legal power to authorize UAS strikes. And because the targets are engaged in combat against us, many legal experts state that the strikes are not in violation of Executive Order 12333's prohibition on assassination.

Are strikes legal according to international law? Mayer reports that, "In order for the U.S. government to legally target civilian terror suspects abroad it has to define a terrorist group as one engaging in armed conflict, and the use of force must be a 'military necessity.' There must be no reasonable alternative to killing, such as capture, and to warrant death the target must be 'directly participating in hostilities.' The use of force has to be considered 'proportionate' to the threat. Finally, the foreign nation in which such targeted killing takes place has to give its permission."

Without going here into a detailed analysis whether or not the United States strikes in all the cases, from Pakistan to Yemen, meet all these criteria, I should point out that international law (and for that matter domestic laws) is rarely that unambiguous. Indeed, there is considerable literature on the subject, which reaches a wide range of conclusions.[5] Nor are the facts always as straightforward as one would need to meet the standards. For instance, the Pakistani government protests publicly the use of UAS, but privately provides bases for them and intelligence to identify targets—does this mean that the foreign power did or did not give consent? And why should a government be expected to seek the consent of a nation that supports terrorism—say

303

if Israel targets a terrorist in Damascus, should it await the consent of Syria?

Most important, laws are not carved in stone. They are living documents. The Constitutional right to privacy did not exist until 1965. Our current understanding of the 1st Amendment's the right to free speech, considered the most absolute right of them all, is an interpretation of the text fashioned in the 1920s. The Geneva Conventions were developed over decades—and thus can be further developed.

Do UAS Alienate the Population?

Prudential arguments against the use of UAS are that they antagonize the population, create martyrs, invite retaliatory attacks, entail the loss of moral high ground, and undermine the legitimacy of the local government (for cooperating with Americans). All this may be true, but the same holds for other means of warfare. Using bombers often generates even more collateral damage and resentment. Attacks by Special Forces are considered more alienating than strikes by UAS because they entail a blatant violation of sovereignty. Nor are there necessarily fewer mistaken targets or less collateral damage when Special Forces or regular forces are used. Last but not least, important segments of the population resent the presence of foreign troops—and the governments they support—for a variety of sentimental, cultural, religious, and nationalistic reasons. No wonder that in areas and periods in which the use of UAS was scaled back, there was no noticeable change in the attitudes of the population.

Hence the main issues are how quickly we can turn over security to native forces and the extent to which we should interfere in the way the people govern themselves—not which means of warfare we use, as long as we stay engaged. Indeed, the reason UAS have recently gained special attention is largely because of their novelty and because their employment is rapidly growing. If they were replaced tomorrow with Autonomous Rotorcraft Sniper Systems, or some other new means of warfare, similar issues would be raised about these technologies.

Also, one should take into account the preferences of the American people and its allies. Using Special Forces or regular troops instead of UAS increases our causalities and tends to undermine the public support of the mission. UAS contribute to staying the course as long as this is called for.

In Cold Blood?

Finally, UAS are criticized on the grounds that they are manned by people sitting in air-conditioned offices, in Nevada or Florida, playing around with a joystick, before they go home for dinner and to coach little league. According to Mayer, ethicist Peter W. Singer believes that the drone technology is "'seductive,' because it creates the perception that war can be 'costless.'" Moreover, the victims (Mayer's term) remain faceless, and the damage caused by the UAS remains unseen. Mary Dudziak of USC's Gould School of Law opines that "Drones are a technological step that further isolates the American people from military action, undermining political checks on . . . endless war."

This kind of cocktail-party sociology does not stand up to minimal critical examination. Would we or the people of Afghanistan and Pakistan—or, for that matter, the terrorists—be better off if they were killed in hot blood? Say knifed by Special Forces, blood and brain matter splashing in their faces? If our troops, to reach the terrorists, had to go through IEDs blowing up their legs and arms and gauntlets of machine gun fire and RPGs, experiences that turn some of them into psychopath-like killers and return many home traumatized?

If all or most fighting were done in a cold-blooded, push-button way, it might well have the effects Mayer suggests. However, as long as what we are talking about are a few hundred drone drivers, what they do or do not feel has no discernable effects on the nation or the leaders who declare war. Indeed, there is no evidence that the introduction of UAS (and before that, high-level bombing and cruise missiles that were criticized on the same grounds) made going to war more likely or extending it more acceptable. Anybody who followed the history of our disengagement in Vietnam after the introduction of high-level bombing, or the difficulties President Obama faced in increasing troop levels in Afghanistan in the fall of 2009—despite the recent increase use in UAS—knows better.

The Moral Turning Point

As someone who lost many friends in combat, and saw many others wounded, and who inflicted such losses on others—I strongly abhor violence. I have written books, essays, and op-eds, testified before Congress, consulted the White House, and demonstrated in the streets to promote peaceful solutions and urge the curbing of the use of arms, from handguns to nuclear bombs.

As I see it, however, the main point of moral judgment must be faced earlier in the chain of action, well before we come to the question of which means are to be used to kill the enemy. The main turning point concerns the question whether we should go to war at all. This is the crucial decision because once we engage in war, we must assume that there is going to be a large number of casualties on all sides and that these may well include many innocent civilians. Often discussions of targeted killings strike me as written by people who yearn for a nice clean war, one in which only bad people will be killed using "surgical" strikes that inflict no collateral damage. Very few armed confrontations unfold in this way. Hence when we deliberate whether or not to fight, we should assume that once we step on this escalator, it is very likely to carry us to places we would rather not go, but must. The UAS are a rather minor, albeit new, stepping stone on this woeful journey.

Notes

1. Jane Mayer, "The Predator War: What Are the Risks of the C.I.A.'s Covert Drone Program?" *New Yorker* (October 26, 2009), http://www.newyorker.com/reporting/2009/10/26/091026fa_fact_mayer.

2. Jane Mayer, *The Dark Side: The Inside Story of How the War on Terror Turned Into a War on American Ideals* (New York: Doubleday, 2008).

3. Ann Scott Tyson, "Rising U.S. Toll in Afghanistan Stirs Unease on Hill, Among Families," *Washington Post* (September 23, 2009), http://www.washingtonpost.com/wp-dyn/content/article/2009/09/22/AR2009092204296.html.

4. Sheldon Richman, "Congress, Obama Codify Indefinite Detention," (December 28, 2011), http://reason.com/archives/2011/12/28/congress-obama-codify-indefinite-detenti.

5. See, for example, Peter M. Cullen, "The Role of Targeted Killing in the Campaign against Terror," *Joint Force Quarterly* 48 (1st Quarter 2008): 22–29; David Kretzmer, "Targeted Killing of Suspected Terrorists: Extra-Judicial Executions or Legitimate Means of Defence?" *The European Journal of International Law* 16, no. 2 (2005): 171–212; and Steven R. Ratner, "Predator and Prey: Seizing and Killing Suspected Terrorists Abroad," *Journal of Political Philosophy* 15, no. 3 (2007): 251–75.

21

Is the Normativity of Human Rights Self-Evident?*

Numerous attempts have been made to justify human rights in terms of other sources of normativity. This essay suggests that such attempts unwittingly weaken the case of human rights and that instead these rights should be treated as moral causes that speak to us directly, as one of those rare precepts that are self-evident.[1] Suggesting that human rights should be treated as self-evident does not deny the value of examining their historical sources, nor the need to spell out what they entail, merely that attempts to support human rights by inserting a foundation underneath them end up undermining their construction. Human rights stand tall on their own.

Weakening Justifications

Michael Ignatieff complains that many in the West have conceded far too much ground to challenges of the universality of human rights (posed both from without and within), bemoaning what he sees as a "desire to water down the individualism of rights discourse." But, to strip rights of their individualism, he argues, is to strip them of their ultimate justification, namely, the preservation of individual agency. He writes: "Rights are universal because they define the universal interests of the powerless, namely, that power be exercised over them in ways that respect their autonomy as agents."[2] This justification raises more questions than it answers. For instance, are those who are not powerless not entitled to have their rights respected? All such arguments do is to move that which needs to be justified over by one notch, relying for support on concepts (e.g., agency) whose normativity is less compelling than that which they are supposed to support, human rights.

Several influential historical writings that prefigure contemporary human rights discourse sought to derive these rights from natural law. In his *Second Treatise on Government,* John Locke claimed that:

> The state of nature has a law of nature to govern it, which obliges every one: and reason, which is that law, teaches all mankind, who will but consult it, that being all equal and independent, no one ought to harm another in his life, health, liberty, or possessions.[3]

But, natural law has been long recognized as a particularly opaque concept. Oliver Wendell Holmes characterized it disparagingly as "a brooding omnipresence in the sky."[4] More recently, legal philosopher Michael S. Moore quipped that natural law theories are "rather like the northern lights . . . but without the lights."[5] In short, the concept of natural law calls for much more explication, and, at this least in this day and age, is inherently much less compelling than human rights.

Some have attempted to argue for human rights as a necessary pre-condition for other values. Joel Feinberg, for instance, argues that human rights must exist because they are a "necessary precondition" for self-respect, respect for others, and for personal dignity.[6] Similarly, one foundational human rights document states that rights "derive from the inherent dignity of the human person."[7] Like other attempts to base the normativity of a given moral claim on its service to other causes, this endeavor ends up making the moral claim contingent; human rights are justified only as long as they serve. If one can show that they are not necessary for, say, respect for others, they lose their normative standing.

Furthermore, it is far from obvious that "self-respect" has a higher, clearer or more compelling moral standing than human rights. The claims entailed by the respect of human rights—that human beings have a right not to be killed, maimed or tortured—seem to be much more sharply etched than the respect of "human dignity" and less open to subjective interpretation. Many devout people hold that human dignity requires shrouding women, preventing them from being educated, condemning homosexuals, avoiding critical thinking, and even "honor" killing. To use self-respect to justify human rights is like arguing that we should look after our children so that we shall sleep better at night. Once again, the proposed foundation is weaker than the structure it is meant to support.

Attempts to base human rights on rationality or the social contract or some kind of Kantian imperative are all precepts that invite the often repeated criticisms of these approaches which need not be repeated here.[8]

An especially weak justification of the universality of human rights seeks to rely on the fact that a global normative consensus exists which supports them. Actually, universal consensus on normative issues is extremely thin. According to one study, the scope of such a consensus does not extend far beyond the agreement that in revenge killing, slaying more than eight people is not acceptable.[9] Although consensus is politically beneficial, it is morally dubious; many people can and do agree on positions that are not morally justified. Thus, sixty years ago there was very broad-based consensus across the world—especially in closed societies and among those of closed minds (see below on these concepts)—that women are at best a second class of citizens. Moreover, predicating the legitimacy of human rights on a global consensus grants de facto veto power to outlier countries. If, say, Myanmar and North Korea do not share the global respect for human rights this should hardly be taken as a challenge to the normativity of these rights. In sum, attempts to undergird human rights with constructions that need more support than these rights themselves is not a constructive way to proceed.

Human Rights Are Self-Evident

Instead, human rights are best recognized as one of the rare moral precepts whose normativity is self-evident, speaks to us directly, unmitigated by other causes, in a compelling manner.[10]

It should be noted that, while the Founding Fathers spoke of "self-evident truths," I deliberately avoid invoking the term "truth" here. The term implies, at least in contemporary context, a logical, empirical, objective and/or scientific validity, which is rather different from an axiomatic nature of self-evident precepts. It concerns "is" statements while I deal here with "ought" statements. I avoid the term "moral truth" because it evokes efforts, like those of David Hume, that seek to base morality on objective foundations. In contrast, my claim that the normativity of human rights is self-evident indicates that they are inherently morally compelling rather than based on some empirical or logical exterior judgments.

Self-evident moral precepts compose a small category of moral claims. Other than human rights, there are not many precepts for which one can credibly make such a claim. Another example of a moral claim that speaks for itself, effectively and directly, is the dictum that we have higher obligations to our own children than to the children of all others. When evaluating this claim, one does not sense that there is a need for a consequentialist explanation, a calculus of harm, or some other form of utilitarian analysis and justification. My observation is not based on the fact that there is very wide consensus on this point, but that when one evaluates this claim, the answer is "obvious"; one does not sense a need for an explanation.[11] To put it in more metaphorical terms, some lights shine so brightly one hardly needs to point them out—unless one's vision is blocked, a point explored below.

I conducted an informal study in several countries with audiences of more than 400 groups of rather different social, intellectual, and political backgrounds and persuasions. In each case, I asked the group to pretend that they were a public school committee that must decide which values to teach in the third grade next year. First, I pointed out that it is impossible to formulate a value-free or neutral curriculum about most matters. Whatever one teaches about slavery, the Holocaust, Washington's cherry tree, and so on will have implied moral judgments (including of course if one tries to present "both" sides objectively). Next, I asked the various audiences if one should teach that truth-telling is superior to lying or vice versa under all but limited conditions (such as when someone is dying from cancer and asks if there is any hope left). Without exception the groups looked puzzled. They wondered: "Where was the question I said I would ask?"; "Was there something else I meant to ask and did not?"; "Why, the answer to the question I did ask was self-evident!"

None of the members of the groups I queried engaged in any kind of philosophical argumentation, such as, "If one tells a lie, soon others will do the same, and then we shall find ourselves in a world of liars, a world we do not wish to live in, therefore, we must not lie": they did not require such a utilitarian, consequentialist explanation.[12] Instead, they found the answer staring them in the face, speaking directly to them. Similarly, when people are asked if one should be free from the fear of death, torture, or have a right to meet with others or practice one's religion, they readily recognize the value of such rights—at least, where their vision is not obscured (more about this shortly).

That some regimes do not observe many human rights does not challenge their status as a self-evident moral claim.[13] To hold that the normativity of human rights is self-evident does not entail assuming that they are self-enforcing, self-implementing, or omnipotent. Rather, they constitute a claim that all regimes face—whether or not they have yet learned to abide by them.

The thesis that there are some select moral causes that present themselves to us as compelling points to something similar to what religious authorities speak of as *revelation*. Importantly, in both religious and secular realms, drawing on such a source does not entail adopting a blind faith in it—it does not mean that one cannot also *reason* about these matters. The fact that some cause appears to one as compelling does not prevent one from examining it. However, here reason follows, buttresses, or challenges revelation, rather than being the source of judgment.[14]

When one recites the dictum that "it is better to let a thousand guilty people walk free rather than hang one innocent person," this may at first seem self-evident. However, when one then notes that these freed criminals are sure to kill at least several innocent people, one finds that the certitude of the initial statement is no longer nearly as strong as it seemed at first blush. In contrast, when one learns that a person reacted to a crime by engaging in revenge, the dictum "two wrongs do not make a right" stands, even after examined.

Charles Taylor writes about this dual nature of morality: "our moral reactions have two facets, as it were. On one side, they are almost like instincts; on the other, they seem to involve claims about the nature and status of human beings."[15] Naturalists and emotivists, Taylor argues, want to forget about the second part[16]; true enough, but it would be equally a mistake to forget about the first part. One must keep in mind that rational explanations of normativity are attempts to, as Taylor puts it, "articulate" the moral sense, but are not its essence.[17]

Human Rights as a Primary Concept

All systems of thought, whether mathematical, scientific, religious, or moral, require at least one starting point, a primary or axiomatic concept or assumption that we must take for granted. Many a philosopher who is critical of the notion of self-evident moral claims may well agree that every moral argument ultimately draws on one or more a priori premises, that there are inevitably premises for which one cannot ask for further foundations[18]—what Alvin Plantinga calls "properly basic beliefs."[19]

In the Jewish tradition, this need to have such a moral anchoring point is expressed in the idea that "every tong is made by a prior tong." For many religions, God is this primary cause. For those who believe, God's commandments, as expressed in tablets or texts, or as interpreted, explained, and specified by God's delegates, identify

311

which acts are moral and which are not, but for those who do not recognize God as a compelling primary source of normativity, the rest does not follow. Other systems of thought employ nature or reason as their primary concept, fulfilling a role analogous to that played by God's commandments in religious systems. Every sustainable moral construction builds on a self-evident foundation.[20] Human rights are the primary normative concept for the construction of international law and norms.

Moral Dialogues and the Opening Effect

A critic may suggest that the concept of self-evident moral claims amounts to an assertion that my moral intuition is better than all others. As I see it, the opposite is the case. All will hear self-evident moral claims unless they have been severely distracted, and even these persons will hear these claims once they are engaged in open moral dialogue. By moral dialogues I mean, drawing on my teacher Martin Buber, conversations about values (as opposed to fact and logic-driven deliberations) in which we truly open up to one another and, in the process, become open to self-evident moral precepts.[21]

German sociologist and social theorist Hans Joas criticized the concept of self-evident moral precepts by suggesting that if these claims were truly self-evident, the founding fathers—and all others who evoke this concept—would not have needed to proclaim it. The fact that they did, Joas says, constitutes *prima facie* evidence that these precepts are not self-evident.[22] Self-evident precepts may indeed elude people whose vision is obscured—either because they live in closed societies (fundamentalist theocracies or secular totalitarian states) or because, although they live in open societies, they have closed minds. In the first case, social pressure and cultural indoctrination have risen to a level that people are unable to hear the normative voice of the moral causes at issue. In the second case, people "under the influence" of one mind modifier or another, whether it is alcohol, drugs, or merely a high dose of mass culture (e.g., watching TV six hours on an average day), or who are mentally handicapped (e.g., psychopathic), are blind to even the most shining normative light. However, even these people can be brought to see the compelling nature of self-evident normative precepts. when their societies are opened up, when they are freed to participate in unencumbered moral dialogues, or they learn to overcome their various mind- (and soul-) numbing addictions.

The preceding statement is supported by the observation that as totalitarian and authoritarian regimes such as Singapore and China open up, due to changes in their regime and technological developments in the realm of communication, they also move toward recognizing human rights—often in word, but also in deed. These regimes, which once dismissed human rights as particularistic, Western notions not applicable to their people, now increasingly pay homage to human rights (a) by abiding by some of them more than they did previously (e.g., allowing some free speech, and increasingly also due process); (b) by presenting various explanations for why their regimes cannot yet abide by the human rights but will do so in the future, or (c), by working to hide the violations of rights, for instance, those of inmates. Thus rather than maintain their original dismissive position, they increasingly accept the normativity of human rights.

Efforts to find texts and narratives in non-Western cultures in support of human rights—for instance, those enumerated by Amartya Sen[23] and Abdullah An-Na'im[24]—are also indications of a growing transcultural base of support. In contrast, in parts of the world where religious fundamentalism is gaining the upper hand—and is moving to close these societies and cut people off from dialogues with others—they lose sight of human rights.

I should note in passing that while open communications and dialogues with people in previously closed societies often moves them toward recognizing human rights, the opposite is not true: as champions of human rights hear from those that are dismissive, they are not won over. Belief systems that reject human rights rely on closed societies and closed minds to do so; all who are open find them compelling.

Social Consequences of Treating Human Rights as Self-Evident

So far, my case against those who seek to provide extraneous foundations to justification human rights has rested on the claim that human rights are self-evident. Oddly, the strongest support for treating them as one of those rare moral claims that are self-evident may well be a consequentialist argument. To argue that human rights are particular to a single culture and thus are, at best, self-evident to people from that culture, and to assert that hence one ought to refrain from rendering transnational moral judgments,[25] greatly weakens if not fully neutralizes the case for human rights and hinders their progress. In contrast, treating human rights as self-evident strengthens the case for human rights.

Social forces make people better or worse than they would be otherwise. A gang encourages its members to pursue anti-social behavior; a religious order to pursue charity work. The same holds true across cultures. Following reports by the global media that a state is violating the human rights of its people—especially if such disclosures are followed by considerable and lasting international criticism and protests—many a state will modify its behavior, at least somewhat. True, in such cases, the parties involved may act largely out of self-interest, seeking to maintain a positive public image for political, commercial or some other self-serving purpose. However, what necessitated these actions, what made it in their self-interest to improve their human rights record are the loud and clear moral voices carried across borders (as well as their own people, as already indicated, who come to see the normativity of human rights as they have access to open moral dialogues). If these voices are silenced or muted, the progress of human rights will be undermined.

While radical cultural relativism argues that we cannot and should not judge others, some moderate relativists hold that one is entitled to judge the policies of others, but not in universalistic terms; one must make it clear that one is merely expressing one's own culturally conditioned normative position and one should recognize that people of other cultures may well readily justify conflicting positions by drawing on their own respective cultures.[26]

Although this position is not as preemptive as radical relativism, it still greatly undermines the very essence of the moral claim; the call for others to heed a given value. In rejecting the transcultural standing of the moral claim, even such moderate relativists end up treating moral judgments like expressions of taste: "I like potatoes and recommend them to you, but you may well have strong reasons to prefer rice and I have no standing to complain about such a preference." Such a move undermines moral claims because one grants those subject to them a license to ignore them in the same breath they are made. Such hedged claims are like speeding tickets handed out to motorists together with the money to pay for them. One further notes that others, say religious fundamentalists, are not going to hedge their claims. Hence, by making our claims contingent and conditional, we yield good part of the transcultural space for moral dialogues to those with unhedged voices. The world would be better off if our claims clashed with those of others in the agora of moral precepts, and let those that are truly self-evident stand out.

It is odd to read a major philosopher arguing that the claim that human rights are universal and self-evident cannot be sustained in part because Friedrich Nietzsche held that such claims "would only have crossed the mind of a slave" as a tool to enfeeble those in power.[27] The notion that the issues at hand could be settled by quoting an authority is surprising; if I come back and quote Locke, Mill and maybe Kant, would the matter be settled by which philosopher ranks higher? By who garners more philosophical votes or citations? Note also that Nietzsche's claim is an empirical one; anyone who takes Nietzsche's notions to apply to contemporary world must answer for the fact that many who are powerful do advocate human rights, and many who are weak (but live in closed societies) have yet to recognize them.

Rorty also argues for abandoning transcultural claims posed by human rights because racists and sexists find it easy to embrace these rights but simply deny that these rights apply to blacks, Jews, and women among others—because they consider them not human beings. It is not particularly difficult to show that the term "human"—those entitled to human rights—is easy to define (surely easier than to define a chair) as featherless bipeds and that minorities and women clearly qualify.

The argument here advanced is not that one should claim a non-relativist status for human rights because such claims are beneficial, although those who subscribe to utilitarian, consequentialist doctrines might consider such a course.[28] Rather, given that human rights are a self-evident moral cause, giving it voice—allowing it to be carried across borders—would make for a better world, one that is more attentive to human rights and other moral causes.

Moreover, without cross-cultural moral judgments one cannot reach the next step—asking what legitimate measures the inchoate global community ought to take to promote these judgments. Thus, key questions concerning the conditions under which it is appropriate to impose economic sanctions and, above all, to engage in armed humanitarian interventions (say to stop genocides and ethnic cleansing) are all are contingent on the recognition that there are actions that are taking place in another nation which violate human rights on a large scale. Only after such a conclusion is reached, can one logically ask about the legitimate ways the global community ought to react to such findings.

Notes

*   I am indebted to Alex Platt for several rounds of comments on previous drafts.

1.   I am not the first to describe human rights as a "self-evident" moral claim. See, e.g., Louis Henkin, *The Age of Rights* (New York: Columbia University Press, 1990), 2.

2.   Michael Ignatieff, "The Attack on Human Rights," *Foreign Affairs* (November/December 2001).

3.   John Locke, *Second Treatise on Government*, trans. C. B. Macphearson (London: Hackett Publishing Company, 1980), Chapter 2, Section 6.

4.   Oliver Wendell Holmes, "Dissenting Opinion," Southern Pacific Company v. Jensen, 244 U.S. 205, 222 (May 21, 1917).

5.   Michael S. Moore, "Law as a Functional Kind," *Natural Law Theory: Contemporary Essays*, ed. Robert George (Oxford: Clarendon Press, 1992), 188–242, 188.

6.   Joel Feinberg, "The Nature and Value of Rights," *The Philosophy of Human Rights*, ed. Patrick Hayden (St. Paul, MN: Paragon House, 2001).

7.   "Preamble to 1966 International Covenant on Civil and Political Rights, and International Covenant on Economic, Social and Cultural Rights," *United Nations Office of the High Commissioner on Human Rights* http://www.unhchr.ch/html/menu3/b/a_cescr.htm 7/8/08.

8.   See, e.g., Alasdair Macintyre *After Virtue* (Notre Dame, IN: University of Notre Dame, 1984).

9.   Rhoda Howard, *Human Rights and the Search for Community* (Boulder, CO: Westview Press, 1995).

10. It might be said that I argue that human rights need no case to be made for them, but I am making one: against those who seek to support human rights by basing them on other concepts.

11. Peter Singer may the only one who contests this point. He writes famously: "if I am walking past a shallow pond and see a child drowning in it, I ought to wade in and pull the child out . . . It makes no moral difference whether the person I can help is a neighbor's child ten yards from me or a Bengali whose name I shall never know ten thousand miles away." Peter Singer, "Famine, Affluence, and Morality," *Philosophy and Public Affairs* 1, no. 3 (1972): 231–32. For a more detailed refutation of Singer on this point, see Amitai Etzioni, "Are Particularistic Obligations Justified?" in *The Review of Politics* 64, no. 4 (Autumn 2002): 573–98.

12. Some added arguments as an afterthought, to examine and account for a moral sense which they already recognized. In other words, this is where ethics and moral philosophy comes in.

13. Louis Henkin, *The Age of Rights* (New York: Columbia University Press, 1990).

14. As epistemologist Robert Audi writes "since premises are not needed as a ground for justified belief of a self-evident proposition, there is also no basis for demanding an independent argument in every case where there is an appeal to the self-evident." Audi, "Self-Evidence" *Philosophical Perspectives* 13 (1999) 205–28, 233.

15. Charles Taylor, *Sources of the Self: The Making of the Modern Identity* (Cambridge: Harvard University Press, 1989), 5.
16. Ibid., 5–8.
17. Ibid., 7.
18. Michael P. Zuckert argues that Jefferson, following John Locke and others, took self-evident truths to "serve as the most fundamental sort of premise, what in mathematics are called axioms." Zuckert, "Self Evident Truth and the Declaration of Independence," *The Review of Politics* 49, no. 3 (Summer, 1987): 319–39, 322.
19. Alvin Plantinga, "Is Belief in God Rational?" *Rationality and Religious Belief*, ed. C. Delaney (Notre Dame, IN: University of Notre Dame Press, 1979).
20. See, for instance, Bernard Williams, *Truth and Truthfulness* (Princeton, NJ: Princeton University Press, 2002). Williams argues that accuracy and sincerity are "virtues of truth."
21. Martin Buber, *I and Thou* (New York: Scribners, 1970).
22. Private communication, Berlin (June 1, 2003).
23. Amartya Sen, "Human Rights and Asian Values," *The New Republic* (July 14–July 21, 1997).
24. Abdullah Ahmed An-Na'im ed., *Human Rights in Cross-Cultural Perspectives: Quest for Consensus* (Philadelphia, PA: University of Pennsylvania Press, 1992).
25. Richard Rorty "Human Rights, Rationality, and Sentimentality," in *The Philosophy of Human Rights*, ed. Patrick Hayden (St. Paul, MN: Paragon House, 2001), 241–57, 246.
26. See, e.g., Rorty, "Human Rights, Rationality and Sentimentality"; Stanley Fish, "Don't Blame Relativism," *The Responsive Community* 12, no. 3 (2002): 27–31.
27. Richard Rorty, Human Rights, Rationality and Sentimentality, 254.
28. See, e.g., Dale Jamieson, "When Utilitarians Should Be Virtue Theorists," *Utilitas* 19, no. 2 (2007): 160–83.

22

Pirates: Too Many Rights?
*

Sometimes a complex issue can be captured in a few very simple words: "Prosecuting suspected pirates detained in international waters has proved difficult" (according to a *Wall Street Journal* reporter).[1] And according to Douglas Burnett, an expert in maritime law, pirates are treated with a "catch and release philosophy that's usually reserved for trout."[2] Indeed, despite the fact that there has been a considerable increase in piracy in the Gulf of Aden and Indian Ocean as of 2007—Somali pirates have taken hundreds of hostages, terrorized commercial and recreational shipping, and imposed a considerable economic burden on seafaring —the majority of pirates who capture hostages were paid off, and even when caught, they were not detained or prosecuted. (Very few pirates have been confronted and killed.)

These observations are puzzling, given that piracy has been considered for centuries a very serious offense, by most if not all nations, and pirates were regularly killed or executed after, at most, a rather perfunctory hearing, by the captain of the ship that captured them. As often is the case, more than one factor helps explain these observations, for instance, the vastness of the area involved. This essay focuses on one set of factors, the effects of the interpretation of the human rights extended to pirates in recent decades.

The main thesis of the paper is that the human rights extended to these pirates were at least initially interpreted in such an expansive way that they prevented proper attention to two basic common goods: the safety and livelihood of civilians and the right to freedom of navigation in international waters. In this way, the expansive interpretation of human rights violated what responsive communitarians consider a legitimate balance between rights and public safety. Moreover, this interpretation of human rights undermines the rights' normativity.

In effect, one can see a parallel between the expansive interpretation of human rights in the case at hand and the expansive interpretations of individual rights in the 1980s. In the 1980s, following vastly

319

overdue and highly justified extension of de jure and de facto rights to minorities, women, handicapped persons, and others, came some trivial extensions of rights that undermined their standing. Telling examples include the claim that the right to play Santa Claus was violated by Macy's when it refused to re-engage a person who had previously played Santa Claus but had started taking psychotropic medications.[3] And, in Santa Monica, a feminist argued that a city ordinance limiting restroom use to the gender noted on the restroom door—unless there were more than three people in line in the women's restroom, at which point a woman could use the men's room—infringed on women's rights, for it restricted their ability to use any bathroom any time.[4] At that time, Mary Ann Glendon's book, *Rights Talk*, spelled out the damage caused by excessively expanding the otherwise cardinal and valuable precept of rights.[5]

The key argument here advanced is not that pirates are without rights, but that the interpretations of these rights have been expanded to the point that it undermines the rights of all other persons and corrodes the rights themselves. Additionally, the rights enjoyed by pirates must be balanced against concerns for the common good.

Others have called attention to the expansive interpretations of pirates' rights and the anti-social results. Eugene Kontorovich, a law professor at Northwestern University wrote,

> While international law has developed to include many new crimes, the successful prosecution of piracy has ironically become more difficult than in the Age of Sail. While international law authorizes and indeed requires the prosecution of piracy, many particular rules as well as practical constraints and considerations create the opposite incentive.[6]

Others have called the treatment of pirates' rights the equivalent of granting "a get out of jail card."[7] John Bolton, a former permanent US representative to the United Nations, added that "due process is only that process that is due, and the pirates have already had more than enough."[8]

Pirates, in recent years, have not been confronted aggressively, and many times, even when they have been caught, they have simply been released. For example, in May 2009, Portuguese forces found dynamite, automatic rifles, and rocket-propelled grenades on the mother ship of pirates they had chased away from seeking to board a German tanker. The Portuguese merely disarmed the pirates and set them free.[9] Danish forces set ten suspected pirates free in September 2008.[10] Canadian forces pursued and then boarded a pirate vessel in April 2009, confiscated the weapons they found, and let the pirates go[11]; in April 2009, Dutch forces even set pirates free who had been holding hostages onboard a ship.[12] In November 2009, Greek forces captured pirates who were believed to have attacked a French cargo ship; the pirates were released within a week. In April 2010, US naval forces captured eleven pirates, ensured that they "had no means to conduct any more attacks," destroyed their mother ship, and then released them onto two small skiffs.[13] *The Sunday Times* reports that between August 2008 and September 2009, 343 suspected pirates were captured, disarmed, and released, compared to the 212 who were held for prosecution.[14] In numerous other cases, pirates were simply paid to let their hostages go.

Since 2007, pirates acted with considerable impunity. In 2007 alone, 433 seafarers were either taken hostage, assaulted, injured, or killed by Somali pirates.[15] In 2008, the incidence of piracy off the Horn of Africa doubled, and pirates attacked 135 ships, seized 44, and took more than 600 seafarers hostage.[16] The trend continued though 2009; as of the year's end, pirates had attacked 200 ships, successfully seizing 42 and taking at least 679 seafarers hostage.[17] In exchange for the release of some of ships and hostages, pirates took in as much as $120 million in 2008[18] and an estimated $100 million in 2009.[19] 2010 appears to be unfolding in a similar manner.

Thousands of employees on commercial ships peacefully navigating the high seas, some carrying food aid and medical supplies to war-torn zones of Africa, now must fear that they may be kidnapped by armed men and injured, killed, or held hostage for months, if not years. The obvious question is, given that security is the first duty of every state, why have the nations of the world not responded more forcefully to this threat? This essay focuses on a sub-question: what role did an expansive interpretation of pirates' human rights play in preventing legitimate and effective peacekeeping in this area?

Section I of this essay deals briefly with the historical background and current status of piracy in international law, pointing to the fact that piracy has been considered for centuries a universal crime of great severity and is only paralleled in the modern law of the high seas by prohibitions on the transport of slaves. Section II discusses the problems that arise from the status of pirates as civilians. Section III deals with the various international human rights interpretations that have greatly limited an effective response to the increase in piracy in 2007–2010. Section IV introduces responsive communitarian ideas that call for balancing rights with concerns for the common good—in the case at hand, elementary safety on the high seas.

Piracy: A Major Crime

For centuries, maritime piracy has been considered a universal crime of great severity. As far back as 1615, British courts had determined that pirates were *hostis humani generic*—enemies of all mankind.[20] Judges in US courts have made similar statements in past centuries.[21] As noted in one eighteenth-century law book, pirates captured on the high seas where it was not possible to obtain a legal judgment were subject to summary execution.[22] Captain Andres Breijo, the Spanish naval officer in Operation Atalanta, the EU's anti-piracy mission, commented, "In the old days, when the navy would catch a pirate, they would tie his hands and feet and throw him back in the sea."[23]

Piracy is a crime subject to universal jurisdiction: any state, regardless of whether or not it has any claim or connection to the property, perpetrators, or victims, may detain and prosecute suspected pirates.[24] With regard to Somalia in particular, the UN Security Council has adopted five resolutions under Chapter VII of the UN Charter to aid in the capture of pirates off the Horn of Africa. In June 2008, with the consent of the Somali government, the SC passed Resolution 1816, which recognizes that states may conduct anti-piracy operations within Somali territorial waters.[25] A few months later, in October, the Security Council passed Resolution 1838, which called upon states with ships or airplanes in the area "to use on the high seas and airspace off the coast of Somalia the necessary means . . . for the repression of acts of piracy."[26] On December 2, the Security Council adopted Resolution 1846, which encouraged states to cooperate in determining jurisdiction, and in the investigation and prosecution of persons responsible for acts of piracy and armed robbery off the coast of Somalia, consistent with applicable international law including international human rights law.[27] Lastly, when resolution 1816 expired in December 2008, the Security Council passed Resolution 1851, which called upon states to deploy military aircrafts and naval vessels to the area and authorized states to "take all necessary measures that are appropriate *in Somalia*" (emphasis added) to suppress "acts of piracy and armed robbery at sea."[28] The resolution was adopted for the period of a year and explicitly approved military raids on Somali land "to interdict those using Somali territory to plan, facilitate or undertake"[29] maritime piracy.

Thus, unlike in more controversial international interventions, including armed humanitarian interventions such as in Kosovo and Sudan, the international law pertaining to the capture and trial of the Somali pirates enjoys a broad consensus and a clear framework, and both the crime itself and the perpetrators of the crime are relatively easily identified. Given the clear and present danger posed by pirates, and given the extensive normative and legal background regarding the ways they ought to be treated, one would expect that there would be few if any obstacles to establishing secure passage for all. (Reference is to legal and normative issues because this essay does not deal with operational and logistical problems, such as the difficulties imposed by the large size of the area involved or that warships no longer have brig facilities.)[30]

Pirates, Civilian Status, and Civilian Rights

In a sort of replay of the debate concerning the rights of suspected terrorists and insurgents— which focused on whether they should be treated like criminals or POWs[31]—the question arises whether pirates should be treated as if they were civilians, with all the rights thereof, as unlawful combatants, or in some other way.

Procedural Rights of Free Nations in Domestic Courts

There is no international court with the jurisdiction to try pirates, and by the framework set forth in the United Nations Convention on the Law of the Sea, pirates are to be prosecuted in the domestic courts of whatever nation seizes them. Thus, pirates are currently treated as if they are entitled to trial in a civilian criminal court, and they are granted the full panoply of criminal procedural rights of the citizens (and residents) of the particular country in which they are tried.

Given that piracy occurs on the high seas, the nature of the confrontations often involved, and the absence of police or other law enforcement agents, adhering to this approach is highly problematic.

For example, collecting evidence on the high seas that will hold up in a criminal court is often impractical. In March 2009, the US Navy released nine suspected pirates, as the evidence against them was "not ironclad," in part, due to their nighttime capture.[32] In November 2009, Belgian Commander Jan De Beurme described rushing to the scene of a pirate attack only to see the suspects in the skiff throw things overboard. Left without evidence, the Commander held that he was forced not only to set the suspected pirates free, but to also fix their broken engine.[33] And the evidence that is collected is difficult to segregate and sequester in order to meet the standards of non-contamination and the evidentiary chain of custody required by law. Nor can one expect that those under attack will read pirates their Miranda rights—and ask them if they understood them—before the pirates blurt out any information that might be used against them in a court of law. Providing merchant ships with the personnel or training required to collect fingerprints, DNA, and other such evidence adds a burden for ships that are often stuffed with low-paid sailors from developing nations. (Nor it is clear that training merchant ship personnel in such matters would be useful, as they are civilians and not law enforcement personnel.)

In one case, FBI agents were flown to the scene to help collect evidence but this often not practical and even these agents may have a hard time collecting evidence under the circumstances. US Coast Guard law enforcement detachments have been assigned to a Navy task force "to help collect and train ship-boarding team members in the best methods of collecting prosecutable evidence."[34] Also, the US Naval Criminal Investigative Service has special agents assigned to Combined Task Force-151 who conduct interviews of suspects and witnesses and coordinate with lawyers and foreign law enforcement.[35]

Consider that even under the less-demanding tribunals that terrorism suspects face, the evidence, often obtained on the battlefield, frequently does not meet the tribunals' standards. Military prosecutors have estimated that under the Military Commissions Act they have enough evidence to be able to bring to trial at best only eighty Guantanamo detainees.[36] Domestic criminal courts' evidentiary standards are higher and hence even more difficult to meet.

All of this means that of those pirates who are detained and turned over to legal authorities, the majority are "unlikely to ever stand trial primarily due to a lack of available evidence and substantial legal hurdles."[37] This seems to be one reason pirates are released rather than detained and prosecuted—and continue to terrorize the high seas.

A Matter of Jurisdiction: Military Pursuit of Civilian Criminals?

As pirates are treated as civilians but function beyond any nation's territory, at least one nation found it difficult to deal with them. Germany was caught in a new catch 22: the German police were not equipped to combat pirates off the coast of Somalia, but the military, which does have the capability to do so, was at first prevented from dealing with them because pirates are considered civilians. Walter Kolbow, a member of the Social Democratic Party, contended that "according to our understanding of the law, police officers but not soldiers may arrest criminals."[38] Other Germans feared that allowing the German navy to take on police duties would open the floodgates for military actions against civilians in Germany. The debate in the German parliament over the response to piracy off the coast of Somalia lasted for the better part of 2008, despite German ships having been attacked and German citizens having been taken hostage on multiple occasions in early to mid-2008.[39] While the German parliament debated the matter, a German naval vessel participating in Operation Enduring Freedom[40] was unable to do anything but provide assistance to ships in emergencies, which in practice meant that the navy could chase away pirates who were engaged in an attack, but could not pursue them if they backed down, catch them, or detain them—let alone shoot them.[41] This situation changed in December 2008, when the German parliament voted to deploy troops as part of the EU's Operation Atalanta, authorizing the use of force to suppress piracy. However, the ambiguities involved continued to hobble German (and other nations') anti-piracy operations. This was one reason, among others, that Germany's GSG-9 federal police unit, which is trained to handle hostage situations, was recalled in 2009 when it set out to free hostages held by pirates off the coast of Somalia.[42]

A new understanding of the legal status of pirates may be called for, as it is for terrorists. Currently, pirates are often treated as if they were entitled to all the rights of the citizens of whatever nation captures or contends with them on the high seas, which in turn is one more reason they are rarely deterred and, in effect, prosper.

Rights Derived from International Law

Imminent Danger

For some of those untutored in legal matters, the best way to deal with pirates may be to shoot them on sight. After all, modern maritime pirates are much like armed intruders who break into one's home. Some have warned against such a response on pragmatic grounds—Somali pirates have been careful not to harm their hostages, as long as they were not confronted. Arming merchant ships might lead to an escalation of violence, and many ports do not allow firearms aboard civilian vessels in port. And while warships and other government-authorized vessels do have a right to defend themselves and others through the use of deadly force if attacked, military personnel are expected to detain and try pirates, if possible, rather than to kill them.[43] This expectation is in line with the domestic policy in democratic society according to which law enforcement officers are often criticized when they discharge their firearms when they could have instead arrested a criminal or convinced him to surrender. Thus, when pirates captured and held Captain Richard Philips hostage on board the Maersk Alabama, President Obama granted the authority for the Navy to use force only if the captain was in "imminent danger."[44] Indeed, the three pirates were shot and killed only when one of them aimed an AK-47 at the hostage.[45]

It should be noted that such criteria maximize danger to the hostage and minimize risk for the hostage takers. This is the case because the pirates could have easily killed the captain out of sight, or the snipers may not have been able to shoot the pirates in the split second it takes to kill an unarmed hostage. Moreover, the pirates were increasingly on edge after the captain tried to escape, the USS Bainbridge closed in, and their supply of narcotic khat leaves dwindled. To limit killing the pirates to visible "imminent danger" is to set a high price on the human rights of pirates at the expense of the rights of the hostage.[46]

One may argue that there is nothing expansive about the imminent danger standard. As one colleague put it, "This is a well established customary international standard for the use of force in maritime law enforcement. This gold standard is mirrored by domestic police forces (including the US) all across the globe." However, the balance between the security of the civilians on ships peacefully negotiating the high seas—and the rights of pirates (and terrorists), is not cast in stone. Throughout legal history, this balance has been re-examined and revised. Given the ease with which pirates operate, it deserves another round of re-examination.

Asylum and Extradition

Another source of legal difficulties in confronting pirates results from asylum and extradition laws. First, if a European nation brings a Somali pirate to its shores for trial, the pirates may be able to remain in the country under asylum laws. At least by the laws of EU countries, a person need not show that he had been specifically targeted in his country of origin; it suffices to show that there is enough indiscriminant violence taking place in the applicant's place of origin that he would face a real risk of his life being in danger if he were returned.[47] It is a standard, authorities fear, pirates may meet and one reason they fear bring pirates to their shores.

That they may qualify for asylum is not an idle legal speculation. In the 1995 case, *Chahal v. The United Kingdom*, the European Court of Human Rights ruled that Article 3 of the Council of Europe's Convention for the Protection of Human Rights and Fundamental Freedoms (ECHR) provides that where there are substantial grounds for believing the deportee would be at risk of torture, "his conduct cannot be a material consideration."[48] Thus, pirates cannot be shipped back to Somalia if they can show that they may be tortured in that country.

Given these rules concerning asylum and Somalia's current political situation—ongoing attacks from the Al Shabaab insurgents that control Kismaayo and the deep south, the sporadic fighting between Puntland and Somaliland—the British Foreign Office, has decided that in order to prevent the possibility that captured pirates could claim asylum in the United Kingdom, the Royal Navy should refrain from bringing pirates to trial in the United Kingdom.[49]

Furthermore, states that capture pirates but that are, like the United Kingdom, either unwilling or unable to prosecute them domestically are effectively barred from extraditing the pirates to Somalia for trial by the Convention against Torture and Other Cruel, Inhuman or Degrading Treatment or Punishment (CAT), and the ECHR. Article 3 of the CAT states "No State Party shall expel, return ("refouler") or extradite a person to another State where there are substantial grounds for believing that he would be in danger of being subjected to torture."[50] Under sharia, which is applied in varying degrees throughout Somalia,[51] the pirates could face very severe punishments, which would constitute torture under international law and under the domestic laws in many of the patrolling countries.[52]

Furthermore, Article 3 of the ECHR bars torture and inhuman or degrading treatment or punishment,[53] and while it does not explicitly state a prohibition on extraditing a person to a state in which he would be in danger of being tortured, in its 1989 decision in the case of *Soering v. The United Kingdom*, the European Court of Human Rights held that

> It would hardly be compatible with the underlying values of the Convention . . . where a contracting state knowingly surrenders a

fugitive to another state where there are substantial grounds for believing that he would be in danger of being subjected to torture, however heinous the crime allegedly committed. Extradition in such circumstances, . . . would plainly be contrary to the spirit and intent of the Article . . .[54]

This decision is binding on all signatories to ECHR, which includes all European states which have deployed warships to the effort to repress piracy off the coast of Somalia.

No Delegation

A nation reluctant to try pirates in its domestic courts and unable to legally extradite them to their country of origin, might seek to turn them over to another nation for trial (and punishment, if convicted). Indeed, the United States, Demark, the EU, and the United Kingdom have all agreed with Kenya that it will accept captured pirates and try them in its courts.[55] And while Kenya has recently stated that it is seeking to cancel these agreements and cease acceptance of pirates for trial, citing the burden to its court and prison systems,[56] the option also faces opposition on human rights grounds. The agreement between the United States and Kenya has led to criticism from Human Rights Watch, which contends that the Kenyan justice system does not guarantee a fair trial. HRW stated, the "[Kenyan] police have a terrible record of long periods of detention without trial," that there are "terrible conditions in the prisons" and "very poor record of access to legal representation" as well as "interminable delays in the court process."[57]

The legal aid network Lawyers of the World, which is representing over forty of the captured pirates in Kenya, says that the agreements between Kenya and other nations and the EU violate the human rights of the suspects.[58] And German lawyers have filed a civil suit in Germany in support of the pirates held in Kenya, claiming that a fair trial is impossible in Kenya because there is no presumption of innocence.[59] In another suit, German lawyers argue that the German government is responsible for ensuring that the pirates receive proper representation in Kenya, suggesting Germany should pay for it, because defendants in the African nation do not have the right to government-provided counsel, except in capital cases.[60]

All said and done, there are no international courts to try pirates; the different roles of national police forces and the military complicate the pursuit of pirates; procedural rights set standards for collection and custody of evidence against pirates that are difficult to meet on the high seas by naval personnel; and various rights—observed by democracies—prevent imprisonment, deportation, extradition, or delegation of trials to other nations. (While Kenya is a democracy, many observers have misgivings about the integrity of its justice system.) To reiterate, the thesis here advanced is not that the extended application of human rights to pirates is the only reason pirates are so often not confronted, detained, and prosecuted, but that these legal considerations seem to be one significant reason piracy thrives.

Balancing Rights and the Common Good

Communitarians, especially responsive communitarians,[61] maintain that we face two strong normative claims: that of individual rights and that of the common good, of which public safety is the prime category. Neither is a priori privileged, and we constantly work to find the proper balance between these two claims. (Courts often proceed by referring to compelling public interest, which they take into account in addition to rights considerations.) Moreover, although rights advocates tend to frame their arguments in strong terms, as if any concession or reinterpretation of what rights entail or the common good demands are a violation, historically, both claims have been modified and rebalanced as conditions change. Thus, the 1st Amendment right to free speech as now understood was largely fashioned in the 1920s and the federal right to privacy was forged only after 1965. After 9/11, the balance between rights and homeland security was modified during the Bush administration, and again recalibrated during the first year of the Obama administration. In the United Kingdom, criminal suspects could be legally held only for forty-eight hours without charge; however, this was extended to up to twenty-eight days for terrorism suspects. Courts and legislatures draw on the fact that the rights themselves are often formulated in ways that suggest limitations and balancing (e.g., the 4th Amendment of the US Constitution reads "The right of the people to be secure . . . against *unreasonable* searches and seizures, shall not be violated . . ." [emphasis added]). And in reference to changes in conditions, particularly relevant to the issue at hand is that after a wave of skyjacking in the early 1970s, the US courts allowed the introduction of screening gates in airports, despite the fact that they constitute searches without individualized suspicion and without a warrant.[62] All this applies to the way pirates are treated. (The ways one decides which consideration is to take precedence—the common good or individual rights—or to what extent the two can be reconciled, is a mater beyond the scope of this article.)[63]

The preceding discussion suggests that the times call for a reexamination of the ways pirates are treated. Few would disagree that they pose a serious threat to the peaceable navigation of the high seas. The level of threat has been rising over time, given that the "business" is very lucrative and the risks and costs imposed by law enforcement authorizes are rather small. This article seeks to point to the problem rather than offer a new interpretation of human rights and an explanation of the extent to which a rebalancing of rights and the common is called for. This work remains to be carried out.

Given that piracy has been considered for centuries a serious offense by most people and nations, given the relative ease with which pirates can be identified (compared, for instance, to terrorists, who pass themselves off as regular civilians), and given the growing harm pirates are inflicting, one would expect that dealing with this threat to the common good could be more readily treated than many others.

Notes

*   I am indebted to Radhika Bhat for extensive research assistance and numerous editorial comments, and to Commander James Kraska for numerous comments on a previous draft.

1.   Sarah Childress, "U.S. Holds Suspects after Pirates standoff," *Wall Street Journal* (April 2, 2010): A11.

2.   *All Things Considered: U.S. Navy Captures Pirates* (NPR radio broadcast, April 1, 2010).

3.   It should be noted that the man here described filed a discrimination claim, contending that Macy's denied him the position on the basis of his HIV+ status and that Macy's fear of his Prozac use was unfounded and a smokescreen. David Margolick, "Man with AIDS Virus Sues To Be a Macy's Santa Again," *N. Y. Times* (August 29, 1991), http://www.nytimes.com/1991/08/29/nyregion/man-with-aids-virus-sues-to-be-a-macy-s-santa-again.html.

4.   Robert Reinhold, "Santa Monica Journal; In Land of Liberals, Restroom Rights Are Rolled Back," *N. Y. Times* (November 15, 1991), http://www.nytimes.com/1991/11/15/us/santa-monica-journal-in-land-of-liberals-restroom-rights-are-rolled-back.html; Nancy Hill-Holtzman, "Santa Monica OKs Restroom Law," *Los Angeles Times* (November 14, 1991), http://articles.latimes.com/1991-11-14/local/me-2074_1_santa-monica.

5.   Mary Ann Glendon, *Rights Talk: The Impoverishment of Political Discourse* (New York: Free Press, 1991).

6.   Eugene Kontorovich, *A Guantanamo on the Sea: The Difficulties of Prosecuting Pirates and Terrorists*, 09-10 Nw. U. Sch. of L. Pub. L. and Legal Theory Series, 19–20 (2009).

7. John S. Burnett, "Captain Kidd, Human-Rights Victim," *N. Y. Times* (April 20, 2008), http://www.nytimes.com/2008/04/20/opinion/20burnett.html?_r=1.

8. John Bolton, "A 'World Turned Upside Down'?; U.S. Now a Judicial Target for Defending Lawful Commerce," *The Washington Times* (April 17, 2009), http://www.washingtontimes.com/news/2009/apr/17/a-world-turned-upside-down/.

9. "Wrong Signals: Piracy," *Economist* (May 9, 2009): 62.

10. Oliver Hawkins, "What To Do with a Captured Pirate," *BBC* (March 10, 2009), http://news.bbc.co.uk /2/hi/in_depth/7932205.stm.

11. Alison Bevege, "Somali Pirates Nabbed, Released by Canadian Frigate," *Reuters Canada.com* (April 19, 2009), http://www2.canada.com/topics/news/story.html?id=1512697.

12. "Dutch Forces Free Pirate Captives," *BBC* (April 18, 2009), http://news.bbc.co.uk/2/hi/africa/8005730.stm.

13. Commander, Combined Maritime Forces Public Affairs, "Combined Maritime Forces Flagship Intercepts Somali Pirates," *NAVY.mil* (April 2, 2010), http://www.navy.mil/search/display.asp?story_id=52370.

14. "Navy Releases Somali Pirates Caught Red-Handed," *Times Online* (November 29, 2009), http://www.timesonline.co.uk/tol/news/world/africa/article6936318.ece.

15. See note 7.

16. International Maritime Organization, "Piracy in Waters Off the Coast of Somalia," http://www.imo.org/home.asp?topic_id=1178.

17. International Maritime Organization, "Reports on Acts of Piracy and Armed Robbery Against Ships: Issued Monthly – Acts Reported During June 2009," (July 7, 2009), http://www.imo.org/includes/blastDataOnly.asp/data_id%3D25980/138.pdf; International Maritime Organization, "Reports on Acts of Piracy and Armed Robbery Against Ships: Issued Monthly – Acts Reported During May 2009," (June 17, 2009), http://www.imo.org/includes/blastDataOnly.asp/data_id%3D25979/137.pdf; International Maritime Organization, "Reports on Acts of Piracy and Armed Robbery Against Ships: Issued Monthly – Acts Reported During April 2009," (May 5, 2009), http://www.imo.org/includes/blastDataOnly.asp/data_id%3D25553/136.pdf; International Maritime Organization, "Reports on Acts of Piracy and Armed Robbery Against Ships: Issued Monthly – Acts Reported During March 2009," (April 6, 2009), http://www.imo.org/includes/blastDataOnly.asp/data_id%3D25552/135.pdf; International Maritime Organization, "Reports on Acts of Piracy and Armed Robbery Against Ships: Issued Monthly – Acts Reported During February 2009," (April 22, 2009), http://www.imo.org/includes/blastDataOnly.asp/data_id%3D25551/134.pdf; International Maritime Organization, "Reports on Acts of Piracy and Armed Robbery Against Ships: Issued Monthly – Acts Reported During July 2009," (October 10, 2009), http://www.imo.org/includes/blastData.asp/doc_id=11908/141.pdf; International Maritime Organization, "Reports on Acts of Piracy and Armed Robbery Against Ships: Issued Monthly – Acts Reported During August 2009," (October 10, 2009), http://www.imo.org/includes/blastData.asp/doc_id=11909/142.pdf; International Maritime Organi-

zation, "Reports on Acts of Piracy and Armed Robbery Against Ships: Issued Monthly – Acts Reported During September 2009," (January 12, 2010), http://www.imo.org/includes/blastData.asp/doc_id=12298/143. pdf; International Maritime Organization, "Reports on Acts of Piracy and Armed Robbery Against Ships: Issued Monthly – Acts Reported During October 2009," (January 12, 2010), http://www.imo.org/includes/blastData. asp/doc_id=12299/145.pdf; International Maritime Organization, "Reports on Acts of Piracy and Armed Robbery Against Ships: Issued Monthly – Acts Reported During November 2009," (January 26, 2010), http://www.imo.org/ includes/blastData.asp/doc_id=12378/146.pdf; International Maritime Organization, "Reports on Acts of Piracy and Armed Robbery Against Ships: Issued Monthly – Acts Reported During December 2009," (January 26, 2010), http://www.imo.org/includes/blastData.asp/doc_id=12379/ 147.pdf.

18. Jerrrey Gettleman, "Pirates Outmaneuver Warships Off Somalia," *N. Y. Times* (December 15, 2008), http://www.nytimes.com/2008/12/16/world/ africa/16pirate.html.

19. "A Long War of the Waters," *Economist* (January 9, 2010): 47.

20. King v. Marsh, 81 Eng. Rep. 23 (K.B. 1615).

21. United States v. Brig Malek Adhel, 43 U.S. (2 How.) 210, 232 (1844); United States v. Smith, 18 U.S. (5 Wheat.) 153, 156 (1820).

22. G. Jacob, *A New Law Dictionary, at "Pirates"* (8th ed. 1762).

23. Justin Stares, "Pirates Protected from EU Task Force by Human Rights," *Telegraph.co.uk* (November 1, 2008), http://www.telegraph.co.uk/news/ worldnews/africaandindianocean/somalia/3363258/Pirates-protected-from-EU-task-force-by-human-rights.html.

24. The modern view of piracy in international law is found in the United Nations Convention on the Law of the Sea. UNCLOS that proclaims that all states have a "duty to cooperate in the repression of piracy," and grants permission for every state to seize pirates and their ships, and use their domestic courts to determine which actions to take with regard to penalties and property. See also US v. Shi, 525 F.3d 709 (9th Cir. 2008) *cert denied* 129 S.Ct. 324 (2008).

25. S.C. Res. 1816, U.N. Doc. S/RES/1816 (June 2, 2008).

26. S.C. Res. 1838, U.N. Doc. S/RES/1838 (Oct. 7, 2008); Security Council Resolution 1844, which is not discussed in this section, places targeted sanctions on individuals or entities "engaging in or providing support for acts that threaten the peace, security or stability of Somalia" or "obstructing the delivery of humanitarian assistance to Somalia, or access to, or distribution of, humanitarian assistance in Somalia." S.C. Res. 1844, U.N. Doc. S/RES/1844 (Nov. 20, 2008).

27. S.C. Res. 1846, U.N. Doc. S/RES/1846 (Dec. 2, 2008).

28. S.C. Res. 1851, U.N. Doc. S/RES/1851 (Dec. 16, 2008).

29. Press Release, Security Council, Security Council Authorizes States to Use Land-Based Operations in Somalia as Part of Fight Against Piracy Off Coast, Unanimously Adopting 1851 (2008), U.N. Doc. SC/9541 (Dec. 16, 2008).

30. James Kraska and Brian Wilson, "Fighting Pirates: The Pen and the Sword," *World Policy Journal* (Winter 2008/09): 46.

31. For more on this as it applies to terrorism, see Benjamin Wittes, *Law and the Long War* (The Penguin Press, 2008); Phillip Bobbitt, *Terror and Consent: The Wars for the Twenty-First Century* (New York: Knopf, 2008); and Amitai Etzioni, *Terrorists: Neither Soldiers nor Criminals*, Mil. Rev (July–Aug. 2009), 108.

32. Kate Wiltrout, "Nine Suspected Pirates Set Free: Others Could Face Trials," *Virginian-Pilot* (Norfolk) (March 3, 2009), http://hamptonroads.com/2009/03/nine-suspected-pirates-set-free-others-could-face-trials.

33. Will Ross, "Drones Scour the Sea for Pirates," *BBC News* (November 10, 2009), http://news.bbc.co.uk/2/hi/8352631.stm.

34. Jacquelyn S. Porth, "Legal Experts Take Action to Prosecute Pirates," *America.gov* (February 27, 2009), http://www.america.gov/st/peacesec-english/2009/February/20090227144346sjhtrop0.3818781.html.

35. Ibid.

36. "Improving Detainee Policy: Handling Terrorism Detainees within the American Justice System: Hearing Before the S. Comm. on the Judiciary, 110th Cong. (2008) http://judiciary.senate.gov/hearings/testimony.cfm?id=3390&wit_id=7214 (Testimony of Benjamin Wittes).

37. Richard Meade, "In the Dock: The Problems with Prosecuting Pirates," *Lloyd's List* (May 1, 2009).

38. "Germany Looks to Battle Pirates," *Speigel Online International* (November 21, 2008), http://www.spiegel.de/international/germany/0,1518,591891,00.html.

39. "Somali Pirates Demand $2 Million Ransom for German Hostages," *Deutsche Welle* (January 7, 2008), http://www.dw-world.de/dw/article/0,,3453015,00.html; "Somali Pirates Release German, Japanese Ships: Maritime Group," *AFP* (September 11, 2008), http://afp.google.com/article/ALeqM5jVT4IZc-mwMTPV. m1yw2hKbb7Aqm-g; "Berlin Looks at Ways to Battle Somali Kidnappers," *Speigel Online International* (June 26, 2008), http://www.spiegel.de/international/germany/0,1518,562204,00.html.

40. Berlin Looks at Ways to Battle Somali Kidnappers.

41. "Monday German Navy Inspector Discusses Expansion of Navy Powers to Combat Piracy," *BBC Monitoring Europe* (April 28, 2008).

42. "Are German Anti-Pirate Forces Hampered by Bureaucrats?" *Speigel Online International* (May 14, 2009), http://www.spiegel.de/international/germany/0,1518,624908,00.html.

43. The laws of war (and the US army field manual) stipulate that "The law of war . . . requires that belligerents refrain from employing any kind or degree of violence which is not actually necessary for military purposes . . ." Field Manual No. 27-10, the Law of Land Warfare, Department of the Army (July 18, 1956), http://www.globalsecurity.org/military/library/policy/army/fm/27-10/Ch1.htm.

44. Robert D. McFadden and Scott Shane, "Navy Rescues Captain, Killing 3 Pirate Captors," *New York Times* (April 13, 2009): A1.

45. Ibid.

46. The rights of pirates involved are spelled out in Article 3 and Article 6 of the Universal Declaration of Human Rights: "Everyone has the right to life,

liberty and security of person" and "Everyone has the right to recognition everywhere as a person before the law."

47. Meki Elgafaji and Noor Elgafaji v. Staatssecretaris van Justitie, Eur. Ct. H.R., www.ehcr.coe.int/eng.

48. Chahal v. The United Kingdom (No. 22), 1996-V Eur. Ct. H.R. 21.

49. Marie Woolf, "Pirates Can Claim UK Asylum," *Sunday Times* (London) (April 13, 2008), http://www.timesonline.co.uk/tol/news/uk/article3736239. ece.

50. Convention against Torture and Other Cruel, Inhuman or Degrading Treatment or Punishment art. 3, Dec. 10, 1984, 1465 U.N.T.S. 85.

51. United Nations Political Office for Somalia, "Human Rights in Somalia," (September. 15, 2009), http://www.un-somalia.org/Human_Rights/index. asp; "Somali Region to Switch to Sharia," *BBC* (November 20, 2006), http://news.bbc.co.uk/2/hi/africa/6166960.stm; "Sharia Imposed at Somali MPs Base," *BBC* (January 27, 2009), http://news.bbc.co.uk/2/hi/africa/ 7854527.stm.

52. While the Transitional Government of Somalia could offer countries assurances that the captured pirates would not be subject to torture, the acceptance of these assurances depends the judgment that they are valid. As a side note, the pirates operating off the coast of Somalia have not fallen inside the protections of the Geneva Conventions up to date. For a treatment of situations in which the Geneva Conventions might apply, see Michael H. Passman, "Protections Afforded to Captured Pirates Under the Law of War and International Law," 33 *Tulane Maritime Law Journal* 1 (Winter 2008): 1.

53. Convention for the Protection of Human Rights and Fundamental Freedoms, art. 3 (November 4, 1950), CETS 005.

54. Seoring v. The United Kingdom, 161 Eur. Ct. H. R. (ser. A) (198.9).

55. One should note that Kenya will not accept all cases, and it decides which cases it is willing to pursue. Sarah Childress, *Pact with Kenya on Piracy Trials Gets First Test, Wall Street Journal* (February 17, 2009), http://online. wsj.com/article/SB123482019865794481.html.

56. "Kenya Seeks to Cancel Deals for Trying Somali Pirates," *AFP* (April 1, 2010), http://www.google.com/hostednews/afp/article/ALeqM5jDQgV-LTDR4BjimFIUAs_1mFVk8OA.

57. Alisha Ryu, "Rights Group Questions US Deal to Send Pirates to Kenya," *Voice of America* (February 13, 2009), http://www.voanews.com/english/ archive/2009-02/2009-02-13-voa43.cfm?CFID=263096949&CFTOKEN= 12225224&jsessionid=6630520c6c29dd8d32fb533945714f95a2b7.

58. Alisha Ryu, "Paris-Based Group Says Accused Somali Pirates Denied Rights," *Voice of Ame*rica (August 27, 2009), http://www.voanews.com/ english/2009-08-27-voa36.cfm.

59. Jeffrey White, "German Lawyers Launch Pirate Defense Team," *Christian Science Monitor* (April 15, 2009), http://www.csmonitor.com/2009/0416/ p06s01-wogn.html.

60. M Matthias Gebauer, "Attorneys File Suit in Germany on Behalf of Alleged Pirates," *Spiegel Online International* (April 15, 2009), http://www.spiegel. de/international/europe/0,1518,619103,00.html; The vast majority of

defendants in Kenya are tried without legal counsel, as they cannot afford representation. US Department of State, "2008 Human Rights Report: Kenya," (February 25, 2009), http://www.state.gov/g/drl/rls/hrrpt/2008/af/119007.htm.

61. For more discussion of responsive communitarianism, please visit http://www.gwu.edu/~icps/About%20Com2.html. To read the "Responsive Communitarian Platform," please visit http://www.gwu.edu/~icps/RCP%20text.html and for the list of founding platform endorsers, please visit http://www.gwu.edu/~icps/RCP%20founding.html. Also, see Part IV of Amitai Etzioni's *My Brother's Keeper.*

62. United States v. Davis, 482 F.2d 893 (9th Cir. 1973).

63. This topic is further discussed by the author in *The Limits of Privacy* (New York: Basic Books, 1999) and *How Patriotic is the Patriot Act?* (New York: Routledge, 2004).

Bibliography

60 Minutes, "Cyber War: Sabotaging the System," (November 8, 2009).

ABC, "Transcript: President Obama's Address to the Nation on Military Action in Libya," *ABC.com* (March 28, 2011). http://abcnews.go.com/Politics/transcript-president-obamas-address-nation-military-action-libya/story?id=132 42776&page=4#.Txl_mIHpbTo (accessed January 20, 2012).

Abdul-Zahra, Qassim and Lara Jakes, "Anti-American Cleric Vies for More Power in Iraq," *Washington Post* (October 2, 2010), http://www.washingtonpost.com/wp-dyn/content/article/2010/10/01/AR2010100101360.html.

Abi-Habib, Maria, Yaroslav Trofimov, and Jay Solomon, "Iran Cash Trail Highlights Battle for Kabul Sway," *The Wall Street Journal* (October 25, 2010), http://online.wsj.com/article/SB10001424052702304388304575574001362056346.html.

Abizaid, General John, "Iran Is Not a Suicide State," *New Perspectives Quarterly* 25, no. 4 (Fall 2008). http://www.digitalnpq.org/archive/2008_fall/14_abizaid.html (accessed January 20, 2012).

Adams, Jonathan, "China's Climate Change Talks: What's Changed since Copenhagen," *The Christian Science Monitor* (October 5, 2010).

Addis, Casey L. et al., *Iran: Regional Perspectives and U.S. Policy* (Washington, DC: Congressional Research Service, January 13, 2010), http://www.fas.org/sgp/crs/mideast/R40849.pdf.

Agence France-Presse, "Kenya Seeks to Cancel Deals for Trying Somali Pirates," *AFP* (April 1, 2010), http://www.google.com/hostednews/afp/article/ALeqM-5jDQgVLTDR4BjimFIUAs_1mFVk8OA.

———, "No 'Risk' from Iran's Russian-Built Nuclear Plant: US," *AFP* (August 22, 2010). http://www.spacewar.com/afp/100822000307.4fud8zcj.html.

———, "Somali Pirates Release German, Japanese Ships: Maritime Group," *AFP* (September 11, 2008). http://afp.google.com/article/ALeqM5jVT4IZcmw-MTPV. m1yw2hKbb7Aqm-g.

Al 'Afghani, Mohamad Mova, "Access to Water Is a Fundamental Human Right," *The Jakarta Post* (July 10, 2007).

al-Banna, Hassan, "On Jihad"; transl C Wendell, in *Five Tracts of Hasan al-Banna* (Berkeley and Los Angeles: University of California Press, 1978), 142.

al-Qaradawi, Yusuf, *Islamic Awakening between Rejection and Extremism*; transl AS Al Shaikh-Ali and MBE Wafsy (1991) (Herndon: American Trust Publications and the International Institute of Islamic Thought, 1981), 21.

Albright, David and Jacqueline Shire, "Misconceptions about Iran's Nuclear Program," Institute for Science and International Security (July 8, 2009). http://www.isisnucleariran.org/static/297/.

Ali, Ayaan Hirsi, "Is Islam Compatible with Liberal Democracy?" Interview at the Aspen Institute (July 2007). http://fora.tv/2007/07/06/Is_Islam_Compatible_with_Liberal_Democracy (accessed January 25, 2012).

Altman, Roger and Richard Haass, "American Profligacy and American Power," *Foreign Affairs* 89, no. 6 (November/December 2010): 30.

Amartya Sen, "Human Rights and Asian Values," *The New Republic* (July 14–July 21, 1997).

American Physical Society and the American Association for the Advancement of Science, *Nuclear Forensics Role, State of the Art, Program Needs* (2008), 23, http://www.aps.org/policy/reports/upload/Nuclear-Forensics-Report-FINAL.pdf.

Amnesty International, "The Battle for Libya: Killings, Disappearances, and Torture," *Amnesty International Report* (September 13, 2011). http://www.amnesty.org/en/library/info/MDE19/025/2011/en.

Amos, Deborah and Robert Siegel, "Saudis Uneasy Amid Arab Unrest," NPR *All Things Considered* (February 21, 2011), http://www.npr.org/2011/02/21/133943624/Arab-Unrest-Makes-Saudi-Arabia-Nervous.

An-Na'im, Abdullah Ahmed ed., *Human Rights in Cross-Cultural Perspectives: Quest for Consensus* (Philadelphia, PA: University of Pennsylvania Press, 1992).

An-Na'im, Abdullahi, "Toward an Islamic Hermeneutics for Human Rights," in *Human Rights and Religious Values: An Uneasy Relationship?* eds. Abdullahi A. Na'im, Jerald D. Gort, Henry M. Vroom (Amsterdam: Editions Rodopi; Grand Rapids: William B. Eerdmans Publishing Company, 1995), 233.

Anderson, Benedict, *Imagined Communities: Reflections on the Origin and Spread of Nationalism* (New York: Verso, 1983).

Anwar Sadat Chair for Peace and Development at the University of Maryland and Zogby International (May 2004), http://www.bsos.umd.edu/SADAT/pub/Arab%20Attitudes%20Towards%20Political%20and%20Social %20Issues,%20 Foreign%20Policy%20and%20the%20Media.htm. (accessed April 18, 2006).

Applebaum, Anne, "Making the World Safe for China," *Slate* (September 27, 2010), http://www.slate.com/id/2268833/ (accessed October 18, 2010).

Aquinas, Thomas, Summa Theologiae II–II, 11:1.

Archik, Kristin and Paul Gallis, "NATO and the European Union," Report by *Congressional Research Services* (January 29, 2008). http://www.fas.org/sgp/crs/row/RL32342.pdf.

Armitage, Richard L. and Samuel R. Berger, "U.S. Strategy for Pakistan and Afghanistan," *Independent Task Fore Report No. 65, Council of Foreign Relations* (2010), 21.

Arnoldy, Ben, "How the Afghanistan War Became Tangled in India vs. Pakistan Rivalry," *Christian Science Monitor* (January 20, 2011), http://www.csmonitor.com/World/Asia-South-Central/2011/0120/How-the-Afghanistan-war-became-tangled-in-India-vs.-Pakistan-rivalry.

Ashcroft, John, "Success and Strategies in the Effort to Liberate Iraq" (April 17, 2003), http://www.usdoj.gov/archive/ag/speeches/2003/041703effortsliberateIraq.htm (accessed April 23, 2010).

Asia Times, "US Lashes Out at Chinese Piracy," (January 15, 2005), http://www.atimes.com/atimes/China/GA15Ad03.html (accessed November 15, 2010).

Associated Press, "China to Sell 50 Fighter Jets to Pakistan," Associated Press (May 20, 2011). http://www.thenational.ae/news/worldwide/south-asia/china-to-sell-50-fighter-jets-to-pakistan.

Audi, Robert, "Self-Evidence" *Philosophical Perspectives* 13 (1999): 205–28, 233.

Audley, John J. and Hans Anker, "Reconciling Trade and Poverty Reduction," *The German Marshall Fund of the United States* (2004), http://www.gmfus.org/galleries/ct_publication_attachments/TAAudlyTrade_and_Poverty.pdf.

Babylonian Talmud, Baba Kama 83 b.

——, Sanhedrin 4:8 (37a).

Bainton, Roland H. *Hunted Heretic: The Life and Death of Michael Servetus* (Boston, MA: Beacon Press, 1953), 170.

Baker, Peter and Eric Schmitt, "Afghan War Debate Now Leans to Focus on Al Qaeda," *The New York Times* (October 7, 2009): A1. http://www.nytimes.com/2009/10/08/world/asia/08prexy.html.

Balfour, Frederik, "U.S. Takes Piracy Pushback to WTO," *Bloomberg Business Week* 10 (April 2007), http://www.businessweek.com/globalbiz/content/apr2007/gb20070410_466097.htm (accessed November 15, 2010).

Bance, Alan, "The Idea of Europe: From Erasmus to ERASMUS," *Journal of European Studies* 22, no. 1 (March 1992): 1–19.

Bangert, Christoph, "Pakistanis View U.S. Aid Warily," *The New York Times* (October 7, 2009).

Banks, Martin, "Mixed Response to EU Plans for Shake-Up of Schengen Area," *The Parliament* (September 19, 2011), http://www.theparliament.com/latest-news/article/newsarticle/mixed-response-to-eu-plans-for-shake-up-of-schengen-area.

Barcelona European Council, "Presidency Conclusions," *Barcelona European Council,* in Barcelona, Spain, March 15 and 16, 2002, http://ec.europa.eu/research/era/docs/en/council-eu-30.pdf.

Barrowclough, Anne, "China Sends Navy to Fight Somali Pirates," *The Times* (December 26, 2008).

Bast, Andrew, "Pakistan's Nuclear Surge," *Newsweek* (May 30, 2011).

BBC, "Cleric Condemns Suicide Attacks," *BBC* (July 11, 2003). http://news.bbc.co.uk/1/hi/world/middle_east/3059365.stm. (accessed April 2, 2006).

——, "Double Veto for Burma Resolution," *BBC* (January 12, 2007). http://news.bbc.co.uk/2/hi/6257921.stm (accessed January 20, 2012).

——, "Dutch Forces Free Pirate Captives," *BBC* (April 18, 2009). http://news.bbc.co.uk/2/hi/africa/8005730.stm.

——, "German Interior Ministers Seek Ban on Far-Right NPD," *BBC* (December 9, 2011), http://www.bbc.co.uk/news/world-europe-16113372 (accessed January 11, 2012).

——, "Monday German Navy Inspector Discusses Expansion of Navy Powers to Combat Piracy," *BBC Monitoring Europe* (April 28, 2008).

——, "Somali Region to Switch to Sharia," *BBC* (November 20, 2006). http://news.bbc.co.uk/2/hi/africa/6166960.stm.

——, "Sharia Imposed at Somali MPs Base," *BBC* (January 27, 2009). http://news.bbc.co.uk/2/hi/africa/7854527.stm.

——, "U.S. Envoy William Burns Says Syria Talks Were Candid," *BBC* (February 17, 2010), http://news.bbc.co.uk/2/hi/8519506.stm.

——, "US 'sure' of Brazil Nuclear Plans," *BBC* (October 5, 2004). http://news.bbc.co.uk/2/hi/americas/3715556.stm.

——, "Writers Issue Cartoon Row Warning," *BBC* (March 1, 2006). http://news.bbc.co.uk/2/hi/europe/4763520.stm. (accessed April 10, 2006).

Begley, Sharon, "Deterring a 'Dirty Bomb," *Newsweek* (April 26, 2010).

Beinart, P., *The Icarus Syndrome: A History of American Hubris* (New York: HarperCollins, 2010).

Bellamy, Richard and Dario Castiglione, "Lacroix's European Constitutional Patriotism: A Response," *Political Studies* 52 (2004): 190.

Bendix, Reinhard, "Max Weber: An Intellectual Portrait," 124.

Benhorin, Yitzhak, "Report: Iran's Uranium Supply Nearly Out," *Ynetnews* (April 28, 2010). http://www.ynetnews.com/articles/0,7340,L-3881821,00.html.

Bergesen, Albert J. and Omar Lizardo, "International Terrorism and the World-System," *Sociological Theory* 22 (2004): 50.

Bergsten, C. Fred, "Two's Company," *Foreign Affairs* 88, no. 5 (September/October 2009): 169–70.

Bevege, Alison, *Somali Pirates Nabbed, Released by Canadian Frigate*, Reuters *Canada.com* (April 19, 2009). http://www2.canada.com/topics/news/story.html?id=1512697.

Bijian, Zheng, "China's 'Peaceful Rise' to Great-Power Status," *Foreign Affairs* 84, no. 5 (2005): 18–24.

BIPPI Independent Pro-Peace Initiative, "Wars, Conflicts, International and Intra-national Crises," (February 2008), http://www.bippi.org/bippi/menu_left/conflicts.htm (accessed June 11, 2009).

Blaker, James R., "Avoiding another Cold War: The Case for Collaboration with China," *Perspectives* American Security Project (November 2008).

Blaker, James R. and Steven J. Nider, "Why It's Time to Revolutionize the Military," *Blueprint Magazine* (February 7, 2001).

Blodget, Henry, "How to Solve China's Piracy Problem," *Slate* (April 12, 2005), http://www.slate.com/id/2116629/ (accessed November 17, 2010).

Bloomberg Business Week, "The Runaway Trade Giant," (April 24, 2006), http://www.businessweek.com/magazine/content/06_17/b3981039.htm (accessed November 15, 2010).

Bowman, Tom, "Obama Sets More Modest Goals for Afghanistan," *NPR* (February 6, 2009). http://www.npr.org/templates/story/story.php?storyId=100279589.

Blumenthal, Dan, "Detecting Subtle Shifts in the Balance of Power," American Enterprise Institute (September 3, 2010).

Bobbitt, Phillip, *Terror and Consent: The Wars for the Twenty-First Century* (New York: Knopf, 2008).

Bok, Derek, *The Politics of Happiness: What Government Can Learn from the New Research on Well Being* (Princeton, NJ: Princeton University Press, 2010), 20–22.

Bolton, John, *A "World Turned Upside Down"?; U.S. Now a Judicial Target for Defending Lawful Commerce*, *The Washington Times* (April 17, 2009), http://www.washingtontimes.com/news/2009/apr/17/a-world-turned-upside-down/.

Bondevik, Kjell, Magne Speech at the conference "Europe: A Beautiful Idea?" The Hague (September 7, 2004).

Bondurant, J, *Conquest of Violence: The Gandhian Philosophy of Conflict* (Princeton, NJ: Princeton University Press, 1988).

Boone, Jon, "WikiLeaks: Afghan MPs and Religious Scholars 'On Iran Payroll,'" *Guardian* (London) (December 2, 2010), http://www.guardian.co.uk/world/2010/dec/02/afghan-mps-scholars-iran-payroll.

Bourne, Angela K., "Democratisation and the Illegalisation of Political Parties in Europe," *Working Paper Series on the Legal Regulation of Political Parties* no. 7 (February 2011), http://www.partylaw.leidenuniv.nl/uploads/wp0711.pdf (accessed January 12, 2012).

Bowman, Tom, "Bahrain: Key U.S. Military Hub," NPR *Weekend Edition Saturday* (February 19, 2011), http://www.npr.org/templates/transcript/transcript. php?storyId=133893941.

Bradsher, Keith, "Sitting Out the China Trade Battles," *New York Times* (December 23, 2010).

Brazilian Constitution, art. 2, sec. XLIII, http://www.v-brazil.com/government/laws/constitution.html (accessed June 11, 2009).

Breitman, G, *Malcolm X Speaks: Selected Speeches and Statements* (New York: Merit, 1965), 9, 12, 57, 165.

Brockett, Charles, "A Hierarchy of Human Rights," Paper presented at Annual Meeting of the American Political Science Association (New York, August 31–September 3, 1978).

Brookes, Peter, "National Review: Beijing's Build-up and New START," *National Public Radio* (December 9, 2010), http://www.npr.org/2010/12/09/131928912/national-review-beijing-s-build-up-and-new-start.

Buber, Martin, *I and Thou* (New York: Scribners, 1970).

Buchanan, Patrick, "The Chinese Century," *American Conservative* (April 22, 2010).

Buckley, Chris, "China Military Paper Spells Out Nuclear Arms Stance," *Reuters* (April 22, 2010).

Bukhari 9.84.57.

Bull, Hedley, Kai Alderson and Andrew Hurrell, eds, *Hedley Bull on International Society* (Basingstoke: Palgrave Macmillan, 2000).

Bumiller, Elisabeth, "Gates Plays Down Idea of U.S. Force in Libya," *The New York Times* (March 1, 2011): A11. http://www.nytimes.com/2011/03/02/world/africa/02military.html.

Burnett, John S., "Captain Kidd, Human-Rights Victim," *N. Y. Times* (April 20, 2008), http://www.nytimes.com/2008/04/20/opinion/20burnett.html?_r=1.

Bush, George W. "Second Presidential Debate," (October 11, 2000). http://www.fas.org/news/usa/2000/usa-001011.htm (retrieved July 14, 2011).

———, "Remarks by President George W. Bush at the Islamic Center of Washington, DC," (September 17, 2001). http://www.whitehouse.gov/news/releases/2001/09/20010917-11.html. (accessed March 5, 2006).

BusinessGreen, "Green Groups Take EU to Court over Biofuels—Again," *The Guardian* (May 26, 2011), http://www.guardian.co.uk/environment/2011/may/26/biofuels-energy.

Caplan, Brian, "Terrorism: The Relevance of the Rational Choice Model," *Public Choice* 128 (2006): 92.

Caporaso, James, "The European Union and Forms of State: Westphalian, Regulatory or Post-Modern? A Logical and Empirical Assessment" *Journal of Common Market Studies* 34, no. 1 (1996): 29–52.

Carey, Sean, "Undivided Loyalties: Is National Identity an Obstacle to European Integration?" *European Union Politics* 3, no. 4 (2002): 387–413.

Carr, Caleb, *The Lessons of Terror: A History of Warfare against Civilians*, Revised edition. (New York: Random House, 2003), 6.

Carroll, Dean, "Strengthened Schengen to 'Europeanise' Borders," *Public Service Europe* (September 16, 2011), http://www.publicserviceeurope.com/article/864/strengthened-schengen-to-europeanise-borders.

CASF, "About Us," http://rtsf.wordpress.com/about/ (accessed July 24, 2009).

Cassata, Donna and Lolita Baldor, "Gates Calls For Limited Role Aiding Libyan Rebels," *Associated Press* (March 31, 2011). http://abcnews.go.com/US/wireStory?id=13264595.

CBS, "Qaddafi: I Will Fight Protests, Die a Martyr," *CBS News* (February 22, 2011). http://www.cbsnews.com/stories/2011/02/22/501364/main20034785.shtml.

Cederman, Lars-Erik, "Nationalism and Bounded Integration: What It Would Take to Construct a European Demos," *European Journal of International Relations* 7(2001): 139–74.

Chahal v. The United Kingdom (No. 22), 1996-V Eur. Ct. H.R. 21.

Chan, Sewell, "China Agrees to Intellectual Property Protections," *The New York Times* (December 15, 2010).

Chandrasekaran, Rajiv, "From Captive to Suicide Bomber" *Washington Post* (February 28, 2009). Terrorism Act 2006, 2006, c. 11, §25 (U.K.).

Chari, P. R. and Hasan Askari Rizvi, "Making Borders Irrelevant in Kashmir," United States Institute of Peace, Special Report 210 (September 2008).

Chase, Michael, "The Dragon's Dilemma: A Closer Look at China's Defense Budget and Priorities," Policy Memo, The Progressive Policy Institute (March 4, 2010), 3.

———, "Not in Our Backyard: China's Emerging Anti-Access Strategy," Policy Memo, The Progressive Policy Institute (October 2010), 5.

Chatterjee, Margaret, *Gandhi's Religious Thought* (Notre Dame: University of Notre Dame Press, 1983).

Chesluk, Benjamin, "Community Policing in New York City," *Cultural Anthropology* 19, no. 2 (2004): 250–74.

Chesney, Robert and Jack Goldsmith, "Terrorism and the Convergence of Criminal and Military Detention Models," *Stanford Law Review* 60 (2008): 1081.

Childress, Sarah, "Pact with Kenya on Piracy Trials Gets First Test," *Wall Street Journal* (February 17, 2009), http://online.wsj.com/article/SB123482019865794481.html.

———, "U.S. Holds Suspects after Pirates Standoff," *Wall Street Journal* (April 2, 2010): A11.

China.org, "UN Needs to Help All Nations Develop," *China.org* (September 7, 2000). http://www.china.org.cn/english/2000/Sep/1605.htm (accessed January 20, 2012).

CIA World Factbook, https://www.cia.gov/library/publications/the-world-factbook/rankorder/2004rank.html (accessed November 17, 2010).

———, "GDP Per Capita (PPP)," CIA World Factbook. https://www.cia.gov/library/publications/the-world-factbook/rankorder/2004rank.html.

Clairvaux, Bernard, *On the Song of Songs III*; transl K. Walsh and I. Edmonds (Kalamazoo, MI: Cistercian Publications, 1979), 175.

Clark, Wesley K. and Kal Raustiala, "Why Terrorists Aren't Soldiers," *The New York Times* (August 8, 2007), http://www.nytimes.com/2007/08/08/opinion/08clark.html (accessed April 23, 2010).

Clinton, Hillary, "Remarks with Afghan Women Ministers before Their Meeting," U.S. Department of State (May 13, 2010). http://www.state.gov/secretary/rm/2010/05/141806.htm (accessed January 25, 2012).

———, Response to Citizens for Global Solutions 2008 Presidential Candidate Questionnaire, Citizens for Global Solutions. http://globalsolutions.org/08orbust/pcq/clinton (accessed January 20, 2012).

———, "Secretary Clinton on Libya," at Andrews Air Force Base (February 27, 2011).

———, "Secretary of State Hillary Rodham Clinton's Remarks on Receiving the George C. Marshall Foundation Award," http://www.marshallfoundation.org/SecretaryClintonremarksJune22011.htm (accessed June 2, 2011).

———, "Senator Clinton's Remarks at the U.S. Islamic World Forum," (April 12, 2011).

CNN, "CBS Hit with $550K Super Bowl Fine," *CNN Money* (September 22, 2004). http://money.cnn.com/2004/09/22/news/fortune500/viacom_fcc/ (accessed January 24, 2012).

Coates, Sam, "China to Blame for Failure of Copenhagen Climate Deal, says Ed Miliband," *The Times* (December 21, 2009).

Cohen, Jerome A. and Jon M. Van Dyke, "Finding Its Sea Legs," *The South China Morning Post* (October 26, 2010).

Coll, Steve, "The Back Channel: India and Pakistan's Secret Kashmir Talks," *The New Yorker* (March 2, 2009).

Collier, Paul, "Dead Aid, by Dambisa Moyo," *The Independent* (January 30, 2009), http://www.independent.co.uk/arts-entertainment/books/reviews/dead-aid-by-dambisa-moyo-1519875.html.

Colvin, R. "Obama Rights Record Questioned Ahead of Nobel Prize." (2009) http://www.reuters.com/article/idUSTRE5B82TM20091209 (retrieved January 10, 2010).

Combined Maritime Forces Public Affairs, *Combined Maritime Forces Flagship Intercepts Somali Pirates*, NAVY.mil (April 2, 2010), http://www.navy.mil/search/display.asp?story_id=52370.

Committee on Foreign Relations, "Evaluating U.S. Foreign Aid to Afghanistan: A Majority Staff Report," *Committee on Foreign Relations, United States Senate* (June 8, 2011).

Connolly, Kate, "Germany Accuses China of Industrial Espionage," *The Guardian* July 22, 2009).

Cook, Samuel D., "Coercion and Social Change," in *Coercion*, eds. James R. Pennock and John W. Chapman (Chicago, IL: Aldin, 1972), 116.

Cooper, Helene, "Allies in War, but the Goals Clash," *The New York Times* (October 9, 2010). http://www.nytimes.com/2010/10/10/weekinreview/10cooper.html (accessed June 19, 2012).

———, "Washington Asks: What to Do About Israel?" *New York Times* (June 5, 2010). http://www.nytimes.com/2010/06/06/weekinreview/06cooper .html.

Cooper, Helene and Landler, M., "For Obama, Pressure To Strike Firmer Tone," *New York Times* (June 18, 2009): A16.

Cooper, Helene and Steven Lee Myers, "U.S. Tactics in Libya May Be a Model for Use of Force," *The New York Times* (August 28, 2011): A9. http://www.nytimes. com/2011/08/29/world/africa/29diplo.html.

Council of Europe, "Convention for the Protection of Human Rights and Fundamental Freedoms," art. 3 (November 4, 1950), CETS 005. http://www.echr. coe.int/NR/rdonlyres/D5CC24A7-DC13-4318-B457-5C9014916D7A/0/ ENG_CONV.pdf.

Council on Foreign Relations, "China's Military Power," Independent Task Force on Chinese Military Power (May 2003), 1; 6–7.

———, "Scheinman: Iran, North Korea, and the NPT's Loopholes," Council on Foreign Relations. http://www.cfr.org/publication/7661/scheinman.html.

———, "U.S.-China Relations: An Affirmative Agenda, a Responsible Course," Task Force Report (April 2007).

Cox, Timothy and Alex van Gelder, "Trade, Not Aid, Is the Best Way Out of Poverty," *South China Morning Post* (June 29, 2010), http://www.policynetwork. net/development/media/trade-not-aid-best-way-out-poverty.

Crenshaw, Martha, "Explaining Suicide Terrorism: A Review Essay," *Security Studies* 16, no. 1 (January–March 2007): 141.

Crittenden, Michael R. and Shayndi Rice, "Chinese Firm 'Hijacked' Data," *The New York Times* (November 18, 2010): A8.

Cromwell, Richard S., "Rightist Extremism in Postwar West Germany," *Western Political Quarterly* 17, no. 2 (1964).

Cullen, Peter M., "The Role of Targeted Killing in the Campaign against Terror," *Joint Force Quarterly* 48 (1st Quarter 2008): 22–29.

D3 Systems and Afghan Center for Social and Opinion Research, WorldPublic Opinion.org survey (November 27–December 4, 2005), http://65.109.167.118/ pipa/pdf/jan06/Afghanistan_Jan06_quaire.pdf. (accessed April 18, 2006).

Dagher, Sam, "Iraq Wants the U.S. Out," *Wall Street Journal* (December 28, 2010), http://online.wsj.com/article/SB10001424052970204685004576045700275218580.html.

Davis, David, "A 21st-Century Marshall Plan," *Prospect* (July 2011): 12–13.

Davis, Jonathan E., "From Ideology to Pragmatism: China's Position on Humanitarian Intervention in the Post-Cold War Era," *Vanderbilt Journal of Transnational Law* 44, no. 2 (March 2011): 243, 251.

DeHousse, Renaud, "Constitutional Reform in the European Community: Are There Alternatives to the Majoritarian Avenue?" *The Crisis of Representation in Europe*, Jack Ernest and Shalom Hayward (1995).

De Luce, Dan, "Afghans Pose Awkward Questions for U.S. Military Chief." *Agence France Presse* (July 26, 2010), http://www.google.com/hostednews/afp/article/ALeqM5hyyMeTjC4oof3Bg5idtZZuEXLO4Q.

Deng, Francis M., Sadikiel Kimaro, Terrence Lyons, Donald Rothchild, and I. William Zartman, *Sovereignty as Responsibility: Conflict Management in Africa* (Washington, DC: Brookings Institution Press, 1996), 223.

Denyer, Simon and Karin Brulliard, "India, Pakistan Agree to Resume Peace Talks," *Washington Post* (February 11, 2011), http://www.washingtonpost.com/wp-dyn/content/article/2011/02/10/AR2011021007207.html.

Dershowitz, Alan, "The Case against Jordan," *Jerusalem Post* (October 7, 2003). http://archive.frontpagemag.com/readArticle.aspx?ARTID=15992

Desch, Michael, "Apocalypse Not," *The American Conservative* (May 19, 2009), http://www.theamericanconservative.com/article/2009/may/18/00006/ (accessed January 20, 2012).

Deudney, Daniel H., *Bounding Power* (Princeton, NJ: Princeton University Press, 2007), 1, 3.

Deudney, Daniel and G. John Ikenberry, "The Myth of the Autocratic Revival: Why Liberal Democracy Will Prevail," *Foreign Affairs* 88, no. 1 (January/February 2009).

Diehl, Jackson, "Obama's National Security Strategy Is Light on Human Rights," *The Washington Post* (May 31, 2010).

Drew, Christopher, "New Targets for Spies: Employers' Trade Secrets," *International Herald Tribune* (October 19, 2010).

Drummond, David, "A New Approach to China," *Googleblog* (January 12, 2010), http://googleblog.blogspot.com/2010/01/new-approach-to-china.html (accessed November 17, 2010).

Deutsche Welle, "Somali Pirates Demand $2 Million Ransom for German Hostages," Deutsche Welle (January 7, 2008), http://www.dw-world.de/dw/article/0,,3453015,00.html.

Dyer, Geoff and Farhan Bokhari, "China-Pakistan Reactor Deal to Open Fresh US Rift," *Financial Times* (September 23, 2010).

Easterbrook, Gregg, "The Pentagon and Wasteful Defense Spending," *New Republic* (November 10, 2010).

Easterlin, Richard, "Diminishing Marginal Utility of Income? Caveat Emptor," *Social Indicators Research* (2005).

———, "Does Money Buy Happiness," *The Public Interest* 30 (Winter 1973).

Easterly, William, *The White Man's Burden: Why the West's Efforts to Aid the Rest Have Done so Much Ill and So Little Good* (New York: Penguin Press, 2006), 136.

Economist, "China's Thing about Numbers: How an Emerging Superpower Dragged Its Feet, Then Dictated Terms, at a Draining Diplomatic Marathon," *The Economist* (December 30, 2009).

———, "The Fourth Modernization," 397, no. 8711 (December 4, 2010): 7.

———, "A Long War of the Waters," *Economist* (January 9, 2010): 47.

———, "NATO after Libya: A Troubling Victory," *Economist* (September 3, 2011), http://www.economist.com/node/21528248.

——, "Protecting the Vulnerable: What Congo Means for Obama," *Economist* (November 18, 2008), http://www.economist.com/node/12601948 (accessed January 20, 2012).

——, "A War of Money as well as Bullets," *Economist* (May 22, 2008).

——, "India and Pakistan: A Willow Branch," *Economist* (March 31, 2011), http://www.economist.com/node/18485995?story_id=18485995.

——, "Wrong Signals: Piracy," *Economist* (May 9, 2009): 62.

Economy, Elizabeth C., "The Game Changer: Coping with China's Foreign Policy Revolution," *Foreign Affairs* (November/December 2010): 142, 144.

Economy, Elizabeth C. and Adam Segal, "The G-2 Mirage," *Foreign Affairs* 88, no. 3 (May/June 2009): 14-23.

Egyptian State Information Service, "International Support for Egypt's Plan of Bridging Budget Deficit," Egyptian State Information Service, http://www.sis.gov.eg/en/Story.aspx?sid=54900 (accessed April 17, 2011).

Eichenberg, Richard C. and Russell J. Dalton, "Post-Maastricht Blues: The Transformation of Citizen Support for European Integration, 1973–2004," *Acta Politica* 42 (2007): 128–52, Figure 1.

Eland, Ivan, "Is Chinese Military Modernization a Threat to the United States?" *Policy Analysis* no. 465 (January 23, 2003) The Cato Institute.

Elgafaji Meki and Noor Elgafaji v. Staatssecretaris van Justitie, Eur. Ct. H.R., http://www.ehcr.coe.int/eng.

Elliott, Michael, "The Chinese Century" *Time* (January 11, 2007).

Ellison, Keith, H.Res.157.IH, 112th Congress (March 9, 2011).

Elyan, Tamim and Muhammad al-Yamani, "Egypt Salafis Want No Pact with Muslim Brotherhood," (December 4, 2011), http://www.reuters.com/article/2011/12/04/us-egypt-salafi-idUSTRE7B30MN20111204 (accessed January 12, 2012).

Enders, David, "African Women Say Rebels Raped Them in Libyan Camp," *McClatchy* (September 7, 2011). http://www.mcclatchydc.com/2011/09/07/123403/african-women-say-rebels-raped.html.

——, "Empty Village Raises Concerns about Fate of Black Libyans," *McClatchy* (September 13, 2011). http://www.mcclatchydc.com/2011/09/13/123999/empty-village-raises-concerns.html.

Etzioni, Amitai, "Are Particularistic Obligations Justified?" *The Review of Politics* 64, no. 4 (Autumn 2002): 573–98.

——, *A Comparative Analysis of Complex Organizations* (New York: The Free Press, 1961 and revised edition 1975).

——, *From Empire to Community* (New York: Palgrave Macmillan, 2004).

——, *The Hard Way to Peace: A New Strategy* (New York: Collier, 1962).

——, *How Patriotic is the Patriot Act? Freedom versus Security in the Age of Terrorism* (New York: Routledge, 2004), 38–39.

——, "Is China a Responsible Stakeholder?" *International Affairs* 87, no. 3 (May 2011): 539–53.

——, *My Brother's Keeper: A Memoir and a Message* (Lanham: Rowman & Littlefield, 2003).

——, *The New Golden Rule: Community and Morality in a Democratic Society* (New York: Basic Books, 1996).

———, *Security First* (New Haven, CT: Yale University Press, 2007), 44, 15–19, 31, 37–85, 236–37.

———, *Terrorists: Neither Soldiers nor Criminals*, Mil. Rev (July–August 2009), 108.

———, *Winning Without War* (Garden City, NY: Doubleday, 1964).

EUR-Lex, "On a New Approach to Technical Harmonization and Standards," *Council Resolution* (May 7, 1985), http://eur-lex.europa.eu/LexUriServ/LexUriServ.do?uri=CELEX:31985Y0604(01):EN:HTML.

European Commission, "Eurobarometer" http://ec.europa.eu/public_opinion/index_en.htm.

———, "European Standards" *European Commission: Enterprise and Industry*, http://ec.europa.eu/enterprise/policies/european-standards/documents/harmonised-standards-legislation/list-references/index_en.htm.

———, "General Publications: Young People," *European Commission Website* http://ec.europa.eu/publications/archives/young/01/index_en.htm (accessed September 30, 2011).

European Parliament, "Symbols of the Union To Be Adopted by Parliament," press release, *Committee on Constitutional Affairs* European Parliament, http://www.europarl.europa.eu/sides/getDoc.do?language=en&type=IM-PRESS&reference=20080909IPR36656 (September 11, 2008).

Evans, Gareth, Mohamed Sahnoun, et al., "The Responsibility to Protect," Report of the International Commission on Intervention and State Sovereignty (December 2001), 13. http://responsibilitytoprotect.org/ICISS%20Report.pdf (accessed January 19, 2012).

Ewing, Jack and Niki Kitsantonis, "Trichet Urges Creation of Euro Oversight Panel," *The New York Times* (June 2, 2011). http://www.nytimes.com/2011/06/03/business/global/03euro.html?_r=1.

Fadel, Leila, "After Government Collapse, Hezbollah Works to Get More Power in Lebanon," *Washington Post* (January 13, 2011). http://www.washingtonpost.com/wp-dyn/content/article/2011/01/13/AR2011011306737.html (accessed June 19, 2012)

Falkner, Gerda and Oliver Treib, "Three Worlds of Compliance or Four? The EU-15 Compared to New Member States." *Journal of Common Market Studies* 46, no. 2 (March 2008): 293–313.

Fan, Maureen, "China to Aid in Fighting Somali Pirates," *The Washington Post* (December 18, 2008).

FAO Newsroom, "The Most Fundamental Human Right Is the Right to Food," (June 26, 2007), http://www.fao.org/newsroom/EN/news/2007/1000610/index.html (accessed July 24, 2009).

Feigenbaum, Evan A., "Beijing's Billions," *Foreign Policy* (May 20, 2010), http://www.foreignpolicy.com/articles/2010/05/19/beijings_billions (accessed October 18, 2010).

Feinberg, Joel, "The Nature and Value of Rights," *The Philosophy of Human Rights*, ed. Patrick Hayden (St. Paul: Paragon House, 2001).

Feinstein, Lee and Anne-Marie Slaughter, "A Duty to Prevent," *Foreign Affairs* (January/February 2004). http://www.foreignaffairs.com/articles/59540/lee-feinstein-and-anne-marie-slaughter/a-duty-to-prevent (accessed January 19, 2012).

Ferguson, Niall, "What 'Chimerica' Hath Wrought," *American Interest* 4, no. 3 (January/February 2009), http://www.the-american-interest.com/article.cfm?piece=533.

Ferry, Jean-Marc, "Ten Normative Theses on the European Union," *Ethical Perspectives* 15, no. 4 (2008): 527–44.

Filkins, Dexter and Mark Landler, "Afghan Leader Is Seen to Flout Influence of U.S.," *New York Times* (March 29, 2010). http://www.nytimes.com/2010/03/30/world/asia/30karzai.html.

Findley, Michael G., Darren Hawkins, Robert L. Hicks, Daniel L. Nielson, Bradley C. Parks, Ryan M. Powers, J. Timmons Roberts, Michael J. Tierney, and Sven Wilson. "*AidData: Tracking Development Finance*," presented at the PLAID Data Vetting Workshop, Washington, DC (September 2009).

Fischer, Joschka, "From Confederacy to Federation: Thoughts on the Finality of European Integration," delivered at the Humboldt University, Berlin, Germany (May 12, 2000).

Fischer, Norman, "The Moral Core of U.S. Constitutional Ban on Hate Speech Codes," (Twentieth World Congress of Philosophy, Boston, MA, August 10–15, 1998), http://www.bu.edu/wcp/Papers/Law/LawFisc.htm (accessed June 11, 2009).

Fish, Stanley, "Don't Blame Relativism," *The Responsive Community* 12, no. 3 (2002): 27–31.

Fishman, Ted, "The Chinese Century," *New York Times Magazine* (July 4, 2004).

Flannery, Kent V., "The Cultural Evolution of Civilizations," *Annual Review of Ecology and Systematics* 3 (1972): 399–426.

Fogh, Anders, "Libya Operation Coming to an End," Secretary General's Video Blog (September 5, 2011), http://andersfogh.info/2011/09/05/libya-operation-coming-to-an-end.

Follath, Erich, "The Dragon's Embrace: China's Soft Power Is a Threat to the West," *Der Spiegel* (July 28, 2010). http://www.spiegel.de/international/world/0,1518,708645,00.html.

Foulger, Matthew, "No to Further Cuts in the Defense Budget," *The Foundry*, The Heritage Foundation (November 22, 2010), http://blog.heritage.org/?p=47081.

Fox News, "Odierno: U.S. Might Seek U.N. Peacekeepers in Iraq After 2011," *Fox News* (July 6, 2010), http://www.foxnews.com/world/2010/07/06/general-iraq-ponders-peacekeepers-defuse-kurd-arab-tensions/.

Fravel, M. Taylor, "China's Search for Military Power," *Washington Quarterly* 31, no. 3 (Summer 2008), 137.

———, "Regime Insecurity and International Cooperation: Explaining China's Compromises in Territorial Disputes," *International Security* 30, no. 2 (2005): 46.

Friedberg, Aaron, "Here Be Dragons," *National Interest* no. 103 (September/October 2009): 19–34.

Friedmann, Yohanan, *Tolerance and Coercion in Islam: Interfaith Relations in the Muslim Tradition* (New York: Cambridge University Press, 2003): 98, 123, 103.

Gabel, Matthew, "Public Support for European Integration: An Empirical Test of Five Theories," *The Journal of Politics* 60, no. 2 (May 1998): 333–54.

Gady, Franz-Stefan, "Pakistan Moves East," *The National Interest* (June 3, 2011), http://nationalinterest.org/commentary/the-china-pakistan-alliance-5400.

Gamal, Rania El, "Libyan Rebel Commander Killed by Allied Militia," *Reuters* (July 30, 2011), http://www.reuters.com/article/2011/07/30/us-libya-idUS-TRE76Q76620110730.

Gandhi, Mahatma, *The Collected Works of Mahatma Gandhi*, vol. 35 (Delhi: Government of India, 1969), 255, 166.

Ganor, Boaz, "Defining Terrorism: Is One Man's Terrorist another Man's Freedom Fighter?" International Policy Institute for Counter-Terrorism, Herzlia, Israel (September 24, 1998), http://www.ict.org.il/ResearchPublications/tabid/64/Articlsid/432/currentpage/1/Default.aspx.

———, "The Relationship between International and Localized Terrorism," *Jerusalem Center for Public Affairs Jerusalem Issue Brief* 4, no. 26 (2005): http://www.jcpa.org/brief/brief004-26.htm.

Gates, Robert, "Landon Lecture," Kansas State University (November 26, 2007).

———, Testimony on Libya to House Armed Services Committee (March 31, 2011).

Gebauer, M. Matthias, *Attorneys File Suit in Germany on Behalf of Alleged Pirates*, Spiegel Online International (April 15, 2009), http://www.spiegel.de/international/europe/0,1518,619103,00.html.

Gelling, Peter, "Indonesia Passes Broad Anti-Pornography Bill," *New York Times* (October 30, 2008), http://www.nytimes.com/2008/10/30/world/asia/30iht-indo.1.17378031.html (accessed January 25, 2012).

German Marshall Fund of the United States, "Transatlantic Trends 2011," German Marshall Fund of the United States and Compagnia di San Paolo (2011). http://trends.gmfus.org.php5-23.dfw1-2.websitetestlink.com/?page_id=3189 (accessed January 20, 2012).

Gertz, Bill, "Harsh Words from Chinese Military Raise Threat Concerns," *The Washington Times* (March 5, 2010).

Gettleman, Jeffrey, "Obama in Africa: Welcome Back, Son. Now Don't Forget Us," *New York Times* (July 11, 2009).

———, "Pirates Outmaneuver Warships Off Somalia," *N. Y. Times* (December 15, 2008), http://www.nytimes.com/2008/12/16/world/africa/16pirate.html.

Ghosh, Tapan, *The Gandhi Murder Trial* (New York: Asia, 1975).

Gienger, Viola, "'Iran Gives Weapons, $200 Million a Year to Help Lebanese Hezbollah Re-Arm," *Bloomberg* (April 20, 2010), http://www.businessweek.com/news/2010-04-20/iran-gives-weapons-funds-to-help-lebanese-hezbollah-re-arm.html.

Gill, Bates, "China Becoming a Responsible Stakeholder," event resource, The Carnegie Endowment for International Peace (June 11, 2007), http://carnegieendowment.org/files/Bates_paper.pdf (accessed October 20, 2010).

———, "China's Evolving Regional Security Strategy," in Shambaugh, ed., *Power Shift* (Berkeley, CA: University of California Press, 2005), 257.

————, *Rising Star: China's New Security Diplomacy* (Washington DC: Brookings Institution Press, 2007).

Gishkori, Zahid, "Indo-Pak Composite Dialogue: No Movement on Sir Creek Talks," *The Express Tribune* (May 22, 2011), http://tribune.com.pk/story/173672/indo-pak-composite-dialogue-no-movement-on-sir-creek-talks/.

Glendon, Mary Ann, *Rights Talk: The Impoverishment of Political Discourse* (New York: Free Press, 1991).

Global Competitiveness Report 2010–2011 (Geneva: The World Economic Forum, 2011).

Global Competitiveness Report 2008–2009 (Geneva: The World Economic Forum, 2009).

Global Security, "Bushehr," Globalsecurity.org, http://www.globalsecurity.org/wmd/world/iran/bushehr-opp.htm.

————, "South China Sea/Spratly Islands," GlobalSecurity.org, http://www.globalsecurity.org/military/world/war/spratly.htm (accessed November 17, 2010).

Godwin, Paul, "Perspective: Asia's Dangerous Security Dilemma," *Current History* no. 728 (September 2010): 264.

Goldsmith, Jack and Neal Katyal, "The Terrorist' Court," *The New York Times* (July 11, 2007).

Goldstein, Avery, "Testimony before the U.S. Economic and Security Review Commission," (July 21, 2005).

Goodman, Peter, "The Persistently Poor: An Internal Report Criticizes World Bank's Efforts on Poverty," *Washington Post* (December 8, 2006).

Gordon, Michael, "A Nation Challenged: Military; Tora Bora Attack Advances Slowly in Tough Fighting," *The New York Times* (December 16, 2001): B2. http://www.nytimes.com/2001/12/16/world/a-nation-challenged-military-tora-bora-attack-advances-slowly-in-tough-fighting.html.

Gorman, Siobhan, "Electricity Grid in U.S. Penetrated By Spies," *The Wall Street Journal* (April 8, 2009).

Gregg v. Georgia 428 U.S. 153 (1976).

Griswold v. Connecticut, 381 U.S. 479 (1965).

Grossman, Emiliano and Patrick LeBlond, "European Financial Integration: Finally the Great Leap Forward?" *Journal of Common Market Studies* 49, no. 2 (2011): 413–35.

Guangya, Wang, "Statement by H.E. Vice Foreign Minister Wang Guangya at the 58th Session of the United Nations Commission on Human Rights," (April 2, 2002), http://www.china-un.org/eng/zghlhg/jjhshsw/rqwt/t29329.htm. (accessed January 19, 2012).

Guardian, "U.S. Embassy Cables: Iranian Influence at Afghanistan Parliament," *Guardian* (London) (December 2, 2010), http://www.guardian.co.uk/world/us-embassy-cables-documents/194913.

Guiora, Amos N., "Quirin to Hamdan: Creating a Hybrid Paradigm for the Detention of Terrorists," *Florida Journal of International Law* 19 (2007): 521, 529.

Gul, Ayaz, "Pakistan Claims Progress against Tribal Area Militants," *Voice of America* (June 9, 2011), http://www.voanews.com/english/news/asia/Pakistan-Claims-Progress-Against-Tribal-Area-Militants-123654394.html.

Guoxing, Ji, "The Legality of the 'Impeccable Incident," http://www.chinasecurity.
us/pdfs/jiguoxing.pdf (accessed October 5, 2010).

Habermas, Jürgen, *The Postnational Constellation: Political Essays* (Cambridge,
MA: MIT Press, 2001), 49, 54, 81.

———, "Why Europe Needs a Constitution," *New Left Review* 11 (September–
October 2001).

Hadar, Leon, "Don't Fear China," *American Conservative* (December 17, 2010),
http://www.amconmag.com/blog/dont-fear-china/.

Hakura, Fadi, "What Can Rescue the Arab Spring?" *Christian Science Monitor*
(May 10, 2011), http://www.csmonitor.com/Commentary/Opinion/2011/0510/
What-can-rescue-the-Arab-Spring (accessed January 25, 2012).

Halper, Stefan, *The Beijing Consensus: How China's Authoritarian Model Will
Dominate the Twenty-First Century* (New York: Basic Books, 2010), 210.

Harcourt, Bernard E., *Illusion of Order: The False Promises of Broken Windows
Policing* (Cambridge, MA: Harvard University Press, 2001).

Harel, Amos, "Iran Is Celebrating Mubarak Downfall with Suez Crossing," *Ha'aretz*
(Tel Aviv) (February 23, 2011), http://www.haaretz.com/print-edition/news/
iran-is-celebrating-mubarak-downfall-with-suez-crossing-1.345103.

Hawkins, Oliver, "What to Do with a Captured Pirate," *BBC* (March 10, 2009),
http://news.bbc.co.uk /2/hi/in_depth/7932205.stm.

Hayward, Allison R., "Revisiting the Fable of Reform," *Harvard Journal on
Legislation* 45 (2008): 429.

Hedgpeth, Dana, "Spending on Iraq Poorly Tracked," *Washington Post* (May
23, 2008); "Section 4 Official Corruption and Government Transparency," in
2009 Human Rights Report: Afghanistan, U.S. Department of State Bureau of
Democracy, Human Rights, and Labor (March 11, 2010).

Helliwell, John F., "Well-Being, Social Capital and Public Policy: What's New?"
Economic Modelling 20, no. 2 (March 2003): 331–60.

Henkin, Louis, *The Age of Rights* (New York: Columbia University Press, 1990),
2.

Hersh, Seymour M., "The Online Threat," *The New Yorker* (November 1, 2010).

Hibbs, Mark, "Moving Forward on the U.S.-India Nuclear Deal," *Carnegie Endowment for International Peace* (April 5, 2010), http://www.carnegieendowment.
org/publications/?fa=view&id=40491.

Higgins, Andrew, "China Showcasing Its Softer Side," *The Washington Post*
(December 2, 2009).

Hill, Tim. "Muammar Gaddafi Son Killed by NATO Air Strike—Libyan Government," *The Guardian* (April 30, 2011), http://www.guardian.co.uk/world/2011/
may/01/libya-muammar-gaddafi-son-nato.

Hill-Holtzman, Nancy, "Santa Monica OKs Restroom Law," *Los Angeles
Times* (November 14, 1991), http://articles.latimes.com/1991-11-14/local/
me-2074_1_santa-monica.

Hirschkorn, Phil, "Civil Rights Attorney Convicted in Terror Trial," *CNN.com*
(February 14, 2005), http://www.cnn.com/2005/LAW/02/10/terror.trial.
lawyer/.

Hoffman, Bruce, *Inside Terrorism* (New York: Columbia University Press, 1998),
43.

Holmes, Oliver Wendell, "Dissenting Opinion," *Southern Pacific Company v. Jensen,* 244 U.S. 205, 222 (May 21, 1917).

Holslag, Jonathan, "Embracing Chinese Global Security Ambitions," *Washington Quarterly* 32, no. 3 (July 2009): 105–18.

Holt-Lunstad, Julianne, Timothy B. Smith, and J. Bradley Layton, "Social Relationships and Mortality Risk: A Meta-Analytic Review," *PLoS Medicine* 7, no. 7 (July 2010).

Hooghe, Liesbet and Gary Marks, "A Postfunctionalist Theory of European Integration: From Permissive Consensus to Constraining Dissensus," *British Journal of Political Science* 39 (2009): 1–23.

Hopkins, Michael, *The Planetary Bargain: Corporate Social Responsibility Matters* (London: Earthscan Publications, 2003), 18.

Höpfl, Harro, *The Christian Polity of John Calvin* (New York: Cambridge University Press, 1982), 183.

Howard, Michael E., *The Franco-Prussian War: The German Invasion of France, 1870–1871* (New York: Routledge, 2001), 11, 235.

Howard, Rhoda, *Human Rights and the Search for Community* (Boulder, CO: Westview Press, 1995).

Hubbard, Glenn and Bill Duggan, "A Marshall Plan for the Middle East?" *The Huffington Post* (February 28, 2011), http://www.huffingtonpost.com/glenn-hubbard/marshall_plan_mid_east_b_829411.html.

Hubbard, Ben and Maggie Michael, "Hard-Line Islamist Gains Surprise in Egypt Vote," (December 6, 2011), http://www.salon.com/2011/12/06/hard_line_islamist_gains_surprise_in_egypt_vote/singleton/. (accessed January 12, 2012).

Hugh Hevitt Show, "Mitt Romney's Analysis of Barack Obama's Libyan Policy," *The Hugh Hewitt Show* (March 21, 2011), http://www.hughhewitt.com/transcripts.aspx?id=e3bf5a59-b9c6-4a10-846b-f573a9a9d74d.

Human Rights First, "Charter," http://www.humanrightsfirst.org/about_us/charter.aspx.

Human Rights Watch, "About Us," http://www.hrw.org/en/about (accessed July 22, 2009).

———, "Libya: Opposition Forces Should Protect Civilians and Hospitals," *Human Rights Watch* (July 13, 2011), http://www.hrw.org/news/2011/07/13/libya-opposition-forces-should-protect-civilians-and-hospitals.

———, *Politics by Other Means: Attacks against Christians in India* (New York: Human Rights Watch, 1999).

———, "We Have No Orders to Save You: State Participation and Complicity in Communal Violence in Gujarat," *Human Rights Watch Report* 14, no. 3 (2002).

Hunter, James D., "Fundamentalism: An Introduction to a General Theory," in *Jewish Fundamentalism in Comparative Perspective,* ed. Laurence J. Silberstein (New York: New York University Press, 1993), 33.

Huntington, Samuel P., *The Clash of Civilizations and the Remaking of the World Order* (New York: Touchstone Books, 1996), 209.

Huntington, Sam, *Who Are We? The Challenges to America's National Identity* (New York: Simon & Schuster, 2004), 92–98.

Hurriyet Daily News, "Don't Overshadow Dynamic Elections, Turkish FM Advises Iranian People," *Hurriyet Daily News* (June 22, 2009), http://www. hurriyetdailynews.com/n.php?n=don8217t-overshadow-dynamic-elections-turkish-fm-advises-iranian-people.

Husain, Ed, "Why Egypt's Salafis Are Not the Amish," *Council on Foreign Relations* (December 1, 2011), http://blogs.cfr.org/husain/2011/12/01/why-egypt%E2%80%99s-salafis-are-not-the-amish/. (accessed January 12, 2012).

Husain, Syed Anwar, "Max Weber's Sociology of Islam: A Critique," http://www. bangladeshsociology.org/Max%20Weber-Anwar%20Hosain.htm.

Hussein, King, "The Jordanian Palestinian Peace Initiative: Mutual Recognition and Territory for Peace," *Journal of Palestine Studies* 14, no. 4 (Summer 1985): 15–22, http://www.jstor.org/stable/2537118.

Ianotta, Ben, "Navy Intel Chief: Chinese Missile Is Effective," *C4ISR Journal* (January 5, 2011).

Ignatieff, Michael, "The Attack on Human Rights," *Foreign Affairs* (November/ December 2001).

Ignatius, David, "Signs of an Afghan Deal," *Washington Post* (May 26, 2011): A23.

Ikenberry, G. John, "Is a "One World" Order Possible? The Rise of China, the West, and the Future of Liberal Internationalism," Centre on Asia and Globalisation working paper 030 (June 2011): 13. http://www.caglkyschool. com/pdf/working%20papers/2011/CAG_WorkingPaper_30.pdf. (accessed January 19, 2012).

Ikenberry, G. John, "The Rise of China and the Future of the West: Can the Liberal System Survive?" *Foreign Affairs* (January/February 2008). http://www. foreignaffairs.com/articles/63042/g-john-ikenberry/the-rise-of-china-and-the-future-of-the-west (accessed January 19, 2012).

Indian Express, "Conditions in Kerry-Lugar Bill Is Stated Policy of Pak: US," *Indian Express* (October 9, 2009), http://www.indianexpress.com/news/conditions-in-kerrylugar-bill-is-stated-policy-of-pak-us/527107/0.

International Atomic Energy Agency, "Additional Protocols to Nuclear Safeguards Agreements," IAEA, http://www.iaea.org/OurWork/SV/Safeguards/sg_protocol.html.

International Maritime Organization, "Piracy in Waters Off the Coast of Somalia," http://www.imo.org/home.asp?topic_id=1178.

———, *Reports on Acts of Piracy and Armed Robbery against Ships: Issued Monthly – Acts Reported during June 2009* (July 7, 2009), http://www.imo.org/includes/ blastDataOnly.asp/data_id%3D25980/138.pdf.

———, *Reports on Acts of Piracy and Armed Robbery against Ships: Issued Monthly – Acts Reported during May 2009* (June 17, 2009), http://www.imo.org/in-cludes/blastDataOnly.asp/data_id%3D25979/137.pdf.

———, *Reports on Acts of Piracy and Armed Robbery against Ships: Issued Monthly – Acts Reported during April 2009* (May 5, 2009), http://www.imo.org/includes/ blastDataOnly.asp/data_id%3D25553/136.pdf.

———, *Reports on Acts of Piracy and Armed Robbery against Ships: Issued Monthly – Acts Reported during March 2009* (April 6, 2009), http://www.imo.org/ includes/blastDataOnly.asp/data_id%3D25552/135.pdf.

————, *Reports on Acts of Piracy and Armed Robbery against Ships: Issued Monthly – Acts Reported during February 2009* (April 22, 2009), http://www.imo.org/includes/blastDataOnly.asp/data_id%3D25551/134.pdf.

————, *Reports on Acts of Piracy and Armed Robbery against Ships: Issued Monthly – Acts Reported during July 2009* (October 10, 2009), http://www.imo.org/includes/blastData.asp/doc_id=11908/141.pdf.

————, *Reports on Acts of Piracy and Armed Robbery against Ships: Issued Monthly – Acts Reported during August 2009* (October 10, 2009), http://www.imo.org/includes/blastData.asp/doc_id=11909/142.pdf.

————, *Reports on Acts of Piracy and Armed Robbery against Ships: Issued Monthly – Acts Reported during September 2009* (January 12, 2010), http://www.imo.org/includes/blastData.asp/doc_id=12298/143.pdf.

————, *Reports on Acts of Piracy and Armed Robbery against Ships: Issued Monthly – Acts Reported during October 2009* (January 12, 2010), http://www.imo.org/includes/blastData.asp/doc_id=12299/145.pdf.

————, *Reports on Acts of Piracy and Armed Robbery against Ships: Issued Monthly – Acts Reported during November 2009* (January 26, 2010), http://www.imo.org/includes/blastData.asp/doc_id=12378/146.pdf.

————, *Reports on Acts of Piracy and Armed Robbery against Ships: Issued Monthly – Acts Reported during December 2009* (January 26, 2010), http://www.imo.org/includes/blastData.asp/doc_id=12379/147.pdf.

International Security Advisory Board, "China's Strategic Modernization," Report of the International Security Advisory Board (ISAB) task force, United States Department of State (October, 2008), 1.

Irish Human Rights Commission, "Press Release: Urgent Action needed to address Unsafe and Degrading nature of Irish Prisons," http://www.ihrc.ie/press_releases/newsarticle.asp?NID=221&NCID=12&T=N (accessed July 24, 2009).

IslamOnline "Muslim Leaders Urge Calm; End of Cartoon Riots," *IslamOnline* (February 8, 2006) http://www.islamonline.com. (accessed April 1, 2006).

Jacob, G., *A New Law Dictionary*, at "Pirates" (8th edn. 1762).

Jacques, Martin, *When China Rules the World: The End of the Western World and the Birth of a New Global Order* (New York: Penguin Press, 2009).

Jamieson, Dale, "When Utilitarians Should Be Virtue Theorists," *Utilitas* 19, no. 2 (2007): 160–83.

Joffe, Josef, "The Default Power: The False Prophecy of America's Decline," *Foreign Affairs* (September/October 2009).

Johnson, Ian and Martin Fackler, "China Addresses Rising Korean Tensions," *New York Times* (November 26, 2010).

Johnston, Alastair Iain, "Is China a Status Quo Power?" *International Security* 27, no. 4 (Spring 2003): 6–7, 28.

Jones, Ann, *Kabul in Winter: Life without Peace in Afghanistan* (New York: Metropolitan Books, 2006).

Jones, James, "Comment of General James Jones" at Stimson Center Chairman's Forum on International Security Issues (June 14, 2011).

Jordens, JTF, *Gandhi's Religion: a Homespun Shawl* (New York: St Martin's Press, 1998): 130.

Juergensmeyer, Mark, *Fighting with Gandhi* (San Francisco: Harper & Row, 1984).

———, "Religious Nationalism and Transnationalism in a Global World."

Kagamem, Paul, "Africa Has to Find Its Own Road to Prosperity," *Financial Times* (May 7, 2009), http://www.ft.com/intl/cms/s/0/0d1218c8-3b35-11de-ba91-00144feabdc0.html#axzz1QsyTnIdk.

Kaplan, Robert D., "Beijing's Afghan Gamble," *The New York Times* (October 6, 2009).

———, *The Coming Anarchy: Shattering the Dreams of the Post Cold War* (New York: Random House, 2000).

———, "Don't Panic About China," *The Atlantic* (January 28, 2010). http://www.theatlantic.com/magazine/archive/2010/01/don-apos-t-panic-about-china/7926/

———, "How We Would Fight China," *Atlantic* 295, no. 5 (June 2005): 49–64.

———, "While U.S. Is Distracted, China Develops Sea Power," *Washington Post* (September 26, 2010).

Kapur, Anuradha, "Deity to Crusader: Changing Iconography of Ram," in *Hindus and Others: The Question of Identity in India Today*, ed. G Pandey (New Delhi: Viking, 1993), 74–109.

Kelemen, Michele, "President Obama Praises Libya's Political Transition," *NPR* (September 20, 2011). http://www.npr.org/2011/09/20/140642290/president-obama-praises-libyas-political-transition.

Kelling, George, *Fixing Broken Windows* (New York: Free Press, 1996).

Kelling, George and James Q. Wilson, "Broken Windows," *Atlantic Monthly* (March 1982).

Kennedy, Paul, *The Rise and Fall of the Great Powers: Economic Change and Military Conflict from 1500 to 2000* (New York: Random House, 1987).

Keping, Yu, *Democracy Is a Good Thing* (Washington, DC: Brookings Institution Press, 2008).

Kerry, John, "Senator John Kerry Addresses the Fletcher School Graduating Class of 2011," *The Fletcher School* (May 21, 2011), http://fletcher.tufts.edu/news/2011/05/news-update/Kerry-May26.shtml.

Kershner, Isabel, "Israel Silent as Iranian Ships Transit Suez Canal," *New York Times* (February 22, 2011), http://www.nytimes.com/2011/02/23/world/middleeast/23suez.html?hp.

Khalil, Lydia, "Al-Qaeda and the Muslim Brotherhood: United by Strategy, Divided by Tactics," Jamestown Foundation *Terrorism Monitor* 4, no. 6 (March 23, 2006), http://www.jamestown.org/single/?no_cache=1&tx_ttnews[tt_news]=714.

Khalilzad, Zalmay, John White, and Andy W. Marshall, eds. *Strategic Appraisal: The Changing Role of Information in Warfare* (Santa Monica, CA: RAND Corporation, 1999).

Khan, Mubarak Zeb, "Pakistan Offers MFN Status to India," *Dawn* (April 29, 2011), http://www.dawn.com/2011/04/29/pakistan-offers-mfn-status-to-india.html.

Kim, Lau Guan, "A Lie Repeated Often Becomes Truth," *China Daily* (April 14, 2004), http://www.chinadaily.com.cn/english/doc/2004-04/14/content_323217.htm (accessed December 3, 2010).

King v. Marsh, 81 Eng. Rep. 23 (K.B. 1615).

King, Jr., Martin Luther, "Pilgrimage to Nonviolence," in *Stride Towards Freedom* (New York: Harper, 1958): 90.

Kirkpatrick, David D., "Egypt's Rural Voters Get Their Turn in Elections," *New York Times* (December 14, 2011), http://www.nytimes.com/2011/12/15/world/middleeast/egyption-vote-enters-second-round-in-rural-areas.html?ref=egypt (accessed January 11, 2012).

———, "Egypt's Vote Puts Emphasis on Split Over Religious Rule," *New York Times* (December 3, 2011), http://www.nytimes.com/2011/12/04/world/middleeast/egypts-vote-propels-islamic-law-into-spotlight.html?n=Top/Reference/Times%20Topics/Subjects/I/Islam?ref=islam&pagewanted=all (accessed January 12, 2012).

Kirkpatrick, David D. and Michael Slackman, "Egyptian Youths Drive the Revolt against Mubarak," (January 26, 2011), http://www.nytimes.com/2011/01/27/world/middleeast/27opposition.html?pagewanted=all (accessed January 25, 2012).

Kissinger, Henry, *On China* (New York: Penguin, 2011).

Klein, Eckart, "Establishing a Hierarchy of Human Rights: Ideal Solution or Fallacy?" *Israel Law Review* 41 (2008): 477–88. 486.

Kleine-Ahlbrandt, Stephanie T., "Beijing, Global Free Rider," *Foreign Policy* (November 12, 2009), http://www.foreignpolicy.com/articles/2009/11/12/beijing_global_free_rider (accessed October 18, 2010).

Klüver, Jürgen, "The Socio-Cultural Evolution of Human Societies and Civilizations," *EMBO Reports* 9 (2008): S55–S58.

Knill, Christoph, "European Politics: Impact of National Administrative Traditions," *Journal of Public Policy* 18, no. 1 (January–April 1998): 11.

Kondapalli, Srikanth, "Tsunami and China: Relief with Chinese Characteristics," *Asian Affairs* (January 17, 2005). http://rudar.ruc.dk/bitstream/1800/1446/4/Dokument.pdf

Kontorovich, Eugene, *A Guantanamo on the Sea: The Difficulties of Prosecuting Pirates and Terrorists*, 09-10 Nw. U. Sch. of L. Pub. L. and Legal Theory Series, 19–20 (2009).

Koopmans, Ruud and Paul Statham, "Challenging the Liberal Nation-State? Post-nationalism, Multiculturalism, and the Collective Claims Making of Migrants and Ethnic Minorities in Britain and Germany," *American Journal of Sociology* 105, no. 3 (November 1999), 652–96.

Koran, (5:32).

Kraft, Dina, "Israel Warns Iran Is 'Taking Advantage' of Middle East Unrest," *Telegraph* (London) (February 20, 2011), http://www.telegraph.co.uk/news/worldnews/middleeast/iran/8336712/Israel-warns-Iran-is-taking-advantage-of-Middle-East-unrest.html.

Kraska, James, "How the United States Lost the Naval War of 2015," *Orbis* 54, no. 1 (2010): 35–45.

Kraska, James and Brian Wilson, "Fighting Pirates: The Pen and the Sword," *World Pol'y J.* (Winter 2008/09), 46.

Krastev, Nikola, "NPT Review Conference Struggles to Find Common Ground," *Radio Free Europe* (May 28, 2010), http://www.rferl.org/content/NPT_Review_Conference_Struggles_To_Find_Common_Ground/2055636.html.

Kretzmer, David, "Targeted Killing of Suspected Terrorists: Extra-Judicial Executions or Legitimate Means of Defence?" *The European Journal of International Law* 16, no. 2 (2005).

Kristensen, Hans M., "China's Noisy Nuclear Submarines", Strategic Security blog, Federation of American Scientists (November 21, 2009). http://www.fas.org/blog/ssp/2009/11/subnoise.php.

Kristof, Nicholas D., "Democracy in the Brotherhood's Birthplace," *New York Times* (December 10, 2011), http://www.nytimes.com/2011/12/11/opinion/sunday/kristof-Democracy-in-the-Muslim-Brotherhoods-Birthplace.html (accessed January 11, 2012).

———, "The Big Military Taboo," *New York Times* (December 26, 2010).

Kristol, W. "The Long War," *The Weekly Standard* 11, no. 24 (2006): 9; see also Fukuyama, F. *End of History and the Last Man* (New York: Free Press, 1992).

Kurlantzick, Joshua, "A Beijing Backlash: China Is Starting to Face Consequences for Its Newly Aggressive Stance," *Newsweek* (October 4, 2010).

Kurniawati, Dewi, "Shariah in Aceh: Eroding Indonesia's Secular Freedoms," *Jakarta Globe* (August 18, 2010) (accessed January 25, 2012).

Kurth, James, "Humanitarian Intervention After Iraq: Legal Ideals vs. Military Realities," *Orbis* 50, no. 1 (Winter 2006): 87–101.

Kurzman, Charles, ed, *Liberal Islam: A Sourcebook* (New York: Oxford University Press, 1998), 196.

Lacroix, Justine, "For a European Constitutional Patriotism," *Political Studies* 50 (2002): 944–58.

Lampton, David, *The Three Faces of Chinese Power: Might, Money, and Minds* (Berkeley, CA: University of California Press, 2008), 111, 253.

Landler, Mark, "Clinton Seeks Shift on China," *New York Times* (February 13, 2009).

———, "Hillary Clinton Is Obama's Key Link to Afghan Leader," *The New York Times* (November 19, 2009): A12, http://www.nytimes.com/2009/11/20/world/asia/20clinton.html.

Landler, Mark and David E. Sanger, "Clinton Speaks of Shielding Mideast From Iran," *New York Times* (July 22, 2009). http://www.nytimes.com/2009/07/23/world/asia/23diplo.html (accessed January 20, 2012).

Lane, Robert E., "Does Money Buy Happiness?" *Public Interest* (Fall 1993): 58.

Lawson, J. M., "We Are Trying to Raise the Moral Issue," in *Negro Protest Thought in the Twentieth Century*, eds. F. L. Broderick and A. Meier (Indianapolis: Bobbs-Merrill, 1965), 278.

Lee, John, "China Won't Be a Responsible Stakeholder," *The Wall Street Journal* (February 1, 2010). http://online.wsj.com/article/SB10001424052748704722304575037931817880328.html

Leiby, Richard, "Egyptian Voters Say 'Yes' to Speedy Elections," *Washington Post* (March 20, 2011). http://www.washingtonpost.com/world/egyptian_voters_say_yes_to_speedy_elections (accessed January 25, 2012).

Lerner, Daniel, *The Passing of Traditional Society: Modernizing the Middle East* (New York, 1958).

Levinson, Charles, "'Brothers' in Egypt Present Two Faces," *Wall Street Journal* (February 15, 2011), http://online.wsj.com/article/SB1000142405274870462 9004576135882819143872.html.

———, "Iran Arms Syria with Radar," *Wall Street Journal* (June 30, 2010). http://online.wsj.com/article/SB100014240527487034260045753389231064 85984.html

Lewis, James, "To Protect the U.S. against Cyberwar, Best Defense Is a Good Offense," *U.S. News and World Report* (March 29, 2010).

Liberal International, "Oxford Manifesto 1997," Liberal International, adopted November 1997. http://www.liberal-international.org/editorial.asp?ia_id=537 (accessed January 19, 2012).

Lieber, Keir A. and Daryl G. Press, "The Rise of U.S. Nuclear Primacy," *Foreign Affairs* (March/April 2006): 48–49.

Lieberthal, Kenneth, "Is China Catching Up with the US?" *ETHOS* no. 8 (August 2010): 8.

———, "Connect the World," *CNN International Transcript* (January 20, 2011), http://archives.cnn.com/TRANSCRIPTS/1101/20/ctw.01.html.

Lipset, Seymour Martin, *Political Man: The Social Basis of Politics* (New York: Doubleday, 1960): 77.

Lipsey, R.G. and Kelvin Lancaster, "The General Theory of Second Best," *Review of Economic Studies* 24, no. 1 (1956): 11-32.

Lobeira, Pablo Jiménez, "Exploring Cosmopolitan Communitarianist: Eu Citizenship – An Analogical Reading," *Open Insight: Revista de Filosofía* 2, no. 2 (June 2011): 145.

Locke, John, *Second Treatise on Government*, trans. C. B. Macphearson (London: Hackett Publishing Company, 1980), Chapter 2, Section 6.

Lowi, Theodore J., "Globalization, War, and the Withering Away of the State," *Brown Journal of World Affairs* 17, no. 2 (Spring/Summer 2011), 243.

Luedke, Adam, "European Integration, Public Opinion and Immigration Policy: Testing the Impact of National Identity," *European Union Politics* 6, no. 1 (2005): 83–112.

Luo, Michael, "Reform Jews Hope to Unmix Mixed Marriages," *New York Times* (February 12, 2006): A1.

Lynd, S. ed., "Student Nonviolent Coordinating Committee, Statement of Purpose," in *Nonviolence in America: A Documentary History* (Indianapolis, IN: Bobbs-Merrill, 1966), 399.

Lyons, Adm. James A., "China's One World?" *Washington Times* (August 24, 2008).

———, "Countering China's Aggression: Communist Dictatorship Presents Trouble in Asia and Abroad," *Washington Times* (October 18, 2010).

Macintyre, Alasdair, *After Virtue* (Notre Dame: University of Notre Dame, 1984).

Maclean, William, "Libya Islamist Takes Inclusive Stance," *Reuters* (September 19, 2011), http://in.reuters.com/article/2011/09/19/idINIndia-59413620110919.

Maddox, Bronwen, "Will Barack Obama Give Way When He Meets Binyamin Netanyahu in Washington?" *Times of London* (May 13, 2009), http://thedai-

lyrepublican.com/index.php?option=com_content&task=view&id=5978&I
temid=2.

Magnezi, Aviel, "Could U.S. Abandon Israel Too?" *Yediot Ahronot* (Tel Aviv) (January 2, 2011), http://www.ynetnews.com/articles/0,7340,L-4022102,00.html.

Makovsky, Michael and Blaise Misztal, "Obama's Iran Policy Shifts to Containment," *Washington Post* (December 9, 2011), http://www.washingtonpost.com/opinions/obamas-iran-policy-shifts-to-containment/2011/12/09/gIQA-UD8DjO_story.html (accessed January 20, 2012).

Mandelbaum, Michael, *The Frugal Superpower: America's Global Leadership in a Cash-Strapped Age* (New York: Public Affairs, 2010), 4–5.

Mann, James, *The China Fantasy: How Our Leaders Explain Away Chinese Repression* (New York: Viking Adult, 2007). '

Margolick, David, "Man with AIDS Virus Sues To Be a Macy's Santa Again," *N. Y. Times* (August 29, 1991), http://www.nytimes.com/1991/08/29/nyregion/man-with-aids-virus-sues-to-be-a-macy-s-santa-again.html.

Marquand, Robert, "Could NATO's Libya Mission Be Its Last Hurrah?" *The Christian Science Monitor* (August 24, 2011), http://www.csmonitor.com/World/Europe/2011/0824/Could-NATO-s-Libya-mission-be-its-last-hurrah.

Matthew, Philip, "Thailand: 'Freedom of Poverty Is a Fundamental Human Right,' says Consultation," *Human Rights Solidarity* (September 1996), http://www.hrsolidarity.net/mainfile.php/1996vol06no03/184/ (accessed July 24, 2009).

Mayer, Jane, *The Dark Side: The Inside Story of How the War on Terror Turned Into a War on American Ideals* (New York: Doubleday, 2008).

———, "The Predator War: What Are the Risks of the C.I.A.'s Covert Drone Program?" *New Yorker* (October 26, 2009), http://www.newyorker.com/reporting/2009/10/26/091026fa_fact_mayer.

Mazzetti, Mark, "A Shooting in Pakistan Reveals Fraying Alliance," *New York Times* (March 12, 2011), http://www.nytimes.com/2011/03/13/weekinreview/13lashkar.html.

———, "Should (Could) America and Pakistan's Bond Be Broken?" *New York Times* (June 4, 2011). http://www.nytimes.com/2011/06/05/weekinreview/05pakistan.html?pagewanted=all

McCord, Joan, "Introduction: Coercion and Punishment in the Fabric of Social Relations," in *Coercion and Punishment in Long-term Perspectives*, ed. Joan McCord (New York: Cambridge University Press, 1995), 1.

McDermid, Charles and Khalid Waleed, "Dark Days for Iraq as Power Crisis Bites," *Asia Times* (June 26, 2010), http://www.atimes.com/atimes/Middle_East/LF26Ak01.html.

McDonnell, Patrick, "David Cameron, Nicolas Sarkozy Visit Post-Kadafi Libya," *Los Angeles Times* (September 15, 2011), http://articles.latimes.com/2011/sep/15/world/la-fg-libya-cameron-sarkozy-20110916.

McFadden, Robert D. and Scott Shane, "Navy Rescues Captain, Killing 3 Pirate Captors," *N. Y. Times* (April 13, 2009): A1.

McGreal, Chris, "US and Vietnam in Controversial Nuclear Negotiations," *Guardian* (August 5, 2010), http://www.guardian.co.uk/world/2010/aug/05/us-vietnam-nuclear-negotiations.

McMichael, William H., "Gates: Strike on Iran Would Create Backlash," *Army Times* (April 14, 2009), http://www.armytimes.com/news/2009/04/military_iran_gates_041309/ (accessed January 20, 2012).

McMillan, Robert, "Google Attack Part of Widespread Spying Effort," *Computerworld* (January 13, 2010), http://www.computerworld.com/s/article/9144221/Google_attack_part_of_widespread_spying_effort (accessed November 15, 2010).

Meade, Richard, "In the Dock: The Problems with Prosecuting Pirates," *Lloyd's List* (May 1, 2009).

Mearsheimer, John, "Pull Those Boots Off the Ground," *Newsweek* (December 30, 2008), http://www.newsweek.com/id/177380.

———, "The Rise of China Will Not Be Peaceful at All," *Australian* (November 18, 2005).

Medeiros, Evan S., "Strategic Hedging and the Future of Asia-Pacific Stability," *Washington Quarterly* 29, no. 1 (Winter 2005/2006): 145–67.

Meisels, Tamar, "The Trouble with Terror: The Apologetics of Terrorism—a Refutation," *Terrorism and Political Violence* 18 (2006): 480.

Merry, Robert W., "American Exceptionalism and the Universality Fallacy," *National Interest* (September 30, 2011), http://nationalinterest.org/commentary/american-exceptionalism-the-universality-fallacy-5956 (accessed January 24, 2012).

Meyer, Michael A., *Response to Modernity: A History of the Reform Jewish Movement* (New York: Oxford University Press, 1998), 390.

Miles, Barry, "Spirit of the Underground: the 60s Rebel," *Guardian* (January 30, 2011), http://www.guardian.co.uk/culture/2011/jan/30/underground-arts-60s-rebel-counterculture (accessed January 26, 2012).

Miles, Tom and Tim Pearce, "Niger Asks Help Fighting Terrorism after Libya Conflict," *Reuters* (September 19, 2011), http://old.news.yahoo.com/s/nm/20110919/wl_nm/us_niger_libya_security.

Miller, Talea, "Russia to Deliver Uranium Fuel for Iran Plant, Raising New Nukes Concerns," *PBS* (August 13, 2010), http://www.pbs.org/newshour/rundown/2010/08/russia-to-deliver-nuclear-fuel-for-iran-plant.html.

Mintz, Alex and Nehemia Geva, "Why Don't Democracies Fight Each Other?" *The Journal of Conflict* Resolution 37, no. 3 (September 1993): 484–503.

Mogahed, Dalia, "Islam and Democracy: Muslim World Residents See No Conflict between Religious Principles and Democratic Values," *Gallup Center for Muslim Studies* (2006), http://media.gallup.com/MuslimWestFacts/PDF/GALLUPMUSLIMSTUDIESIslamandDemocracy030607rev.pdf (accessed January 25, 2012).

Moore, Michael S., "Law as a Functional Kind," in *Natural Law Theory: Contemporary Essays* ed. Robert George (Oxford: Clarendon Press, 1992), 188–242, 188.

Moravcsik, Andrew, "In Defense of the 'Democratic Deficit': Reassessing Legitimacy in the EU," *Journal of Common Market Studies* 40, no. 4 (November 2002): 603–24.

Mosk, M., "Obama too Polite in Shanghai for Some Rights Defenders See Forum as a Key 'Missed Opportunity.'" *Washington Times* (November 17, 2009): A3.

Moyo, Dambisa, *Dead Aid: Why Aid Is Not Working and How There Is a Better Way for Africa* (New York: Farrar, Straus, and Giroux, 2009).

MSNBC "Obama Unveils Afghanistan Plan," *MSNBC* (March 27, 2009), http://www.msnbc.msn.com/id/29898698/ns/world_news-south_and_central_asia/t/obama-unveils-afghanistan-plan/#.TyBUY4HpbTo (accessed January 25, 2012).

Mukasey, Michael B., "Remarks Prepared for Delivery by Attorney General Michael B. Mukasey at the American Enterprise Institute for Public Policy Research," (remarks, American Enterprise Institute, Washington, DC, July 21, 2008).

Murphy, Dan, "Qaddafi Threatens Libya Rebels as UN No-Fly Vote Nears," *Christian Science Monitor* (March 17, 2011), http://www.csmonitor.com/World/Middle-East/2011/0317/Qaddafi-threatens-Libya-rebels-as-UN-no-fly-vote-nears.

Museveni, Yoweri K., "We Want Trade, Not Aid," *The Wall Street Journal* (November 6, 2003).

Musharraf, Pervez, "Pakistan: A Reality Check Amid the Terror and Chaos," *CNN* (June 8, 2011), http://articles.cnn.com/2011-06-08/opinion/pakistan.pervez.musharraf.islamism_1_today-pakistan-religious-militancy-afghanistan?_s=PM:OPINION.

Nagl, John, "Let's Win the Wars We're In," *Joint Force Quarterly* 52 (First Quarter 2009): 20–26.

Nandy, Ashis, "Final Encounter: The Politics of the Assassination of Gandhi," in *At the Edge of Psychology: Essays in Politics and Culture* (New Delhi: Oxford University Press), 83.

Nandy, Ashis et al., "Creating a Nationality: the Ramjanmbhumi Movement and Fear of the Self," in *Exiled at Home* (New Delhi: Oxford University Press, 2002), 53.

Narine, Shaun, "State, Sovereignty, Political Legitimacy and Regional Institutionalism in the Asia-Pacific," *The Pacific Review* 17, no. 3 (2004): 14.

Nathan, Andrew J., "Authoritarian Resilience," *Journal of Democracy* 14, no. 1 (2003): 6–17.

National Park Service, "The Shakers," *National Park Service* http://www.nps.gov/nr/travel/shaker/shakers.htm.

Nawaz, Shuja, "Raging at Rawalpindi," *Foreign Policy* (May 13, 2011), http://www.foreignpolicy.com/articles/2011/05/13/raging_at_rawalpindi?page=full.

New Revised Standard Version Bible (1989), Division of Christian Education of the National Council of the Churches of Christ in the United States of America.

New York Times, "China to Buy $50 Billion of First I.M.F. Bonds," *The New York Times* (September 3, 2009).

———, "'Day of Rage' For Syrians Fails to Draw Protesters," *New York Times* (February 4, 2011), http://www.nytimes.com/2011/02/05/world/middleeast/05syria.html.

New York Times v. United States, 403 U.S. 713 (1971).

New York Times Co. v. Sullivan, 376 U.S. 254 (1964).

Nixon, Richard, "Asia after Viet Nam," *Foreign Affairs* (October 1967): 111–125.

Nocera, Joe, "4 Questions He Leaves Behind," *New York Times* (May 2, 2011), http://www.nytimes.com/2011/05/03/opinion/03nocera.html (accessed January 25, 2012).

Norris, John and Connie Veillette, "Five Steps to Make Our Aid More Effective and Save More Than $2 Billion," brief for *Center for American Progress* (April 2011).

NPR, "All Things Considered: U.S. Navy Captures Pirates," *NPR Radio Broadcast* (April 1, 2010).

———, "Egyptian Activist Discusses Recent Elections," *NPR* (December 2, 2011), http://www.npr.org/2011/12/02/143062999/activist-discusses-egyptian-elections (accessed January 11, 2012).

Nye, Joseph, "The Case against Containment: Treat China Like an Enemy and That's What It Will Be," *Global Beat* (June 22, 1998).

O'Byrne, Darren J., *Human Rights: An Introduction* (New York: Pearson Education, 2003), 11.

O'Farroll, Tad, "T Minus Bushehr," *Nukes of Hazard* blog (August 18, 2010). http://nukesofhazardblog.com/story/2010/8/18/164241/897.

O'Neill, Caitria, "Revolution and Democracy," *Harvard Political Review* (May, 19, 2011), http://hpronline.org/covers/revolution/revolution-and-democracy/ (accessed January 12, 2012).

O'Rourke, Ronald, "China Naval Modernization: Implications for U.S. Navy Capabilities—Background and Issues for Congress," *Congressional Research Service* (April 22, 2011): 8–14.

Obama, Barack, "President Obama's Remarks on New Strategy for Afghanistan and Pakistan," *New York Times*, Washington, DC (March 27, 2009), http://www.nytimes.com/2009/03/27/us/politics/27obama-text.html.

———, "President Barack Obama's Inaugural Address," *White House Blog* (January 21, 2009). http://www.whitehouse.gov/blog/inaugural-address (January 25, 2012).

———, 2009. "The President's Opening Remarks on Iran." http://www.whitehouse.gov/blog/The-Presidents-Opening-Remarks-on-Iran-with-Persian-Translation/ (retrieved January 10, 2010).

———, 2009. "Remarks by the President on a New Beginning." http://www.whitehouse.gov/the_press_office/Remarks-by-the-President-at-Cairo-University-6-04-09/ (retrieved January 10, 2010).

———, "Remarks by the President on the Situation in Libya," Washington, DC (March 18, 2011), http://www.whitehouse.gov/the-press-office/2011/03/18/remarks-president-situation-libya.

———, "Remarks by the President on the Way Forward in Afghanistan," Washington, DC (June 22, 2011), http://www.whitehouse.gov/the-press-office/2011/06/22/remarks-president-way-forward-afghanistan.

———, "Remarks by President Obama and President Karzai of Afghanistan in Joint Press Availability," Washington, DC (May 12, 2010), http://www.whitehouse.gov/the-press-office/remarks-president-obama-and-president-karzai-afghanistan-joint-press-availability.

———, 2009. "Statement by the President on the Attempted Attack on Christmas Day and Recent Violence in Iran." http://www.whitehouse.gov/the-press-office/statement-president-attempted-attack-christmas-day-and-recent-violence-iran (retrieved January 10, 2010).

———, "Transcript of Obama's Speech in Sderot, Israel," *New York Times* (July 23, 2008), http://www.nytimes.com/2008/07/23/us/politics/23text-obama.html?pagewanted=print (accessed January 20, 2012).

Obama, Barack, David Cameron, and Nicolas Sarkozy, "Libya's Pathway to Peace," *International Herald Tribune* (April 14, 2011) http://www.nytimes.com/2011/04/15/opinion/15iht-edlibya15.html.

Offe, Claus, "Is There, or Can There Be, a 'European Society?'" in *Civil Society: Berlin Perspectives*, ed. John Keane (New York: Berhahn Books, 2007), 169–88.

Orban, Leonard and Jan Figel, "Key Data on Teaching Languages at School in Europe," *Eurydice Network* (2008 edition).

Osgood, Charles E., "Reciprocal Initiative," *Liberal Papers* (New York: Doubleday & Company, 1962).

Ottolenghi, Emanuele, "Life after the 'Game-Changer,'" *Standpoint* (April 2009), http://standpointmag.co.uk/node/1063/full (accessed January 20, 2012).

Oxford Analytica, "Aid vs. Trade," *Forbes* (March 30, 2005), http://www.forbes.com/2005/03/30/cz_0330oxan_aid.html.

Page, Jeremy, Patrick Barta, and Jay Solomon, "U.S., Asean to Push Back against China," *Wall Street Journal* (September 22, 2010).

Pape, R. (1997) "Why Economic Sanctions Do Not Work," *International Security* 22, no. 2: 90–136.

Parrish, Karen, "Navy Intel Chief Discusses China's Military Advances," *American Forces Press Service* (January 6, 2011).

Parrull, "BJP Sees Red after Bush's Fuel Supply Comment," *CNN-IBN* (September 13, 2008), http://ibnlive.in.com/news/bjp-sees-red-after-bushs-comment-on-fuel-supply/73462-3.html.

Parsons, Talcott, ed. Bryan S. Turner, *The Talcott Parsons Reader* (Hoboken: Wiley-Blackwell, 1999).

Passman, Michael H., "Protections Afforded to Captured Pirates Under the Law of War and International Law," *Tulane Maritime Law Journal* 33, no. 1 (Winter 2008): 1.

Patrick, Stewart, "Irresponsible Stakeholders? The Difficulty of Integrating Rising Powers," *Foreign Affairs* (November/December 2010), http://www.foreignaffairs.com/articles/66793/stewart-patrick/irresponsible-stakeholders. (accessed January 19, 2012).

PBS, "Summer of Love Program Transcript," *PBS,* http://www.pbs.org/wgbh/amex/love/filmmore/pt.html (accessed January 26, 2012).

Peerenboom, Randal, *China Modernizes: Threat to the West or Model for the Rest?* (Oxford University Press, 2008).

Pei, Minxin, "China: The Big Free Rider," *Newsweek* (January 22, 2010).

Pei, M. and Kasper, S. "Lessons from the Past: The American Record on Nation-building," Carnegie Endowment Policy Brief No. 24 (2003).

People Daily English, "China Supports Joint Declaration by France, Germany, Russia on Iraq," *People Daily English* (February 12, 2003), http://english.peopledaily.com.cn/200302/12/eng20030212_111535.shtml (accessed January 20, 2012).

Percival, Bronson, "Threat or Partner: Southeast Asian Perceptions of China," Testimony before the U.S.-China Economic & Security Review Commission, United States Congress (February 4, 2010).

Perlez, Jane, "Pakistan's Chief of Army Fights to Keep His Job," *New York Times* (June 15, 2011), http://www.nytimes.com/2011/06/16/world/asia/16pakistan. html.

Perlez, Jane and Helene Cooper, "Signaling Tensions, Pakistan Shuts NATO Route," *New York Times* (September 30, 2010).

Perlez, Jane and Ismail Khan, "Pakistan Tells U.S. It Must Sharply Cut CIA Activities," *New York Times* (April 11, 2011), http://www.nytimes.com/2011/04/12/world/asia/12pakistan.html.

Perry, William and Stephen Hadley, statement before the House Armed Services Committee, Hearing on Quadrennial Defense Review Independent Panel, United States Congress (August 3, 2010), 4.

Peters, Edward, *Heresy and Authority in Medieval Europe* (Philadelphia, PA: University of Pennsylvania Press, 1980), 165.

Pew Research Center, "Egyptians Embrace Revolt Leaders, Religious Parties, and Military, As Well," Pew *Research Center* (April 25, 2011), http://www.pewglobal.org/2011/04/25/egyptians-embrace-revolt-leaders-religious-parties-and-military-as-well/ (accessed January 25, 2012).

———, "Islamic Extremism: Common Concern for Muslim and Western Publics," *Pew Global Attitudes Survey* (July 14, 2005), http://www.pewglobal.org/2005/07/14/islamic-extremism-common-concern-for-muslim-and-western-publics/ (accessed January 24, 2012).

———, "Most Embrace a Role for Islam in Politics," *Pew Research Center* (December 2, 2010), http://www.pewglobal.org/2010/12/02/muslims-around-the-world-divided-on-hamas-and-hezbollah/ (accessed January 25, 2012).

———, "World Publics Welcome Global Trade—But Not Immigration," Pew Research Center, Global Attitudes Project, Washington, DC (October 4, 2007), http://www.pewglobal.org/2007/10/04/world-publics-welcome-global-trade-but-not-immigration/ (accessed January 25, 2012).

Pildes, Richard, "Political Parties and Constitutionalism," *New York University Public Law and Legal Theory Working Papers*, Paper 179 (2010): 12.

Plantinga, Alvin, "Is Belief in God Rational?" *Rationality and Religious Belief*, ed. C. Delaney (Notre Dame, IN: University of Notre Dame Press, 1979).

Polachek, Solomon W., "Why Democracies Cooperate More and Fight Less: The Relationship between International Trade and Cooperation," *Review of International Economics* 5, no. 3 (December 2002): 295–309.

Pomfret, John, "Beijing Claims 'Indisputable Sovereignty' Over South China Sea," *The Washington Post* (July 31, 2010).

———, "Military Strength Eludes China, Which Looks Overseas for Arms," *Washington Post* (December 25, 2010).

Pope Paul VI, "Dignitatis Humanae," On The Right Of The Person And Of Communities To Social And Civil Freedom In Matters Religious Promulgated By His Holiness Pope Paul VI (December 7, 1965), http://www.vatican.va/archive/hist_councils/ii_vatican_council/documents/vat-ii_decl_19651207_dignitatis-humanae_en.html (accessed April 1, 2006).

Porth, Jacquelyn S., "Legal Experts Take Action to Prosecute Pirates," *America. gov* (February 27, 2009), http://www.america.gov/st/peacesec-english/2009/February/20090227144346sjhtrop0.3818781.html.

Power, Samantha, "Our War on Terror," *New York Times* (July 29, 2007), http://www.nytimes.com/2007/07/29/books/review/Power-t.html?_r=1 (accessed April 23, 2010).

———, *The Problem From Hell* (New York: Basic Books, 2002).

Privacy International, "About Privacy International," http://www.privacy international.org/article.shtml?cmd[347]=x-347-65428 (accessed July 24, 2009).

PPI, "India, Pakistan to Ease Visa Restrictions," *The Express Tribune* (June 7, 2011), http://tribune.com.pk/story/184215/india-pakistan-to-ease-visa-restrictions/.

Putnam, Robert D. and David E. Campbell, *American Grace: How Religion Divides and Unites Us* (New York, Simon and Schuster, 2010), 491.

Raghu, Sanil, "India's 11 Nuclear Power Units Short of Local Uranium," *Wall Street Journal* (December 9, 2009), http://online.wsj.com/article/NA_WSJ_PUB: SB126034438674983263.html.

Raines, Howell, *My Soul Is Rested: Movement Days in the Deep South Remembered* (New York: Penguin Books, 1983), 79.

Ramadan, Tariq, *Western Muslims and the Future of Islam* (New York: Oxford University Press, 2005).

Ramcharan, B. G., *The Right to Life in International Law* (Leiden, The Netherlands: Martinus Nijhoff Publishers, 1985).

Rapp, Tobias, Christian Schwägerl, and Gerald Traufetter, "How China and India Sabotaged the UN Climate Summit," *Der Spiegel* (May 5, 2010).

Raslan, Karim, "The Islam Gap," *New York Times* (February 15, 2006), http://www.nytimes.com/2006/02/15/opinion/15raslan.html?th=&emc=th&pagewanted =print. (accessed January 20, 2012).

Ratner, Steven R., "Predator and Prey: Seizing and Killing Suspected Terrorists Abroad," *Journal of Political Philosophy* 15, no. 3 (2007).

Raychaudhuri, Tapan, "Shadows of the Swastika: Historical Reflections on the Politics of Hindu Communalism," *Contention* 4, no. 2 (1995): 145.

Reinhold, Robert, "Santa Monica Journal: In Land of Liberals, Restroom Rights Are Rolled Back," *N. Y. Times* (November 15, 1991), http://www.nytimes. com/1991/11/15/us/santa-monica-journal-in-land-of-liberals-restroom-rights-are-rolled-back.html.

Rengger, N. J., "Toward a Culture of Democracy? Democratic Theory and Democratization in Eastern and Central Europe," in *Building Democracy? The International Dimension of Democratization in Eastern Europe*, ed Geoffrey Pridham, Eric Herring, and George Sanford (London: Continuum International Publishing Group, 1997), 63.

Rhoads, Christopher and Laura Meckler, "International Leaders Pledge to Back New Libya," *Wall Street Journal* (September 21, 2011): A9.

Richardson, Michael, "China Tips the Nuclear Balance," *NZ Herald* (February 3, 2011), http://www.nzherald.co.nz/world/news/article.cfm? c_id=2&objectid=10385486.

Richman, Sheldon, "Congress, Obama Codify Indefinite Detention," (December 28, 2011), http://reason.com/archives/2011/12/28/congress-obama-codify-indefinite-detenti.

Rieff, David, "Policing Terrorism," *The New York Times* (July 22, 2007), late edition, sec. 6.

Rorty, Richard, "Human Rights, Rationality, and Sentimentality" in *The Philosophy of Human Rights*, ed. Patrick Hayden (St. Paul: Paragon House, 2001), 241–257, 246.

Rosenberg, Matthew, "Corruption Suspected in Airlift of Billions in Cash from Kabul," *Wall Street Journal* (June 25, 2010).

Ross, Robert, "Beijing as a Conservative Power," *Foreign Affairs* (March/April 1997): 33-44.

———, "Myth," *National Interest* no. 103 (September/October 2009).

———, "The Rise of Chinese Power and the Implications for the Regional Security Order," *Orbis* 54, no. 4 (2010): 540, 541, 545.

Ross, Robert and Zhu Feng, eds., *China's Ascent: Power, Security, and the Future of International Politics* (Ithaca, NY: Cornell University Press, 2008).

Ross, Will, "Drones Scour the Sea for Pirates," *BBC News* (November 10, 2009), http://news.bbc.co.uk/2/hi/8352631.stm.

Roth, Felix, Felicitas Nowak-Lehmann D., and Thomas Otter, "Has the Financial Crisis Shattered Citizens' Trust in National and European Governmental Institutions? Evidence from the EU Member States, 1999–2010," *Center for European Policy Studies* no. 343 (June 2011).

Rubin, Alissa J., "British Link Iran to Rockets Found in Afghan Province," *New York Times* (March 9, 2011), http://www.nytimes.com/2011/03/10/world/middleeast/10iran.html.

Rummel, R.J., "Democracies Don't Fight Democracies," *Peace Magazine* (May–June 1999): 10.

Ryu, Alisha, "Paris-based Group Says Accused Somali Pirates Denied Rights," *Voice of America* (August 27, 2009), http://www.voanews.com/english/2009-08-27-voa36.cfm.

———, "Rights Group Questions US Deal to Send Pirates to Kenya," *Voice of America* (February 13, 2009), http://www.voanews.com/english/archive/2009-02/2009-02-13-voa43.cfm?CFID=263096949&CFTOKEN=12225224&jsessionid=6630520c6c29dd8d32fb533945714f95a2b7.

Sagan, Scott, Kenneth Waltz, and Richard K. Betts, "A Nuclear Iran: Promoting Stability or Courting Disaster?" *Journal of International Affairs* 60, no. 2 (Spring/Summer 2007): 137–38, 143.

Saragosa, Manuela, "Greece Warned on False Euro Data," *BBC News* (December 1, 2004), http://news.bbc.co.uk/2/hi/business/4058327.stm.

Sarhan, Saad and Aaron C. Davis, "Cleric Moqtada al-Sadr Returns to Iraq After Self-Imposed Exile," *Washington Post* (January 6, 2011), http://www.washingtonpost.com/wp-dyn/content/article/2011/01/05/AR2011010500724.html.

Sarkozy, Nicolas and David Cameron, "Letter from David Cameron and Nicolas Sarkozy to Herman Van Rompuy," (March 10, 2011), http://www.guardian.co.uk/world/2011/mar/10/libya-middleeast.

Sarmiento, Atty. Rene V., "Human Rights: Universal? Indivisible? Interdependent?" (speech, PAHRA-Sponsored Forum on Human Rights, Quezon City, Philippines, June 20, 1995), http://www.hrsolidarity.net/mainfile.php/1995vol05no02/92/.

Save Darfur "China Must End UN 'Interference,'" http://www.savedarfur.org/pages/press/china_must_end_un_interference/ (accessed November 17, 2010).

Sayers, Eric, "Military Dissuasion: A Framework for Influencing PLA Procurement Trends," *Joint Force Quarterly* 58 (July, 2010): 89–93.

S.C. Res. 1816, U.N. Doc. S/RES/1816 (June 2, 2008).

S.C. Res. 1838, U.N. Doc. S/RES/1838 (Oct. 7, 2008).

S.C. Res. 1844, U.N. Doc. S/RES/1844 (Nov. 20, 2008).

S.C. Res. 1846, U.N. Doc. S/RES/1846 (Dec. 2, 2008).

S.C. Res. 1851, U.N. Doc. S/RES/1851 (Dec. 16, 2008).

Schaff, Philip, ed. *A Select Library of the Nicene and Post-Nicene Fathers of the Christian Church, Vol 4, Augustine: The Writings against the Manicheans and the Donatists* (Buffalo, NY: Christian Literature, 1886), 816.

Schmitt, Carl, "The Concept of the Political" (1932).

Schneider, Howard, "Iran, Syria Mock U.S. Policy; Ahmadinejad Speaks of Israel's 'Annihilation.'" *Washington Post* (February 26, 2010), http://www.washingtonpost.com/wp-dyn/content/article/2010/02/25/AR2010022505089.html.

Schrag, Claudia, "The Quest for EU Legitimacy: How to Study a Never-Ending Crisis," *Perspectives on Europe* 40, no. 2 (Autumn 2010): 27–34.

Schwartz, John, "Path to Justice, but Bumpy, for Terrorists," *The New York Times* (May 1, 2009).

Schwartz, Thomas and Kiron K. Skinner, "The Myth of Democratic Pacifism," *Hoover Digest* (April 30, 1999).

Seib, Gerald F., "An Exit off Iran's Atom Highway," *Wall Street Journal* (August 24, 2010): A2.

———, "An Expert's Long View on Iran," *Wall Street Journal* (March 5, 2010), http://online.wsj.com/article/SB20001424052748704187204575101560801756150.html (accessed January 20, 2012).

Seoring v. The United Kingdom, 161 Eur. Ct. H. R. (ser. A) (198.9).

Shah, Aqil, "Getting the Military out of Pakistani Politics," *Foreign Affairs* (May/June 2011), http://www.foreignaffairs.com/articles/67742/aqil-shah/getting-the-military-out-of-pakistani-politics.

Shambaugh, David, "Introduction" in *Power Shift: China and Asia's New Dynamics* (Berkeley, CA: University of California Press, 2005), 15.

———, "Return to the Middle Kingdom? China and Asia in the Early Twenty-First Century," in Shambaugh, ed., *Power Shift* (Berkeley, CA: University of California Press, 2005), 24.

Shanker, Thom and Helene Cooper, "Doctrine for Libya: Not Carved in Stone," *New York Times* (March 29, 2011), http://www.nytimes.com/2011/03/30/world/africa/30doctrine.html (accessed January 20, 2012).

Shanker, Thom and David E. Sanger, "NATO Plans to Take Libya War to Qaddafi's Doorstep," *The New York Times* (April 26, 2011), http://www.nytimes.com/2011/04/27/world/middleeast/27strategy.html.

Shanker, Thom and David E. Sanger, "North Korean Fuel Identified as Plutonium," *New York Times* (October 17, 2006), http://www.nytimes.com/2006/10/17/world/asia/17diplo.html?_r=1.

Shavit, Ari, and Haaretz Correspondent, "Israel Fears Obama Heading for Imposed Mideast Settlement." *Ha'aretz* (Tel Aviv) (March 29, 2010), http://www.haaretz.com/print-edition/news/israel-fears-obama-heading-for-imposed-mideast-settlement-1.265466.

Shlapak, David A., David T. Orletsky, Toy I. Reid, Murray Scot Tanner, Barry Wilson, "A Question of Balance: Political Context and Military Aspects of the China-Taiwan Dispute," Rand Corporation (2009).

Singer, Peter, "Famine, Affluence, and Morality," *Philosophy and Public Affairs* 1, no. 3 (1972): 231–32.

Sinkaya, Bayram, "Turkey and Iran Relations on the Eve of President Gul's Visit: The Steady Improvement of a Pragmatic Relationship," *ORSAM* (February 10, 2011), http://www.orsam.org.tr/en/showArticle.aspx?ID=408.

Skinner, G. William and Edwin A. Winckler, "Compliance Succession in Rural Communist China: A Cyclical Theory," in *A Sociological Reader on Complex Organizations*, 2nd ed., edited by Amitai Etzioni (New York: Holt, Rinehart, and Winston, 1969), 410–38.

Slackman, Michael, "Poland, Lacking External Enemies, Turns on Itself," *New York Times* (November 27, 2010).

Sly, Liz, "Calls in Syria for Weapons, NATO Intervention," *The Washington Post* (August 28, 2011), http://www.washingtonpost.com/world/middle-east/calls-in-syria-for-weapons-nato-intervention/2011/08/26/gIQA3WAslJ_story.html.

Smith, Ben, "A victory for 'Leading from Behind?" *POLITICO* (August 22, 2011), http://www.politico.com/news/stories/0811/61849.html.

Smith, Rhona, *Textbook on International Human Rights* (Oxford: Blackstone Press, 2003).

Solomon, Jay, "Jordan's Nuclear Ambitions Pose Quandary for the U.S.," *Wall Street Journal* (June 12, 2010), http://online.wsj.com/article/NA_WSJ_PUB:SB10001424052748704414504575244712375657640.html.

———, "U.S., Hanoi in Nuclear Talks," *Wall Street Journal* (August 3, 2010), http://online.wsj.com/article/SB10001424052748704741904575409261840078780.html.

Solomon, Jay and Bill Spindle, "Syria Strongman: 'Time for Reform,'" *Wall Street Journal* (January 31, 2011), http://online.wsj.com/article/SB10001424052748704832704576114340735033236.html.

Somerville, Margaret, "Children's Human Rights and Unlinking Child-Parent Biological Bonds with Adoption, Same-Sex Marriage and New Reproductive Technologies," *Journal of Family Studies* (November–December 2007), http://findarticles.com/p/articles/mi_6968/is_2_13/ai_n28469751/ (accessed July 24, 2009).

Spetalnick, Matt and Laura MacInnis, "Obama Urges Gaddafi Forces to Give Up, Vows Libya Aid," *Reuters* (September 20, 2011), http://www.reuters.com/article/2011/09/20/us-libya-obama-idUSTRE78J31H20110920.

Spiegel, "Are German Anti-Pirate Forces Hampered by Bureaucrats?" *Speigel Online International* (May 14, 2009), http://www.spiegel.de/international/germany/0,1518,624908,00.html.

———, "Berlin Looks at Ways to Battle Somali Kidnappers," *Speigel Online International* (June 26, 2008), http://www.spiegel.de/international/germany/0,1518,562204,00.html.

———, "Germany Looks to Battle Pirates," *Spiegel Online International* (November 21, 2008), http://www.spiegel.de/international/germany/0,1518,591891,00.html.

Sprinzak, Ehud, *The Ascendance of Israel's Radical Right* (New York: Oxford University Press, 1991): 53.

———, "Extremism and Violence in Israel: The Crisis of Messianic Politics," *Annals of the American Academy of Political and Social Science* 555, no. 1 (January 1998): 120.

Stares, Justin, "Pirates Protected from EU Task Force by Human Rights," *Telegraph.co.uk* (November 1, 2008), http://www.telegraph.co.uk/news/worldnews/africaandindianocean/somalia/3363258/Pirates-protected-from-EU-task-force-by-human-rights.html.

Steorts, Jason Lee, "Can Iran Be Deterred? A Question We Cannot Afford to Get Wrong," *National Review* 58, no. 19 (October 23, 2006): 35.

Stephens, B. "Does Obama Believe in Human Rights?" *Wall Street Journal* (October 20, 2009): A19.

Stevenson, Betsey and Justin Wolfers, "Economic Growth and Subjective Well-Being: Reassessing the Easterlin Paradox," *Brookings Papers on Economic Activity* 69 (Spring 2008): 1–87.

Stigler, George J., *The Theory of Price*, 3rd edn. (New York: Macmillan, 1966): 57.

Talent, Jim, "Don't Cut Military Spending," *National Review* (November 4, 2010), http://www.nationalreview.com/articles/252458/don-t-cut-military-spending-jim-talent.

Talent, Jim and Mackenzie Eaglen, "Shaping the Future: The Urgent Need to Match Military Modernization to National Commitments," The Heritage Foundation (November 4, 2010), http://www.heritage.org/Research/Reports/2010/11/Shaping-the-Future-The-Urgent-Need-to-Match-Military-Modernization-to-National-Commitments.

Tanenhaus, S, "The World: From Vietnam to Iraq: The Rise and Fall and Rise of the Domino Theory," *New York Times* (March 23, 2003).

Tannenwald, Nina, *The Nuclear Taboo: The United States and the Non-Use of Nuclear Weapons Since 1945* (Cambridge: Cambridge University Press, 2007).

Taranto, James, "The Bin Laden Raid and the 'Virtues of Boldness'," *Wall Street Journal* (May 7, 2011), http://online.wsj.com/article/SB10001424052748703937104576304002029268570.html (accessed January 25, 2012).

Tarzi, Amin, "Afghanistan: Kabul's India Ties Worry Pakistan," *Radio Free Europe/Radio Liberty* (April 16, 2006), http://www.rferl.org/content/article/1067690.html.

Tavernise, Sabrina and Lehren, Andrew W. "A Grim Portrait of Civilian Deaths in Iraq." *The New York Times* (October 22, 2009) http://www.nytimes.com/2010/10/23/world/middleeast/23casualties.html.

Taylor, Charles, *Sources of the Self: The Making of the Modern Identity* (Cambridge: Harvard University Press, 1989), 5–8.

Telegraph, "NATO in Libya a 'Model' for Euro-US Cooperation: US Official," *Telegraph* (September 15, 2011),http://www.telegraph.co.uk/news/worldnews/africaandindianocean/libya/8764812/NATO-in-Libya-a-model-for-Euro-US-cooperation-US-official.html.

Teraya, Koji, "Emerging Hierarchy in International Human Rights and Beyond: From the Perspective of Non-derogable Rights," *European Journal of International Law* 12, no. 5 (2001): 917–41.

Thakur, Ramesh, "Law, Legitimacy and United Nations," *Melbourne Journal of International Law* 1 (2010), http://www.austlii.edu.au/au/journals/MelbJIL/2010/1.html#fn59 (accessed January 20, 2012).

Theiler, Tobias, "Viewers into Europeans? How the European Union Tried to Europeanize the Audiovisual Sector, and Why It Failed," *Canadian Journal of Communication* 24 no. 4 (1999), http://www.cjc-online.ca/index.php/journal/article/view/1126/1035.

Thompson, Drew, "Think Again: China's Military," *Foreign Policy* no. 178 (March/April 2010): 86–90.

———, "Tsunami Relief Reflects China's Regional Aspirations," *China Brief* Jamestown Foundation (January. 17, 2005), http://www.jamestown.org/single/?no_cache=1&tx_ttnews[tt_news]=27394 (accessed October 21, 2010).

Thompson, Mark, "Whatever Happened to Asian Values?" *Journal of Democracy* 12, no. 4 (October 2001): 155.

Tiffert, Glenn, "By Provocatively Engaging the US Navy, Beijing May Be Trying to Change the International Rules," *Yale Global* (27 Mar. 2009). http://yaleglobal.yale.edu/content/china-rises-again-%E2%80%93-part-ii

Timberlake, Edward and William C. Triplett, *Red Dragon Rising: Communist China's Military Threat to America* (Washington, DC: Regnery Pub, 1999), 42.

Times Online, "Navy Releases Somali Pirates Caught Red-Handed," *Times Online* (November 29, 2009), http://www.timesonline.co.uk/tol/news/world/africa/article6936318.ece.

Tol, Gonul, "Turkey's Warm Ties with Iran: A Brief History," *InsideIran.org* (March 17, 2010), http://www.insideiran.org/news/turkey%E2%80%99s-warm-ties-with-iran-a-brief-history/.

Topol, Sarah A., "Egypt's Salafi Surge," *Foreign Policy* (January 4, 2012), http://www.foreignpolicy.com/articles/2012/01/04/egypt_s_salafi_surge (accessed January 12, 2012).

Trager, Robert F. and Dessislava P. Zagorcheva, "Deterring Terrorism: It Can Be Done," *International Security* 30, no. 3 (Winter 2005/2006): 93–94.

Tran, Mark, "Iran to Gain Nuclear Power as Russia Loads Fuel into Bushehr Reactor," *Guardian* (August 13, 2010), http://www.guardian.co.uk/world/2010/aug/13/iran-nuclear-power-plant-russia.

Transparency International, "Corruption Perception Index," *Transparency International* (October 26, 2010), http://www.transparency.org/policy_research/surveys_indices/cpi.

Travis, Hannibal, "Freedom or Theocracy? Constitutionalism in Afghanistan and Iraq," *Northwestern University Journal of International Human Rights* 3 (Spring 2005): 1.

Trichet, Jean-Claude, "Speech by Jean-Claude Trichet, President of the ECB on Receiving the Karlspreis 2011," delivered in Aachen, Germany (June 2, 2011), http://www.ecb.int/press/key/date/2011/html/sp110602.en.html.

Trofimov, Yaroslav, "Egypt Opposes U.S.'s Democracy Funding," *Wall Street Journal* (June 14, 2011).

Tufts University, "Senator John Kerry Addresses the Fletcher School Graduating Class of 2011," *The Fletcher School* (May 21, 2011), http://fletcher.tufts.edu/news/2011/05/news-update/Kerry-May26.shtml.

Turner, Bryan, "Rights and Communities: Prolegomenon to a Sociology of Rights," *Australian and New Zealand Journal of Sociology* 31, no. 2 (1995): 1–8.

Tushnet, Mark, "Potentially Misleading Metaphors in Comparative Constitutionalism: Moments and Enthusiasm," in Weiler and Eisgruber, eds., *Altneuland: The EU Constitution in a Contextual Perspective*, Jean Monnet Working Paper 5/04, http://centers.law.nyu.edu/jeanmonnet/papers/04/040501-04.pdf (accessed January 12, 2012).

Tyson, Ann S., "Rising U.S. Toll in Afghanistan Stirs Unease on Hill, Among Families," *Washington Post* (September 23, 2009), http://www.washingtonpost.com/wp-dyn/content/article/2009/09/22/AR2009092204296.html.

Union for Reform Jews: Board of Trustees (2004) "Resolution on Unilateral Withdrawals, Security Barriers, and Home Demolitions: Striving for Security and Peace for Israel and the Middle East."

United Nations, Convention against Torture and Other Cruel, Inhuman or Degrading Treatment or Punishment art. 3 (December 10, 1984), 1465 U.N.T.S. 85. http://www2.ohchr.org/english/law/cat.htm.

——, "A More Secure World: Our shared responsibility," Report of the High-level Panel on Threats, Challenges and Change (2004), http://www.un.org/secureworld/ (accessed January 19, 2012).

——, "Preamble to 1966 International Covenant on Civil and Political Rights, and International Covenant on Economic, Social and Cultural Rights", *United Nations Office of the High Commissioner on Human Rights* http://www.unhchr.ch/html/menu3/b/a_cescr.htm 7/8/08.

——, "A United Nations Priority: Universal Declaration of Human Rights," http://www.un.org/rights/HRToday/declar.htm (accessed June 11, 2009).

——, "The Universal Declaration of Human Rights," (December 10, 1948), http://www.un.org/en/documents/udhr/ (accessed July 22, 2009).

——, *Vienna Declaration and Programme of Action at the World Conference on Human Rights*, 1993, http://www.unhchr.ch/huridocda/huridoca.nsf/(Symbol)/A.CONF.157.23.En?OpenDocument.

——, United Nations Convention on the Law of the Sea, http://www.un.org/depts/los/convention_agreements/convention_overview_convention.htm.

United Nations Political Office for Somalia, *Human Rights in Somalia* (September 15, 2009), http://www.un-somalia.org/Human_Rights/index.asp.

United Nations Population Fund, Human Rights Principles, http://www.unfpa. org/rights/principles.htm (accessed June 11, 2009).

United Nations Security Council, Press Release, Security Council Authorizes States to Use Land-Based Operations in Somalia as Part of Fight Against Piracy Off Coast, Unanimously Adopting 1851 (2008), U.N. Doc. SC/9541 (December 16, 2008).

United States Army, Field Manual No. 27-10, the Law of Land Warfare, Department of the Army (July. 18, 1956), http://www.globalsecurity.org/military/ library/policy/army/fm/27-10/Ch1.htm.

United States v. Brig Malek Adhel, 43 U.S. (2 How.) 210, 232 (1844).

United States v. Davis, 482 F.2d 893 (9th Cir. 1973).

United States v. Shi, 525 F.3d 709 (9th Cir. 2008) *cert denied* 129 S.Ct. 324 (2008).

United States v. Smith, 18 U.S. (5 Wheat.) 153, 156 (1820).

United States Conference of Catholic Bishops, "Respect for Unborn Human Life: The Church's Constant Teaching," http://www.usccb.org/prolife/ constantchurchteaching.shtml (accessed June 11, 2009).

United States-China Economic and Security Review Commission (USCC), 2010 Report to Congress (November 2010), http://www.uscc.gov/annual_ report/2010/annual_report_full_10.pdf (accessed November 2010).

United States Department of Defense, "Annual Report to Congress: Military and Security Developments Involving the People's Republic of China, 2010", Office of the Secretary of Defense., 34. http://www.defense.gov/pubs/pdfs/2010_ CMPR_Final.pdf.

———, *Nuclear Posture Review Report* (April 2010), 10, http://www.defense.gov/ npr/docs/2010%20Nuclear%20Posture%20Review%20Report.pdf.

———, *Quadrennial Defense Review Report* (February 2010), 31.

United States Department of Energy, U.S. Energy Information Administration, "World Oil Transit Chokepoints," (December 30, 2011), http://www.eia.doe. gov/cabs/world_oil_transit_chokepoints/pdf.pdf.

United States Department of Justice, "Effect of a Recent United Nations Security Council Resolution on the Authority of the President Under International Law to Use Military Force Against Iraq," *Opinions of the Office of Legal Counsel in Volume 26* (November 8, 2002), http://www.justice.gov/olc/2002/iraq-unscr-final.pdf (accessed January 20, 2012).

United States Department of State, *2008 Human Rights Report: Kenya* (February 25, 2009), http://www.state.gov/g/drl/rls/hrrpt/2008/af/119007.htm.

———, "U.S.-Vietnam Cooperation on Civil Nuclear Power and Nuclear Security," U.S. Department of State (March 30, 2010), http://www.state.gov/r/pa/prs/ ps/2010/03/139255.htm.

United States Department of State: Office of the Coordinator for Counterterrorism, "Chapter 3: State Sponsors of Terrorism," in *Country Reports on Terrorism 2009* (Washington, DC: U.S. Department of State, August 5, 2010), http://www. state.gov/j/ct/rls/crt/2009/140889.htm.

United States House of Representatives, Select Committee on U.S. National Security and Military/Commercial Concerns with the People's Republic of China, *U.S. National Security and Military/Commercial Concerns With the People's Republic of China*, 106 Cong., 1 sess., 1999, 60.

United States House of Representatives, Subcommittee on National Security and Foreign Affairs, "Afghanistan and Pakistan: Understanding and Engaging Regional Stakeholders," *Hearing Before the House Subcommittee on National Security and Foreign Affairs* (March 31, 2009), https://house.resource.org/111/gov.house.ogr.fa.20090331.pdf, 16.

United States Office of Management and Budget, "The President's Budget for Fiscal Year 2012," http://www.whitehouse.gov/omb/budget (accessed June 24, 2011).

Office of the Press Secretary, "Press Conference with President Obama and President Hu of the People's Republic of China," the White House (January 19, 2011), http://www.whitehouse.gov/the-press-office/2011/01/19/press-conference-president-obama-and-president-hu-peoples-republic-china.

———, "Remarks by the President in Address to the Nation on Libya," Transcript from the Office of the Press Secretary (March 28, 2011), http://www.whitehouse.gov/the-press-office/2011/03/28/remarks-president-address-nation-libya (accessed January 20, 2012).

United States Office of the Press Secretary, The White House, *Statement of President Barack Obama on Military Commissions* (May 15, 2009), http://www.whitehouse.gov/the_press_office/Statement-of-President-Barack-Obama-on-Military-Commissions/ (accessed April 23, 2010).

Vale, Tim, "Are Bans on Political Parties Bound to Turn Out Badly? A Comparative Investigation of Three 'Intolerant' Democracies: Turkey, Spain, and Belgium," *Comparative European Politics* 5 (2010): 141–57.

van Tol, Jan with Mark Gunzinger, Andrew Krepinevich, and Jim Thomas, "Air Sea Battle: A Point-of-Departure Operational Concept," Center for Strategic and Budgetary Assessment (May 18, 2010).

Veenhoven, Ruut and Michael Hagerty, "Rising Happiness in Nations 1946–2004," *Social Indicators Research* 79, no. 3: 421–36.

Vincent, R.J., *Human Rights and International Relations* (New York: Cambridge University Press, 1986), 87.

Vogel, Ezra F., "Pax Nipponica?" *Foreign Affairs* 64, no. 4 (Spring 1986): 752-767.

Walker, Neil, "After the Constitutional Moment," *The Federal Trust Constitutional Online Paper Series* 32 (November 2003), http://papers.ssrn.com/sol3/papers.cfm?abstract_id=516783 (accessed January 12, 2012).

Waraich, Omar, "Pakistan's Reaction to Obama's Plan: Departure Is Key," *Time* (December 2, 2009), http://www.time.com/time/world/article/0,8599,1945134,00.html.

Washington Post, "President Obama Delivers Joint Press Statement with President Hu Jintao of China," (November 17, 2009).

Waxman, Matthew, "Administrative Detention of Terrorists: *Why* Detain, and Detain *Whom*?" *Journal of National Security Law and Policy* 3 (2009): 11–13.

Weber, Max, "The Social Psychology of the World Religions," in *Essays in Sociology* (London: Psychology Press, 1991).

Wedgwood, Ruth and Kenneth Roth, "Combatants or Criminals? How Washington Should Handle Terrorists" *Foreign Affairs* (May/June 2004), http://www.foreign

affairs.com/articles/59902/ruth-wedgwood-kenneth-roth/combatants-or-criminals-how-washington-should-handle-terrorists.

Weiler, J. H. H., "A Constitution for Europe? Some Hard Choices" *Journal for Common Market Studies* 40, no. 4 (2002): 563–80.

Weiss, Davis E., "Striking a Difficult Balance: Combating the Threat of Neo-Nazism in Germany While Preserving Individual Liberties," *Vanderbilt Journal of Transnational Law* 27 (1994).

Westerwelt, Eric, "NATO's Intervention in Libya: A New Model?" *NPR* (September 12, 2011), http://www.npr.org/2011/09/12/140292920/natos-intervention-in-libya-a-new-model.

White, Jeffrey, "German Lawyers Launch Pirate Defense Team," *Christian Sci. Monitor* (April 15, 2009), http://www.csmonitor.com/2009/0416/p06s01-wogn.html.

Whitney v. California, 274 U.S. 357 (1927).

Williams, Bernard, *Truth and Truthfulness* (Princeton, NJ: Princeton University Press, 2002).

Williams, Walter, "Property Rights Are a Fundamental Right," *Capitalism Magazine* (August 3, 2005). http://www.capmag.com/article.asp?ID=4341 (accessed July 24, 2009).

Wiltrout, Kate, "Nine Suspected Pirates Set Free; Others Could Face Trials," *Virginian-Pilot* (Norfolk) (March 3, 2009), http://hamptonroads.com/2009/03/nine-suspected-pirates-set-free-others-could-face-trials.

Wines, Michael, "Chinese State Media, in a Show of Openness, Print Jet Photos," *New York Times* (April 25, 2011), http://www.nytimes.com/2011/04/26/world/asia/26fighter.html?_r=1.

Winston, Morton, "On the Indivisibility and Interdependence of Human Rights," (Twentieth World Congress of Philosophy, Boston, MA, August 10–15, 1998), http://www.bu.edu/wcp/Papers/Huma/HumaWins.htm.

Witte, Griff, "Pakistan Courts China as Relations with the U.S. Grow Strained," *Washington Post* (June 22, 2011), http://www.washingtonpost.com/world/asia-pacific/pakistan-courts-china-as-relations-with-us-grow-strained/2011/06/19/AGDCyWfH_story.html.

Wittes, Benjamin, *Law and the Long War* (New York: The Penguin Press, 2008), 11–16, 164–78.

———, "Testimony before the Senate Committee on the Judiciary," *Improving Detainee Policy: Handling Terrorism Detainees within the American Justice System*, 110th Cong., 2nd sess. (2008).

Wittes, Benjamin and Zaahira Wyne. The Current Detainee Population of Guantánamo: An Empirical Study. *The Brookings Institution* (October 21, 2009), 1, http://www.brookings.edu/reports/2008/~/media/Files/rc/reports/2008/1216_detainees_wittes/1216_detainees_wittes_supplement.pdf.

Wong, Edward, "China's Disputes in Asia Buttress Influence of U.S.," *The New York Times* (September 22, 2010).

———, "China: Government Tells U.N. Agency Not to Interfere," *New York Times* (March 29, 2011), http://www.nytimes.com/2011/03/30/world/asia/30briefs-ART-zhisheng.html (accessed January 20, 2012).

Woolf, Marie, "Pirates Can Claim UK Asylum," *Sunday Times* (London) (April 13, 2008), http://www.timesonline.co.uk/tol/news/uk/article3736239.ece.

World Bank, "Assessing Aid—What Works, What Doesn't, and Why," *Policy Research Report* (1998).

World Bank Independent Evaluation Group, "Annual Review of Development Effectiveness 2006: Getting Results," World Bank Independent Evaluation Group, Washington, DC (2006).

Wright, Lawrence, "The Double Game," *New Yorker* (May 16, 2011), http://www.newyorker.com/reporting/2011/05/16/110516fa_fact_wright.

Wyatt, Caroline, "Afghan Burden Tasks NATO Allies," *BBC News* (October 27, 2007), http://news.bbc.co.uk/2/hi/south_asia/7061061.stm.

Yahuda, Michael, "The Evolving Asian Order" in *Power Shift: China and Asia's New Dynamics*, ed. David Shambaugh (Berkeley, CA: University of California Press, 2005), 347.

Yale University Indonesia Forum, "Workshop on Islam, Freedom, and Democracy in Contemporary Indonesia," *Yale University Indonesia Forum*, http://www.yale.edu/seas/IslamWorkshop.htm (accessed January 25, 2012).

Yale University Law School, "A Decade of American Foreign Policy 1941–1949 Potsdam Conference," *The Avalon Project*, http://avalon.law.yale.edu/20th_century/decade17.asp (accessed January 11, 2012).

Yao, Yang, "The End of the Beijing Consensus: Can China's Model of Authoritarian Growth Survive?" *Foreign Affairs* (February 2, 2010), http://www.foreignaffairs.com/articles/65947/the-end-of-the-beijing-consensus.

Yin, Tung, "Ending the War on Terrorism One Terrorist at a Time: A Noncriminal Detention Model for Holding and Releasing Guantanamo Bay Detainees," *Harvard Journal of Law and Public Policy* 29 (2005): 155.

Yusuf, Huma, "US Concerned about China's Military Investments," *The Christian Science Monitor* (June 10, 2010).

Yusuf, Moeed and Adil Najam, "Kashmir: Ripe for Resolution?" *Third World Quarterly* 30, no. 8 (2009): 1503–28.

Zakaria, Fareed, "Containing a Nuclear Iran," *Daily Beast* (October 2, 2009), http://www.thedailybeast.com/newsweek/2009/10/03/containing-a-nuclear-iran.html (accessed January 20, 2012).

———, "Don't Scramble the Jets: Why Iran's Dictators Can Be Deterred," *Daily Beast* (February 18, 2010), http://www.thedailybeast.com/newsweek/2010/02/18/don-t-scramble-the-jets.html (accessed January 20, 2012).

———, *The Future of Freedom: Illiberal Democracy at Home and Abroad* (New York: W. W. Norton & Company, 2003).

———, "A Military for the Real World" *Newsweek* (July 26, 2009), http://newsweek.washingtonpost.com/postglobal/fareed_zakaria/.

———, "The Radicalization of Pakistan's Military," *The Washington Post* (June 22), http://www.washingtonpost.com/opinions/the-radicalization-of-pakistans-military/2011/06/22/AGbCBSgH_story.html.

Zemin, Jiang, "Statement by President Jiang Zemin of the People's Republic of China at the Millennium Summit of the United Nations," (September 6, 2000). http://www.un.org/millennium/webcast/statements/china.htm. (accessed January 19, 2012).

Zirulnick, Ariel, "Pakistani Militants Infiltrate Naval Base Just 15 Miles from Suspected Nuclear Site," *Christian Science Monitor* (May 23, 2011), http://www.csmonitor.com/World/terrorism-security/2011/0523/Pakistani-militants-infiltrate-naval-base-just-15-miles-from-suspected-nuclear-site.

Zuckert, Michael P. "Self Evident Truth and the Declaration of Independence" *The Review of Politics* 49, no. 3 (Summer, 1987): 319–39, 322.

Index